Praise for *About Teaching Mathematics, Fourth Edition* . .

Marilyn Burns has done it again. I started teaching math to children with her first edition of *About Teaching Mathematics* more than thirty years ago. Then I delved into her second edition for many years, especially for the rich collection of problem-solving activities. I embraced her third edition with graduate students in teacher education programs, specifically the "Raising the Issues (Starting Points)" and "Questions Teachers Ask" sections because they caused me to think hard about my own practices. Now in the fourth edition Marilyn has expanded the whole-class lessons, including "sticky note" teaching tips and management suggestions. It's like she's always there for me, helping me teach the way I want to teach math. Thank you, Marilyn. I couldn't do what I do without your resources.

> —Ann Carlyle, coauthor of *Teaching Preschool and Kindergarten Math* and Continuing Lecturer,
> Teacher Education Program, Department of Education, University of California,
> Santa Barbara, California

I think this resource and the *About Teaching Mathematics* course is the best resource and professional development available. Per Marilyn, "We can't teach what we don't know, and we can't teach well what we don't understand." As in previous editions, Marilyn addresses this critical issue; however, throughout this fourth edition she has added even more learning journeys, gently guiding readers to expand their mathematical understanding by engaging in the mathematics, written as only Marilyn can write—with clarity, warmth, and a touch of humor.

> —Maryann Wickett, math consultant, author, and retired teacher, grades preK–6,
> San Marcos Unified School District, San Diego County, California

"Don't mess with a good thing!" You know the saying? Marilyn Burns must disagree because she has been updating and adding to a "good thing," *About Teaching Mathematics*, for more than twenty years . . . and the fourth edition is no exception. Who wouldn't want to peek at Marilyn's personal notes? What a gift! This is a book that continues to enhance and guide my teaching, learning, and consulting. Thank you, Marilyn, for messing with a good thing . . . and continuing to make a difference in my professional and personal life.

> —Beth Terry, mathematics educator and consultant, Singapore; and
> former Math Solutions instructor

I'm often in awe of how versatile *About Teaching Mathematics* is. Its contents have helped me communicate with parents about effective arithmetic instruction, plan professional development workshops for teachers, and craft problem-based lessons for students from kindergarten through grade 8. After fifteen years working as a math coach, workshop leader, and classroom teacher, it remains one of my top "go-to" resources for K–8 mathematics instruction.

> —Nancy Anderson, K–8 Mathematics Coordinator, Milton Academy, Massachusetts;
> and coauthor of *Classroom Discussions in Math*

Who'd have dreamed that this essential book could get even better? Beyond the foundational ideas for how to teach mathematics, Marilyn's personal thoughts and insights make this an incredible resource that speaks to all of us. This fourth edition of *About Teaching Mathematics* needs to be the centerpiece of the library of every teacher and everyone who supports those teachers.

> —Cathy Seeley, NCTM Past President and author of *Faster Isn't Smarter*
> and *Smarter Than We Think*

About Teaching Mathematics is *the* most important resource in my teaching library; I've been using it for more than twenty-five years. This fourth edition will especially help teachers and administrators wrap their brains around the Common Core content and practice standards. It provides educators with a host of rich math tasks and includes clear and relatable reflections about math teaching and learning.

—Rusty Bresser, Lecturer and Supervisor of Teacher Education, Education Studies Department,
    University of California, San Diego, California

About Teaching Mathematics is my first choice in resources when I want to make effective instructional decisions and improve children's ability to think and reason mathematically. Each revision of *About Teaching Mathematics* has offered more ideas, discussions, explanations, investigations, management suggestions, and guidance. This fourth edition is the best yet.

—Jane Crawford, author of *Math Reads* and *Why Can't I Have Everything? Teaching Today's
    Children to Be Financially and Mathematically Savvy*

Marilyn's ability to continually reflect upon and improve the teaching of mathematics for more than fifty years is a gift that keeps on giving. The heart of every edition of *About Teaching Mathematics* has been to provide mathematics instruction that develops the concepts and skills that students need to think, reason, and understand math, and to help teachers better understand the math they teach. This fourth edition is no exception.

—Lynne Zolli, classroom teacher grades 1–6, San Francisco Unified School District, California;
    and author of the *Math Reasoning Inventory (MRI)* and the *Do the Math* intervention program

I have heard Marilyn say that we can only teach what we know and understand. Marilyn has helped me really know and understand mathematics through the wide range of lessons and experiences she shares in *About Teaching Mathematics*. This fourth edition is a must-have resource for all teachers.

—Dana Islas, 2009 recipient of the Presidential Award for Excellence in Mathematics Teaching
    and author of *How to Assess While You Teach Math, Grades K–2*

I gained new appreciation for the words perseverance and respect from Marilyn Burns. Through the years I have watched Marilyn encourage both children and their teachers as mathematical learners. Marilyn accepts struggle as a natural part of learning. I have personally experienced frustration as a mathematical learner; it is a great gift to be treated with respect during those moments and to be encouraged to persevere. This beautiful resource makes it clear that Marilyn perseveres in her own learning as well. I have the deepest respect for my favorite teacher, Marilyn Burns.

—Vicki Bachman, elementary school teacher, Iowa City Community School District, Iowa;
    Math Solutions instructor; Cognitively Guided Instruction (CGI) instructor; and
    K–5 curriculum consultant

In this comprehensive guide to teaching elementary mathematics, Marilyn Burns shows how to weave together lessons that are hands-on, engaging, and require students to think critically. The stand-alone lessons are also the perfect companion to any curriculum, Common Core or otherwise. *About Teaching Mathematics* is an ideal guide for new teachers, but also includes lessons and activities that will enhance the repertoire of the most veteran teacher.

—Jenny Wickett, first-grade teacher, Pajaro Valley Unified School District, Watsonville, California

In 1985 I attended my first *About Teaching Mathematics* course. The experiences Marilyn gave me in that course forever changed me as a teacher, as a mother, and as a presenter of professional development. First, Marilyn single-handedly opened the vault doors on my mathematical potential. Then, she taught me to think about how people learn. I am a better educator because of Marilyn. Additionally, her uncanny intuition is supernatural!

—Brenda Mercado, early childhood teacher, Tucson, Arizona; Math Solutions instructor;
    and coauthor of *Teaching Preschool and Kindergarten Math*

ABOUT TEACHING Mathematics

A K–8 RESOURCE
Fourth Edition

Marilyn Burns

Math Solutions
Sausalito, California, USA

Math Solutions
One Harbor Drive, Suite 101
Sausalito, California, USA 94965
www.mathsolutions.com

Credits and acknowledgments appear on page 506, which constitutes an extension of this copyright page.

ISBN-13: 978-1-935099-32-1
ISBN-10: 1-935099-32-9

Editor: Jamie Ann Cross
Production: Denise A. Botelho
Cover design: Vicki Tagliatela, DandiLion Designs
Interior design: Susan Barclay/Barclay Design
Composition: Susan Barclay/Barclay Design
Cover images: main image by Kara Brodgesell; background images by Bob Adler, Jim Franco/Jim Franco Photography, and collected from Math Solutions archives

Printed in China.

3 4 5 6 7 8 9 10   38   24 23 22 21 20 19 18 17 16 15

A Message from Math Solutions

We at Math Solutions believe that teaching math well calls for increasing our understanding of the math we teach, seeking deeper insights into how students learn mathematics, and refining our lessons to best promote students' learning.

Math Solutions shares classroom-tested lessons and teaching expertise from our faculty of professional development consultants as well as from other respected math educators. Our publications are part of the nationwide effort we've made since 1984 that now includes

- more than five hundred face-to-face professional development programs each year for teachers and administrators in districts across the country;

- professional development books that span all math topics taught in kindergarten through high school;

- videos for teachers and for parents that show math lessons taught in actual classrooms;

- on-site visits to schools to help refine teaching strategies and assess student learning; and

- free online support, including grade-level lessons, book reviews, inservice information, and district feedback, all in our Math Solutions Online Newsletter.

For information about all of the products and services we have available, please visit our website at *www.mathsolutions.com.* You can also contact us to discuss math professional development needs by calling (800) 868-9092 or by sending an email to *info@mathsolutions.com.*

We're always eager for your feedback and interested in learning about your particular needs. We look forward to hearing from you.

CONTENTS OVERVIEW

*Reproducibles are available online
at mathsolutions.com/atm4theditionreproducibles.*

CONTENTS

About the Mathematics

This icon indicates that I've written a mathematical commentary for the investigation. I've written these explanations in response to queries from teachers asking for math help with particular problems. I encourage you to try the investigation first before reading my explanation.

— MSB

Problem-Solving Investigations: Patterns and Algebraic Thinking

Problem-Solving Investigations: Number and Operations — 263

*Reproducibles are available online
at mathsolutions.com/atm4theditionreproducibles.*

LIST OF REPRODUCIBLES

Reproducibles are available online at
mathsolutions.com/atm4theditionreproducibles.

Preface

How I Came to Write This Book

My goal when entering college was to become a teacher. I'd always liked school, often played school at home with my sister and friends, and earned good grades. I'd always done particularly well in math and was interested in learning more. So I decided to major in mathematics and become a math teacher.

When I got to college, I was especially curious about the mysteries of calculus (which wasn't taught in my high school). But while math always made sense to me in my earlier studies, when I began studying calculus, I had a very different experience. I was completely lost. My first professor was caring and kind. She gave lectures and filled the chalkboard with symbols often new to me to reveal ideas that were also new.

In her lectures and in those other professors gave in subsequent classes, there always was a moment that triggered my downfall. The professor would say, nearing the end of an explanation or proof, "So you can now see that . . . " or "It's now obvious that . . . " or "Because of this, it's now clear that . . ." But for me, "now" rarely came. I often didn't "see" what they saw, nothing was "obvious" to me, and little was "clear." I earned my math degree, but it was very, very difficult.

I hit my mathematical wall in calculus, the way many teachers have told me they experienced in their math learning, sometimes with subtraction, sometimes with fractions, other times with algebra or geometry. Many elementary teachers have shared with me that in college they took only the math that they absolutely had to take. Many have taken the oath that math is not their thing.

With the difficulty I was experiencing, I stuck with math in college. In my classes, I copied down everything the professors wrote with the diligence I had developed in high school. I filled notebooks. I did my homework and prepared for exams, more times resorting to memorizing than understanding. I earned the degree. Today I'm fine with the content of math through high school, but I still feel inadequate with much of what I studied in college. And while these experiences in college were more than fifty years ago, I can still conjure up the feeling of being a poor math student. In a way, I think that my feelings mirror what some teachers have told me they remember about being sent to the board in elementary math classes. The feelings run deep.

There's an upside to this story. When I became a teacher, I made some promises to myself. I would never, never cause a student in my math class to feel deficient. I wouldn't tolerate students feeling demeaned by math. I would do all that I could to help students build the understanding of the math they were learning as I had somehow built successfully through high school math. I would never say things like "So you can now see that . . ." or "It's now obvious that . . ." or "Because of this, it's now clear that . . ." I was going to be a different kind of teacher.

But what it meant to be a different kind of teacher wasn't clear to me, and the journey to figure it out has been the main quest of my teaching career. Even with this goal, in my beginning years of teaching when I taught eighth and ninth graders, I reverted to teaching the way I had been taught. I filled the board as I taught, the students listened, and then I circulated as they did assignments. I planned my lessons carefully, working on how to explain fractions, algebra, or geometry by relying on how these topics had been explained to me. Explaining was the only way I knew to try to make things plain for students. Oh, my, how much time I took to plan those lessons.

My lessons worked for some students, as they had worked for me when I learned math before attending college. But I was painfully aware that they didn't work for other students. I realized that I was doing to some of my students just what my well-meaning math professors in college had done to me.

That's when I started my search for how to be a better math teacher. And that search took me in several directions: I had to learn more about the math I was teaching—more about whole numbers, fractions, algebra, and geometry. As I became fascinated by how younger children dealt with math and moved down to the earlier grades, I thought more about what it really takes for students to learn the basics of mathematics, both to understand concepts and also to develop a repertoire of skills. And, of course, I had to figure out how to establish and manage a classroom that gave students access to the mathematical content and also helped them become mathematical learners.

There was not a straightforward path for this learning. There was no sign saying "Marilyn, this way." I engaged with colleagues, learned from my students, took classes and workshops, attended conferences, and read many resources. I studied in earnest, this time not to pass exams to get a degree. I already had the degree. Now I studied so I could feel like a good teacher of mathematics. And that meant being more than just adequate, but really, really effective. I wanted my students to become competent and confident mathematically. But I also wanted them to be interested in math, curious about new math ideas, willing to take risks and plunge into solving new math problems, and also see math as engaging and playful.

It's in this spirit that I offer this resource, which has been a work in progress for more than half of my teaching career. I wrote the first version in 1981, revised it in 2000, and then again in 2007. And here, in 2015, is my newest edition. So, in an important way for me, this resource has been a major part of my journey as a teacher. I'm still on that journey, and I invite you to come along with me. I hope that this fourth edition of *About Teaching Mathematics* helps you meet the challenge of helping your students become successful learners of mathematics.

Introduction to the Fourth Edition

Many documents have been made available over the years to help teachers think about teaching elementary mathematics. In 2000, the National Council of Teachers of Mathematics (NCTM) published *Principles and Standards for School Mathematics* to address teaching mathematics in all the grades. In 2001, the National Research Council released its report, *Adding It Up: Helping Children Learn Mathematics*, to explore how students in pre-K through eighth grade learn mathematics. In 2006, NCTM published *Curriculum Focal Points for Pre-Kindergarten Through Grade 8 Mathematics* offering a step toward a national dialogue about a coherent curriculum and defining the content to be emphasized at each grade level. In 2010, supported by the Council of Chief State School Officers (CCSSO) and the National Governors Association Center for Best Practices (NGA Center), the *Common Core State Standards for Mathematics* were released to define what students in kindergarten through grade 12 should understand and be able to do in their study of mathematics.

Along with these major documents, states and school districts have prepared frameworks of specific expectations about what teachers are to teach and when. Instructional programs and other curriculum resource materials provide teachers suggestions and road maps for teaching math. Online websites make available teaching ideas and video examples. State and local tests further impacts teaching choices.

It's a dizzying amount of material, daunting for teachers to sift through, digest, and use to help students successfully acquire the math knowledge, skill, and confidence they need.

My goal in writing *About Teaching Mathematics* has been to connect the major ideas and suggestions from these many documents to the reality of classroom teaching. In a way, I've tried to translate the major ideas in the documents to best instructional practices, to make these ideas accessible and helpful for classroom instruction. I realize, and confess, that a particular point of view has evolved for me over the more than fifty years I've been involved with mathematics education, which is to offer students opportunities to think, reason, and make sense of mathematics and to settle for nothing less. With that in mind, I've written this book to help teachers

- deep their knowledge and appreciation of mathematics;
- understand how students learn mathematics;
- implement effective instructional strategies for teaching mathematics;
- make assessment an integral part of informing mathematics instruction; and
- establish classroom environments that support students' learning of mathematics.

What's New in the Fourth Edition?

Over the years, I've often dipped into my own copy of *About Teaching Mathematics, Third Edition*, for ideas as I've prepared to teach classroom lessons. My personal copy is woefully dog-eared and filled with notes, some scribbled in the margins and some on sticky notes. In this fourth edition, I've reproduced many of these notes from my own copy of the book and added new ones as well. (This idea came from a gift I received from a friend a few years ago. She gave me a copy of her favorite cookbook that included her own notes written throughout the book. Her annotations were enormously helpful and made the cookbook more personal and accessible.) Some of my notes are reminders of improvements I've made to teaching ideas, some are references to other related parts of the resource, and some are references to other resources I found helpful or informative. I offer them as assistance for planning lessons, and I encourage you to add your own notes and share them with colleagues.

Overview of Changes and Additions

Part 1

I've made a major overhaul to Part 1, "Starting Points," to present how my thinking has evolved on some of the issues that were included in the third edition and to add sections that reflect my current thinking on other issues. Organized into six categories, each of the twenty-three Starting Points engages with a particular issue and draws on my years of teaching experience to tie it to classroom instruction.

Part 2

In Part 2, "Problem-Solving Investigations," I continue to draw on my classroom teaching experiences, here organized not by issues but by the content areas of math instruction—measurement, data, geometry, patterns and algebraic thinking, and number and operations. Each content area includes sample whole-class lessons, additional investigations for whole-class lessons, and independent investigations. I've also written About the Mathematics sections that offer commentary about some of the problem-solving investigations and address the underlying mathematics.

Part 3

Part 3, "Teaching Arithmetic," focuses on the cornerstone of elementary math teaching. Here I draw on the issues in Part 1 and embrace the problem-solving instruction emphasized in Part 2 to offer classroom teaching suggestions for developing students' arithmetic understanding and skills. The nine sections span the content from beginning number concepts through decimals and percents. In each section, suggestions are included for whole-class instruction, partner or small group experiences, and assessing students' understanding.

Part 4

Part 4, "Questions Teachers Ask" is a compilation of questions from teachers and responses I've provided over the years.

Reproducibles

More than forty reproducibles have been created to help you prepare lessons.

Getting Started

About Teaching Mathematics, Fourth Edition, offers more than 250 mathematical investigations and teaching suggestions. I realize that this is a huge resource to add to your professional library. I don't expect, or advise, that you feel the need to read the resource from beginning to end. Rather, scan the issues in Part 1, the content areas in Part 2, and the specific areas of arithmetic in Part 3, and dig in to an area that best meets your needs.

Starting Points

Overview

Part 1 of this resource addresses issues that are at the foundation of teaching mathematics in kindergarten through grade 8. As shown in the "At a Glance" list, twenty-three sections are organized into six categories to help you locate issues that address your specific interests and concerns. I've labeled these sections "Starting Points," and in each I offer my thoughts, perspectives, and observations as points of departure or starting points for your own thinking.

While each "Starting Point" addresses a specific topic, overlapping themes occur in them to help provide an overview and coherence. Also, included in some of the "Starting Points" are "Try This Now" activities for you to engage firsthand with the ideas presented as well as suggestions to help connect the big picture to the realities of classroom teaching.

General Pedagogical Issues

Starting Point 1

Getting Started: Connecting Content, Practices, and Instruction

"How much is one hundred minus three?" I asked Sara, a second grader, near the end of the school year. I asked Sara to try solving the problem in her head, but I also assured her, "You can use paper and pencil if you need to."

After a moment, Sara responded confidently and correctly, "Ninety-seven."

"How did you figure it out?" I probed.

"It was easy," Sara responded. "I just counted back—ninety-nine, ninety-eight, ninety-seven." She used her fingers to show how she had counted back three numbers.

I then gave Sara another problem. "How much is one hundred minus ninety-eight?"

Sara thought for a bit, then frowned and said, "I'll have to use paper and pencil. I can't count back that far." She wrote the problem on her paper and subtracted, regrouping as she had learned, and got the correct answer of 2.

Sara's response indicated that she hadn't learned about the relationship between addition and subtraction. She didn't think, "I know that ninety-eight plus two equals one hundred, so one hundred minus ninety-eight has to be two." On numerous assignments, Sara demonstrated proficiency with paper-and-pencil skills for both addition and subtraction. Her written work, however, hid this important gap in her understanding.

I interviewed Jessica, a kindergartener, near the middle of the school year. Her teacher was concerned about her mathematics progress. At one point during the interview, I asked Jessica to put eight cubes on a sheet of paper. She did this easily.

"Watch as I take away one cube," I said to her. I removed one cube and placed it on the table next to the paper. "How many cubes are on the paper now?"

Jessica counted the cubes remaining on the paper, carefully moving one at a time to the side. "Seven," she answered correctly.

"Watch as I take away another cube," I said. I removed another cube and asked, "How many cubes are on the paper now?"

Again, Jessica counted the cubes remaining on the paper and answered correctly, "Six."

"Now I'll put a cube back," I said. I added a cube to the six cubes on the paper and asked, "Can you tell me how many cubes are on the paper now without counting?"

Jessica looked at the paper, then shook her head no and said, "I need to count." I assured her that it was OK to do so.

Jessica wasn't able to identify numbers that were one more or one less, which indicated that she didn't yet understand that smaller numbers are contained within greater numbers. Jessica needed more experiences to help her learn how quantities relate to each other.

I showed Hugo, a fourth grader, two fractions—$\frac{6}{10}$ and $\frac{7}{10}$. "Which fraction is greater?" I asked.

Hugo answered quickly, but incorrectly, "Six-tenths."

"How did you decide?" I probed.

"The smaller the number, the bigger the fraction," he replied confidently. Hugo incorrectly applied what he had learned about comparing fractions with different denominators, such as $\frac{1}{8}$ and $\frac{1}{5}$. He knew that one piece of a whole cut into five equal pieces is greater than one piece of the same whole cut into eight equal pieces.

Hugo would most likely have given the incorrect answer on a written assignment if asked to circle the greater fraction. However, without talking to Hugo and having the opportunity to probe his thinking, I wouldn't have known that his misconception was a result of inappropriately applying something he had learned about fractions.

I asked Gerald, a sixth grader, to solve a problem I had written on a card: *12.6 × 10*. Gerald looked at the problem and said, "Twelve point sixty."

"How did you figure it out?" I asked.

Gerald explained, "I know that when you multiply a number by ten, you just add a zero." Gerald inappropriately applied a rule he had learned about whole numbers, not noticing that his answer of 12.60 was the same as 12.6 in the problem, so it couldn't be ten times greater. Similar to Hugo applying a fraction concept erroneously, here Gerald was inappropriately applying a property of whole number multiplication to decimals.

The responses from these students aren't unusual when students haven't developed the mathematical understandings they need.

Understanding the Mathematical Content Students Need to Learn

All of the questions I asked these students relate to number and operations, the major emphasis of the mathematics content through grade 5. As one of the time-honored "Three R's", arithmetic has long been the cornerstone of mathematics instruction in the elementary grades.

The questions I asked these students were specific to grade-level content. Asking Sara to solve 100 − 98 relates to second-grade content about numbers and operations. Specifically, second-grade students should learn to add and subtract with numbers within one hundred using strategies based on place value, properties of operations, and the relationship between addition and subtraction. The questions I asked Jessica are related to the kindergarten content of counting and cardinality that expects students to understand that each successive number name refers to a quantity that is one greater. Asking Hugo to compare $\frac{6}{10}$ and $\frac{7}{10}$ relates to the understanding of fractions, specifically to fraction equivalence and ordering. Hugo was a fourth grader, but students in third grade typically are expected to learn to compare fractions with the same denominator, a necessary prerequisite for ordering fractions. Solving 12.6 × 10 required Gerald to understand place value and be able to multiply with whole numbers and decimals, which is typically part of the mathematics content for fifth graders.

Understanding the Mathematical Thinking and Reasoning Skills Students Need to Develop

While the math content guided me in selecting the questions to ask these students, I was also interested in learning about their ability to think and reason. It's important for teachers to know the math content for their particular grade level, but it's equally important for teachers to know the general mathematical processes and proficiencies students need to develop for learning the content. These are the general mathematical practices that are important to students in all grade levels. They are the thinking and reasoning skills that are essential for doing mathematics, the ways we want students to engage with the mathematics they're learning.

The content of the mathematics curriculum is different for each grade level, but the same set of mathematical practices applies to students in all grade levels. The Common Core State Standards lists eight Mathematical Practices that promote reasoning and conceptual understanding of mathematical content.

THE COMMON CORE STATE STANDARDS FOR MATHEMATICAL PRACTICE

1. Make sense of problems and persevere in solving them.
2. Reason abstractly and quantitatively.
3. Construct viable arguments and critique the reasoning of others.
4. Model with mathematics.
5. Use appropriate tools strategically.
6. Attend to precision.
7. Look for and make use of structure.
8. Look for and express regularity in repeated reasoning.

When focusing on number and operations and teaching the basics of arithmetic, perhaps especially when teaching the basics of arithmetic, these thinking and reasoning skills should be at the forefront of instruction. This means that students should do more than produce correct answers. For example, when responding to the questions I asked, the students had to make sense of a problem that required them to reason numerically, construct a viable argument, communicate their ideas, and attend to the precision of their solution.

Instructional Practices for Effective Math Teaching

Effective mathematics teaching calls for attention to mathematical content and practices—both are essential and important to understand, embrace, and incorporate into math instruction. A major challenge for teachers is to develop instructional practices that connect the mathematical content for the particular grade they teach and the mathematical practices important for all students.

The National Council of Teachers of Mathematics (NCTM) provides guidance for teachers in *Principles to Action: Ensuring Mathematical Success for All* (NCTM, 2014). Based on the premise that effective mathematics instruction must help all students become mathematical thinkers prepared for any academic or professional path they choose, *Principles to Action* presents a list of mathematics teaching practices as a framework for strengthening the teaching and learning of mathematics.

NCTM MATHEMATICS TEACHING PRACTICES

Establish mathematics goals to focus learning.

Implement tasks that promote reasoning and problem solving.

Use and connect mathematical representations.

Facilitate meaningful mathematical discourse.

Pose purposeful questions.

Build procedural fluency from conceptual understanding.

Support productive struggle in learning mathematics.

Elicit and use evidence of student thinking.

Wrapping It Up

In her August 2014 President's Message, Diane Briars, president of the National Council of Teachers of Mathematics, offered back-to-school advice about what teachers should communicate to parents about their children's math learning:

> *First and foremost, parents need to know that being prepared for the 21st-century workforce requires being able to do more than simply compute or carry out procedures. Children need conceptual understanding as well as procedural fluency, and they need to know how, why, and when to apply this knowledge to answer questions and solve problems. They need to be able to reason mathematically and communicate their reasoning effectively to others.*

The remainder of this resource is dedicated to helping teachers meet this challenge.

Starting Point 2
Uncovering the Curriculum

Teachers have often told me that they don't have time for many of the rich math investigations that promote problem solving and number sense because they have to "cover the curriculum." Drawing on one of my favorite quotes, I respond, "You don't want to cover a subject; you want to uncover it." This quote is from *"The Having of Wonderful Ideas" and Other Essays on Teaching and Learning* by Eleanor Duckworth, a book on my shelf that I return to time and again for inspiration and guidance about teaching and learning. Eleanor Duckworth is one of my educational heroes, and another is David Hawkins, who she credits with the quote.

One of the steps in my own growth as a math teacher, actually one of the most important steps, has been to understand the difference between "covering" and "uncovering" the curriculum. I've given much thought to how to incorporate this difference into my teaching practice. In the next few pages, I address this aspect of my teaching journey through suggestions of investigations enhanced with firsthand experience based on the idea of uncovering the curriculum.

Most of my early teaching experience was in middle school and circles was a topic I needed to "cover" as part of the curriculum. In my early years of teaching, I primarily taught the way I had been taught. I presented the formulas for circumference ($c = \pi d$ or $2\pi r$) and area ($A = \pi r^2$), introduced π as the symbol for pi, explained that we could use either 3.14 or or $3\frac{1}{7}$ for the value of π, and then had students apply the formulas to solve problems. I "covered" the subject.

What was lacking in my teaching was attention to developing students' understanding. I didn't help students learn where pi came from, that it's the result of dividing the circumference by the diameter of any circle. I didn't give them opportunities to learn why the formulas for area and circumference made sense. I "covered" the subject, but I didn't "uncover" it. That is, I taught the formulas and how to apply them, but I didn't help develop students' understanding about circles. It's this difference that I've thought about a great deal since my early years of teaching.

As a beginning teacher, along with figuring out how to manage students and organize my classroom, I focused on honing my lessons. I mostly taught by explaining to my students what I wanted them to learn. It's long been believed that you know something best when you teach it, and I think there's truth to this. In order to be able to explain something, I have to think through the material for myself first, dig in to understand it deeply, and come up with a lesson sequence for presenting it clearly and precisely. Preparing for lessons calls for making sense of the content thoroughly, and that process of making sense of the content for myself strengthens my own knowledge.

But I've come to understand that my challenge as a teacher is also to find ways for students to make sense of what they're learning for *themselves*, so that they connect new concepts to the existing foundation of what they've already learned. In order to engage students actively in making sense of what they're learning, they need to do more than listen to explanations. An old Chinese proverb speaks to this: "I hear and I forget; I see and I remember; I do and I understand." When giving explanations, I'm covering the curriculum for the students, but not necessarily giving them opportunities and the support to uncover the curriculum for themselves.

Thinking About Uncovering the Curriculum: Investigations on Circles

Back to thinking about circles. Next I suggest some investigations that offer you support for uncovering important concepts about circles for yourself. After these, I return to the classroom and provide teaching ideas that I've found are useful for helping students uncover important concepts about circles for themselves.

Try This Now: Circle Investigation #1

Height/Circumference of a Soft Drink Can

Imagine a soft drink can. Suppose you take a piece of yarn or string and wrap it around the can to measure its circumference. Do you think the circumference is longer, shorter, or about the same as the height of the can? Indicate on the drawing how high you think the circumference measure will reach.

> **FYI**
> In the spirit of "I do and I understand," be sure to try Circle Investigation #1. If you cut a length of yarn or string about equal to your height, you'll have it for a later investigation as well.
>
> — MSB

I've done this experiment with many adults and children, and most guess incorrectly. The most common response is that the yarn wrapped around the can will be about the same length as the height of the can. There's an element of surprise not only when that perception is proved to be incorrect, but also about how much longer the wrapped-around yarn is than the height of the can. More than surprise, there's often a feeling of consternation, of being puzzled about what has been shown to be true about a common object that you've handled many times.

Realizing a misperception like this often results in a feeling of confusion. The new information you have from actually seeing how the yarn around the can compared to the height of the can doesn't fit with what you had predicted. You now have a problem—you've been faced with a contradiction. This state of confusion is what Jean Piaget called disequilibrium. At this moment, you have the greatest potential to learn, to gain new understanding about a relationship, to develop the understanding that takes you beyond your misperception to what is really so. This requires that you reorganize your thinking about the relationship between the distance around and the height of a soft drink can that led you to the erroneous conclusion in the first place.

Accomplishing this reorganization calls for making an internal adjustment in your thinking. The source of the new understanding lies inside you. Then, when you come to new understanding—based in reality rather than on how you perceived reality—you no longer are confused. It's as if your intellectual balance is restored. You no longer experience discomfort or confusion. You are in what Piaget terms the state of *equilibrium*.

One experience is not generally sufficient to cement understanding of a new relationship. To follow up the exploration of measuring with a soft drink can, experiment with other cylinders that have different proportions.

Try This Now: Circle Investigation #2

Height/Circumference of Other Cylinders

Repeat the experiment you did with the soft drink can with at least six other cylindrical containers. Use glasses or jars from your cupboard, paper cups, a roll of paper towels, wastepaper baskets—whatever is available. For each, make a sketch of the object and predict before measuring how the distance around the base compares with the height. Record your prediction (longer, shorter, or same) and the actual result for each.

What conclusion can you now make about the relationship of the circumference and the height of a cylindrical container? If it's not possible for you to make a conclusion, what more might you do?

_____

_____

_____

The process of resolving disequilibrium is called *equilibration*. This process is supported through ample concrete experiences. It's generally not sufficient to be taught a concept abstractly. Actually, when you studied about circles in school, you were "taught" what you needed for success on assignments and quizzes. You were taught the formulas $c = \pi d$ or $c = 2\pi r$, that the circumference of a circle is equal to pi times the diameter, or pi times the radius doubled. You used an approximate value for pi, $3\frac{1}{7}$ or 3.14. You plugged in pi and applied the formulas, but you may not have uncovered more about pi or the formulas in a way that was useful in this new situation.

What's important to understand about pi is that it's the ratio of the circumference of a circle to its diameter; that is, pi is equivalent to the circumference of a circle divided by the circle's diameter, or $\pi = \frac{c}{d}$. Pi is a mathematical constant that has always existed in our natural world, waiting to be discovered. It's a constant because the same number results from dividing the circumference by the diameter of any circle, no matter how large or small. The circumference of all circles is always equal to π times its diameter, or $c = \pi d$.

The diameter of the bottom of a soft drink is a little longer than my pinky finger. I know that the distance around a can, its circumference, is a little more than three times as long as its diameter. That means it's a little more than three times the length of my pinky. By comparing my pinky to the height of the can, I can see that a piece of yarn that measures the same as three of my pinky fingers will be much taller than the height of the can. Because of my understanding that the circumference of a circle is π times its diameter, I can generally predict correctly whether yarn that goes around any cylindrical container will be longer, shorter, or about the same length as the container's height. However, if I only had knowledge about how to use the formula, I wouldn't necessarily have the understanding to apply the formula in this new situation.

Can you imagine what a container looks like when the yarn around the container is just about as long as the height of the container? Think of a can of three tennis balls. The can is just about as tall as the diameters of the three tennis balls, which is very close to pi times the diameter, which is how we figure the circumference of a circle when we know the diameter.

Here's one more investigation for you to try. For this, you'll need just the yarn or string you cut that's equal to your height. But first think about the following:

Try This Now: Circle Investigation #3

The Ratio of Your Height to Your Head

How many times do you think a piece of yarn or string equal to your height would wrap around your head as a headband? Predict first and then measure.

As with the soft drink can experiment, unless you've tried this before, your initial response may be based purely on your perceptions, based on your own mental picture of your body. The answers that I've gotten over the years range between two and ten. (Ask at least five other people this same question.) Few people make an accurate estimate when the estimate is based solely on their perceptions.

Instead of making a guess based on my perception, I could make use of what I know about circles, π, and hat sizes. I know that hat-bands are more or less circular and that hats come in different sizes. Although many are sized small, medium, or large, some hats still come in numerical sizes that range from 6 to 8. Where do these sizes come from? The diameters of circles! I know that the circumference of a circle is equal to π times its diameter ($c = \pi d$). If you measure around your head, where a hatband would sit, that's more or less a circumference. Then if you divide the circumference of your head by π, you'll get a number that's about equal to the diameter of your head, about the distance across from one ear to the other. That's your hat size.

Back to comparing the distance around my head with my height: When I look in a mirror, I estimate that my head diameter is more than 6 inches, maybe even 7 inches. Also, I know that π is a little more than 3, so if I multiply 7 inches times 3, I get 21 inches, which is about the circumference of my head or the length of a hatband that would fit me. My height is about 65 inches, which is a little more than three times 21 inches. So a piece of yarn or string equal to my height will wrap around my head about three times.

Perceptions are not always based in reality. We see this with young children who are shown five objects and claim that there are more when the objects are spread out. This is what they perceive. Their response is not based on reasoning logically but on their perception.

If you've never explored the ratio between your height and your head, there's no reason to assume you have learned that relationship. You most likely need to do the measurement to find out the ratio. To learn concepts, experience in the real world is often useful.

The mathematics instruction we provide to students should emphasize meaning, relationships, and connections to help them "uncover" the curriculum. We must attend to what students understand, not merely what they can do. It's useful to keep in mind the importance during instruction of balancing procedures and understanding. When students lack understanding, they're more likely to grasp for a procedure and less likely to consider similar problems, step back to evaluate their answers, think about how math can relate to practical situations, or use more efficient shortcuts when appropriate.

In the Classroom

What might classroom instruction look like that uncovers the curriculum to develop both understanding about circles and why the formulas make sense? I presented the soft drink can as a professional learning experience, but it's also an appropriate investigation that I've used in many classrooms and at different grade levels.

For Younger Students

With younger students, I keep the mathematical focus on comparing and measuring, not on the characteristics of circles. For example, second graders gleefully predict as I wrap the yarn around the can and compare its length to the height of different containers. They're then eager to explore other containers on their own. I collect an ample supply, labeling them A, B, C, and so on, and give a length of yarn to each student. Working in pairs, students measure and compare, record their results, and sort the containers into three groups according to whether the distance around each is longer, shorter, or about the same length as the container's height. (Because not all containers are cylindrical, such as plastic cups that are wider at the top than at the bottom, I direct students to measure around the bottoms so that they all produce the same results for each container.) I have them decide how to represent their results and then have the class compare their different ways of recording.

For Third and Fourth Graders

For third and fourth graders, I broaden the mathematical focus to include measuring with standard units. I provide them tape measures and rulers and ask them to record the actual measurements of the circumferences and heights of the containers. This not only provides them practice with measuring lengths but also engages them with the important idea of approximation when measuring.

For Fifth Graders and Older

Fifth graders and older students also use standard measures to compare the circumferences of the containers' bottoms with their heights, but I take the investigation deeper. The students measure the diameters of the bottoms of the containers, divide the measures of their circumferences by their diameters, and then compare the quotients. They're typically surprised that the quotients are all close to 3. I build

For a description of and my commentary on the investigation for third and fourth graders, as well as a suggested way for students to record, see *Round Things* in Part 2 on page 152.

on that experience to introduce pi as the ratio of the circumference and diameter of all circles. Not only are the older students engaged in useful practice with measuring and division, they also gain experience with the approximate nature of measurement while developing understanding of the standard formula for figuring out the circumference of circles, $c = \pi d$.

Students in grade 7 are also expected to learn about the formula for figuring out the area of circles, $A = \pi r^2$.

Wrapping It Up

In a nutshell: When mathematical knowledge is based in logic, it requires students to make sense in order to develop understanding, to interact with the knowledge in ways that help them uncover its meaning for themselves. Uncovering knowledge is supported by engaging in firsthand investigations, working with physical materials when appropriate, and having opportunities to interact with others. It calls for thinking and reasoning, and the process is unique to each learner; that is, the source of *logical knowledge* is internal.

It's also true that some mathematical knowledge doesn't rely on the internal process of figuring something out to make sense of it, but instead is *social knowledge*, based on agreed-upon conventions, not logic. Students acquire social knowledge by relying on outside sources—a book, another person, TV, the internet. No amount of thinking and reasoning alone will reveal knowledge about conventions; that is, the source of *social knowledge* is external.

Using the Greek letter pi to represent the ratio of the circumference to diameter of circles is not based in logic. It's a social convention, as is using the symbol π for pi. This is material that I have to "cover." I tell them. But the ratio of the circumference to the diameter is a mathematical constant that exists in the physical world for all circles. Students can "uncover" this for themselves through firsthand learning experiences. And they should.

For a follow-up investigation and my commentary, see *Wraparound* in Part 2 on page 161.

For a unit that presents how to uncover for students why the formula for figuring out the area of circles makes sense, see "Finding the Area of a Circle" from *A Collection of Math Lessons from Grades 6 through 8*, a book I coauthored with Cathy Humphreys (1991).

Starting Point 3

You Can't Teach What You Don't Understand

A friend of mine, also a math teacher, has a tee shirt with this message on it:

Those who can, do.

Those who understand, teach.

I agree with this message. An important element of teaching math well is to understand deeply the mathematics that students are learning. Even with elementary math topics that seem to be fairly uncomplicated and easy to understand, unexpected twists, turns, and difficulties can emerge during classroom teaching. Our math knowledge as teachers has to be robust enough so that we are prepared to confront complications when they arise.

I earned my undergraduate degree in mathematics and took a hefty number of upper division math courses. After I became a teacher, I attended professional learning sessions and talks at conferences, which provided me opportunities to learn more about the mathematics content taught in kindergarten through eighth grade, content that wasn't included in my university math courses. I was able to revisit old content and deepen my understanding in important ways.

Understanding What You Teach: Investigations with Cylinders

Here's an example of an exploration I experienced at a workshop many years ago. The exploration was about cylinders, a topic that I "thought" I understood. But confronted with a new problem, what had seemed straightforward to me turned out to increase my understanding. I encourage you to try the investigation so that you can better understand what I describe.

Try This Now: Cylinder Investigation #1

Take two 5-by-8-inch cards, tape, and dried beans or rice. Roll and tape each card into a tube, rolling one the short way and the other the long way. You'll have two cylinders, one shorter and wider, and the other taller and thinner.

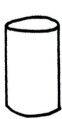 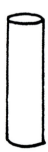

Imagine that these cylinders are both glasses and you were going to choose one to enjoy some iced tea. Will they hold the same amount? If not, which do you think would hold more than the other? Why? Jot down what you think.

_____

_____

Now measure by first placing the taller thinner tube on a piece of paper (for easier cleanup afterward) and filling it to the top with the beans or rice. Then place the shorter wider tube over it. Slowly lift out the thinner tube so the beans or rice are transferred to the wider tube. What do you notice?

_____

_____

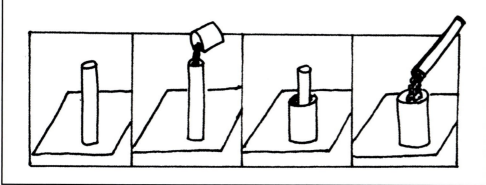

While I can't remember when I was introduced to this investigation or by whom, I do remember how startled I was that what happened was so different from what I had predicted. What I had thought was that since the containers were made from identical 5-by-8-inch index cards, they'd hold the same amount. This seemed obvious to me. But then, after I lifted out the thinner container, I noticed that the wider container was only a little more than half full. Well, maybe it was two-thirds full. Either way, it was now clear to me that the shorter, wider container would be a much better choice if I wanted a larger amount of iced tea.

My experience with the two cylinders made me curious about my own confusion. I was invested in the situation, ready and eager to learn more. I knew that I had to reorganize how I had been thinking, which was that since both containers were made from the same size card, both would hold the same amount. That is, because they had the same surface area, I thought their volumes would also be the same. When I measured with beans, it was made clear to me that their volumes were different. Now I thought that the volume of a cylinder isn't determined only by its surface area, but also by its shape.

What did I do? I reached out to friends to talk about the problem, and together we decided to experiment further.

The area of a 5-by-8-inch index card is 40 square inches, so my colleagues and I decided to make other shaped cylinders with that same surface area. (Investigating ideas with physical materials provides valuable feedback for developing understanding.) What we did is take another 5-by-8-inch index card, cut it in half (hamburger cut, not hotdog cut) so we had two 5-by-4-inch rectangles, and then taped the two rectangles together into a 4-by-10-inch rectangle. This new rectangle still had the same area of 40 square inches, but it wasn't the same shape as the 5-by-8-inch index card. We rolled and taped it into a tall, thin cylinder. We then cut another 5-by-8-inch index card the same way but rolled the resulting 4-by-10-inch rectangle into a shorter, wider cylinder. Now we were ready to continue our investigation.

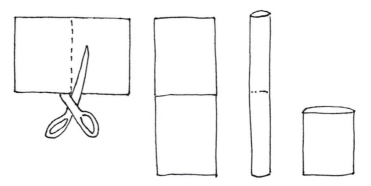

We decided to use beans to compare the volumes of all four cylinders by using a standard measuring cup to measure and record how much each held. (This seemed more efficient than counting the beans.) We studied our data. We talked more. We related our measurements to the formula for the volume of a cylinder: $V = \pi r^2 h$. We worked over a period of time, taking breaks when we felt overloaded or stuck, but sticking with it until we finally made sense of what was happening.

Try This Now: Cylinder Investigation #2

Use two more 5-by-8-inch cards to make two additional cylinders as shown earlier. Before rolling and taping them, cut each card in half (hamburger cut, not hotdog cut), tape each into a 5-by-4-inch rectangle, and then roll and tape each into a cylinder.

Use a standard measuring cup to measure the beans that fill these two cylinders and also the two cylinders from Cylinder Investigation #1. Record. What can you learn from the data?

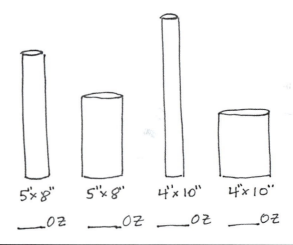

5"x 8"   5"x 8"   4"x 10"   4"x 10"

___oz   ___oz   ___oz   ___oz

It's just this process of investigation that I strive to offer to students. I seek to create situations that engage students' interest in pursuing ideas the way I was engaged by this investigation with cylinders. I encourage students to take risks, make predictions, and not get discouraged when their predictions turned out to be wrong. I remind them that confusion and partial understanding are part of learning. I strive to inspire them to be interested, curious, and invested in learning more.

Solving problems that involve surface area and volume is part of middle school math, which I taught for my first eight years of teaching. Although I was familiar with the formulas when I began teaching, that knowledge wasn't sufficient for preparing me to introduce this investigation about cylinders to students. It was only after exploring cylinders as I described, going beyond applying the formulas and thinking about a situation that was new for me, that my own understanding was sufficiently deepened. I then felt prepared to present this exploration to students, confident that I could understand students' approaches and ways of thinking, field questions they might have, and guide them to persevere.

Connecting New Ideas to Previous Understandings

In K–5 mathematics instruction, the content of number and operations receives the major emphasis. And even though we think of this content as "elementary" math, it too has complexities and demands in-depth content knowledge in order to teach for understanding. This knowledge extends beyond basic facts and procedures.

For example, think about multiplying fractions. As students ourselves, we learned the procedure for multiplying fractions: You multiply across the numerators and across the denominators. But why? Frankly, it's easier and more expedient to teach students the procedure than to help them make sense of why multiplying the numerators and denominators produces a correct answer.

Teaching for expediency, however, is not sufficient for developing understanding. We need to connect new ideas to previous understandings. Students learn about multiplying fractions in grades 4 and 5, initially applying what they've learned about multiplying whole numbers to multiplying whole numbers by fractions, and then extending their learning to multiplying fractions by fractions. In both grades, the starting point is on *understandings*. Teaching the "why" requires that teachers themselves have thought deeply about multiplying fractions, which means connecting new ideas to previous understandings.

Here's one approach for making such a connection. When we multiply whole numbers, for example 6×4, one way we interpret this is to think of "6 groups of 4," which we can interpret as $4 + 4 + 4 + 4 + 4 + 4$, or 24. Similarly, to multiply a fraction by a whole number, $6 \times \frac{1}{4}$, as included in the Common Core content standards in grades 4 and 5, we can think of "6 groups of $\frac{1}{4}$" as $\frac{1}{4} + \frac{1}{4} + \frac{1}{4} + \frac{1}{4} + \frac{1}{4} + \frac{1}{4}$, which is $\frac{6}{4}$. And this is the answer we get from multiplying across the numerators and denominators of $\frac{6}{1} \times \frac{1}{4}$. This starting point helps students make sense of multiplying a whole number by a fraction.

In *Teaching Arithmetic: Lessons for Multiplying and Dividing Fractions, Grades 5–6* (2003), I present lessons I've taught that are designed specifically to help develop students' understandings and skills with multiplying and dividing fractions.

Helping Students Understand "Why?"

The underpinnings of numerical concepts are essential for building the mathematical foundations that students need, for helping them understand "why" things work the way they do. To that end, it's important for teachers to have opportunities to think deeply about these underpinnings. Here are some examples of "why" questions to contemplate, with brief explanations to get you started thinking about them:

1. *Why is it OK to add a zero when multiplying whole numbers by ten but not when multiplying decimals by ten?* This calls for knowing that tacking a zero onto a whole number increases it tenfold since it shifts the digits in the original number each one place to the left; for example, tacking on a zero changes 25 to 250, which is ten times greater. But with decimals, tacking on zeroes after the decimal point doesn't change the value; for example, 2.5 and 2.50 are equivalent, both equal to $2\frac{1}{2}$.

2. *Why, when multiplying whole numbers, do we always get an odd product when we multiply two odd numbers, but an even product when we multiply an odd number times an even number or we multiply two even numbers?* I've often had students in grade 3 and up investigate this. From trying examples, students generally decide that it's true that multiplying two odd numbers results in an odd product. But giving examples isn't a conclusive proof. A proof calls for constructing a viable argument, which is an important mathematical practice. Kelly, a third grader, tried to give a convincing explanation. She chose an example—3 × 5—and drew five groups of three circles to interpret it.

   Then Kelly separated each group of three circles into two groups, one with two circles and one with one circle. She reasoned, "So fifteen is equal to five groups of two circles plus five groups of one circle. If you add five twos, you get an even number, ten, because adding any number of twos will always be even. The five ones add up to five, which is odd because it's an odd number of ones. And ten plus five is odd because when you add an even number to an odd number, you always get an odd number." I wasn't able to follow Kelly's reasoning when she explained it to me, so I asked her to write it down. Her writing appears on the next page.

> **FYI**
> We typically interpret
> 3 × 5 as three groups of five,
> but Kelly didn't follow this
> convention for her argument.
> Still, her interpretation is
> mathematically correct.
>
> — MSB

For more on interpreting multiplication, see one teacher's question in Part 4 on page 482.

> Proof for Odd × Odd = Odd
>
> 3 × 7 = 21
> 5 × 7 = 35
> 7 × 7 = 49
> 5 × 5 = 25
>
> Odd × Odd = Odd becaus if you take 1 odd number and do it a number of odd times and take 1 away from the odd number you get a even number done a odd number of times. So if you add all the even number you get a even number
>
> oo + oo + oo + oo + o͜o = 10   10+5=15
>   5
>
> 3×5=15
>
> then you add all the ones together. you get a.. odd number so if you add the even number the odd number you get a odd number. So Odd × Odd = Odd because it's the same thing as what I did to find the awnser just without all the work.

3. *Why is the sum of two odd numbers always even?* This question combines investigating how the parity of numbers—that is, whether they are odd or even—connects to the operation of addition. Questions like this help students develop understanding of the properties of numbers and of operations while building their number sense. Before students discuss this, it's important to give them time to verify that adding two odd numbers results in an even sum. I typically have students do this in pairs, and also discuss with their partners why this might be so. This helps them prepare to offer ideas in a classroom discussion. I've seen students come up with several explanations for why the sum of an odd number plus an odd number is even. For instance, one student explained that when you take an odd number of things and put them in pairs, there will always be one extra without a partner. But when you put two odd numbers of things in pairs, each of them will have one extra without a partner. These two extras can always be paired, so there won't be an extra anymore.

> **Teaching Tip**
> I often follow up this conversation on other days with different but related questions: Why is the sum of two even numbers always even? Why is the sum of an odd number and an even number always odd? What happens when we subtract two odd numbers, two even numbers, or one of each?
>
> —MSB

4. *Why is zero an even number?* Even numbers describe integers that are divisible by 2; for example $26 \div 2 = 13$, so 26 is even. (A number is divisible by another when the result is a whole number without a remainder.) Using multiplication instead of division, an integer is even if you can write it as two times something; for example, $26 = 2 \times 13$, so 26 is even. Or you can use addition—even numbers can be represented as a number plus itself ($13 + 13 = 26$, so 26 is even). Zero passes all three tests; it's divisible by 2 ($0 \div 2 = 0$), $2 \times 0 = 0$, and $0 + 0 = 0$. One way young children can think about even numbers, before they have learned about multiplication or division is by using what they know about addition. For example, 6 is an even number because they physically can divide six objects into two equal groups with three in each, and $3 + 3 = 6$. It's hard to relate physically to zero counters, but you can write $0 + 0 = 0$, so it follows the pattern.

5. *Why don't we classify fractions as odd or even?* As I described earlier, you can use division, or multiplication, and addition to determine whether an integer is even. If you apply these tests to fractions, you would determine that all fractions are even. Take $\frac{6}{10}$, for example. You can divide it by 2 ($\frac{6}{10} \div 2 = \frac{3}{10}$ or $\frac{6}{20}$); you can represent it as 2 times something ($2 \times \frac{3}{10} = \frac{6}{10}$); you can split it into two equal parts ($\frac{3}{10} + \frac{3}{10} = \frac{6}{10}$). Well, you might be skeptical because the numerator and denominator of $\frac{6}{10}$ are both even. So take another fraction like $\frac{5}{7}$, which sort of seems as if it should be odd. The tests work again: $\frac{5}{7} \div 2 = \frac{5}{14}$; $2 \times \frac{5}{14} = \frac{10}{14}$, which is the same as $\frac{5}{7}$; $\frac{5}{14} + \frac{5}{14} = \frac{5}{7}$. You can apply the three tests to any fraction in the same way, which means we would have to classify all fractions as even, which isn't very useful. So the designation of odd or even only applies to integers.

6. *Why does "canceling" zeros in the fraction $\frac{10}{20}$ produce an equivalent fraction, but not in the fraction $\frac{101}{201}$?* I presented this question to a class of fourth graders. First, we discussed several examples of equivalent fractions that demonstrated we could "cancel" zeroes in their numerators and denominators and have equivalent fractions:

$$\frac{10}{20} = \frac{1}{2} \qquad \frac{20}{40} = \frac{2}{4} \qquad \frac{20}{30} = \frac{2}{3}$$

Then I presented another fraction and asked if it was OK to "cancel" the zeroes and still have an equivalent fraction:

$$\frac{101}{201} \quad ? \quad \frac{11}{21}$$

Some initially thought yes and others thought no, and we had a spirited discussion. Trey argued for yes because, "It works for $\frac{102}{204}$ and $\frac{12}{24}$ because both would be $\frac{12}{24}$ and that's $\frac{1}{2}$." Russell supported Trey with another example, $\frac{100}{200}$ and $\frac{10}{20}$, saying, "It doesn't matter which zeroes you cancel." Elissa argued that those examples were different because you could reduce those fractions to $\frac{1}{2}$. "But you can't reduce $\frac{101}{201}$ or $\frac{11}{21}$ to any-

For a suggestion about how to help young children learn about even and odd numbers, see "Starting Point 18: The Role of Manipulative Materials" in Part 1 on page 99.

thing," she said. Tina argued that the fractions should be the same because, "If you add 1 to each denominator, you get $\frac{101}{202}$ and $\frac{11}{22}$, and these both are equal to $\frac{1}{2}$." Sophia used a calculator to divide and reported that it didn't work because $101 + 201$ was 0.5024875 and $11 \div 21$ was 0.5238095. She came up to the board and recorded these numbers. Then Nick came to the board and wrote the sequence of equivalent fractions he had written starting with $\frac{11}{21}$ to show that $\frac{101}{201}$ wasn't in the sequence:

$$\frac{11}{21}, \ \frac{22}{42}, \ \frac{33}{63}, \ \frac{44}{84}, \ \frac{55}{105}, \ \frac{66}{126}, \ \frac{77}{147}, \ \frac{88}{168}, \ \frac{99}{189}, \ \frac{110}{210}$$

Emmy gave a place value argument for why you can't cross out the middle zeroes. She said, "If you cross out the zeroes, you suddenly are making hundreds into tens, and math doesn't work like that."

Actually, there were three sides, with Leslie offering a minority opinion that the discussion was moot since both fractions were very, very close to $\frac{1}{2}$, so you should just say that they're just about the same.

Wrapping It Up

Glenda Lappan, a past president of the National Council of Teachers of Mathematics, addressed the importance of teacher knowledge in her article "Knowing What We Teach and Teaching What We Know" (n.d.). She wrote:

> *Our own content knowledge affects how we interpret the content goals we are expected to reach with our students. It affects the way we hear and respond to our students and their questions. It affects our ability to explain clearly and to ask good questions. It affects our ability to approach a mathematical idea flexibly with our students and to make connections. It affects our ability to push each student at that special moment when he or she is ready or curious. And it affects our ability to make those moments happen more often for our students.*

When teachers are asked to think deeply about how to multiply one fraction by another fraction, they may wonder, *What's the point of understanding that when students are tested only on the answer to the problem?* Being able to compute answers without also understanding the underlying mathematics is an insufficient and shallow goal for students' mathematics learning. It builds the erroneous notion for students that math is all about learning procedures, rather than learning math is about making sense of ideas. Also, it runs the risk that learning procedures becomes the end goal of math instruction, while the mathematical expertise we should seek to develop in our students is much broader and embraces understanding as well as procedures. All instruction must foster students' ability to think, reason, and solve problems.

There are opportunities throughout this resource to help you deepen your own mathematical knowledge. It's important to bring a sense of curiosity to these opportunities and pursue making sense of ideas that are new for you. The payoff will be not only for you but for your students as well.

Starting Point 4
Helping Students Become Effective Math Learners

Many years ago, when I was beginning to lead professional learning sessions about math for K–8 teachers, I was asked to conduct six after-school sessions for the kindergarten teachers in the county where I live. I agreed, and seventeen teachers signed up for the series. Then I panicked. I had never taught kindergarten. What could I possibly have been thinking when I agreed? Yes, I knew what children were supposed to learn in kindergarten math and I had ideas about instruction that would support their learning, but my firsthand understanding of the demands of kindergarten teaching were limited to the few visits I had made to observe kindergarten classes.

One of the teachers who had enrolled was a close friend. She had actually been the impetus for organizing this class, and I sought help from her. What resulted was the decision to hold the six sessions in six of the seventeen kindergarten teachers' classrooms. I would plan the bulk of each session, and the hosting teacher would also contribute by talking about her classroom—why she arranged the classroom furniture as she did, how she organized children for math lessons, what she thought about when planning daily instruction, and what math content she was focusing on at the time we met. I sent out a note to each teacher who had enrolled and recruited volunteers.

It turned out to be a wonderfully successful experience for us all. What was especially beneficial for me was what I gleaned from being in the different classrooms, learning how seasoned teachers organized for instruction. It made sitting in those teeny kindergarten chairs for two hours after school well worth it.

After this experience, I made the commitment to spend more time learning from teachers in their classrooms. I no longer was teaching full time and instead was devoting my time to writing and providing inservice. I keenly felt the need to be connected with actual classroom instruction. Since then, I've used a variety of ways to keep in touch. Some years I've "adopted" a class nearby, becoming a partner teacher for math time. Some years I've established a relationship with several teachers, at times supporting them by presenting lessons for them to observe, at times observing their lessons, and at other times "borrowing" their classes to try out new lessons I'm working on.

These experiences have given me the opportunity to be in different classrooms and observe a wide variety of effective teaching practices in action, something that wasn't possible when I was teaching full time. The experiences have been invaluable for helping me understand the characteristics that are important for students to develop:

- interest to figure out solutions to problems
- willingness to persevere when solutions are not immediate
- ability to check solutions by solving problems in a different way

- understanding that incorrect answers are valuable for learning and, therefore, be willing to risk making errors at times
- ability to accept frustrations that come from not knowing
- understanding that there's a difference between not knowing an answer and not having figuring it out *yet*

This is a substantial list of characteristics, and the amount of time and effort needed to develop them depends on the students themselves and their previous learning experiences. What I've learned from my many classroom visits is that in order to help students develop these characteristics, it's essential that they see them regularly modeled and encouraged by their teachers. Only then will students feel that their teacher values their thinking and that the classroom is a safe place for them to participate openly and fully.

Present Problems That Have Different Possible Answers or Outcomes

To encourage the attitudes of "let's try" and "we can," I've found it helpful to present problems or initiate investigations that have more than one particular correct answer or outcome. For example, many teachers use the number of the day for a warm-up routine. The investigation asks students to think of equations that use the number of the day, and the possibilities are endless. For younger children, using the day of the month for the number of the day relates the investigation to the calendar and limits the range of the numbers. Keeping track of which day of school it is, perhaps planning for a 100th day of school celebration, extends the numbers. Setting parameters structures the investigation further: "Use subtraction." "Use at least two operations." "Think of an equation that involves multiplication." "Include fractions (or decimals)." "Make the number of the day the remainder of a division problem." "Include at least one exponent." Teachers use the investigation in different ways—having students work individually or in pairs, having students give equations orally and recording them on the board, or asking students to write three equations when math time begins and then having a few report what they wrote.

Encourage Students to Verify Solutions for Themselves

It's important for students to develop the mathematical practice of checking their answers to problems using different methods to decide if their answers make sense. To this end, it's important to encourage students to find ways to verify solutions for themselves. Having students think about problems in more than one way, by talking with a partner or hearing others' ideas in a classroom discussion, can provide alternate views on solutions.

Not only is this good practice for classroom instruction, it's also a helpful skill in most life situations. For many problems we face, there isn't one correct solution but several possibilities. Often, an exact solution isn't required and being close enough is sufficient. Most

For tips about incorporating children's books in math lessons, see "Starting Point 23: Using Children's Literature to Teach Math" in Part 1 on page 126.

In *Lessons for Algebraic Thinking: Grades K–2*, see *Two Handfuls* (Burns and von Rotz 2002, 128–156) for useful ideas to help students build their understanding of the equivalence relationship.

For an example of verifying a solution by acting it out, see the *Dealing in Horses* problem in "Starting Point 8: Word Problems: Developing Understanding of Arithmetic Operations" in Part 1 on page 36.

importantly, in real life, it's often up to the problem solver to decide when a solution is right or best. (Life has no answer book!) In light of those issues, it's important to urge students to evaluate their own solutions and to provide them support for doing so.

Ask Students to Explain Their Approaches and Results

Along with not providing answers, I'm diligent about encouraging students to explain their approaches and results, even when they are totally correct. Often, teachers nod and affirm students' correct responses and question them when there are errors. If we question students only when their responses are wrong, the students soon catch on. Instruction should be structured so students describe their methods and solutions not only to the teacher but to their classmates as well. Time for discussions is needed, and students should be encouraged to listen, question, and learn from one another's ideas.

Value Errors as Opportunities for Learning

It's important to address the issue of making mistakes. Students need to see errors as opportunities for learning, not as unfortunate occurrences. They must feel that it's OK to offer an idea that might be incorrect and know that they'll have the support of their teacher and classmates to resolve errors in their thinking. I consistently emphasize, when asking students to think about an idea or solve a problem, that I value persistence, not speed, which relates to the mathematical practice of making sense of problems and persevering in solving them. Putting the value on quick, right responses does not help establish a classroom environment that supports students' learning.

Wrapping It Up

One thing I've learned is that there isn't one best way to manage math instruction. As teachers, we all have different teaching styles and ideas. I've also learned that thinking about how to help students become effective math learners calls for thinking about all that's required to support and facilitate student learning—establishing a safe environment for learning, arranging the classroom furniture, defining how students are to participate in lessons, helping students establish productive learning habits, and managing materials for storage and use. Helping students become effective learners of mathematics requires consistent and ongoing reinforcement. With time, a classroom culture of curiosity, inquiry, and communication can become the norm.

Number and Operations: The Mathematical Cornerstone

Starting Point 5
Reasoning: A Perspective on Arithmetic

As a child, I was bothered that "arithmetic" was the third R in the 3R's of Reading, Writing, and Arithmetic. It was clear that "arithmetic" didn't begin with an "r" and even when it appeared as "rithmetic" the R seemed wrong to me. (Using an R for Writing wasn't as offensive to me—maybe the phonetics of writing made it more OK.)

I did some digging into the origins of the 3R's phrase and traced it to Sir William Curtis, who was born in London in 1752 and served as a member of the London parliament for 28 years, from 1790 through 1818. He used the 3R's phrase in a speech he made at a Board of Education dinner in 1795, and it seems that it slipped into common usage.

I also found references, maybe more pleas than references, for changing the third R of Arithmetic to Reasoning. One reference that I found to be particularly interesting is from Louis Benezet, who was superintendent of schools in Manchester, New Hampshire. In 1936, he published "The Teaching of Arithmetic I, II, III: The Story of an Experiment" in the *Journal of the National Education Association*. He presented his new version of the 3R's as "Reading, Reasoning, and Reciting." About "reciting," he explained that he was referring to speaking the English language, not giving back words verbatim from teachers or textbooks. He made a firm case for the focus of arithmetic instruction to be on reasoning, and he abandoned the teaching of formal arithmetic procedures in his district prior to the seventh grade. It was a radical idea that, obviously, hasn't taken hold.

The idea of changing the traditional third R from arithmetic to reasoning, however, delights me. Arithmetic still holds its place as the emphasis of the mathematics content for kindergarten through grade 5, but now with a broader view than developing proficiency with paper-and-pencil computation. Computational procedures are still important, of course, and students learn algorithms for computing accurately and efficiently. Algorithms are useful when problems are too complex for reasoning mentally, and being able to reason mentally is rooted in understanding. For instruction, this translates to developing understanding that builds the reasoning strategies students need for dealing flexibly with numbers.

In order to make the case for reasoning, it's helpful to consider the role of arithmetic in our daily lives. We all know that being able to compute is a necessary life tool. On a daily basis, we face situations that call for doing arithmetic. I've asked teachers at professional learning sessions and parents at back-to-school nights to list situations when they use arithmetic—that is, when they have to add, subtract, multiply, and/or divide to figure out something they need to know. The responses typically include the following: when I calculate my checkbook balance, when I'm in the supermarket figuring how much I'm spending or doing price comparisons, when I'm estimating the price of a sale item with the discount, when I need to know how much wallpaper or floor covering I need, when I'm deciding on the tip in a

To learn more about Benezet's version of the 3R's (Reading, Reasoning, and Reciting), visit inference.phy.cam.ac.uk/sanjoy/benezet

restaurant, when I want to know the mileage I'm getting on my car, when I'm figuring out what time to put the roast in the oven, when I'm deciding what time to leave to arrive at the movies on time.

When I've asked them to review their lists to see how they typically do the arithmetic required, people report that they most often either figure mentally, or they use a calculator or computer. Relying on paper and pencil is always a less common choice. When people evaluate their lists to decide when being accurate is necessary (such as when keeping score in games) and when an estimate does fine or is even more appropriate (such as when tipping in restaurants), they generally find a fifty-fifty split between the two.

Thinking About Your Use of Arithmetic

Complete the following questionnaire to analyze your own use of arithmetic.

Try This Now

How You Use Arithmetic

1. List all the situations outside of school responsibilities during the past month for which you've used arithmetic—that is, you've had to add, subtract, multiply, and/or divide.

   _____   _____

   _____   _____

   _____   _____

   _____   _____

   _____   _____

2. There are three methods people generally use when doing arithmetic:

   (1) calculator or computer
   (2) paper and pencil
   (3) figure mentally

   Using 1, 2, or 3 as described above, number each item on your list to indicate the method you usually use in that situation. Which method do you use

   most often? _____

   least often? _____

3. Review your list once more and mark each item with E for estimate or A for accurate to show which is usually required for that situation.

   What percentage of your items did you mark estimate? _____

   What percentage of your items did you mark accurate? _____

Wrapping It Up

Learning to do paper-and-pencil arithmetic on isolated examples does not ensure that students will truly develop understanding of concepts or develop the number sense they need to reason mentally. This becomes obvious when assigning addition practice and a student asks, "Do I have to carry on this page?" It's obvious when assigning word problems and a student asks, "Do I need to add or subtract?" It's clear when a student makes a division error, omitting a zero in the quotient so the answer is ten times too small, and doesn't even notice. All of these examples indicate students' lack of understanding and are substantiated by research findings.

I'm not implying that students don't need to learn arithmetic procedures. Instead, students need to learn more about arithmetic, including which operations to use when solving problems, how to choose a method for computing that's appropriate for the numbers at hand, and how to determine whether an answer makes sense. Can students determine whether it's cheaper to buy things two for a nickel or three for a dime? Can they name a fraction that is larger than one-third yet smaller than one-half? Can they figure out what to do when halving a recipe that calls for $\frac{3}{4}$ cup of sugar? (What would you do?) Merely learning paper-and-pencil arithmetic algorithms is not sufficient preparation for students' future mathematical success—reasoning is essential to arithmetic instruction.

Starting Point 6
Why Do Students Make Common Arithmetic Errors?

Emphasizing computational procedures without adequate attention to developing understanding runs the risk of failing to help students develop the reasoning skills they also need. The importance of reasoning became clear and compelling to me after I began to think about the common errors I noticed students made when doing paper-and-pencil computations.

Try This Now

Investigating Incorrect Answers

For each of the arithmetic exercises below, purposely record an incorrect answer that reflects an error that you've seen students make.

1. $3 + \boxed{} = 7$	2. $\begin{array}{r} 35 \\ +67 \\ \hline \end{array}$
3. $\begin{array}{r} 42 \\ -17 \\ \hline \end{array}$	4. $\begin{array}{r} 300 \\ -136 \\ \hline \end{array}$
5. $12\overline{)3840}$	6. $\dfrac{1}{2} + \dfrac{2}{3} =$
7. $2.06 + 1.3 + 0.38 =$	8. $\begin{array}{r} \$5.40 \\ \times 0.15 \\ \hline \end{array}$

With the exception of errors that result from carelessness, typically with basic facts, most errors that students make are not random. They are remarkably consistent. Teachers see the same mistakes over and over, year after year. In most instances, students' errors relate to rules they've learned, but have applied incorrectly or in inappropriate situations. They often are guided by logic, but the logic is often incorrect for the problem being solved. The following errors and explanations are examples of students' incorrect thinking.

1. $3 + \boxed{10} = 7$ A plus sign means to add.

2. $\begin{array}{r} 35 \\ +67 \\ \hline 912 \end{array}$ Add the numbers in each column and write the sums under the line.

3. $\begin{array}{r} 42 \\ -17 \\ \hline 35 \end{array}$ When you subtract, you take the smaller number from the larger.

4.
$$\begin{array}{r} \overset{299}{\cancel{300}} \\ -136 \\ \hline 163 \end{array}$$ You can't subtract a number from zero, so you change the zeros into nines.

or

$$\begin{array}{r} \overset{2}{\cancel{3}}\overset{1}{0}0 \\ -136 \\ \hline 174 \end{array}$$ You can't subtract from zero, so you borrow from the three and the zeros become tens.

5.
$$\begin{array}{r} 32 \\ 12\overline{)3840} \end{array}$$ You can drop the zero at the end of the problem.

6. $\frac{1}{2} + \frac{2}{3} = \frac{3}{5}$ When you add fractions, you add across the top and across the bottom.

7.
$$\begin{array}{r} 2.06 \\ 1.3 \\ .38 \\ \hline 2.57 \end{array}$$ Line up the numbers and add.

8.
$$\begin{array}{r} \$5.40 \\ \times 0.15 \\ \hline \$81.00 \end{array}$$ After you figure the problem, bring down the decimal point.

Thinking about possible causes for these examples of erroneous reasoning is helpful for informing instruction. When learning arithmetic procedures, students focus on the numerals and symbols in problems and tend to see arithmetic as doing something with them to get the right answers. The same students who incorrectly put 10 in the box for the first example, $3 + \square = 7$, most likely know that $3 + 10$ is not equal to 7. When tackling a missing-addend problem, students who make the common error aren't focusing on the meaning of the problem but on the symbols in the problem. They learned that a plus sign means to add, so they combined 3 and 7 to get the sum instead of figuring out how much more was needed to add to 3 to get 7. However, the error doesn't typically occur when children think about the same numerical problem set in a context: *You have three birthday candles, but you need seven altogether. How many more birthday candles do you need?* When given this problem, students generally interpret the situation and correctly figure out that they need three more birthday candles. Here they don't make the error they commonly do when dealing with the same problem presented only numerically.

Integrating Understanding and Procedures

The implication from the examples of arithmetic errors is that students rely on following procedures without reasoning. (Yours is not to question why; just invert and multiply.) Applying procedures without reasoning results from learning arithmetic as a collection of specific steps for figuring out answers, rather than thinking about what makes sense. Many teachers express concern when students come to class and want to know if they can do the division using a method someone at home showed them. It's not uncommon for a teacher to believe that children must learn to divide only the way their textbook says. The implication is that the specific algorithm is important, not that students should understand that different algorithms are possible and they should make sense of any method they use. It's important to keep in mind the need for an instructional balance of procedures and understanding, so that students don't rely on procedures that are inappropriate for the numbers at hand because of a lack of understanding.

Focus on Doing the Math, Not Doing the Page

When making errors, students rarely notice or even seem to care when they arrive at an absurd answer. Though teachers urge students to estimate or check their answers, students are generally more concerned with finishing the assignment. Their goal is to get the problem or page done, not to evaluate answers. Our goal should be to keep the focus on "do the math," not on "do the page." Some students when figuring out 15 percent of $5.40 will get the result of $81.00 (as shown on the previous page), and accept the answer without question, even though $81.00 is fifteen times greater than $5.40. (The correct answer would be $81.00 if the problem were to figure out what is 1500% of $5.40!) If students believe that getting quick, right answers is what's valued in school, then this response is an obvious result. Instruction should aim not toward an answer-oriented curriculum but toward one that values reasoning processes and calls for evaluating answers as an essential part of any assignment.

Wrapping It Up

Not only is the mastery of algorithms often seen as the most important goal in elementary mathematics instruction, the algorithms taught are often presented as if they are the only way to perform a calculation. In this light, the following exercise is revealing:

┌─ **Try This Now** ───

Calculating Mentally
Mentally double 38.
Then analyze the method you used in order to arrive at the answer.

└──

When adults are asked to double 38 mentally and then describe how they figured it out, their methods vary. Some visualize the problem symbolically, seeing two 38s lined up on their mental chalkboards and applying the algorithm mentally by adding the 8s, carrying the 1, and so on. Some use this approach, but mentally multiply 38 by 2 instead of adding. Some first add 30 + 30 and then add on 16. Some double 40 and subtract 4. Some double 35 and then add 6. All of these strategies are effective and comparably efficient. Why then, in school, is the implication that there is one right way to do arithmetic? And why is the procedure used to produce arithmetic results so often disconnected from its logic, without attention to developing reasoning?

When Observing
I've observed over the years that even though we typically teach students to add the numbers in the ones place before those in the tens place, when adding mentally they more often add the tens first. It makes me yearn for having students' paper-and-pencil recording reflect their natural way of thinking, rather than follow a set procedure.

— MSB

Starting Point 7
The Equal Sign: What It Really Means

Students tend to see the equal sign as a signal that the answer to an arithmetic problem is coming next, instead of as a symbol of equivalence. That is, instead of seeing the equals sign as expressing the relationship "is the same as," students often think it means that they should do something to the numbers before it and write the answer after it. They often read an equation like $6 + 1 = 7$ as "six plus one *makes* seven." I've read various research studies about the common and serious misconception students have about the meaning of the equal sign, a misconception that can result in difficulties when students later study algebra. Following is an account of ways that I've supported students across grade levels in understanding what the equal sign really means.

Investigating the Equal Sign in Grades K–1

Students begin learning about the equal sign in the early grades, and *Quack and Count* by Keith Baker (1999) is a terrific children's book for helping with this. The book is ideal for kindergarten and grade 1. Students love the rhymes and the illustrations of seven ducklings slipping, sliding, leaping, diving, and finally flying away.

The first combination introduced in the book is $6 + 1$, shown with six ducklings on the left-hand page and one duckling on the right-hand page. The text reads:

Slipping, sliding, having fun

7 ducklings, 6 plus 1

My typical lesson plan is first to read the book in its entirety for students to enjoy. Then I revisit the book and, for each spread, have the students count the ducks on the left, then on the right, and then altogether. For each combination, I write an equation on the board or on chart paper to represent the rhyme and illustration mathematically. For the combination above, for example, I'd typically write $6 + 1 = 7$. But after my own experiences and becoming aware of research about the equals sign, I changed that and now write the equation as $7 = 6 + 1$.

The first time I taught the lesson with this change gave me a first-hand experience with what the research reported. I was teaching the lesson in a first-grade class. After I wrote $7 = 6 + 1$ and read the equation aloud, Russell frowned and emphatically shook his head back and forth. "No," he said, "you wrote it backwards. It's supposed to go six plus one equals seven." It was as if Russell had leapt off the pages of the research articles.

"Yes, that's another way I could write the equation," I said and recorded Russell's suggestion.

Then, for each of the other combinations in the book, I wrote the equations both ways. At the end of the rereading of the book, I had written two columns of equations.

Literature Connection
Quack and Count by Keith Baker is one of my favorite children's books. Along with helping to develop understanding of the equal sign, it also helps children learn about decomposing seven in a way that also emphasizes thinking about patterns. Also, the illustrations and rhymes are wonderful.

— MB

For tips about using other children's books in math lessons, see "Starting Point 23: Using Children's Literature to Teach Math" in Part 1 on page 126.

$$7 = 6 + 1 \qquad 6 + 1 = 7$$
$$7 = 5 + 2 \qquad 5 + 2 = 7$$
$$7 = 4 + 3 \qquad 4 + 3 = 7$$
$$7 = 3 + 4 \qquad 3 + 4 = 7$$
$$7 = 2 + 5 \qquad 2 + 5 = 7$$
$$7 = 1 + 6 \qquad 1 + 6 = 7$$

Also, as I read each equation aloud two ways, I alternated using "equals" and "is the same as" for the equal sign, hoping to develop understanding of its correct meaning. For subsequent lessons, to continue building the students' understanding of the equivalence relationship, I relied on some of the lessons from *Lessons for Algebraic Thinking: Grades K–2*, a book I coauthored with Leyani von Rotz (Math Solutions, 2002).

In *Lessons for Algebraic Thinking: Grades K–2*, see *Two Handfuls* (Burns and von Rotz 2002, 128–156) for useful ideas to help students build their understanding of the equivalence relationship.

Investigating the Equal Sign in Grade 3

The research I had read, and my experience with first graders, was the impetus for focusing on the equal sign with third graders. I gave students in six different classes an assignment that would give their teachers and me insights into their thinking about the equal sign. The assignment had three parts—the first to figure out the missing number in an equation, and the other two parts for them to explain their thinking. I duplicated the assignment on half sheets of paper, leaving space for the students to write.

$$7 + 5 = \underline{} + 4$$

How did you figure it out?

The equal sign (=) means _____.

Of 96 students, just under half, 46, correctly wrote *8* in the blank. Most of them wrote an explanation similar to Nick's. He wrote: *7 + 5 = 12 so the number in the blank would be 8 because 8 + 4 = 12.* The most common incorrect response given by 42 of the 50 students who answered incorrectly was 12, and their explanations completely ignored the "+ 4" in the problem. For example, Elianna wrote: *I got 12 because 7 + 5 is 12 because 5 + 5 is 10 and 2 more makes 12.* Julio wrote: *I just took the seven and counted on five and got 12.* Some students extended the equation and wrote: *7 + 5 = 12 + 4 = 16*, showing that they noticed that 12 + 4 was equal to 16, but still misinterpreting the problem. Jack wrote *16* in the blank and wrote: *I added 7 + 5 and then I add 4 to 12 so I got my anser.* (This was the student's misspelling.) Three students wrote *35*, thinking about multiplication, which they were then studying in their class. One student wrote *2* in the blank and didn't complete the rest of the assignment.

When explaining the meaning of the equal sign, 78 of the students wrote responses like these (with the students' misspellings):

The equal sign means the answer. Equal means what is the anser to the problem.

Add up the two numbers then put the answer behind the equal sign.

Equal means that there is about to be an answer.

It means "give me you'r anser!"

The equal sign means you wright the answer right next to it.

Of the 13 students who wrote that the equal sign meant the same, only seven gave the correct response of *8* and the others wrote *12* in the blank. Several students offered two possible meanings. Robin wrote: *The = sign means if you are trying to figure out an equation then the = sign means what the anser is or it could mean that the two equations on either side of it equwel the same number.* Cal wrote: *It is the sign that goes before the answer and it means the same as.*

Helping Students Understand the Equal Sign

If I hadn't had the previous experiences, I don't think I would have understood how important it is to provide instruction that helps students understand what the equal sign really means.

It's tricky. When students learn about addition, they associate the operation with the action of combining quantities. They learn to write equations using the plus sign to describe that action and the equal sign to indicate the answer. As Mike wrote on his paper: *You put the equal sign at the end so it's not 7 + 5 13 so you know where it splits 7 + 5 = 13.* (He correctly wrote *8* in the blank for *7 + 5 = __ + 4*, but he indicated, incorrectly, that both *7 + 5* and *8 + 4* were equal to 13.) Also, when learning about subtraction, students often begin with the action of taking away, using the minus sign to describe the action and the equal sign to indicate the answer. The plus and minus signs are *operation* symbols, indicating an action to be performed to the numbers at hand. The equal sign, however, is a *relational* symbol, not an operation symbol. No action is associated with it. Instead, it describes the relationship of equivalence between two expressions, a state of being, not the result of an action.

In this situation, what gets in the way of developing relational thinking is that students are used to focusing on computation to get answers, and also to read equations from left to right the way they read sentences. They've had much practice with both, so it's no surprise that they see the equal sign as an indication that they need to write an answer. The suggestion I made for using the children's book *Quack and Count* is helpful, but it's not sufficient for helping students broaden their concept of equals so that they understand that it's an indicator of equivalence, not always a signal to write an answer. Following are a few other instructional suggestions.

Lead Number Talks to Evaluate Equations

Write equations on the board and lead number talks about whether the equations are true or false. Engaging students in talking about their ideas provides the kind of social interaction that supports learning. I allow all students to present their ideas, and then end the discussion for each by telling the students what "mathematicians" would think and why they might think that. I vary the equations, depending on the grade level of the students and what they're studying at the time. When equations are false, I draw a line through the equal sign to change it to ≠. Students are accustomed to seeing this convention on other signs, and it's a good opportunity to introduce the mathematical symbol for "not equal to." Also, I sometimes give reasons that mathematicians might provide, as often as possible giving explanations that avoid doing the computations but rather suggest other ways to reason. For example, these equations are appropriate for third graders:

- 28 + 32 = 150 (False, when you add two numbers under 50, they can't add up to more than 100)

- 175 + 35 = 175 + 25 + 10 (True, since 35 = 25 + 10, splitting 35 this way would be an easier way to add and get the same sums.)

- 214 + 107 − 107 = 214 (True, since 107 − 107 equals zero and any number plus zero stays the same.)

- 82 = 70 − 12 (False, since 70 + 12 is 82, not 70 − 12. Also, subtracting 12 from 70 has to be less than 70, so it also has to be less than 82).

- 3 × 7 = 7 + 7 + 6 (False, since 3 × 7 means "three groups of seven" which is 7 + 7 + 7.)

After students have analyzed equations, I ask them to write their own equations for others to evaluate whether they are true or false. This engages them in using the equal sign for themselves. I've found it helpful to have students work in pairs to do this. I ask them to work together to write five equations, agree on whether they are true or false, and think of how to explain why. Then I have pairs of students lead number talks for the class as I had done.

Introduce Open Sentences

Open sentences—equations that are neither true nor false—help prepare students for later solving algebraic equations. Ask students to figure out how to make the equations true. Here are samples, all using blanks for the missing numbers. It's also possible to vary them and use boxes or letters. I keep the numbers simple so that students can focus on the meaning of the equations:

- __ = 20 + 30

- __ + 10 = 20 + 30

- 20 + 30 = 70 − __

- 8 + __ = 4 + 4 + 4

- 3 × 4 = 12 ÷ __

Wrapping It Up

Learning about students' confusion about the meaning of the equals sign was an important lesson for me. Not only did it awaken me to students' misconceptions, it made me more mindful about things that I've taken for granted about students' understanding. I'm more careful in my teaching to check for understanding and not make assumptions about what students know. Also, doing my own classroom research helps make research I read more meaningful and useful.

Starting Point 8

Word Problems: Developing Understanding of Arithmetic Operations

A long-standing tradition when teaching arithmetic has been to teach computational procedures first and then have students apply these pencil-and-paper skills to solve word problems. This is actually backward. It doesn't make sense to teach arithmetic skills in isolation from contextual situations that help students develop understanding of the arithmetic operations for which those skills are useful. Research findings have shown that this pedagogical version of putting the cart before the horse doesn't work.

When research studies examined why students' ability to solve word problems falls far below their ability to compute, they found certain commonly held notions to be untrue. For example, students' difficulties are not caused primarily by poor computation skills or by insufficient reading ability. Instead, when given a word problem, students don't know what arithmetic problem to solve. They're not able to "mathematize" word problem situations by connecting contexts to the related arithmetic operations. Although students can perform the computations adequately, they don't understand the meanings of the arithmetic operations in ways that enable them to identify which are appropriate to word problem situations.

To experience the sort of difficulty that students encounter when they face word problems and aren't sure how to proceed, solve the *Dealing in Horses* problem.

Investigating Student Difficulties with Word Problems

> **Try This Now**
>
> *Solving the Dealing in Horses Problem*
>
> A man bought a horse for $50 and sold it for $60. He then bought the horse back for $70 and sold it again for $80. What do you think was the financial outcome of these transactions?
>
> ❑ Lost $20 ❑ Earned $10
>
> ❑ Lost $10 ❑ Earned $20
>
> ❑ Came out even ❑ Earned $30
>
> ❑ Other (describe) _____
>
> Explain your reasoning: _____
>
> _____
>
> _____

Generally, people offer different solutions and explanations for the *Dealing in Horses* problem. It's important to note that this problem isn't typical of the word problems students face. Although the situation can be translated into an arithmetic problem and solved by computation, it involves more than word problems typically demand. However, the difficulty adults have deciding on the solution is similar to the difficulty many students have when trying to connect their arithmetic skills to the word problems they are assigned to solve.

Understanding the situation is not the difficulty with *Dealing in Horses*—the scenario is clear. Adding and subtracting the numbers in the problem also is not difficult—the numbers are easy to handle, even mentally without having to rely on paper and pencil. Yet deciding precisely what to do with the numbers isn't obvious to everyone. The difficulty lies in knowing how to choose appropriate arithmetic operations for the situation at hand in order to arrive at a correct solution. The confusion that adults experience with this situation is similar to the confusion that students experience when presented with a page of mixed word problems that leads them to ask, *Do I need to add or subtract?*

Using Word Problems to Introduce Operations

Facility with computation does not ensure students' ability to know when to apply those skills to solve problems. Word problems should be the starting place for developing understanding of each of the four basic operations of arithmetic—addition, subtraction, multiplication, and division—thereby establishing the need and context for computation skills. Students need to see that they learn to compute for the purpose of solving problems. Too often, the message is reversed, and students see word problems as a way of providing computation practice, and a mysterious way at that.

Several of the mathematical practices important to students at all grade levels relate directly to students solving word problems. Making sense of problems and persevering in solving them calls for students to explain to themselves the meaning of a problem and look for entry points to its solution. Reasoning abstractly and quantitatively calls for students to make sense of quantities and their relationships in problem situations. Modeling with mathematics calls for students to apply mathematics to solve problems arising in everyday situations.

Developing understanding of the operations of arithmetic, essential for solving word problems, is one of the basic expectations for students. But this shouldn't translate into teachers beginning arithmetic instruction by assigning word problems from the textbook. This accomplishes no more than testing students' abilities to solve those problems. It's teaching that's needed, not testing. More effective is to present word problems for students to discuss and solve, initially for young children without the distraction of numerical symbols. Doing this frequently, several times a week throughout the entire year, provides experience for helping students learn to generalize for themselves how the arithmetic operations are described in the language of the real world.

Parent Suggestion
The *Dealing in Horses* problem is useful for a back-to-school night experience, to engage parents in doing some math and understanding how solving problems and reasoning are important to their children's math learning. When using this problem with parents, it's important to assure them that right answers are indeed important, but also that there can be different ways to solve a problem correctly. Point out that an answer book doesn't exist for most real-life problems, so have some cut-out $10 bills, maybe also a plastic horse, for them to use to act out the problem. *Dealing in Horses* is also an interesting problem to present to a class, if the students can deal comfortably with the numbers.
—MBB

For help with presenting word problems to young children in the classroom, see "Introducing Addition and Subtraction with Word Problems" in Part 3 on page 333.

Supporting Students' Reasoning

Also, students should be encouraged to figure their own ways to arrive at solutions and make sense of situations numerically. My colleague Lynne Zolli described a student who was frustrated on a standardized test by the problem below. Students weren't supposed to figure out a numerical answer, but rather indicate which operation they would use. Choose which you think is the correct operation.

Try This Now

Word Problem: Chairs and Tables

There are 40 chairs and 10 tables. If each table has the same number of chairs, how many chairs will there be at each table? What do you need to do to solve this problem?

- ❑ Add
- ❑ Subtract
- ❑ Multiply
- ❑ Divide

The "correct" answer is to divide, expecting students to think about dividing 40 by 10 ($40 \div 10 = 4$) in order to figure out that there would be four chairs at each table. But the student argued with Lynne that the problem could be solved by any of the operations.

After Lynne described this experience to me, I thought about how the student might have solved this problem using each of the other operations. As I did for division, think about how you could solve the problem by adding, subtracting, or multiplying, and record an equation for each operation.

Try This Now

Chairs and Tables Investigation

There are 40 chairs and 10 tables. If each table has the same number of chairs, how many chairs will there be at each table? Record an equation to show how to solve the problem for addition, subtraction, and multiplication.

Addition   _____

Subtraction   _____

Multiplication   _____

Division $40 \div 10 = 4$

For me, it was easiest to think of how to use multiplication. I thought about what number I could multiply by 10 to get 40, and I represented that as $10 \times 4 = 40$. For addition, I thought that I would first put one chair at each table, which used up 10 chairs. Then I'd put another at each table, which meant I had used 20 chairs. And I'd continue: $10 + 10 + 10 + 10 = 40$. I was stuck a bit longer thinking about subtraction until I related it to the addition solution. Instead of adding 10s, I'd subtract 10 from 40, leaving 30, and then keep subtracting 10 until I used up all 40 chairs and had zero chairs left. I subtracted 10 four times, so there would be four chairs at each table: $40 - 10 - 10 - 10 - 10 = 0$.

The Problem with Word Cues

Some teachers resort to helping students solve textbook problems by providing word cues—for example, when it says "altogether," you are supposed to add and "how many more" means to subtract. Teachers provide these cues to help students be more successful with word problems. However, instruction of this type does little more than offer students tricks for figuring out answers. Students focus on doing something with the numbers, instead of making sense of the situation and modeling it mathematically. I've often shown students the cartoon below and asked them why they think that I find it funny.

Even worse, cues can result in students' development of misconceptions about the operations. The implication is that getting the answer is most important and that relying on tricks is an effective strategy for finding those answers. This message often results in students looking for tricks, rather than trying to make sense out of problems.

Wrapping It Up

Thinking about word problems as vehicles for learning about the operations of arithmetic, rather than exercises for students, results in keeping the focus on developing understanding. The goal is "word problems without tears," with the extra benefit of deeper mathematical knowledge.

For a revealing example of how word cues can interfere, watch this online, one-minute video clip of a fifth grader inappropriately using word cues: mathreasoninginventory.com/Home/VideoLibrary (find "Marisa" under "Search by Student" and select the video "295 students, 25 on each bus").

From Arithmetic to Problem Solving

Starting Point 9
From Word Problems to Problem Solving: A Broader View

Solving problems is the ultimate reason for students to study mathematics. In order to function in our complex and ever-changing society, students need to be able to solve a wide variety of problems. And as adults, all of today's students will face problems to solve that call for reasoning mathematically.

In the real-life problems students will encounter, they'll rarely have all the information they need in one tidy package the way word problems typically provide—instead, students will have to collect the data, often from a variety of sources. There's rarely only one possible method or strategy that emerges from real-life problems—usually students will choose one from several viable possibilities. They won't always know for sure if the solution they decide upon is the right or best one—they'll commit to a plausible solution and it may be only later when they evaluate their choice and make a change, if needed. Sometimes they'll never be sure about a solution—life has no answer book.

When we solve problems in real life, we have to call upon all the resources we've developed in other situations—knowledge, previous experience, intuition, and more. We analyze, predict, make decisions, and evaluate. The elementary math curriculum must prepare students to become effective problem solvers.

Word problems are an important aspect of students' experiences as they learn mathematics at all grade levels. Typically, word problems require students to connect situations to arithmetic operations and rely on understanding the meanings of addition, subtraction, multiplication, and division. To solve a word problem, a student has to translate a situation into an arithmetic problem (or sometimes more than one problem), and then perform the computations called for. There's always an exact right answer.

Making traditional word problems the only or main emphasis of the problems students encounter, however, is not sufficient for preparing them mathematically. Doing so communicates an unrealistic message to students about the way mathematics will serve them as adults. Most daily problems adults face that require mathematical reasoning and skills aren't solved merely by translating the available information into arithmetic problems and then performing the needed calculations. A broader range of skills is needed.

Teaching students to be problem solvers does not minimize the importance of arithmetic or of solving word problems. Arithmetic is necessary for solving many problems in life. Also, not all the problems students deal with in school need to be real-life problems. Although many situations that arise daily in classrooms afford opportunities for the application of math skills—collecting lunch money, deciding on how many cars are needed for a field trip, taking attendance, and so on—students also benefit from other opportunities to build their problem-solving abilities. A challenge when planning instruction is to pose problems that motivate students, spark their natural curiosity, and allow them to use, in a safe and supportive environment, the skills they'll need later.

One classroom example of a problem-solving experience is a twist on what we usually think of as word problem—the *$1.00 Word Search*. Stop and try this problem before continuing to read.

Try This Now

$1.00 Word Search

1. If A = $0.01, B = $0.02, C = $0.03, and so on, what is the value of your first name?

2. Using this alphabet system, one of the days of the week is worth exactly $1.00. Which one is it?

3. Find other words that are worth exactly $1.00.

Ask students to figure out the value of their first names and, as a follow-up, figure out which day of the week is worth exactly $1.00. After students have had the opportunity to investigate, use the following questions to discuss their results and processes:

- *How did you go about figuring the value of your name?*

- *Did you list all the letters of the alphabet with the value of each, or just of the letters you needed?*

- *How did you go about finding which day of the week is the $1.00 word?*

Discussing questions such as these gives students the opportunity to hear that there are different ways to approach solving a problem.

Finding $1.00 words opens up addition practice to a multitude of possibilities. Some teachers have organized class or school $1.00 word searches. More than one thousand $1.00 words have been discovered by students and teachers across the country. (Examples include *Wednesday, pumpkin, inflation, elephants, quarter, mittens, telescope, double-header*). Some teachers have simplified the problem for young children to one of finding the most expensive and least expensive three- or four-letter words, or asking children to brainstorm pairs of three- and four-letter words that have some relationship to each other—*dog/cat, hot/cold, up/down, one/two, big/tiny*, and so on—and figure out which in each pair is worth more. Some teachers have students report and demonstrate the different strategies they used when searching for $1.00 words.

One of the unique features of the *$1.00 Word Search* problem is that students don't need to refer to an answer book to determine whether a word is worth exactly $1.00. Their work is the verification. Another investigation with this same characteristic is *The 1–10 Card Investigation*. This is sort of a puzzle to be solved with ten cards, numbered 1 through 10. Before introducing this investigation to students, I first arrange the cards into a deck, with the numbers facedown, so that I can deal them to follow the directions.

Teaching Tip

When I present these problems to students, rather than providing them with a list of the alphabet letters and their values, or organizing for them how to approach the problem, I ask them to collect the data they need and decide how to move forward. This is an important experience for them.

—MSB

The riddles in *The $1.00 Word Riddle Book* I wrote (Burns 1990) present clues for finding $1.00 words. The caption that describes the book's cover illustration is a sentence composed entirely of $1.00 words: *Whenever Henrietta whistled, thirty trembling costumed elephants merrily performed.*

Teaching Tip

Your firsthand experience is important before asking your students to attempt the investigation.

—MSB

The 1–10 Card Investigation

Arrange a set of ten cards, numbered 1 to 10, facedown so that the following occurs:

1. When you turn over the top card, it should be a 1. Place it faceup on the table.

2. Move the next card to the bottom of the deck, keeping it facedown.

3. When you turn over the third card, it should be a 2. Place it faceup on the table.

4. Move the next card to the bottom of the deck, keeping it facedown.

5. Continue this way, turning over a card, placing it faceup on the table, and moving the next card to the bottom of the deck.

6. When you're done, all of the cards on the table should be faceup in order from 1 to 10.

> **Management Suggestion**
> So that each student can have their own cards, I distribute five 3-by-5-inch cards to each student to cut in half and number from 1 to 10. Then students can take the cards home to share the puzzle with their families.
> — MSB

I demonstrate the investigation by having the class watch as I deal out the cards I've prearranged so they wind up in order from 1 to 10, as described. This helps students understand exactly what they are supposed to accomplish. Then I let them work on the problem, either individually or in pairs.

There are several things I especially like about this problem. One is that it doesn't depend on students having a particular mathematical skill that could make the problem inaccessible or inappropriate—they all know how to put numbers in order. Another is that there are different ways to figure out how to arrange the cards in order to accomplish the task, including using trial and error, and learning from unsuccessful arrangements. Students typically learn fairly quickly that they need some way of keeping track of their arrangements to learn from their unsuccessful tries, and it's valuable experience for them to decide how to represent their thinking in a way that's useful to them. In a way, this is a low-stakes problem in that it doesn't address core skills or understandings, but has a big payoff in terms of engaging students' interest and giving them experience with making sense of problems and persevering in solving them. The investigation gives students experience with monitoring and evaluating their progress and changing course as necessary. Plus it has a playful aspect that too often is lost during students' math studies.

> **For Younger Students**
> To make the 1–10 Card Investigation more accessible for younger students, have them try it with three cards, numbered from 1 to 3. Then, if they're able and interested, extend to five cards, numbered from 1 to 5.
> — MSB

Criteria for Mathematical Problems

Textbooks often present word problems so that all those on the same page are solved with the same operation. The first one on the page may challenge a student. But when the student realizes that the same procedure can be used for all the others (and students are quick to notice this), the rest are not problems. They don't require thinking or reasoning but rather routine application of the same algorithms.

Although arithmetic is essential for solving many problems in life, it's not the only mathematical skill generally needed. Figuring how much floor covering is needed for a room requires applying both geometry and measurement skills. Deciding on the best place to put savings involves ideas in the areas of probability and statistics. Assembling a bicycle that arrives in a crate calls for the application of logical thinking skills. These are examples of problems for which a suitable course of action may not be immediately apparent.

Nonroutine problems, like the $1.00 word investigation, demand that students develop a plan for solving the problem and then execute that plan. Problem-solving techniques do exist, but they are general approaches, not algorithms that can be routinely applied to specific problems. When selecting problems for students to solve, I refer to four criteria:

CRITERIA FOR MATHEMATICAL PROBLEMS

1. There is a perplexing situation that the student understands.
2. The student is interested in finding a solution.
3. The student is unable to proceed directly toward a solution.
4. The solution requires use of mathematical ideas.

Refer to the above four criteria as you reflect on the following questions.

Try This Now

Reflecting on Problems

1. Was the *Dealing in Horses* problem (page 36) a problem for you? Why or why not?

2. Was finding the value of your first name (*$1.00 Word Search*, page 42) a problem for you? Why or why not?

3. Was finding $1.00 words (*$1.00 Word Search*, page 42) a problem for you? Why or why not?

4. Was arranging the 1–10 cards (*The 1–10 Card Investigation*, page 43) a problem for you? Why or why not?

5. Would the following be problems for your students? Why or why not?

   Solving *Dealing in Horses*: Yes ❑ No ❑

   Finding the value of your first name: Yes ❑ No ❑

   Finding $1.00 words: Yes ❑ No ❑

   The 1–10 Card Investigation: Yes ❑ No ❑

Wrapping It Up

In the context of the mathematics curriculum, a problem is a situation requiring that mathematical concepts, skills, and procedures be used to arrive at a solution. Whether a situation poses a problem is an individual matter, depending on a student's reaction or relationship to that situation. A student must understand the situation and be interested in resolving it, yet there must be some block preventing immediate resolution. If there isn't a block, then the situation is not a problem for that student. What may be a problem for one student may not be a problem for another.

Starting Point 10
Tackling Problem-Solving Strategies and Issues

Students benefit from learning problem-solving strategies that are useful for analyzing and solving problems. Strategies are not specific to particular problems or to particular areas of the mathematics curriculum but can be applied alone or in combination with other strategies to solve a wide variety of problems. Students use many strategies intuitively when they solve problems. However, gaining familiarity with a collection of strategies, by seeing them modeled and then practicing applying them, helps students develop useful tools for tackling problems and strengthens their problem-solving abilities. The following is a list of useful problem-solving strategies.

> ### PROBLEM-SOLVING STRATEGIES
> - Look for a pattern.
> - Construct a table.
> - Make an organized list.
> - Act it out.
> - Draw a picture.
> - Use objects.
> - Guess and check.
> - Work backward.
> - Write an equation.
> - Solve a simpler (or similar) problem.
> - Make a model.

Usually, it's possible to use different strategies or a combination of strategies to solve a particular problem. Try solving the three problems that follow. For each, decide which strategies are possible or reasonable to use and record them. Then, after recording the strategies, choose one or a combination of strategies to solve the problem and record.

Try This Now

Problem 1: Fifteen Objects

Show all the ways that fifteen objects can be put into four piles so that each pile has a different number of objects in it.

Possible or reasonable strategies:

_____

_____

_____

Which strategy or combination of strategies will you try first to solve the problem?

_____

_____

Solution: _____

_____

Did you change strategies or use others as well? Describe.

_____

_____

Try This Now

Problem 2: Playing a Game

Lisa and David are playing a game. At the end of each round, the loser gives the winner a penny. After a while, David has won three games, and Lisa has three more pennies than she did when she began. How many rounds did they play?

Possible or reasonable strategies:

_____

_____

_____

Which strategy or combination of strategies will you try first to solve the problem?

_____

_____

Solution: _____

_____

Did you change strategies or use others as well? Describe.

_____

_____

If these problems are appropriate for your students, have them solve them. Working in pairs provides support. Also, it's important to discuss with students both the specific strategies they use to solve problems and why those strategies are effective choices. Classroom discussions are useful because they provide opportunities for students to hear others points of view, which can help them cement and/or extend their own thinking.

Problem-Solving Issues

Teachers agree that problem solving has an important role in mathematics instruction, but have raised various concerns: There isn't enough time; parents expect school to teach arithmetic; problem solving is too hard for students who struggle with basic skills; I was never very good in math myself and I don't feel comfortable teaching what I don't understand. It's valuable to examine each of these issues.

Issue 1: There isn't enough time.

The reality of classroom instruction is that teaching the basic skills of arithmetic is time-consuming. There is only so much time in the school day and, over the years, more and more curriculum responsibilities have been added. A focus on problem solving is too much to expect and isn't realistic. Besides, the major complaint of secondary math teachers is that the students aren't well enough prepared with basic arithmetic skills.

There's no quarrel with the reality of how difficult and time-consuming teaching is. It has never been easy. But that's no excuse for not taking a serious and critical look at how the math instructional time, no matter how limited, is spent. Spending the bulk of mathematics instructional time to teach arithmetic skills does not prepare students to solve problems. Teachers are well aware of this when they assign even the most rudimentary of word problems and find that students are unable to solve them. Continuing to emphasize arithmetic in isolation rather than in the context of problem solving makes little sense, especially when this choice is considered in the perspective of what children need to function in our complex world.

Issue 2: Parents expect school to teach arithmetic.

Parents are concerned about their children's arithmetic skills. They want their children to bring home papers that show the arithmetic work they are doing in school. Parents argue that they learned arithmetic when they were in school without all this fuss about problem solving, and that should be good enough for their children.

Teachers need to explain the full scope of math instructional goals to parents, stated in the context of what children require for success in higher education and in our changing society. The world differs greatly today from when parents were in elementary school; the technological explosion has affected all areas of everyone's life. To cling to what was suitable when parents were in school is clinging to nostalgia rather than examining what is currently essential. Professional educators have the job of reeducating parents, not just complying with demands that are obsolete.

Issue 3: Problem solving is too hard for students who have difficulty with the basic skills.

For many students, mastering basic computation requires both more instructional time and more practice. Without this, they are not able to perform arithmetic calculations. It's better for students who learn more slowly to concentrate on the skills rather than attempt to do even more complicated problem solving.

Instead of merely considering how to give struggling students more instructional time for arithmetic skills, why not examine what is really basic for those students? Skills are tools. The value of a tool is its usefulness. Being able to do paper-and-pencil computation will not serve students without the ability to interpret a problem, analyze what needs to be done, and evaluate the solution. What's needed is a redefinition of what is really basic to mathematics instruction.

Issue 4: Some teachers are not very good in math and do not feel comfortable teaching problem solving.

Some teachers studied mathematics only as long as it was a requirement, and for some this means that their last math course was high school geometry. To be afraid of mathematics, to feel inadequate, and even to dislike it are not uncommon reactions from people, professional educators included. All teachers can do arithmetic; not all have that same facility in the other strands of mathematics. It's not fair to expect teachers to teach what they don't understand themselves.

Indeed, there are professional educators who are not comfortable with mathematics. Too often, it's taken for granted that teachers have a firm grasp of the content of grades K–12 mathematics when they leave high school. This isn't always the case. Many teachers feel that they don't have full understanding of the mathematics taught in the high school curriculum. It's a myth that some people do not have a mathematical mind and therefore cannot learn mathematics. All teachers responsible for teaching mathematics face the challenge of introducing children to important mathematics concepts and motivating them to enjoy and appreciate mathematics. Teachers who have never been at all interested in mathematics or who have a limited background in it can continue their learning of mathematics through mathematics courses, conferences, workshops, and other professional learning opportunities.

Wrapping It Up

It's important to keep in mind that the overall purpose of studying mathematics is to learn to solve problems. This requires that students learn to reflect on and justify their solutions, communicate their solution strategies, and respond to others' explanations. Only then are students truly mathematically proficient.

Starting Point 11
Building Number Sense

Along with developing numerical understandings and skills, number sense is an important goal of instruction related to concepts and procedures in the content area of number and operations. Number sense relates to students' ability to make sense of numerical relationships. It's helpful to consider characteristics that are indicators of number sense.

INDICATORS OF NUMBER SENSE

Students with good number sense can:

- reason flexibly with numbers,
- use numbers to solve problems,
- spot unreasonable answers,
- understand numerical relationships,
- take numbers apart and put them together in different ways,
- make connections among operations,
- figure mentally,
- make reasonable estimates, and
- see numbers as useful.

This isn't a definitive list of characteristics of number sense, nor is it meant to be a checklist. Rather, the list is a starting point for thinking about those qualities that we want to foster in students to help develop their number sense. In contrast, students with poor number sense tend to rely on procedures rather than reasoning, often do not notice when answers or estimates are unreasonable, and have limited numerical intuition or common sense.

Instructional Strategies for Developing Students' Number Sense

How can you integrate instruction that develops number sense into the curriculum? First, here's a classroom example. When beginning instruction about multiplication in a third-grade class, I asked the students to figure out, in their heads, how many chopsticks we needed for the upcoming Chinese New Year celebration so that everyone in the class had two chopsticks. First, we determined that we needed chopsticks for twenty-eight people.

Try This Now

Chopsticks Problem

Stop for a moment and figure out mentally how many chopsticks are needed for twenty-eight people.

I posed this problem to the class and gave them time to think. After a few moments, many of them wanted to answer. Eddie's hand was up, eager as always. He said, "I guess seventy-five chopsticks."

Rosa also volunteered a guess, "Maybe eighty."

Jayden said, "Those guesses are too big because if there were thirty people, we'd only need sixty chopsticks." Jayden had reasoned quantitatively, using a friendlier number to make an estimate that he then compared to Eddie's and Rosa's guesses.

Josh chimed in, "It can't be seventy-five because the answer has to be even." Josh's response indicated that he knew that multiples of two are all even, an indication of applying an important numerical structure.

Rebecca reported that she had counted by 2s, and showed how she used her fingers to keep track. She said, "I think fifty-six."

Carla agreed with Rebecca's answer and explained how she reasoned, "I know that twenty-five plus twenty-five is fifty, and we have three more people, so we need six more chopsticks." Carla had decomposed 28 into 25 + 3, numbers that were easier for her to reason with mentally.

Jayden's, Josh's, Rebecca's, and Carla's responses demonstrated indicators of number sense. I didn't ask Eddie or Rosa to explain their guesses, so it wasn't possible to assess their ability to reason.

The problem I posed gave me the opportunity to use several instructional strategies that help build students' number sense.

INSTRUCTIONAL STRATEGIES FOR BUILDING NUMBER SENSE

1. Model different methods for computing.
2. Ask students regularly to calculate mentally.
3. Have classroom discussions about strategies for computing.
4. Make estimation an integral part of computing.
5. Question students about how they reason numerically.
6. Pose numerical problems that have more than one possible answer.

Instructional Strategy #1: Model different methods for computing.

When children think that there's one right way to compute, they focus on learning and applying it, rather than on thinking about what makes sense for the numbers at hand. A one-way approach doesn't help students learn to think flexibly, which is essential to developing number sense. Also, recording on the board models for students how to represent their ideas mathematically. For example, for the chopsticks problem, when Rebecca kept track as she counted by 2s, I recorded *2, 4, 6, 8, 10,* and so on, up to *56.* When Carla reported, I recorded:

$$25 + 25 = 50$$

$$50 + 6 = 56$$

Sometimes I introduce a method of my own. For example, I added on to Jayden's suggestion about thirty people requiring sixty chopsticks by explaining that I could subtract four chopsticks for the two extra people:

$$60 - 4 = 56$$

Instructional Strategy #2: Ask students regularly to calculate mentally.

Examining our everyday uses of arithmetic reveals that we most often rely on mental computation when we use arithmetic—to get to the movies on time, figure the tip in restaurants, double or halve a recipe, and so on. As a regular routine, I present a problem and the students solve it by relying only on their ability to reason mentally. For example, in a second-grade class, I had each child put two cubes into a jar. Then I asked them to work with their partner and figure out the number of cubes in the jar altogether. To verify, we counted the cubes by 2s, 5s, and 10s.

With fifth graders, I used a coffee scoop to fill a jar with beans, having the students count as I did so to see how many scoopfuls it took. I set the jar aside and gave each pair of students a scoop of beans to count. They reported their counts and we discussed what number to use for an average number of beans in a scoop. Then the students mentally calculated about how many beans were in the jar.

Instructional Strategy #3: Have classroom discussions about strategies for computing.

When students report answers, I ask them to explain how they reasoned. When others report, I don't worry if they give the same reason as another student—explaining in their own words supports their learning. Also, as I guide the discussion, I keep track of students' ideas on the board. This helps model for students how to numerically represent their different ways of figuring.

Instructional Strategy #4: Make estimation an integral part of computing.

I ask students for an "about number" when posing a problem. For example, a multidigit multiplication problem, such as 148×21, isn't an appropriate mental computation problem if the goal is to find the exact answer. However, asking fourth or fifth graders to decide if the answer is closer to 1000, 2000, 3000, 4000, or 5000 is a good challenge that gives students important practice with estimating.

When students give an estimate, I write it in a wavy cloud. Then, when we figure out an answer, we refer back to the estimate. Sometimes an estimate helps confirm that an answer is reasonable. Other times, when an estimate is far off, it provides the basis for a rich discussion about why it didn't make sense. For example, in a fifth-grade class, I wrote on the board: $2\frac{2}{3} \times 1\frac{3}{4}$.

"We haven't learned that yet," Jackson blurted out. The students had some experience multiplying fractions by whole numbers, such as $6 \times 4\frac{1}{2}$, but had not yet been asked to solve problems like the one I wrote on the board.

When observing
I was surprised to learn that some children thought that we'd get different answers when county by 2s, 5s, and 10s. This convinced me of the importance of repeating the experience with other numbers and objects.
—MBB

I responded, "What I'm interested in is what you think might be a good estimate for the answer." I had them think by themselves for a moment, then confer with a partner, and then offer possibilities. As students reported, I wrote each suggestion in its own wavy cloud.

I then said, "Now I'm interested in hearing your reasons for why each of these estimates might be close to the answer."

Cassie explained why 4 could make sense. She said, "Two times 1 is 2, but there are fractions so it has to be more." Vera gave the same reason for the estimate of 3. Harry explained how he arrived at $2\frac{1}{2}$, "I did 2 times 1 is 2, and I know that when you multiply two fractions (he was referring to the $\frac{2}{3}$ and $\frac{3}{4}$), the fraction gets small, so I think $2\frac{1}{2}$." Julio gave a reason for his estimate of 6, "I rounded $2\frac{2}{3}$ to 3, and $1\frac{3}{4}$ to 2, and 3 times 2 is 6." Emma used the same reasoning for her estimate of 5, "I did the same as Julio, but I went down a little bit because the numbers are smaller than 3 and 2."

I used their estimates as a jumping-off point to discuss how to think about getting an exact answer. Not only was it a good experience for the students to explain their reasoning, they now were invested in knowing the "real" answer and how to figure it out.

Instructional Strategy #5: Question students about how they reason numerically.

I probe students' thinking by saying, *Why do you think that? Explain why that makes sense,* and *Tell more about how you reasoned.* I pursue students' thinking regularly, not just when they make errors. This gives students the message that thinking numerically is about reasoning, not just memorizing. Also, their responses can provide important feedback about their understanding that can help inform my instructional decisions.

Instructional Strategy #6: Pose numerical problems that have more than one possible answer.

For example, I tell children that I have $1.00 and pose one of these problems:

> *How could I spend exactly $1.00 by buying two things with different prices?*
>
> *How could I spend exactly $1.00 by buying three things with different prices?*
>
> *How could I spend exactly $1.00 by buying three things with different prices if one of them costs $0.39?*

There are multiple correct answers to each of these problems, making them especially useful for giving students a good deal of practice figuring mentally.

Wrapping It Up

Number sense rests on the premise that there are multiple ways to reason numerically, and the selection of a particular approach depends on the numbers at hand. Students' number sense develops over time and from many experiences with reasoning numerically. It's enhanced by knowing the basic facts so that students can calculate more efficiently. During classroom instruction, students benefit from many opportunities to reason numerically, explain their reasoning, and listen to others' ideas.

Starting Point 12
Developing Mental Math Skills

Being able to calculate mentally, both for making estimates and figuring exact answers, is an important life skill that deserves a regular place in math instruction. I've found it useful to establish a classroom routine for helping students work on mental math skills. It's a simple routine to introduce. "No paper, no pencils, no manipulatives, no books," I tell them. And when they're ready, I present a problem for them to solve in their heads, usually writing it on the board.

First, I give the students time to think about the problem individually, then to turn and talk with a partner. But I'm clear that figuring out ways to solve the problem will be a class effort. I explain, "You'll share how you reason. You'll listen to each other's ideas. And I'll record on the board so we can review our thinking together." Recording gives me the opportunity to model for the students how to represent their mathematical ideas.

Choosing Problems Appropriate for Mental Math

Different types of problems are appropriate for students to solve mentally. I've asked young students to figure out the sum of two single-digit numbers, 6 + 7, for example, always asking each student who gives an answer to explain how he or she figured it out. Or I give an addition problem with two two-digit numbers, 26 + 57, and have students explain how they find the sum. Sometimes I write a two-digit number on the board, 47, for example, and have the students figure out how much more is needed to make 100. Even though problems like these call for exact answers, there are multiple strategies students can use to figure out solutions.

I also present problems that have more than one possible answer. I give students a number, 53, for example, and ask them how to rename it as the sum of two smaller numbers. For older students, I give a greater number, for example, 500 or 1275, and ask how to rename it as the sum of two smaller numbers or, if appropriate, as the sum of three smaller numbers. From hearing others' ideas, students have the opportunity to broaden their own repertoire for computing, which helps build their number sense.

Problems that don't immediately seem suited for mental math can be turned into problems for mental math. For example, mentally figuring out the answer to a multiplication problem like 148 × 21 isn't appropriate if the goal is to find the exact answer. However, presenting it as an estimation problem is a good challenge for fourth or fifth graders.

A Multiplication Estimation Problem

Which answer is closest to the product?

148 × 21

a. *1000*

b. *2000*

c. *3000*

d. *4000*

e. *5000*

As with all problems, I give students a few moments to think quietly by themselves, next ask them to turn and talk with a partner, and then begin a classroom discussion. As students explain their thinking, I record on the board to represent their ideas mathematically.

When I presented this problem to a class of fifth graders, I ascertained from listening as they talked in pairs that it was difficult for many of them. When I began a classroom discussion, I said, "If you're not sure about which answer is closest, it's OK to tell something you notice that could help us decide. Talk about what you know so far." Doing this opened up the discussion in a way that gave more students entry.

Josh had a beginning thought. He said, "I know that 148 times 10 is 1480, so 1000 can't be closest because 148 × 20 would be 1480 again, and that's more than 2000." I wrote on the board:

148 × 10 = 1480

148 × 21 > 2000

"I think it's between 2000 and 3000," Lucy said. She added, "Like Josh said, it's more than 2000, but I think it's less than 3000 because 3000 would be 1500 plus 1500." First I wrote Lucy's idea on the board about adding 1500 and 1500:

1500 + 1500 = 3000, so 1480 + 1480 is less than 3000

"Is this part of what you said?" I asked her. Lucy nodded yes. Then I recorded in a different way to review the greater than and less than signs. Lucy gave a nod of approval.

148 × 21 > 2000

148 × 21 < 3000

Then Jackson said, "I think the closest has to be 3000, because 148 is close to 150, and 21 is close to 20, and 150 x 20 is 3000." I recorded on the board:

150 × 20 = 3000

Some of the students reacted with "Oh, yeah," and others with "I don't get it." I again had them talk in pairs and then reconvened the whole-class discussion so others could present their ideas. We continued for a while longer and then finally resolved the problem by ending our mental math restriction and using paper and pencil to figure the exact product of 3108.

Sometimes I realize that I've given a problem that's too difficult for most students in a class. Then I move on to another problem. Just as there is usually more than one way to solve a problem, there's always another problem that can help you address the same concept or skill. This happened to me when I gave fourth graders the problem on page 57 of estimating 148×21. Most students were stumped. So I changed the choices for the estimates so that it was an easier problem.

Which answer is closest to the product?

148×21

a. 30

b. 300

c. 3000

d. 30,000

Solving this new problem was more appropriate and led to a fruitful discussion about place value and multiplying by 10 and multiples of 10, important for reasoning mentally.

During classroom discussions, sometimes a student will give an explanation that expresses the same idea as another student, but with different wording. I reinforce for students that even though their explanation might be the same or similar to someone else's, it's good to hear all of their thoughts.

As a follow-up, I sometimes give a writing assignment, asking students to explain at least one way to solve the problem. I tell them that it's fine for them to refer to what I've recorded on the board, but I encourage them to choose something that makes sense to them. I ask them to make their responses as detailed as possible to help me see what they do and don't understand. Having students complete the assignment on their own gives me the opportunity to assess their work and decide whether to revisit the problem or present another similar problem with different numbers.

Some problems don't require that students do one particular calculation, but engage them in doing multiple calculations to test different possibilities in order to come up with an answer. For example, sometimes I write different quantities on the board and ask students to come up with a number sentence. The following problem uses money as a context, providing a way to connect with students' real-world experiences and giving a problem for which there is more than one possible correct answer.

A number sentence uses three of the following.

$1.50   2 $3.75   50 cents   6 $3.00   75 cents

What could the number sentence be?

(One possible solution is $3.00 ÷ 2 = $1.50.)

Some problems don't require computing, but still encourage interesting discussions that build students' understanding about numbers. Here is one example of a number riddle that has multiple possible correct answers.

A number has been rounded off to 1200.

What could the number be?

And here's another example.

I wrote down a number with one zero in it, but I can't remember what it was.

I know it was between 500 and 800. What could the number be?

For all problems, I encourage students to explain their reasoning, whether or not they give correct answers. Too often students learn that teachers only ask students to explain their thinking when they're wrong. However, explaining is important for all students at all times. Their explanations help them solidify their own thinking and are valuable for their classmates to hear.

Mental Math Guidelines

When encouraging mental math, I find it's useful to present clear guidelines to the students:

- We don't use paper, pencil, or any other materials to solve a problem—we use just our heads.
- We'll talk together about different ways to solve the problem.
- Your job is to be willing to share your ideas and to listen to everyone else's ideas.
- My job is to help us keep track of everyone's ideas by keeping track of them where everyone can see them.
- Sometimes I post shortened versions of the guidelines on a chart and review them from time to time.

MENTAL MATH GUIDELINES

1. We use our heads.
2. We talk together.
3. We need everyone's help.
4. I record students' thinking for everyone to see.

For ideas for mental math problems, I've found two Math Solutions resources to be especially helpful—*Good Questions for Math Teaching, Grades K–6* by Peter Sullivan and Pat Lilburn (2002), and *Good Questions for Math Teaching, Grades 5–8* by Lainie Schuster and Nancy Canavan Anderson (2005).

There have been times when a student gives an incorrect answer or gives an explanation with faulty or confusing reasoning. I've learned not to interrupt immediately. Many times, students self-correct as they explain. Sometimes, if I record on the board and restate what a student has said, the students see the error and make a correction. Sometimes another student can explain. Of course, I'm careful not to end a lesson with a misconception still existing, but I don't rush into resolving problems. I let discussions evolve.

Wrapping It Up

Being able to calculate mentally is an important and useful life skill. Regular classroom practice helps students learn to rely on their own ability to reason in their heads and builds their confidence for doing so.

Assessing Understanding and Skills

Starting Point 13
Making Formative Assessment Integral to Instruction

First a confession: Only in the second half of my teaching career have I given significant thought and attention to assessing students' understanding and learning progress. As a beginning teacher, my focus was on learning to manage the classroom, plan lessons, and hold students' attention. Later, my focus moved toward improving my lessons and expanding my instructional repertoire. During those years, my attention was always on my teaching. Assessment was not one of my concerns. Yes, I gave assignments and quizzes and examined the results, but I did so more to determine grades than to figure out what students were thinking.

Assessment now plays a much different role in my teaching. Although I'm no longer a full-time classroom teacher, I still spend time teaching lessons in classrooms to try out new instructional ideas. I now include assessment in these lessons in a determined and intentional way. I'm no longer satisfied merely with using students' responses on assignments and quizzes to judge what they've learned. My goal now is to find out what students understand and how they think so that I can judge my own teaching. What students reveal informs my subsequent teaching decisions. I'm still interested in honing my instruction, but along with planning sequences of learning investigations, I also plan for making formative assessment an integral part of all lessons.

The Importance of Probing Students' Answers (Whether Correct or Not)

In my early teaching years, I was a devotee of discovery learning, sometimes called inquiry learning. This instructional approach involves designing learning investigations that help students discover concepts and make sense of facts and principles for themselves, rather than relying on textbook or teacher explanations. I implemented this approach by asking the class a carefully prepared sequence of questions, in the style of Socrates. If a student's response was correct, I continued to the next question. If a student's response was incorrect, other students would typically raise their hands to disagree, and I'd let a classroom discussion unfold until someone proposed the correct response. Then I'd continue with the next question. If no students objected to an incorrect response, I'd ask a slightly different question to lead students to the right answer.

Years later, I thought about why the discovery method of instruction seemed flawed. The problem was that when a student gave a correct response, I assumed that both the student who had answered correctly and the rest of the students understood the mathematics behind the problem and the reasoning behind the correct response. Actually, I rarely probed students' responses to understand how they were thinking—I just continued on my planned teaching trajectory of questions. As a result, I never really knew how students were reasoning or whether their correct answers masked incorrect ideas. I only knew that they had given the answer I sought and I could continue with my lesson plan.

I no longer teach this way. I still believe in the value and importance of using questions to present ideas for students to consider, but I've broadened my use of questions so that I now probe as well as stimulate students' thinking.

Probing Fifth Graders' Thinking: A Fractions Lesson

As an example, when teaching fractions to a class of fifth graders, I wrote five fractions on the board—$\frac{1}{4}$, $\frac{11}{16}$, $\frac{3}{8}$, $\frac{1}{16}$, and $\frac{3}{4}$—and asked the students to write the fractions in order from smallest to largest. First I gave them time to work individually, next I had them talk with a partner, and then I initiated a classroom discussion.

I began the classroom discussion with a direction to the class. "Rather than giving the order of all five fractions," I said, "explain something you think about just one or two of the fractions."

I called on Isabella. She said, "I know that $\frac{11}{16}$ has to be the biggest." I asked Isabella to explain how she decided.

"It's closest to one," she said. "See, you only need one-sixteenth more to make it one, and none of the other fractions are even close." In former discussions, we had talked about comparing fractions by comparing them to a whole, and Isabella used this strategy when she thought about these five fractions. To be sure that others followed her reasoning, we discussed how far each of the other fractions were from a whole, and why those amounts were always less than $\frac{1}{16}$.

Next I called on Robert. "One-sixteenth is the smallest fraction," he said, with confidence.

"How do you know that?" I asked, again probing to keep reasoning at the forefront of the lesson.

Robert answered, again with confidence, "Because one-sixteenth is the lowest number in fractions."

This example points out the value of probing students' thinking. Robert correctly identified the smallest of the five fractions in the set, but his explanation revealed a serious misconception. When the students had earlier made fraction kits, $\frac{1}{16}$ was the smallest piece they had cut and labeled. The fraction kit, one of my favorite teaching tools, had led Robert to an erroneous generalization!

This experience had a direct influence on informing my subsequent teaching. I used it to improve upon the fraction kit lessons to avoid this problem in the future. I now always have students consider how to name pieces that are smaller than $\frac{1}{16}$. I talk with them about how we can continue to cut smaller and smaller pieces and find fraction names for even the teeniest of slivers.

Also, as a result, I made time later to talk with Robert individually, further probing his understanding about fractions to learn more about what he did and didn't understand to ensure that he wouldn't continue to embrace misconceptions.

After this discussion, I gave the class an assignment, asking them individually to order five different fractions. I also asked them to write

Often referred to as "think, pair, share" or "turn and talk," this procedure has become standard to my teaching. For more information, see "Starting Point 14: The Importance of Classroom Discussions" in Part 1 on page 67.

Teaching Tip
The students had previously cut and labeled strips of paper to make fraction kits, and they had a helpful model for thinking about fractions. The fraction kit is a standard in my instructional repertoire that I've always found effective for developing students' understanding of fractions.

— MSB

For more about fractions kits, see Part 3 on page 422.

For more about fraction assessment, which can provide in-depth information about students' understanding, see Part 3 on page 437. Or, check out the fraction assessment in the free online Math Reasoning Inventory, mathreasoninginventory.com.

about their reasons for how they ordered the fractions. This way, their work would help avoid risk of a correct answer covering a misconception, or an incorrect answer masking understanding.

Probing Second Graders' Thinking: A Word Problem Lesson

Here's another example of how probing students' thinking provided me valuable information about the instruction needed. In a second-grade class, I began a lesson about solving word problems by writing on the board:

> *Emily sold _____ tickets to the school play.*
>
> *James sold _____ tickets to the school play.*
>
> *Together they sold a total of _____ tickets.*

The blanks allowed me to vary the numbers and also the position of the unknown. Students were used to seeing word problems presented in this way and comfortable with the routine I had established. First we'd read the problem aloud together, saying "blank" for the missing numbers. Next I'd write numbers in two of the blanks and ask them to think by themselves about what might be the missing number. After a few moments, they'd talk in pairs about their answers and how they figured them out. Then I'd lead a classroom discussion, beginning by asking them to say the answer together softly, which gave me the opportunity to assess whether there was disagreement. Then I'd ask students to explain their reasoning.

My particular focus on this day was on computing with multiples of 10. I began by writing *10* and *30* into the blanks for the number of tickets Emily and James sold:

> *Emily sold __10__ tickets to the school play.*
>
> *James sold __30__ tickets to the school play.*
>
> *Together they sold a total of _____ tickets.*

Figuring out the answer to this problem was easy for the class, as I had expected. The students were unanimous in reporting 40 when I asked them for the answer. To explain, Josie said, "You just add 1 plus 3 and add on the 0." Antonio said, "I switched it around to 30 plus 10 and just went up 10 to get 40." I wrote on the board: *10 + 30 = 40*, underlining the answer.

For the next problem, I erased the number of tickets that Emily sold, replaced it with a blank, left 30 for the number of tickets James sold, and inserted 50 for the total:

> *Emily sold _____ tickets to the school play.*
>
> *James sold __30__ tickets to the school play.*
>
> *Together they sold a total of __50__ tickets.*

This problem was also easy for the students and I heard a chorus of 20 when I asked for the answer. Nick explained how he figured by counting up by 10s from 30 to 50. Anna said, "You do 30 plus what number is 50, and it's 20." I wrote two equations on the board—*20 + 30 = 50, 50 − 30 = 20*—and underlined the answer in each.

After a few more problems like these, I gave a problem that had an answer greater than 100:

Emily sold __80__ tickets to the school play.

James sold __50__ tickets to the school play.

Together they sold a total of ____ tickets.

When I asked students to say the answer aloud, I heard two different responses—*130* and *113*. Crossing over into the hundreds typically poses problems for some students, and this was the situation here. Because I noticed that some students hadn't given an answer, I asked who wasn't sure, and about a third of the students raised a hand.

I wrote *130* and *113* on the board and commented, "I agree that the total has to be greater than 100. I know that 50 plus 50 is 100, so 80 plus 50 has to be more than 100. Let's listen to some explanations and see if that helps us decide which answer is right." I asked students to explain their reasoning for one or the other.

Students who figured out the correct answer of 130 did so in several ways. Isaac said, "I broke the 80 into 50 plus 30, then I did 50 plus 50 to get 100, and added on the 30 to get 130." Marina counted up from 80 by tens, using her fingers to keep track of counting five tens, "Ninety, one hundred, one hundred ten, one hundred twenty, one hundred thirty." These were typical of the explanations for correct responses.

The students who arrived at the incorrect response of 113 all used the same reasoning. Ali explained, "I added 8 plus 5, and that's 13. The answer is over 100, so it's 113." Those who also thought 113 was the correct answer nodded.

But Brian's hand shot up. "That can't be right," he said. "The answer has to end in a 0, like all of the others, because we're adding tens." Brian's understanding of the structure of the problems was impressive.

"I can prove that it's 130," Bella said. She came to the board, wrote the numbers one under the other as she would do when adding with paper and pencil, and then added. Russell concurred, "That's how I did it in my head."

Here I learned several important things. One was that the problem wasn't accessible at all for some of the students, which told me that I needed to provide experiences for them with problems that crossed over into the hundreds. Another was that those who came up with an answer could explain how they reasoned. Even though the answer of 113 is incorrect, those students were applying a version of the strategy Josie had used earlier to add 30 and 10 by first figuring 3 plus 1. However, they didn't add a 0 to get 130 but added on 100 to get 113. It's not correct, but it's not illogical. I've learned that children's errors are more often based in some logic that isn't appropriate to the problem at hand than being random, and this was the case. The lesson gave me important information about additional experiences the students needed with solving problems like these. And, after more experiences, I identified four students who needed further support and arranged to work with them further on problems like these.

Teaching Tip
One way I like to vary this lesson is to write a number in only one of the three blanks; for example: Together they sold a total of 27 tickets. Then students decide what numbers would work in the other two blanks. This provides them experience with solving a problem that has more than one right answer.
—MBB

For additional thoughts about using classroom discussions for assessment, see "Starting Point 14: The Importance of Classroom Discussions" in Part 1 on page 67.

Wrapping It Up

Probing students' thinking is essential for making assessment an integral and ongoing aspect of classroom teaching. Over the years, I've expanded and refined how I assess what students are learning, and now assessment is a staple of my math teaching. Without having students explain (even when they answer questions correctly), we risk erroneously concluding that their correct answers show understanding. Also, when they answer incorrectly, learning how they thought is valuable for understanding the source or reason for their error.

Starting Point 14
The Importance of Classroom Discussions

I have several memories from learning math in elementary school. I can picture Miss Collins in second grade at the board teaching us subtraction, showing us how to "borrow," write the "little" 1s, and check our answers by adding. I listened and watched as she wrote on the board, always a bit distracted and fascinated by the complicated arrangement of her pulled-back blonde hair. I remember Mrs. Friedman in third grade sternly telling us when we were doing seat work, "No talking, and cover your paper." I remember her reminding me, as she circulated around the room, to cup my left hand alongside my paper to hide what I was writing. And in Mrs. DeSimoni's fourth-grade class I remember being sent to the board with half the class to solve a multiplication problem, assigned to my own slice of the blackboard between two of the vertical lines she had ruled, always relieved when I could return to my seat. In all of these classes, except for calling on students to give answers to a problem, I don't remember the teachers leading any discussions.

As beginning teachers, we all tend to teach the way we were taught. In my beginning years, I spent most of my math instructional time the way Miss Collins, Mrs. Friedman, and Mrs. DeSimoni did, teaching from the chalkboard, then giving students assignments to complete individually, and correcting their papers.

It was only after I began attending professional learning workshops and conferences that I learned about other approaches to classroom instruction and made major changes in my own teaching practices, including making classroom discussions integral to classroom instruction. I experienced how classroom discussions gave students opportunities to explain what they knew and how they reasoned, ask questions, try out new ideas, and get feedback on their thinking, both from other students and from me. From workshops, reading I've done, and my own teaching experiences, I've learned how discussions can give students access to mathematical ideas and give me access to what they understand. I've come to believe that discussions are vital for supporting students' mathematics learning.

However, talking about mathematical ideas may not come naturally to students. I've found that it's important, and often essential, to provide explicit guidelines to help students learn to talk about their mathematical ideas.

Establishing a Classroom Atmosphere That Supports Discussion

First of all, it's important to establish a classroom atmosphere that supports student participation in discussions, and I've learned to be deliberate about establishing that atmosphere. This includes giving students time to collect their thoughts, listening attentively to students when they talk, being curious about their ideas, and allowing them ample time to finish their thoughts. It also calls for being clear to the

Teaching Tip
I've often wondered about how much time to give students to think before talking with a partner. A colleague, Leo Kostelnik, gave me a useful tip about how to let the students decide. He tells students to look at their partner to signal when they're ready to talk. If their partner isn't looking back, then they know they have to give him or her more time.

— MSB

class about expectations. I tell students, and reinforce often, that it's OK for them to change their minds about answers or ideas at any time, but that they also have to explain why. I tell them that it's OK to make mistakes, that errors are opportunities for learning. And I tell them that I expect them to listen to each other with respect and show patience when someone is searching for a thought.

It helps students collect their thoughts for a classroom discussion by first thinking on their own and then talking with a partner. Some teachers refer to this as "think, pair, share." Some ask students to "turn and talk" or "talk with their *shoulder partner*" (in contrast to their face partner). Explain to students that communicating in this way helps them try out ideas and prepare to present their ideas to the whole class. I always make sure that students know who their partner is so that when I say, "Turn and talk," or "Talk with your partner," there's no confusion about who talks with whom. When there's an odd number of students, I either form one group of three, or I become the partner for one of the students.

These ideas are useful only when they are put into practice consistently. It's helpful to post a chart so the guidelines are available for reference.

GUIDELINES FOR CLASSROOM DISCUSSIONS

- Share your ideas.
- Explain how you reason.
- Listen, with your hand down, when someone else is talking.
- Ask questions.
- Offer your comments about others' ideas.

Guidelines for discussions will mean more to students after they've had experience with how you lead discussions. It's useful to review the guidelines from time to time and add any additional suggestions that come up during the course of lessons.

A Beginning Classroom Discussion with Fourth Graders

To give a class of fourth graders a beginning experience with participating in a classroom discussion, I chose a problem for them to solve and then discuss: 99 + 17. I chose this problem because it was accessible to the students and typically leads to different mental computation strategies. I wrote the problem on the board and first asked them to think about the answer by themselves. After a few moments, I had them turn and talk to a partner to share their answers and strategies. And then I called the class to attention.

To begin the classroom discussion, I told them, "I'm going to count to three. When I say 'three,' please softly say the answer you got to the problem." I counted and heard a quiet chorus of 116. I did this both to get a read on the students' answers and also so that I could turn their attention to the strategies they used to figure out the answer.

Then I called on students to explain how they figured and recorded on the board to translate their ideas into appropriate mathematical representations. In this class, I recorded seven different methods.

$$99 + 17$$

Celina
$$99 + 10 = 109$$
$$109 + 7 = 116$$

Jake
$$9 + 7 = 16$$
$$16 + 10 = 26$$
$$90 + 26 = 116$$

Elena
$$9 + 7 = 16$$
$$90 + 10 = 100$$
$$16 + 100 = 116$$

Dean
$$100 + 17 = 117$$
$$117 - 1 = 116$$

Pedro
$$90 + 17 = 107$$
$$107 + 9 = 116$$

Celeste
$$90 + 10 = 100$$
$$9 + 7 = 16$$
$$100 + 16 = 116$$

Stephanie
99 is 1 less than 100
$$17 - 1 = 16$$
$$99 + 1 = 100$$
$$100 + 16 = 116$$

After recording the students' strategies, I showed the class video clips of four students from a different class—Alberto, Amir, Dina, and Manuel—each solving the same problem and getting the correct answer but using a variety of strategies. The students were curious about the videos and got interested in watching them. After each, I referred them back to the board to see if the method they observed matched one that they had thought of.

The students Alberto, Amir, Dina, and Manuel were interviewed for the Math Reasoning Inventory (MRI). The videos are available online at mathreasoninginventory .com/Home/VideoLibrary. Click on "Search by Interview Question" and select "99 + 17." All of the videos available for this problem are interesting, but the four I chose are particularly useful for showing how other students used strategies appropriate to the numbers at hand.

Questions for Classroom Discussions

In addition to posting guidelines for classroom discussions, it's also useful for students to be familiar with the kinds of questions you'll ask during classroom discussions. I've found it helpful to post a list of questions that help in classroom discussions, and I encourage students to use these when they are talking in pairs or small groups.

QUESTIONS FOR CLASSROOM DISCUSSIONS

- How did you figure out the answer?
- Why do you think the answer is reasonable?
- Who has another way to explain? (Or who has a different answer?)
- Who can explain what _____ said in your own words?

Modeling What It Means to Explain Your Thinking

Sometimes it's helpful to model for students what it means to explain how they figured out an answer. For example, I was teaching a lesson to second graders about adding two-digit numbers mentally. The children already had experience solving problems like 19 + 6, where they took 1 from the 6, added it to 19 to make 20, and then added 20 + 5 to make 25. Also, they had experience with adding multiples of 10, such as 20 + 70 and 40 + 30, with sums up to 100. Now I was interested in helping them think about adding other pairs of two-digit numbers, all with sums within 100, using multiples of 10 as friendly (or landmark or benchmark) numbers.

I began a number talk with something that was familiar to the children. I asked them to watch as I wrote a list of numbers, and to say the numbers along with me as they figured out the pattern. I listed the multiples of 10. By the time I wrote *30*, the class was chanting along with me:

10

20

30

40

50

60

70

80

90

100

I said, "These numbers are called *multiples of 10*, and they are friendly numbers that we can use as *landmark numbers* or *benchmark numbers*. I use them to help me when I solve problems." I wrote *multiples of 10, landmark numbers*, and *benchmark numbers* on our Math Words chart.

I then wrote *29 + 15* on the board and said to the class, "Listen and watch as I explain one way that I can figure out the answer using one of the multiples of 10, the number 30." I recorded as I explained, "It would be easier to add 30 plus 15, so first I'll add one more to 29 to make it 30. Then 30 plus 15 is 45. But because I added on 1 extra, 45 is 1 too much, so I have to subtract 45 minus 1 to get 44. The answer is 44."

29 + 15

29 + 1 = 30

30 + 15 = 45

45 − 1 = 44

I asked the students to turn and talk about what I had explained and written and had a few explain in their own words.

Next I said, "I have another way to solve the problem. Listen and watch as I explain. This time I'm going to use the friendly numbers 20 and 10 to help. I know that 29 is equal to 20 plus 9, and 15 is equal to 10 + 5. First I add the multiples of 10, 20 plus 10 equals 30, and then I add the leftovers, 9 plus 5 = 14. Finally, I'll add 30 plus 14 to get 44. And that's the same answer I got the other way."

$29 + 15$

$29 = 20 + 9$

$15 = 10 + 5$

$20 + 10 = 30$

$9 + 5 = 14$

$30 + 14 = 44$

I repeated this explanation, recording in a slightly different way. This gave students another opportunity to hear me explain and also to see another option for how I could keep track of my thinking.

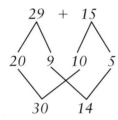

$30 + 14 = 44$

Again, I asked the students to turn and talk and then had several explain what I had done in their own words.

I then wrote another similar problem on the board with one addend close to a multiple of 10: $39 + 12$. I said, "Turn and talk with your partner. See if you can think of at least two ways to figure out the answer. I showed two ways for 29 plus 15, but you might think of other ways for this new problem. Then we'll share our ideas." After giving them time to talk, I recorded as pairs shared their ideas. We repeated this for another problem: $28 + 24$. And we continued practicing on subsequent days.

For ideas about lessons like this, I often rely on *Number Talks: Helping Children Build Mental Math and Computation Strategies, Updated with Common Core Connections* by Sherry Parrish (2014, 2010).

The Talk Moves

In their valuable and important book *Classroom Discussions in Math: A Teacher's Guide for Using Talk Moves to Support the Common Core and More, Third Edition* (2013), Suzanne H. Chapin, Catherine O'Connor, and Nancy Canavan Anderson describe specific tools that teachers can use to support productive classroom conversation. Specifically, they present "talk moves" that provide a solid base for teachers to rely on when leading discussions, and they provide many examples of actual classroom discussions. One talk move is revoicing, in which the teacher repeats what a student has said and then asks the student to verify whether the revoicing is correct. This is especially helpful when you understand what a student said but aren't sure that others have. (It's also helpful when I'm not clear myself

To learn more about the talk moves, see *Classroom Discussions in Math: A Teacher's Guide for Using Talk Moves to Support the Common Core* (Chapin, O'Connor, and Anderson 2013). This book and DVD were enormously useful for helping me improve my own skills at leading productive math discussions.

For additional thoughts about using classroom discussions for assessment, see "Starting Point 13: Making Formative Assessment Integral to Instruction" in Part 1 on page 62.

about a student's explanation and I need to "buy time" to try and understand.) Another talk move is to call on a student to revoice by asking, "Can you say what _____ just said?" This gives the rest of the students another version of an idea. A third is to ask "Do you agree or disagree, and why?" This encourages students to apply their thinking to others' ideas. A fourth is to ask for additional input by asking, "What can you add on?" Another talk move is to use wait time, being explicit when a student is struggling by saying, "Take your time . . . we'll wait."

Wrapping It Up

In order for classroom discussions to serve students, it's essential to establish a classroom atmosphere that's safe and guidelines that are clear. Then, with repeated experiences, students will become more comfortable contributing and see the benefits for their own learning from listening to their classmates. Modeling for the students is useful, but their direct practice is the key.

Students should learn that participating in classroom discussions is part of their responsibility as members of the class. I acknowledge that I know that speaking to the whole class is more difficult for some people than for others, but that it's important for everyone to contribute. I assure students that I'll provide the support to help everyone in the class become better communicators.

Starting Point 15
Incorporating Writing into Math Instruction

One reason I chose mathematics for my undergraduate major was that it didn't require writing papers. Math homework called for solving problems or proving theorems, and that was just fine with me. I saw math and writing as oil and water, subjects that seemed to have little in common. And, for my first twenty years of teaching, writing played no role in my math teaching.

My view has changed completely. I can no longer imagine teaching math without making writing an integral aspect of students' learning. This transition occurred over a period of years as I gradually overcame my own writing phobia. After writing children's books, professional books (like this one), and many articles, I've faced my writing dragon. I've even come to appreciate writing as a tool for clarifying my thinking. As William Zinsser states in *Writing to Learn*, "Writing is a way to work yourself into a subject and make it your own" (1988, 16). I think he's right about that.

But the results I experienced with students were what clinched my commitment to making writing a regular part of math instruction. I experienced how writing can help students think more deeply and clearly about math because it requires students to organize, clarify, and reflect on their ideas—all useful processes for making sense of mathematics. I also discovered that students' writing is an invaluable assessment tool. When students write, their papers provide a window into their understandings, their misconceptions, and their feelings about the math they're studying.

Categories for Writing Assignments

When making writing a regular feature of math class, I've found that it helps to offer students a variety of assignments. Writing assignments can fall into various categories, each of which focuses the students on their math learning in a different way, and each of which provides useful information for assessing students' progress.

CATEGORIES FOR WRITING ASSIGNMENTS

- Keeping journals or logs
- Solving math problems
- Explaining mathematical ideas
- Writing about learning processes

Keeping Journals or Logs

When students record regularly about what they're doing and learning in math class, they have a chronological record of their learning experiences. It's helpful, especially for assignments at the beginning of the year, to post suggestions to help students focus their journal writing:

Write about what you did in class.

What did you learn?

What are you unsure about, confused by, or wondering about?

Describe what was easy and what was difficult for you.

At times, I give guidelines that relate to a specific lesson. For example, "Explain why Raul's answer made sense," or "Write about why Kaisha and Robert disagreed."

I've managed students' journal writing in various ways. Sometimes I've had students staple sheets of paper into booklets with construction-paper covers. This system provides the opportunity for students to start new booklets—and thus have a fresh start—several times a year. (Remember the pleasant school ritual of having new notebooks for courses at the start of each semester?) Sometimes I've asked students to write on individual sheets of paper that they later can file in their folders. (This makes reading a class set of papers easier than rummaging through individual journals or logs.) Sometimes I've given each student a notebook. When teaching eighth grade, I made the investment in spiral-bound notebooks with grid paper, which were especially useful for graphing assignments. One year I found notebooks with the pages pre-numbered, and I found this to be useful. I had students write "Table of Contents" at the top of the first page and, during the year as we studied different topics, they listed them on this page, with their page numbers. The next year, I could only find notebooks without page numbers, so when I distributed them, I had the students number the pages.

Whatever the system, I advise keeping the students' journals, logs, folders, or notebooks in the classroom, except when you take them home to read. I instituted this policy after too many students left their journals at home.

Solving Math Problems

Math instruction should engage students in applying a variety of strategies for solving problems and also teach them to monitor and reflect on their problem-solving processes. Writing enhances both of these skills. Even when students work cooperatively to solve a problem, it's beneficial to have each student write his or her own paper. Group work gives students access to other ideas, and writing requires them to clarify and express their own thinking.

For example, I gave fifth graders a problem about mixing red and yellow paint to get orange paint. The problem would engage them with using fractions and provide them a beginning experience with reasoning proportionally. I told them about two different batches of orange paint: Batch A had two parts red paint and two parts yellow paint, and Batch B had three parts red paint and two parts yellow paint.

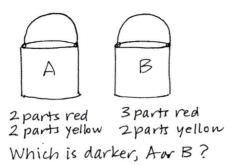

2 parts red   3 parts red
2 parts yellow   2 parts yellow

Which is darker, A or B ?

"How would the colors of the two batches of orange compare?" I asked them. I asked them to think for a moment by themselves and then talk with a partner about their ideas. The students agreed that B would be a darker orange.

Then I asked them to compare two additional batches of paint—Batch C with two parts red and one part yellow, and Batch D with the same three parts red and two parts yellow—and to write about their solutions.

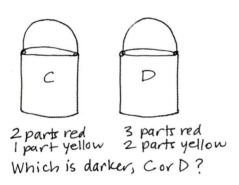

2 parts red   3 parts red
1 part yellow   2 parts yellow

Which is darker, C or D ?

The class was divided in their opinions: Some thought that the two batches would be the same color, and some argued that Batch D would be darker. Becky, for example, wrote about why the colors would be the same: *There is always one more red than yellow, so D should have more parts, but C and D should be the same color.* David, however, reasoned correctly: *C would be darker than D because there is twice as much red as yellow. In D there should be four parts red to make C and D the same color.* The classroom discussion was lively.

For a more complete description of the paint can lesson with samples of actual student writing, see *Writing in Math Class: A Resource for Grades 2–8* (Burns 1995, 70–75).

Explaining Mathematical Ideas

From time to time, I ask students to write what they think about an idea or a math concept. Their responses often provide useful information for assessing what they understand. For example, at the end of a unit on division, I asked the students to write about how multiplication and division are alike and different. Or, partway through a unit, I asked students to write on the topic "What I Know About _____ So Far," a title that conveyed to them that I didn't expect them to know everything yet.

Writing About Learning Processes

Instead of focusing on a math problem or concept, I've also used writing assignments to have students address a general aspect of their learning in math class. For example, I've asked students to write about their favorite and least favorite investigations in a unit, or about what makes a good problem-solving partner in math class. Sometimes, after teaching a game, I've had students write directions for the game and then teach it to someone at home. One year, when we had quite a few visitors coming to class to observe, I had students write letters describing the kinds of things we did in math class. I put the letters into a folder and made them available to visitors.

Strategies for Incorporating Writing

My skill and comfort with making writing integral to math learning evolved over years of experiences, which included many mistakes and discoveries. Here are some classroom strategies I've found to be useful for incorporating writing into math lessons.

STRATEGIES FOR INCORPORATING WRITING

- Establish the purpose for writing in math class.
- Establish yourself as the audience.
- Ask students to include details and to explain their thinking as thoroughly as possible.
- Have students discuss their ideas before writing.
- Post useful mathematics vocabulary.
- Write a prompt on the board to get students started on a writing assignment.
- Give individual assistance as needed.
- Have students share their writing in pairs or small groups.
- Use students' writing in subsequent instruction.
- Use student papers to create class inventories.

Establish the purpose for writing in math class.
Make sure students understand the two basic reasons that writing is an important part of math: to support their learning and to help you assess their progress.

Establish yourself as the audience.
Let students know that their writing will help you teach them better by providing valuable insights into their understandings, misconceptions, and confusions.

Ask students to include details and to explain their thinking as thoroughly as possible.
Encourage them to use words, numbers, and, if they like, pictures to provide as much information as possible.

Have students discuss their ideas before writing.
Most students find talking easier than writing, and opportunities to talk about their thinking can help students formulate ideas that they

can then explain in writing. Classroom discussions are useful, and having students talk in small groups enables more students to express their ideas. After a discussion, remind students that they can write about any idea they heard, as long as it makes sense to them and they can explain it.

Post useful mathematics vocabulary.

Maintain a Math Words chart to post pertinent mathematics-related vocabulary that comes up in classroom discussions. Before students begin work on an assignment, ask if there are other words or phrases they might use that they'd like to see on the chart. Keep this chart posted and add to it during the year.

Write a prompt on the board to get students started on a writing assignment.

Sometimes a general prompt is appropriate: *I think that the answer is____. I think that because _____.* Sometimes you'll want to use a prompt that relates more specifically to the assignment. For example, for third graders solving the problem of how many wheels there are on 15 tricycles, you might write on the board: *There are ___ wheels on 15 tricycles. I figured it out by _____.*

Give individual assistance as needed.

No matter how thoroughly I prepare students for a writing assignment, some will need additional assistance to get started. In this situation, I talk with these students first to ascertain that they understand the assignment. I encourage them to verbalize their thinking by asking them such questions as, *What do you think? What's one idea that you have?* and *What do you remember about what others said?* After students offer an idea, I ask them to repeat it aloud. Then I suggest that they repeat it silently to themselves. Finally, I tell them to write those exact words on their paper. This process often helps jump-start writing. If it doesn't, I may refocus the assignment and ask them to write about what they find confusing.

Have students share their writing in pairs or small groups.

Before handing in an assignment, students benefit from reading their papers to another student or to a small group for feedback. This exercise not only serves the writer but also enables students to hear other points of view.

Use students' writing in subsequent instruction.

Student papers can provide useful springboards for extending lessons, and using them in this way reinforces the idea that I value their writing.

Use student papers to create class inventories.

Reading a set of papers from an assignment can provide a useful overview of how the class responded to particular lessons. Was the experience accessible to all? Did it interest or challenge the more capable students? What additional instruction do students need?

Wrapping It Up

In general, I focus students' writing in math class not on producing polished writing products, but rather on using writing to reflect on their own learning. Most important to me is that students' writing helps them explore, extend, and cement their ideas. My focus is more on what they write than on how they write it. More and more, I've come to rely on students' writing to provide me important insights into their thinking.

Starting Point 16
The Benefits of One-on-One Interviews

I've learned that one-on-one interviews with students reveal valuable information that isn't available to me any other way. Even though I rely on students' participation in classroom discussions and on their written assignments to assess their skills and understanding, the information revealed when talking to a student individually is much more specific. I've found that interviews provide information that's often essential both for guiding classroom instructional decisions and for serving the specific needs of individual students.

Sample Interviews

For a first look at interviews, here I describe students I interviewed in the spring of one school year in a colleague's second-grade class. Number talks were a daily routine of the students' math instruction and they had had many experiences throughout the year solving problems mentally. My goal for the interviews was to learn how individuals reasoned when asked to solve problems without paper and pencil.

Key to these interviews, as with all of the interviews that my colleagues and I have developed, is that each time we ask a student a question, whether or not the student answers correctly, we follow up by asking, *How did you figure it out?* I found that the students' explanations were the most revealing aspects of our interactions. Here I describe four questions I asked and the responses from four students: Scott, Kali, Dianna, and Miguel.

Question #1

The first question I asked each student was, "What is 6 plus 8?" I also showed the problem on an index card.

$$6 + 8$$

All four of the second graders answered correctly, and their explanations revealed three different ways of reasoning. Scott, a strong math student, explained, "I know that 8 plus 8 is 16, and 16 minus 2 is 14." Kali, a student who struggled, explained, "Six plus 6 is 12 so I have to add on 2 more to get 14." Dianna, identified as an average math student, reasoned the same way that Kali did. Miguel, also identified as an average math student, said, "I know 8 and 4 makes 12, and 2 more makes 14."

While all four children gave the correct answer to this first question, this wasn't the case as I continued with the interviews.

<aside>
These interviews were based on a project funded by the Bill & Melinda Gates Foundation that resulted in the Math Reasoning Inventory (MRI), an online tool to assess the numerical reasoning of students in grades 4 and up, available at mathreasoninginventory.com.
</aside>

<aside>
Teaching Tip
When we're teaching language arts, why is it OK, even expected and encouraged, for children to write different once-upon-a-time sentences to begin a story, even a common story like Goldilocks and the Three Bears, but we don't often have the same expectation in math?
— MSB
</aside>

Question #2

Another question I asked was, "What is 34 plus 10?" Again, I showed the problem on a card.

$$34 + 10$$

Scott gave the correct answer of 44 quickly and explained, "It's just 10 more. You just add another ten." Kali counted up from 34 using her fingers to keep track, getting the incorrect answer of 45. (Ah, the inefficiency of counting.) Dianna got the correct answer and reasoned the way Scott did. Miguel also got the correct answer, but it took him a bit. He explained, "I lined them up in my head. I put the 10 under the 34 and added—4 plus 0 is 4 and 3 plus 1 is 4." This showed Miguel could apply the algorithm, but didn't provide information about whether he could make use of place value.

While algorithms are important, it's also important for students to develop reasoning strategies for figuring mentally. With this problem, relying on a procedure isn't appropriate or efficient. We too often see students approaching problems the opposite way, going to the procedure first. I remember years ago asking a class of sixth graders, "How much is 50 percent of 36?" More than half of the students reached for paper and pencil to figure the answer. It made me sad.

Question #3

I was also interested in learning how the students would reason with a problem in context. I showed them the problem on a card and also read it aloud.

> Jake had saved $100.
>
> He spent some and had $85 left.
>
> How much did Jake spend?

It was no surprise that this was easy for Scott and he got the correct answer of $15 quickly. He reasoned by thinking about addition, "$85 and $5 gets you to $90, and then $90 plus $10 is $100, and $10 plus $5 is $15." Kali said, "I think $25, but I just guessed." Dianna got the correct answer by thinking about subtraction and explained, "It's $15 because $100 minus $10 is $90, and $90 minus $5 more is $85." Miguel tried lining the numbers up in his head as he had done for 34 + 10, here to subtract 100 − 85, but he abandoned that as being "too hard to do in my head that way." Then he approached the problem another way and reasoned out loud to explain how he got the incorrect answer of $25. He said, "If you go back $10, you get $90. Then if you go back another $10, you get to $80. But he had $85 left, so you have to add on $5, and the answer is $25."

It's important for students to develop reasoning strategies for figuring mentally. For more information about computing mentally, see "Starting Point 12: Developing Mental Math Skills" on page 56.

Question #4

I gave the students another problem in context that, similar to the problem about Jake, could also be solved by thinking about either addition or subtraction.

> Alicia wanted to sell 150 tickets.
>
> She already sold 30 tickets.
>
> How many more does Alicia need to sell?

Scott, as I predicted, quickly gave the correct answer of 120. He reasoned, "I know that 30 plus 20 is 50, and I need 100 more, so it's 150." My own reaction was interesting to me. I had thought about the problem in a different way. I reasoned that Alicia needed 70 more to sell 100 tickets, and then 50 more to get to 150, so 70 plus 50 is 120. When Scott reasoned that Alicia needed to sell 20 more tickets to get to 50, I had to make a shift from my own way of thinking to follow how Scott reasoned. This reminded me of the importance of listening to how students think instead of listening for an explanation that already makes sense to me. Kali told me that the problem was too hard and I didn't push her for more. Dianna used subtraction and explained, "You go 150 minus 10 and that's 140, then 140 minus 10 is 130, and 130 minus 10 is 120. So she has to sell 120 more." Miguel actually tackled the problem the way I had thought about it, but when he got to the point where he wanted to add 70 plus 50, he was stuck. "I have to line them up to add," he told me. "Is there another way you can think about adding 70 plus 50?" I asked. He thought again and said, "Oh, yeah, 7 plus 5 is 12, so the answer has to be 112." (This is a response I've had from other students whose understanding about place value is still developing.)

Using One-on-One Interviews to Inform Instruction

As I always find when I interview students, the interactions provided specific information about the students' understandings and misunderstandings, and direction for instruction. For example, because of Miguel's erroneous thinking, it made sense for subsequent number talks to include problems about adding multiples of 10 when the answer is greater than 100. Also, while students often develop their personal preferences for reasoning, such as relying more on addition or on subtraction, it's important that students develop the flexibility to choose between the operations depending on the number at hand in the problems. For example, suppose the problem with Jake were rewritten, as follows.

> Jake had saved $100.
>
> He spent $98.
>
> How much did Jake have left?

While the problem seems like a straightforward "take away" subtraction problem, solving it with by thinking about addition (i.e., *How much do I need to add to $98 to get $100?*) is much easier. But suppose this was the problem:

> Jake had saved $100.
>
> He spent $4.
>
> How much did Jake have left?

Then it makes sense to think about subtracting 4 from 100 instead of thinking about how much you'd need to add to $4 to get $100. Of course both addition and subtraction can be used for either, but choosing strategies that are efficient for the numbers in the problem plays an important part in developing numerical reasoning.

Back to interviews. As I found with the second graders I described earlier, I've learned that having one-on-one interviews reveals valuable information that isn't available when I rely solely on students' classroom participation or written work. I've found this information is an essential guide for making appropriate instructional decisions.

Here's some history about how I came to this conclusion. In 1993, I was working on a series of videotapes for teaching mathematics that included individual student interviews. In preparation, I practiced by conducting dozens of one-on-one interviews with students at different grade levels. During the interviews, I probed mathematical strengths and weaknesses so I could construct a mathematical profile of the student. The practice experiences were always revealing and sometimes astonishing, uncovering students' misconceptions and gaps in their understanding that I hadn't realized before.

I was even more stunned during the actual videotaping. In a grade 2 class, the lesson called for the students to time their teacher, Carol Brooks, for one minute as she drew stars on the board. Carol then talked with the students about how they might figure out how many stars she had drawn, which led to circling groups of 10 stars and counting how many 10s and extras there were. During the lesson, the responses of two of the students—Cena and Jonathan—indicated that they had a firm foundation of understanding about place value. However, when I interviewed each of them the next day to probe their understanding one-on-one, I was shocked. The interviews revealed the fragile conceptual base of their understanding in ways that Carol and I had no way of knowing from the context of the classroom lesson. As a result of this experience, I began to incorporate more and more

Interviews with Cena and Jonathan are available online. To view them, visit mathsolutions.com and choose "Free Resources," then "Video Clip Library."

individual interviews into my own teaching. However, I didn't do anything more formal with this experience.

Nine years later, in 2002, while I was visiting an elementary school in Boston, I learned from the principal about one of her greatest concerns: Although all the primary teachers in the school conducted one-on-one assessments in reading with each of their students, no such counterpart existed for mathematics. The principal worried that teachers didn't have the same degree of understanding about their students' mathematical ability as they did about their students' reading ability and therefore might be unable to make appropriate instructional shifts or identify appropriate interventions.

The principal's concern rekindled my interest in student interviews in math. I formed a study group with several colleagues to create and test individual assessments for kindergarten through grade 6 that focused on the basics of number and operations. We met weekly to work on the interviews and separately tested the assessments with students in different schools between our meetings. Part of the work we did was transformed into the Math Reasoning Inventory (MRI) assessment tool for grades 4 and up.

A Closer Look at Interviews

Following are glimpses into what we learned from interviewing students at several grade levels.

Snapshot 1: Understanding Place Value

I asked Jonah, a first grader, to put 14 tiles on the table. He counted out 14 tiles correctly. I asked him to write 14 on his paper, and he correctly wrote the numeral.

"Are there more than 10 tiles?" I asked. Jonah quickly nodded yes.

"If you give me 10 of the 14 tiles, will there be extras?" I continued. Jonah again quickly nodded yes.

"How many extras would there be?" I continued. Jonah was quiet for a moment. Then he looked intently at the tiles, nodding his head as he silently tried to track the tiles with his eyes to count them. But he couldn't manage.

"I'm not sure," he finally said and then added, "maybe 2 or 3."

Understanding our place-value system is an essential foundation for all computations with whole numbers. Teachers talk with students about 10s and 1s, and students learn early on which number is in the 10s place and which is in the 1s place in a two-digit number. However, merely being able to identify the place of the numbers is not a reliable indicator that a student understands the structure of our base ten number system. Students need to understand the role of 10s and learn to see 10 objects both as one group (the 1 in the 10s place) and as 10 individual objects.

What I Learned

The difficulty in developing understanding of place value is compounded because of the language we use for numbers in English, especially for the teens. It would be helpful if we read 11 as "1 ten and 1" instead of "eleven," and 12 as "1 ten and 2" instead of "twelve," and so on. This is the verbal pattern that exists in Chinese languages. Our number names of *eleven*, *twelve*, and *thirteen* do not help to reveal the role of 10 in those numbers. Although this is unfortunate, these are the words we have for numbers and the number names that children have to learn. That said, we can support students' conceptual learning by providing them with many opportunities to count quantities of objects by grouping them into 10s and recording how many there are.

Cena and Jonathan had one such experience when they figured out how many stars Carol had drawn on the board. Now they are ready to reexperience that investigation in pairs, with one child timing while the other draws stars, dollar signs, letters, or any other symbols. They need experience counting other collections of objects in the classroom—cubes, beans, pencils, paperclips, and so on. For each of these experiences, the teacher needs to help the students see the pattern that exists when they record how many there are—that the digit on the left represents the number of groups of 10s and the other digit represents the number of extras.

Snapshot 2: Solving Missing Addend Problems

I took two tiles from a container and showed them to Rosa, a second grader. "How many more do I need so I have 10 tiles?" I asked her. Rather than showing her the problem in written form—2 + ___ = 10—I presented the problem verbally and with the concrete material of the tiles. This question presented Rosa with a missing addend problem: Instead of giving numbers to students and asking them to figure out the sum, students already know the sum and one of the parts and have to figure out the missing part.

"You need 8 tiles," Rosa answered quickly with confidence.

"How did you figure out the answer?" I probed.

Rosa replied, "It's easy. I know that 8 plus 2 makes 10."

Next, I showed Rosa a picture of a jar and explained, "This jar can hold 100 marbles when it's totally filled." I showed her another picture of the same size and shape jar, this one with 30 marbles written underneath. I hadn't drawn actual marbles, but had roughly scribbled to show a jar that was about one-third filled. "Can you figure out in your head how many more marbles I need to put into the jar so there are 100?"

"You need 70 more marbles," Rosa answered, again quickly with confidence.

"How did you figure out the answer?" I asked.

"I know that 7 plus 3 makes 10, so 70 plus 30 makes 100," she replied. I've found that using the known fact of 7 + 3 to figure out the answer to this problem is a typical response.

I gave Rosa another problem. This time I showed her 5 tiles. "Figure out in your head how many more tiles I need so I have 30 tiles in all," I said.

Rosa was quiet. After a moment, she counted softly by 5s to 30, putting up a finger each time. She looked at her six fingers and thought. After another moment, she said, "This one is hard. I don't think that six is right."

What I Learned

The numbers we choose for problems matter. Rosa's correct responses to the first two questions indicated that she understood the structure of the problem. The known fact of 7 + 3 gave her an anchor that helped her reason both problems. Children usually have a good deal of experience with numbers that add to 10, with their fingers as a backup support.

With 5 and 30, however, Rosa had no useful anchor, except for counting by 5s, which didn't help her solve the problem. Rosa understood the structure of the problem—that she was to find the missing addend—but she lacked facility with the particular numbers. Students need experience with developing strategies for mentally computing with numbers that are not "friendly," as are single-digit numbers or multiples of 10.

The marbles-in-the jar problem can help students figure out, in their heads, how many more are needed to make 100. The teacher can start with multiples of 10, then move to numbers that end in 5, and then move to all numbers. A 1–100 chart is a useful visual, and having students share their strategies is valuable. Also useful is providing 10-by-10 grids as a visual model; students can color in the number they have and see how many more 1s and 10s they need to fill the grid. The goal is to help students develop their number sense so they increase the range of their numerical comfort.

Snapshot 3: Interpreting Remainders

"Here's a word problem to solve," I told Randy, a fifth grader. This was at the beginning of the school year, and I was assessing students' understanding and skills with division. I showed Randy a card to help him keep track of the key information in the problem.

```
30 students
4 students in a car
```

Then I presented the problem, *Thirty students are going on a field trip. Four students fit in a car. How many cars are needed to fit all the students?*

"Can I use paper and pencil?" Randy asked. I nodded and watched Randy solve the problem as a long division problem. He wrote the answer as *7 R2*.

"How many cars are needed to fit all the students?" I asked.

"It's 7 remainder 2," he said.

What I Learned

Even though Randy was able to compute correctly, the computation alone wasn't a sufficient indication of his proficiency with division. His answer of "7 remainder 2" made sense numerically but not in the context of the problem. Students often lack experience solving problems that call for relating numbers to the numbers' meanings in real-world situations.

Dividing up things in their lives is a common experience for students, and it's valuable to build on this experience and situate a good deal of their division work in word problems. Randy, like all students, needs many experiences solving division word problems with a focus on making sense of the answer.

Sometimes pictorial representations of problems can help. In my experience, when asking students, like Randy, who don't make sense of their answers to draw a picture that shows the 30 students getting into cars in groups of 4, they often self-correct and give the answer of 8, which does make sense. But if students do the bulk of their division work on naked numbers—numbers without connections to contexts that require that they interpret answers—they may not learn the importance of reasoning to decide what those answers actually mean.

Snapshot 4: Estimating the Sum of Fractions

During a fraction assessment with Heidi, a sixth grader, I wrote a problem on her paper: $\frac{1}{3} + \frac{2}{5}$. I said to her, "Without using paper and pencil, decide if the answer is greater or less than 1."

Heidi considered the problem for a moment and then gave the correct answer, "Less than 1."

I followed up by asking, "How did you figure that out?" I was listening for Heidi to explain that because both fractions were less than $\frac{1}{2}$, their sum had to be less than 1. However, that's not what Heidi offered up. Instead, she made a classic error.

"One plus 2 is 3," she answered, pointing to the numerators of each fraction. Then, as she pointed to the denominators, she added, "three plus 5 is 8, and $\frac{3}{8}$ is less than 1." Heidi didn't notice, or consider, that $\frac{3}{8}$ is also less than $\frac{1}{2}$, so it couldn't possibly be the sum of the two fractions.

What I Learned

Sometimes correct answers hide misconceptions or gaps in learning. Too often, we probe students' thinking only when they answer incorrectly. Students quickly catch on that if we ask them a follow-up question, this indicates that they've made an error. Missing is the opportunity to give all students the experience of communicating how they reason, an important aspect of their math learning. Also, students benefit from hearing one another's ideas. Having students explain their thinking as a general procedure and asking the others to listen and react not only benefits all the students but also makes the important point that often there are different ways to solve a problem. If we don't ask students to explain their reasoning, we can't be sure how they are reasoning or what they truly understand. Heidi's faulty reasoning is a common error, an indication that she was relying on a procedure instead of trying to reason numerically.

Putting One-on-One Interviews into Practice

I can't imagine teaching math without investing time into interviewing students. At the beginning of the year, not only are interviews a valuable formative assessment that provides a mathematical profile of each student, but they're also a wonderful way to form a beginning connection with students. Also, during the year for interim assessments, doing a spot check in the class—asking each student just one question that relates to the math they've been studying—provides important information about the effectiveness of the instruction. With any one-on-one assessment, I'm careful to tell the student that I'm asking the questions so I can be a more effective teacher—not to give them a grade.

Finding the Time

Finding time to interview students is a challenge, but not an impossible one. I tell students what it is I'll be doing (talking with each of them) and why (so that I can learn to be a better teacher). In preparation, I rely on having an assortment of investigations that students can choose and do independently. These can include math games that give students practice with skills and strategic thinking, or explorations about something we're studying. Then the class can be productively engaged while I pull students aside individually. To make this work, however, the students need to understand what I expect them to do independently while I'm talking with individual students. Practicing this first before beginning interviews is useful.

For more information to support you in finding time for one-on-one interviews, see the choice time hints in "Starting Point 20: Four Structures for Organizing and Managing Classroom Instruction" in Part 1 on page 111.

Regularly Probing Students' Thinking

Spending time interviewing students has had a spillover effect on my classroom teaching practices. First of all, I use the information I get from one-on-one assessments to inform the instructional decisions I make. I'm deliberate about taking the time, especially before teaching a new topic, to find out what students do and do not understand. And I'm more careful now about not relying solely on students' written work to gauge what they know.

For more information on asking questions to probe students' thinking, see "Starting Point 14: The Importance of Classroom Discussions" in Part 1 on page 67.

Also, I now regularly probe students' thinking during classroom lessons, even when their answers are correct. I regularly ask them questions such as *Why do you think that? How did you figure that out? How would you explain your answer to someone who disagreed?* I have them comment on their classmates' answers as well, asking them to explain what someone else said in their own words or asking students if they have a different way to explain the answer. If a student is stuck, it's sometimes useful to have them turn and discuss the problem with a partner and then return to a whole-class discussion. This gives more students a chance to practice explaining their thinking. Also, while students are working with partners or in small groups, I often talk with them about what they're doing and thinking.

Wrapping It Up

We know that the students in our classes have a range of mathematical skills, understanding, intuition, interests, approaches to learning, and needs. The challenge we face is to balance the teaching of math with the teaching of students. Talking to students, one on one, and probing their thinking and reasoning, can help teachers find that balance. My mantra: *We ask, we listen, we learn.* The more information I have about students, the better prepared I am to make effective instructional decisions.

Suggestions for Classroom Instruction

Starting Point 17
Using Games in Math Class

Several issues come up regularly when teachers seeking help with their math instruction ask me questions. One is a general question: *How can I motivate all of my students to enjoy math more?* Another relates more to managing instruction in the classroom: *What can I do during math lessons when some students finish their work quickly while others need more time?* Another is a concern about practice: *How can I give students the practice they need without relying on more and more worksheets?*

One suggestion I offer to respond to all of these questions is: Make games an integral part of math instruction. Using games to support students' math learning has long been a standard feature in my teaching, and I have several reasons for doing so. Games address the question about motivating students by capturing their interest and providing alternative ways to engage them in learning math. Games are ideal for engaging students independently and productively when they have extra time. And games are effective options for the paper-and-pencil practice that worksheets often provide.

A Game for Getting Started: Four Strikes and You're Out

One game that has become a standard in my teaching repertoire is *Four Strikes and You're Out.*

I've taught this game at different grade levels to give students practice with mental computation, choosing numbers that are appropriate for the particular class.

When I introduced the game to a class of third graders, I began as I typically do. I wrote *Four Strikes and You're Out* on the board as I explained to the class that this is the name of a game I was going to teach them. Sammy's hand shot up and asked me the question I typically get.

"Don't you mean three strikes?" he asked, thinking about baseball.

And I gave my typical response, "We could play the game with three strikes, but let's try it first with four strikes and then you can see which would be better." Next I wrote a blank frame for a math problem that I knew the children could solve. And next to the problem frame, I listed the numbers from 0 to 9.

Four Strikes and You're Out

___ ___ + ___ ___ = ___ ___   *0 1 2 3 4 5 6 7 8 9*

"One number goes in each blank," I explained, pointing to the six blanks I had drawn, "and your job is to figure out the numbers in the problem." I showed the children a folded slip of paper and told them that inside I had written the problem they were to guess. (I didn't tell them the problem: 35 + 10 = 45.)

This game appears in *Lessons for Addition and Subtraction, Grades 2–3* by Bonnie Tank and Lynne Zolli (2001, 135–136), one of the books in the Teaching Arithmetic series.

"Here's how we play," I continued. "You guess a number, and if it's in my problem, I'll write the number in all the places it belongs. But, if you guess a number that's not in my problem, you get a strike. To win, you have to figure out all of the numbers before you get four strikes."

As with all new investigations, some children were confused. I've found that the best way to resolve confusion is to move forward. "There's no way to know at this point in the game what my numbers may be—you just have to guess," I said. "But after you make some correct guesses, you'll have some clues that can help."

I called on Celia to make the first guess. "Three," she said. I referred to my "cheat sheet" with the problem written on it and said, "Yes, that's one of the numbers in the problem." I wrote 3 where it belonged in the problem and crossed it off the list to indicate that it had been guessed.

Four Strikes and You're Out

$$\underline{3} \ \underline{} \ + \ \underline{} \ \underline{} \ = \ \underline{} \ \underline{} \qquad 0 \ 1 \ 2 \ \cancel{3} \ 4 \ 5 \ 6 \ 7 \ 8 \ 9$$

"Two," Hiroshi guessed next. I referred to my cheat sheet and said, "No, there's no 2 in my problem, so that counts as a strike." I crossed out the 2 and wrote an X next to the title to indicate a strike.

Four Strikes and You're Out   X

$$\underline{3} \ \underline{} \ + \ \underline{} \ \underline{} \ = \ \underline{} \ \underline{} \qquad 0 \ 1 \ \cancel{2} \ \cancel{3} \ 4 \ 5 \ 6 \ 7 \ 8 \ 9$$

"Nine," Amanda guessed next. I referred to my cheat sheet again and said, "No, that's strike two." The children groaned.

"It's good that we have four strikes," Sammy commented. I wrote another X.

Four Strikes and You're Out   X X

$$\underline{3} \ \underline{} \ + \ \underline{} \ \underline{} \ = \ \underline{} \ \underline{} \qquad 0 \ 1 \ \cancel{2} \ \cancel{3} \ 4 \ 5 \ 6 \ 7 \ 8 \ \cancel{9}$$

"Five," Maria guessed. I again referred to my cheat sheet. Even though I had memorized the problem, I checked to model for the students what they were to do after each guess when they later played the game independently.

"That's a useful guess," I said, recording the 5 in the two places it appeared and crossing it out on the list.

Four Strikes and You're Out   X X

$$\underline{3} \ \underline{5} \ + \ \underline{} \ \underline{} \ = \ \underline{} \ \underline{5} \qquad 0 \ 1 \ \cancel{2} \ \cancel{3} \ 4 \ \cancel{5} \ 6 \ 7 \ 8 \ \cancel{9}$$

A buzz of conversation broke out. A few children realized that the two 5s meant that there had to be a zero in the ones place of the second number. Others, however, didn't notice this. I brought the class back to attention. "Now that you have some clues in the problem," I said, "talk at your tables about what you now know, and what might be a good next guess. Raise your hand when you're ready to make the next guess." After a moment or so, about half the hands were raised. I called on Charlotte. "There has to be a 0," she said.

"Can you explain why?" I asked.

"Because you're adding something to 35 and the answer ends in a 5. So the number you're adding has to end in 0." Some children nodded in agreement and others looked confused. I've learned that after playing the game several times, more students begin to reason numerically about how the clues can help. This thinking calls for computing mentally, thinking about numerical structures, and helps develop their number sense. At this point, I focused on being sure they all at least knew how to play.

"So you'd like to guess a 0?" I asked. Charlotte nodded and I recorded.

Four Strikes and You're Out   X X

__3__ __5__ + ___ __0__ = ___ __5__   0̸ 1 2̸ 3̸ 4 5̸ 6 7 8 9̸

Conversation broke out again at their tables. After a few moments, I called the students back to attention and asked, "Who would like to share an idea about what you now know?" I called on Nelson.

"You can't be sure about the missing numbers," he said. "But if you guess one of the numbers right, then you'll know the other."

Anna had something else to add. "Eight won't work in either place," she said. "Can I come up to the board and show why?" I agreed. She came up and pointed at the first remaining blank. "Look," she said, "if it's 35 plus 80, you'd have three numbers in the answer because it would be more than 100." She then pointed at the blank in the sum and continued, "If the answer is 85, the second number would have to be 50, but we already used up the five." I could see that some children didn't follow Anna's explanation, so I asked the students again to turn and talk at their tables about Anna's idea and what they might want to guess next.

After a moment I asked, "Who wants to make the next guess?" I called on Tom

"Lucky 7," he guessed.

I checked the problem and responded, "Strike three." The students groaned as I recorded a strike and crossed out the 7.

Four Strikes and You're Out   X X X

__3__ __5__ + ___ __0__ = ___ __5__   0̸ 1 2̸ 3̸ 4 5̸ 6 7̸ 8 9̸

"Let's see what choices are left," I said. Together we read the numbers that weren't crossed out—1, 4, 6, and 8. Max reminded us that eight wouldn't work, but I didn't cross it out since it hadn't been guessed.

"Six won't work either," Angela said. "We already know nine is wrong, so you can't have 35 plus 60, and if the answer was 65, there would have to be another 3, and we already guessed that number."

"I guess a 1," Beatrice said.

"And the other number is a 4. It has to be 35 plus 10 equals 45," Sammy said.

I recorded the numbers and said, "Let's check the addition to be sure it's right." Everyone agreed that it was correct.

Four Strikes and You're Out   X X X

$\underline{3}\ \underline{5} + \underline{1}\ \underline{0} = \underline{4}\ \underline{5}$ ~~0~~ 1 ~~2~~ ~~3~~ 4 ~~5~~ 6 ~~7~~ 8 ~~9~~

"You figured out the problem with only three strikes," I said, "so you win." The class cheered.

I repeated the game for two more problems (50 + 26 = 76 and 29 + 13 = 42). The next day, we played two more games, and this time I changed the number of blanks in one game and the operation from addition to subtraction in the other (37 + 87 = 124 and 70 − 12 = 58). Later in the year, I used problems that involved multiplication and division, choosing problems that related to what the students were learning and practicing (for example, 6 × 5 − 4 = 26 and 5 = 40 ÷ 8).

This is an example of a game that works well as a whole-class investigation, for the class to play as one team against the teacher. When the students understand how to play, they can learn to play the game independently. For this, I organize the class into partners so that each pair of students could play against another pair.

First I had each pair think of a problem and, as I had modeled, write it on a slip of paper and fold it. On a half sheet of paper, they wrote the blanks for the problem and the list of the numbers from 0 to 9. Then they were ready to play. Pairs took turns, first one pair guessing and then switching roles. I added *Four Strikes and You're Out* to the class list of Math Games and it became a favorite option.

I've learned that it's important that students have the skills they need to play any game I teach, whether the game is intended to develop understanding, provide practice, and/or offer challenges. I was careful to introduce *Four Strikes and You're Out* using an addition problem that I knew the students could solve. When the math is accessible, students can more easily focus on learning how to play.

I've also learned that when I first introduce a game, just as when I present anything new in the classroom, some confusion is typical. For that reason, I like to teach a new game to the entire class so that everyone receives the same information. I play sample games as many times as needed to resolve all issues of confusion before I expect students to be successful independently.

Competitive or Cooperative?

Four Strikes and You're Out is an example of a competitive game where the goal is to win. From their experience playing games like Tic-Tac-Toe, children have learned to play competitive games where someone wins (or sometimes the game ends in a tie). Competitive games help students test their skills, take risks, and learn to be graceful winners and losers. However, it's important to foster communication and cooperation among students. Having the students play in pairs, as I did with *Four Strikes and You're Out*, allows for both cooperation and competition. Throughout the year, I like to teach a mix of games that can be played competitively, cooperatively, or either way.

Teaching Tip

I've found that having students work in pairs helps avoid errors in their responses and encourages communication about how they are reasoning.

— MSB

A Game for Practicing Combinations of 10: Seven Up

Developing fluency with combinations of 10 is essential in the early grades. *Seven Up* is appropriate for students who need practice with the combinations of 10.

For this game, a deck of forty cards is needed—four each of cards numbered 1 to 10 (a deck of playing cards with the face cards removed works well). To play, students deal seven cards faceup in a row. They remove all 10s, either individual cards with the number 10 on them, or pairs of cards that add to 10, and place the cards in a pile separate from the deck. Each time they remove cards, they replace them with cards from the remaining deck. When it's not possible to remove any cards, they deal a new row of seven cards on top of the ones that are there, covering each of them and any blank spaces with a new card. When those cards are removed, it may be possible to use the cards underneath. The game ends when it's no longer possible to make 10s or all of the cards in the deck are used up.

I gathered a group of six first graders to teach them the game and asked Luke to be my partner.

"I play card games at home with my grandma," Genevieve offered.

"I'm glad to know that," I responded, and then explained that I had removed all of the Jacks, Queens, and Kings from the deck we'd be using so it had the cards from Ace to 10.

"The joker, too?" she asked. I nodded yes, and added that for our game, the Ace is worth 1.

I modeled how to shuffle the cards by putting them facedown on the table and stirring to mix them. I've found this to be a good shuffling solution for young children. Then I gathered the cards back into a deck, handed it to Luke, and gave him a beginning direction, "Deal a row of seven cards faceup so that we can see the numbers." After Luke did this, I modeled how to play, introducing the rules, one by one. "First we take away cards with 10 on them and start a pile with them," I said. I removed the two cards with 10 on them and set them aside, facedown. I continued, "Next Luke will put out two more cards where those were." Luke dealt out two more cards. I explained the other part of how to play, "We also look for pairs of cards that add to 10." Owen noticed 9 and 1, and Jake noticed 6 and 4. As I removed each pair and added them to the pile with the 10s, I instructed Luke to deal new cards in their spaces.

We continued in this way. It didn't happen for this game, but I told the children that if you get stuck because there aren't any 10 cards showing, or any pairs of cards that add to 10, then you would deal a new row of seven cards on top of the ones showing, covering each of them. I directed Luke to pretend we were stuck and deal seven new cards this way. Then we continued. I pointed out that any covered-up card was OK to use once it was revealed.

After we finished the game, I organized the students in pairs and gave each pair a deck of cards. I reminded them, "One person should do the job that I had of removing the cards, and the other is the dealer

Seven Up is a game from *Do The Math*, an intervention program I worked on with a team of Math Solutions consultants, geared to help students in grades 2 and up who need to catch up and keep up. For more information on *Do The Math*, visit http://teacher .scholastic.com/products/ dothemath

and puts out the seven cards to start and then new cards to fill the spaces or because you're stuck. You should change jobs for each game." I watched the students as they played to make sure they were following the directions I had given them.

Variations

Unlike *Four Strikes and You're Out*, students can also play *Seven Up* as a game of solitaire. The solitaire feature is especially useful when a student doesn't have a partner to play with. Also, as long as you don't make an error by removing two cards that don't add to 10, you'll use up all of the cards for each game. This is a way to check that students are identifying the correct combinations. I typically limit the game so that children can remove only two cards that add to 10, to reinforce these combinations. It is possible, however, to allow them to remove three cards, but they "win" less often; that is, they wind up stuck with no more possible moves.

Both *Seven Up* and *Four Strikes and You're Out* are games that are suitable for playing multiple times. I remember happily playing the same games over and over when I was a child—checkers, Monopoly, solitaire, Sorry, and others. I've found that the same occurs during the year with math games, and these two are good examples. Students may lose interest in a game after a while but return to it later, enjoying the comfort of their familiarity with how to play.

A Versatile Game: The Greatest Wins

The Greatest Wins is a game that I've used in many grade levels and in many versions over the years. In a fourth-grade class, for example, I chose a multiplication version and asked each student to draw a game board that looks like this:

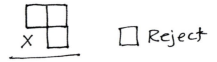

Students take turns rolling a 1–6 number cube and writing the number that comes up in one of the boxes on their game boards. Once a student writes a number, that number can't be changed. Students use the "Reject" box to write a number they think isn't helpful, but they can only do this once. After all players have filled in all of their boxes, students do the calculations and then compare to see who has the greatest answer.

When introducing this version to the fourth graders, after I drew a game board on the board to model for them how to draw their own game boards, I said, "Be sure to draw boxes large enough so you can write a number inside each." As I did when introducing *Four Strikes and You're Out*, I introduced this new game with a game board for a problem that I knew the students could solve—a two-digit number times a one-digit number.

The game works for groups of two, three, or four students to play, but I typically teach it by inviting a volunteer to come up to the board and play with me. Wesley came up and drew a matching game board. I then reminded the students that the goal was to get the greatest answer possible, that after Wesley and I each rolled four times, once for each box, we'd figure the products and see which was more. I rolled the number cube first and a 4 came up. I deliberated aloud about where the best place might be to play the number, "I wonder if I should take the chance that I'll roll 5s or 6s on at least some of my next three rolls so I could play it in the tens place. I think I'll write the 4 in the ones place of the top number and hope that happens. Remember, once I write a number, I can't move it."

Wesley went next and rolled a 1. Several in the class advised him to write it in the Reject box, which he did.

We continued taking turns, with much advice from others in the class. My final problem was 34 × 6 and Wesley's was 52 × 4. The students were surprised to see that Wesley won by only 4 points!

I then organized the 26 students into eight groups of three and one group of two, gave a 1–6 number cube to each group, and had them play a game. I led a discussion about the strategies they had used when placing numbers, asking questions such as, *How did you decide where to play a 1 or 2? What about a 5 or 6? Who has a different idea about where to play these numbers? How would you play the game if you got the same rolls again?*

Variations

Even though students enjoy playing games multiple times, offering different versions of a game not only adds variety to the game but also avoids having to teach new rules for playing. Here are other possible *The Greatest Wins* game boards that work for different grade levels and skills. Notice that for the first game board, no computation is needed; for this game it's important that students read their resulting numbers aloud.

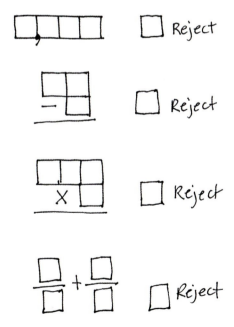

For information about how students can make their own spinners, see "Spinner Experiments" in Part 2 on page 171.

Target 300 appears in *Lessons for Extending Multiplication*, a book in the Teaching Arithmetic series that I coauthored with Maryann Wickett (2001, 92–102). In this resource, you can read a vignette that provides a look at how the game evolved in a classroom setting.

At times I assign students a specific version of a game to play. At other times, I leave the choice of the version up to the students. Not only does this give students control of their learning, their choices also can provide information about their mathematical comfort. Another way to vary *The Greatest Wins* is to exchange the 1–6 number cube for a 0–9 spinner, which generates additional possible numbers. Or sometimes I change the game to a less-is-more version—*The Smallest Wins*. It helps to list all of these options on the class Math Games chart.

A Multiplication Game: Target 300

Target 300 develops students' numbers sense, gives them practice multiplying by 10 and multiples of 10, and supports mental computation. Although the game's focus is multiplication, students also get practice with addition and subtraction. The object of the game is to be the player whose total is closest to 300 after six rolls of a 1–6 number cube. The total can be exactly 300, less than 300, or greater than 300, but players must use all six turns. As with *The Greatest Wins*, I teach students how to organize their own recording sheets, two columns each with a player's name at the top. Each player records what happens for both players, a way for them to have a check on what is happening.

Player 1 rolls the number cube and decides whether to multiply the number that comes up by 10, 20, 30, 40, or 50. Players record their own and each other's problems. For example, if Player 1 rolls a 2 and multiplies it by 20, both players record $2 \times 20 = 40$. Then Player 2 takes a turn. Players keep a running total of their scores. After each has had six turns, they record:

_____ *won.*

_____ *was* ___ *points away from 300.*

_____ *was* ___ *points away from 300.*

When I introduce this game, I am Player 1 and a volunteer is Player 2, which gives me a chance to model first how to play. Also, as a helpful reference, I write on the board:

$\times 10$

$\times 20$

$\times 30$

$\times 40$

$\times 50$

Variations

Games can help with differentiating instruction. To serve the differing needs of students, I change *Target 300* to *Target 200* for some students and to *Target 600* for more of a challenge. Also, using a 0–9 spinner for this game increases the challenge by generating additional possible numbers.

Managing the Classroom During Games

Following are tips for managing the classroom when students are involved playing games.

CLASSROOM MANAGEMENT TIPS FOR USING GAMES

1. Choose games that are accessible to all students.

2. Teach games to the entire class at the same time.

3. Use games competitively and cooperatively.

4. Teach games that are suitable for playing multiple times.

5. If possible, modify games so students can play them individually.

6. Offer different versions of games.

7. Start a Math Games class chart.

8. Have students share games at home.

It's common when giving an assignment in class for some students to finish quickly while other are still working or even struggling to get their footing. Games are ideal for answering the "What do I do now?" question. I start a Math Games class chart and add the names of the games as I teach them. This creates a math repertoire of independent math investigations that I have approved and that are accessible to all. Then, when students have extra time, I direct them to choose one of the games from the chart. Either I have them choose from any on the list or, as the list grows, I indicate the three or four that are particularly appropriate for what they are studying. And an extra tip: The list of games can be a helpful support to a substitute.

Also, having students share a game they've learned with their families is a way to send home information about the kind of math thinking their children are doing in school. When I choose a game for students to play at home, I'm always sure that they have had enough experience to be thoroughly familiar with how to play. Sometimes I give a writing assignment and have students write the rules for playing. Then, in pairs or small groups, students test their rules on one another to be sure they are clear and complete. I've found that it helps to prepare students for writing rules by first modeling how to write rules for a different game—I post rules that are purposely incomplete or unclear, and lead a classroom discussion about how to change them.

When I use games in the classroom, I expect that students will prefer different games and that some students will be more skilled than others. This is fine as long as each game provides math experiences that are within the students' grasp and supports their learning. Games are ideal for engaging students in your class so that you can be free to provide help to those who require additional instruction and more individual attention; they are definitely a win-win option for teachers and students.

For a helpful resource with many ideas for games that work with K–5 students, check out *Math Games for Independent Practice* by Jamee Petersen (2013).

Wrapping It Up

When I choose games to teach, I use a variety and draw from games that promote strategic thinking, provide practice, and support thinking, reasoning, and problem solving. I also look for games where some degree of chance is also involved, such as guessing a number, rolling a number cube, or using a spinner. The chance aspect helps to level the playing field and make it possible for students of varying abilities to enjoy playing together. As a guide, I use the following list of characteristics as criteria when I select games to teach.

CHARACTERISTICS OF EFFECTIVE GAMES

- Easy to teach

- Accessible to all students

- Build number sense, reinforce understanding, and/or provide practice

- Encourage strategic thinking

- Rely on only a few materials in addition to paper and pencil

- Have different versions for differentiation

Starting Point 18
The Role of Manipulative Materials

Physical objects are important tools for teachers to use for teaching mathematics and for students to use for learning mathematics. Supplies of manipulative materials for teaching mathematics exist in most classrooms—tiles, cubes, pattern blocks, Cuisenaire rods, geoboards, tangrams, counters, and others.

Reasons for Using Manipulative Materials

Manipulative materials have long been staples for math instruction, and for good reasons. Here I discuss four of these reasons.

REASONS FOR USING MANIPULATIVE MATERIALS

- Manipulatives help students make sense of abstract concepts.
- Manipulatives provide students ways to test and verify ideas.
- Manipulatives serve as useful tools for solving problems.
- Manipulatives make learning mathematics more engaging and interesting.

Manipulatives help students make sense of abstract concepts.

Just as we say that a picture is worth a thousand words, there's no substitute for firsthand concrete experiences. Manipulative materials provide a way for students to form mental models that they can then connect to abstract symbolic representations. In a way, they give students opportunities to get their hands on abstract ideas so that they can also wrap their minds around them.

For example, young students learn that some numbers are odd and others are even. Often, they are introduced to the idea that when you can split a number into two equal quantities, the number is even. But instead of teaching this idea simply numerically (for example, since $12 = 6 + 6$, 12 is an even number), manipulative materials can engage students concretely with this idea. I ask students each to take a handful of objects, count them, and record how many they have on a sticky note. Then they see if they can split the handful into two equal groups by arranging them into two lines and seeing if each object has a partner. If they can, the number is even; if they can't, then it's odd. Write *Even* and *Odd* on the board and have students come up and post their sticky note under the correct label. Allow enough time so all students investigate at least two numbers. It's fine if more than one student investigates the same number—this provides additional verification for whether it's even or odd. Should the same number wind up under both labels, we investigate further by having all children try that number. Matching up counters in groups or lines for many quantities helps students build mental models that they can then

For Younger Students
An alternative to lining up objects into two lines is to introduce the activity as Two-Hand Take-Away. Students pile the objects on the desk and, at the same time, remove one object with each hand. If they wind up removing all of the objects, there was an even number. If there's an object left, there was an odd number.

— MSB

translate to the abstract concept. Once the class has identified various quantities as even or odd, they can begin to look for patterns in these numbers. When they organize and examine the numbers that turn out to be even, the numerical pattern (2, 4, 6, 8, 10, and so on) emerges.

For older students learning about square numbers, the concept is greatly enhanced when they actually arrange tiles into squares and see how the square numbers grow—2 by 2, 3 by 3, 4 by 4, and so on. (Yes, square numbers are actually square!) Students can then connect their concrete experience to multiplication (2 × 2, 3 × 3, 4 × 4, and so on) and think about the pattern of square numbers (1, 4, 9, 16, 25, and so on) both numerically and visually.

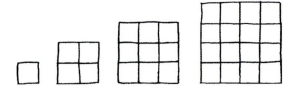

Manipulatives provide students ways to test and verify ideas.

Another reason for using manipulative materials is that they provide students ways to test and verify ideas. We know that partial understanding and confusion are natural to children's learning, and manipulative materials can provide the support students need to develop, cement, and extend their developing understanding. For example, when young children first learn about even and odd numbers, their understanding is typically fragile. I remember Brian, a second grader, telling me that 50 is an odd number. He was sure about this and explained, "I know that 5 is odd because when you line them up, one doesn't have a partner." He concluded, "So 50 has to be odd because it has a 5 in it." While Brian was able mentally to line up the small quantity of 5, thinking about 50 in this way seemed to be out of his reach. I gave Brian 50 pennies and asked him to line them up in two groups. I assigned another student to work with him to help. (Keeping track of so many pennies can be daunting.) Brian was surprised to find out that each penny had a partner, so 50 was an even number. He was confused. I used Brian's idea for a classroom discussion, presenting his conjecture to the others. I wrote on the board: *True or False: 50 is odd because it has a 5 in it and 5 is an odd number.* After giving the students a chance to talk in pairs, I called on some to present their ideas.

Darius began, "It's part true and part false because 5 is odd but 50 is even."

Katie pointed out, emphatically, "It's not the first number that tells, it's the second number."

"Do you mean the number in the ones place is the one that tells?" I asked, to reinforce the place-value structure of 50. Katie nodded in agreement.

Julius pointed out that he knew 50 was an even number because he thought about money. He explained, "It's like two quarters make 50 cents, so you can split 50 cents into two amounts that are the same."

After all students had shared their ideas, I wrote the number *10* on the board. "Is it even or odd?" I asked the class. Everyone, Brian included, knew it was even. I pointed to the 1 in the 10 and said, "Hmm, I agree that the number 10 is even, but I notice that it has the number 1 in it, and I know that 1 is an odd number. My clue for the number 10 is the number in the ones place, the 0, not the other digit." Brian seemed to be convinced about 10, but he still was shaky with greater numbers. Additional experiences using pennies helped with his new learning.

When older students study square numbers, they learn about the pattern of how square numbers relate to sums of consecutive odd numbers. This pattern can be presented numerically:

4 = 1 + 3

9 = 1 + 3 + 5

16 = 1 + 3 + 5 + 7

25 = 1 + 3 + 5 + 7 + 9

and so on.

But it helps students understand how this pattern emerges by building it with tiles. Direct students to place one tile on their desk to represent the first square number, 1. Then ask them to add three tiles of another color, surrounding the original tile on two sides to build the next square number, 4. Record on the board: *4 = 1 + 3*. Then ask them to surround this new square on two sides with tiles of another color to build the next square number, 9. Underneath the first equation on the board, record: *9 = 1 + 3 + 5*. Continue. Then ask students to notice patterns in the list of equations. Finally, ask students to write conclusions about what they notice about how the patterns relate to square numbers. The pattern of adding consecutive odd numbers emerges visually from the students' interaction with the physical materials.

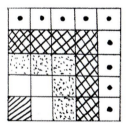

Manipulatives serve as useful tools for solving problems.

A third reason for using manipulative materials is that they are useful tools for solving problems. For example, think about the formulas we learned for calculating areas of geometric shapes. Textbooks provide ample practice for applying the formula to calculate the areas of triangles—$A = \frac{1}{2} b \times h$. Manipulative materials add the dimension of helping students understand the *why*, not just the *how*, of the formula. Students can use rectangles cut from grid paper to help them build understanding by relating the triangle formula to the formula for the area of rectangles— $A = b \times h$. To do this, I model for students, cutting out two congruent 8-by-4 rectangles from grid paper and recording the area, 32 square units, on one of the cut-out rectangles. On the other rectangle, I draw a diagonal to divide the rectangle into two triangles (which will be congruent). Then we talk about the area of each triangle. Some students notice that it's half of the rectangle, but I model how to figure out the area by counting the whole and partial squares. Then I have students do the same, working in pairs, and cutting rectangles with sides less than or equal to 10 units. I label two columns on the board—*Area of Rectangle* and *Area of Triangle*— and have students post their data. We discuss that the triangle areas are always half of the rectangle areas, and I relate this to the formulas. For problems that involve three-dimensional shapes, such as finding the volume and surface area of cubes, using cubes to construct larger cubes and then figuring out their volumes and surface areas are valuable and effective first steps. Concrete materials help students get their hands as well as their minds around many of the mysteries of mathematics.

Manipulatives make learning mathematics more engaging and interesting.

Concrete materials lift mathematics off the pages of textbooks and workbooks. They involve students as active learners. When I first began exploring the use of manipulative materials for teaching math, I remember learning what was described as an ancient Chinese proverb: *I hear and I forget, I see and I remember, I do and I understand*. Using concrete models helps students understand concepts and skills that they then learn to represent abstractly.

Classroom Suggestions for Using Manipulatives

It's important to make manipulative materials part of the regular classroom supplies, available to students as needed. This calls for organization, ground rules, and discussion.

CLASSROOM SUGGESTIONS FOR USING MANIPULATIVES

- Talk with the class about how manipulative materials can help them learn math.
- Set up a storage system.
- Give time for free exploration.
- Set ground rules for using manipulative materials.
- Post a chart of the names of manipulatives.
- Send home a letter to families.

When talking with your class about how manipulative materials can help them learn math, refer to the list of "Reasons for Using Manipulatives Materials" on page 99.

Talk with the class about how manipulative materials can help them learn math.

Talk about the reasons for using manipulatives. These discussions are essential for first-time users and useful refreshers to refocus students from time to time.

Set up a storage system.

Establish a system for labeling and storing manipulative materials and familiarize students with it. It's important that students know where and how to store the materials they use.

Give time for free exploration.

Giving time for free exploration is essential. Free exploration allows students to satisfy their curiosity so they don't later become distracted from assigned tasks. After students explore a manipulative material, ask what they discovered. Record their observations so students can learn from one another's ideas.

Set ground rules for using manipulative materials.

Explain that using manipulative materials in math class won't always be free exploration; students will have specific problems to solve and investigations to do. Then assign a specific task so students can experience the difference. Monitor as they work, reminding students as needed to stay on task.

Post a chart of the names of manipulatives.

For easy reference, listing the names of the manipulative materials as you introduce them helps students learn the materials' names and how to spell them. The chart lets students know that you value manipulative materials.

Send home a letter to families.

Inform parents why their children are using concrete materials in math class. Give parents some firsthand experience with manipulatives during back-to-school night. Also, you might from time to time have students take home materials and investigations to do with family members.

Wrapping It Up

I've found manipulative materials to be indispensable teaching tools for helping students make sense of mathematics. In the lower grades, I rely on interlocking cubes, pattern blocks, counters, color tiles, and more; in the upper grades, I rely on the geoboards, geometric models, pattern blocks, color tiles, algebra tiles, and more. Not only do they support learning, they're especially effective for engaging students' interest and motivating them to explore ideas.

Starting Point 19
Strategies for Intervention Instruction

Paul was floundering in math. He was a fourth grader when I met him and Anne, his teacher, was concerned. She told me that Paul typically worked very slowly in math and "didn't get much done." I agreed to talk with Paul and see if I could figure out the nature of his difficulty.

"Can you tell me something you know about multiplication?" I asked Paul.

Paul thought for a bit and then responded, "Six times 8 is 48."

I nodded to accept his response and asked, "Do you know how much 6 times 9 is?"

Paul shrugged, shook his head to indicate he didn't, and said, "I don't know that one. I didn't learn it yet."

"Can you figure it out some way?" I pursued. Paul sat silently for a moment and then shook his head no again.

"How did you learn 6 times 8?" I asked him, returning to something that Paul did know.

Paul brightened and grinned. "It's easy," he said, "goin' fishing, got no bait, 6 times 8 is 48. My sister taught me."

As I talked more with Paul, I found out that multiplication was a mystery to him. Because of his weak foundation of understanding, he was falling behind his classmates who were multiplying problems like 683 × 4. Paul was not able to explain what expressions like 6 × 8 meant and he didn't know many of the products of two one-digit numbers. Not only didn't Paul know the basic multiplication facts, he had no way to figure out products that he hadn't memorized, like for 6 × 9. Only when he had a foundation of understanding would Paul be prepared to tackle problems like the ones his classmates were solving.

Paul wasn't the only student in this particular class who was floundering; there were several students about whom the teacher was concerned. In talking with teachers, and from my own teaching experience, it seems that it's typical in every class to have at least a handful of students who are at serious risk of failure in mathematics and aren't being adequately served by the classroom instruction. Faced with students like Paul who have fallen through the cracks, what should we do?

Issues Important to Teaching Mathematics

My exchange with Paul reminded me of three issues that are important to teaching mathematics:

- It's important to help students make connections among mathematical ideas so they don't see these ideas as isolated and disconnected from one another. (Paul wasn't able to use addition for figuring products and reason that 6 × 8 could be thought of as adding six 8s—8 + 8 + 8 + 8 + 8 + 8—and 6 × 9 could be thought of as adding six 9s—9 + 9 + 9 + 9 + 9 + 9.)

- It's important to build students' new learning on the foundation of their prior learning. (Paul saw each multiplication fact as a separate piece of information to memorize and didn't use the grouping structure of multiplication to reason that 6×8 could be thought of as 6 groups of 8, so 6×9 could be thought of as 6 groups of 9.)

- It's important to remember that correct answers by themselves, without students' explanations of how they reasoned, aren't sufficient for judging mathematical understanding. (Paul's initial offering of the product of 6×8, without my additional probing, masked his confusion and lack of understanding.)

For many years, my professional focus has been on finding more effective ways to teach arithmetic, the cornerstone of elementary mathematics. My goal, in collaboration with colleagues, has been to create lessons that are accessible to all students and that teach skills in the context of understanding. Of course, even well-planned lessons will require differentiating instruction, and much of the differentiation needed is doable within the context of regular classroom instruction.

But students like Paul present a greater challenge. Many are already at least a year behind and lack the foundation of mathematical understanding on which to build new learning. They may have multiple misconceptions that hamper progress. They have already experienced failure and typically lack confidence. These students not only demand more time and attention but they also need instruction that differs from the regular program and is designed specifically for their success. Intervention instruction, in addition to the regular classroom math instruction, is essential in order for these students to learn the basic mathematics they need.

Nine Essential Strategies for Successful Intervention Instruction

To address the need of intervention instruction, I worked with a team of colleagues designing lessons to provide instruction that would engage students, offer scaffolded instruction in bite-sized learning pieces, be paced for students' success, provide the practice students need to cement fragile understanding and skills, and bolster students' mathematical foundations along with their confidence. We were committed to the notion that "the basics" of number and operations for all students, including those who are in need of intervention, must address understanding and sense making as well as skill proficiency.

We relied on nine strategies to create intervention lessons for students like Paul. Attention to all of these strategies is necessary in order to intervene in ways that reroute students' learning toward understanding and success.

Our work as described here resulted in *Do The Math*, an intervention program I worked on with a team of Math Solutions consultants, geared to help students in grades 2 and up who need to catch up and keep up. For more information on *Do The Math*, visit http://teacher.scholastic.com/products/dothemath

Scaffold the mathematics content.

Determining the essential math content is like peeling an onion—we must identify the concepts and skills we want students to learn and discard what's extraneous. Only then can the content be scaffolded. For Paul to multiply 683×4, for example, he must know the basic multiplication facts. He needs an understanding of place value that allows him to think about 683 as $600 + 80 + 3$. He needs to be able to apply the distributive property to figure out and then combine partial products. For this particular problem, he needs to be able to multiply 4 by 3 (one of the basic facts); understand that when he multiplies 4 by the 8, he's really multiplying 4 by 80; and that multiplying 4×6 is really multiplying 4 by 600.

Pace lessons carefully.

We've all seen the look in students' eyes when they get lost in math class. When it appears, ideally teachers stop, deal with the situation, and move on only when students are ready. Yet curriculum demands often result in pressing forward, even when some students lag behind. Intervention instruction allows for students like Paul who typically need more time to grapple with new ideas and practice new skills in order to internalize them. Many students need to unlearn before they relearn.

Build in a routine of support.

Students are quick to reveal when a lesson hasn't been scaffolded sufficiently or paced slowly enough: As soon as you give an assignment, hands shoot up for help. To avoid this, we need to build in a routine of support before expecting students to complete independent work. We found that it helps when presenting a new idea or skill to think about a four-stage process.

First, we model what students are expected to learn. For example, to give students practice multiplying and also experience applying the associative and commutative properties, we present problems that involve multiplying three single-digit factors. An appropriate first problem is $2 \times 3 \times 4$. It's helpful to think aloud to model, "I could start by multiplying 2 times 3 to get 6 and then multiply 6 times 4 to get 24. Or I could first multiply 2 times 4, and then multiply 8 times 3, which gives 24 again. Or I could do 3 times 4, and then 2 times 12. All three ways produce the same product of 24 and solving a problem in more than one way is a good way to check your answer." It's important to record on the board to illustrate this thinking:

$$2 \times 3 \times 4 \qquad 2 \times 3 \times 4 \qquad 2 \times 3 \times 4$$
$$6 \times 4 = 24 \qquad 8 \times 3 = 24 \qquad 2 \times 12 = 24$$

In the second stage, we model again with a similar problem—for example, $2 \times 4 \times 5$—this time eliciting responses from the students by asking, for example, *Which two factors might you multiply first? What's the product of those two factors? What should we multiply next? What's the product? What's another way to start?* Again, recording on the board is important.

$$2 \times 4 \times 5 \qquad 2 \times 4 \times 5 \qquad 2 \times 4 \times 5$$
$$8 \times 5 = 40 \qquad 10 \times 4 = 40 \qquad 2 \times 20 = 40$$

During the third stage, we present another similar problem—for example, $2 \times 3 \times 5$. After a moment to think on their own, students work in pairs to solve the problem in three different ways and record. Then, when students report, we again record on the board.

$$2 \times 3 \times 5 \qquad 2 \times 3 \times 5 \qquad 2 \times 3 \times 5$$
$$6 \times 5 = 30 \qquad 10 \times 3 = 30 \qquad 2 \times 15 = 30$$

Finally, in the fourth stage, students work independently on similar problems, referring to the recordings on the board.

Foster student interaction.

It's often been said that you know something best once you've taught it. I think that's because teaching calls for verbalizing ideas in order to communicate them coherently, which calls for formulating, reflecting, and clarifying—all processes that support learning. In the same way, giving students opportunities to voice their ideas helps them strengthen, extend, and cement their learning. To this end, it's valuable to make student interaction an integral part of instruction, as in the third phase previously described when students work in pairs to figure out the answer to $2 \times 3 \times 5$ in three ways. Students first are asked to think on their own to collect their thoughts, then they talk with a partner, and finally they share with the whole group. Maximizing students' opportunities to express ideas is also particularly valuable for students who are developing their English language skills.

Make connections explicit.

Students in need of intervention typically don't look on their own for relationships or make connections among ideas. They need help building new learning on what they already know. For example, Paul needed explicit help to understand how thinking about 6×8 could give him access to figuring out 6×9. He needed to connect the meaning of multiplication to what he already knew about addition, that 6×8 can be thought of as combining 6 groups of 8, and that 6×9 could be thought of as combining 6 groups of 9. He needed time and practice to cement this understanding for other multiplication problems. He would benefit from investigating six groups of other numbers—6×2, 6×3, and so on—and looking at the numerical pattern of these products. Paul needs many experiences seeing connections like these and applying them to solve problems.

Encourage mental math.

Calculating mentally builds students' ability to reason and fosters their number sense. It's important after students have a foundation of understanding about multiplication for them to learn the basic multiplication facts, but their experience with multiplying mentally should expand beyond. For example, students should investigate the patterns that help them mentally multiply any number by a power of 10—10, 100, or 1000, and so on. I find it deeply concerning to see students, when needing to multiply 18×10, for example, reach for pencil and paper and follow a procedure they've learned:

$$
\begin{array}{r}
18 \\
\times\ 10 \\
\hline
00 \\
180 \\
\hline
180
\end{array}
$$

(Or sometimes students don't write the zero on this line, or misalign the columns.)

Revisiting students' prior work with multiplying three factors can help develop their skill with multiplying mentally. Making the choice of which way is easiest or most efficient to multiply three factors depends on the numbers at hand. Multiplying $2 \times 9 \times 5$, for example, results in the following options:

$$2 \times 9 \times 5 \qquad 2 \times 9 \times 5 \qquad 2 \times 9 \times 5$$

$$18 \times 5 = 90 \qquad 10 \times 9 = 90 \qquad 2 \times 45 = 90$$

Guiding students to check for factors that produce a product of 10, as shown in the middle solution above, helps them build the tools they need to build their ability to reason.

When students can calculate mentally, they can make estimates before they solve problems so that they can reflect on whether answers make sense. For example, to estimate the product of 683×4, students can figure out the answer to 700×4. Learning to multiply 700×4 mentally can be supported by building on students' prior experience changing three-factor problems to two-factor problems. Now they learn to change a two-factor problem, like 700×4, into a three-factor problem that includes a power of 10—$7 \times 100 \times 4$. Then they multiply by the power of 10 last for easiest computing.

$$7 \times 100 \times 4$$

$$28 \times 100 = 2800$$

For other ideas on encouraging mental math, see "Starting Point 12: Developing Mental Math Skills" in Part 1 on page 56.

Help students use paper and pencil to track thinking.

When computations are too complex to do mentally, paper and pencil is essential. (In our daily lives, this is when we typically use calculators or computers.) Students should be able to multiply 700×4 in their heads, but they'll need paper and pencil to multiply 683×4. When students learn and practice procedures for calculating, their recording with paper and pencil should be rooted in understanding and sense making. They should see paper and pencil as a tool for keeping track of how they think. For example, to multiply 14×6 in their heads, students can first multiply 10×6 to get 60, then 4×6 to get 24, and then combine the two partial products, 60 and 24, to get 84. To keep track of the partial products with paper and pencil, they might write:

14×6

$10 \times 6 = 60$

$4 \times 6 = 24$

$60 + 24 = 84$

They can also use this way of reasoning for problems that involve multiplying by three-digit numbers, like 683×4.

Provide practice.

Regular practice is essential, and intervention students typically need more practice than students who learn more easily. What's important is that practice be directly connected to students' learning experiences, with problems chosen to support the scaffolded instruction, and always with an eye toward promoting understanding as well as skills. In addition to assignments, games can be a motivating and effective way for providing students practice.

For more on regular practice, see "Starting Point 17: Using Games in Math Class" in Part 1 on page 89.

For other ideas on helping improve the math vocabulary of intervention students, see "Starting Point 22: Teaching Math Vocabulary" in Part 1 on page 122.

Build in vocabulary instruction.

The meanings of words in math—for example, *even, odd, difference, product*—often differ from their common use. Many students needing math intervention have weak mathematical vocabularies. It's important to remember that teaching vocabulary should be tied to—and typically follows—teaching mathematical concepts, so that new terminology is grounded in understanding. We should explicitly teach vocabulary in the context of a learning investigation and then use it consistently. A math vocabulary chart can help keep the class focused on the importance and use of math language.

Wrapping It Up

We relied on the previous nine strategies for the lessons published in *Do The Math*, a program for providing intervention instruction for number and operations. Working on *Do The Math* reinforced my belief that instruction—for all students and especially for at-risk students—must emphasize understanding, sense making, and skills. Also, when I thought about how to serve students like Paul, I made substantial shifts in my own teaching of mathematics. While I still rely on the best practices I know for teaching mathematics, I am now much more intentional about creating and teaching lessons that will help intervention students catch up and keep up.

Starting Point 20

Four Structures for Organizing and Managing Classroom Instruction

When I'm planning a lesson, one of the important aspects I consider is how to manage instruction. I find that I rely on four different structures: whole-class instruction, small-group work, individual work, and choice time. The structures serve different purposes, and each helps students learn how to be productive learners in a different way. In this section, I describe the four structures as they have evolved in my own classroom teaching.

FOUR STRUCTURES FOR ORGANIZING AND MANAGING INSTRUCTION

- Whole-class instruction
- Small-group work
- Individual work
- Choice time: math menus

Whole-Class Instruction

From my own math learning as a student, I mostly remember my teachers at the chalkboard teaching lessons to the whole class. They explained, asked questions, called on students for answers, and sometimes asked students to come to the board to solve problems. It was generally one-way teaching—we listened and tried to understand the teacher's explanations. And while whole-class instruction is still an important element of my classroom practice, I've broadened my view of when it's appropriate and how to engage students when teaching to the whole class.

Basically, I think that whole-class instruction is appropriate and useful when the content of the lesson is something I want to communicate to all students in the class. The content might include presenting concepts, demonstrating skills, introducing vocabulary, modeling how to represent math thinking, presenting procedures for an investigation, introducing materials that we'll be using, or giving assignments. During whole-class instruction, I expect students to attend carefully, perhaps take notes or copy down what I've presented. I often find it easier to gather the students in one area, such as on the rug, so that I can more easily maintain eye contact.

A major change I've made over my years of teaching whole-class lessons is to shift from the one-way teaching I experienced as a student. This doesn't pertain to when I'm giving logistical instructions, but it does apply when we're dealing with math content. I've shifted from being the sole or primary presenter of information to engaging students to participate more actively in classroom talk. I expect students to attend carefully to what I'm saying *and* to what their classmates are saying. Rather than being the sole explainer in the classroom, I share

For more information on sharing the role of facilitating discussions, see "Starting Point 14: The Importance of Classroom Discussions" in Part 1 on page 67.

For more on assessing during whole-class instruction, see "Starting Point 13: Making Formative Assessment Integral to Instruction" in Part 1 on page 62.

that role by facilitating discussions during which students are also expected to be explainers. Instead of conducting a series of conversations by calling on students to give answers, I encourage conversations between and among students from which we can all learn. As I've honed my teaching skills over the years, this process of broadening the whole-class lessons I teach has enhanced my listening skills as well.

An important benefit of this shift, along with increasing student engagement, has been that I now receive much more feedback about what students are thinking and learning. Listening to students allows me to guide classroom lessons more effectively and assess what students are learning. And my lesson planning now involves not only the material I plan to present but also the questions I plan to pose for class discussion.

Small-Group Work

I also remember as an elementary student how, after a whole-class lesson, we all worked by ourselves on what the teacher assigned. During these times, talking was not encouraged. Mostly it wasn't allowed. When you didn't know what to do and were stuck, you had to wait for the teacher to come and help.

There are times when individual seatwork is appropriate, as I explain a bit further on in this section. But looking back, it's clear that this structure had its limits for supporting learning. Plus, it was tough on students who were floundering and the teacher who sometimes had more individual needs to meet than was reasonable.

I've found organizing students into small groups when they are working on assignments or involved in investigations to be a much more productive structure for their learning. Small groups maximize the active participation of each student and reduce individuals' isolation. In small groups, students have more opportunities to voice their thinking and to respond to others' ideas. Organizing students into pairs or groups helps establish an environment that is safe and supportive. It provides a setting that encourages and values social interaction, which supports learning by providing more students the opportunity to offer their ideas for reaction and receive feedback than occurs in whole-class lessons or isolated individual work.

Small-group work also provides students with an organized way to get support from one another, rather than depending solely on my feedback. It builds students' independence, which, in turn, can free me to provide attention to individuals.

But I've only been able to realize the benefits of small-group work when I've given sufficient time and attention to implementing and reinforcing the guidelines for the students. There's no guarantee of instant success from seating students in pairs or small groups and explaining the rules. Students need practice, encouragement, and discussion to learn to work together productively. Although students may have heard much about cooperation, functioning cooperatively is not a skill they've necessarily put into practice. And although they've always been told they're responsible for their own work and behavior, meeting that responsibility independently doesn't come naturally. In order for the system to best serve teachers and students, it's important

For specific help with organizing small-group work, refer to "Planning Whole-Class Lessons with Problem-Solving Investigations" in Part 2 on page 134.

to carefully plan instruction that utilizes the benefits of this organizational structure.

Organizing a class for small-group work requires thinking about the classroom space and deciding how to group students. It requires redefining the students' responsibilities as learners. And it calls for a shift in the teacher's role.

Organizing Small Groups

Let's consider the physical organization first. Desks or tables need to be arranged so that groups of two to five students can talk together. This is generally not difficult. Desks can be moved into clusters or, if tables are available, each group can be seated at a table or pairs can share a table. I don't think there's an ideal size for groups—it depends on the students and the investigation.

It's beneficial for students to have the opportunity to work with all of their classmates over the course of time. This is as much to the point of developing good citizenship as it is to learning mathematics and, to this end, I recommend changing groups from time to time. Some teachers like to form groups randomly. Playing cards work well to accomplish this. I label tables or clusters of desks or tables (Ace, 2, 3, 4, and so on) and then pull out the corresponding cards from a deck of playing cards, two, three, or four of each number, depending on the size of the groups. By shuffling the cards, distributing them, and asking students to sit at the table or cluster of desks that matches their card, you can quickly organize the students into groups. Using cards in this way removes the responsibility from the teacher of deciding who works with whom and communicates the message to students that they need to learn to work with all their classmates. (This is good preparation for later experiences in the workplace when we can't choose our coworkers.) Other teachers, however, prefer to make decisions about the composition of groups depending on the particular investigations and interests of the students.

> Management Suggestion
> A confession: Sometimes dealing out cards has resulted in a particularly troublesome combination of students who can't seem to work productively together. In that case, I make a change, but I communicate openly with the students about why I'm doing so.
> — MSB

Establishing Guidelines for Small Groups

Whatever the system, it helps to prepare students to work together by establishing guidelines. I find three rules to be extremely useful.

THREE RULES FOR SMALL-GROUP WORK

1. You are responsible for your own work and behavior.

2. You must be willing to help any group member who asks.

3. You may ask the teacher for help only when everyone in your group has the same question.

These rules are only as useful as they are understood and practiced in actual operation. After explaining them to the class, I discuss them for at least the first half dozen times students work in groups.

Rule #1: You are responsible for your own work and behavior.

The first rule is not new for any student. Even so, it helps to clarify it with further explanation: "You have responsibilities in this class and your job is to meet them. If you don't understand something, your first option is to ask your group for help. If you do understand, don't take over and give answers—listening to others' ideas is also a part of your individual responsibility. Sometimes, although you are sitting with your group, you will have an individual assignment to complete. Other times, your group will have an assignment to complete jointly, and then your responsibility is to contribute to the group effort."

Rule #2: You must be willing to help any group member who asks.

Two comments help clarify the second rule: "Notice that the benefit of this rule is that you have willing helpers at your disposal at all times, with no waiting for help. Also, remember that you are to give help when asked." I caution students not to be pushy or overbearing, to wait for group members to ask, and to help not merely by giving answers, but by asking questions that would help someone focus on the problem at hand.

Rule #3: You may ask the teacher for help only when everyone in your group has the same question.

The third rule eliminates many procedural concerns, such as "What are we supposed to do?" "When is this due?" and "Can we take this home?" This rule directs students to seek help from each other first, avoiding the tedium of having to give the same directions or information over and over again. When I talk to the entire class, it's rare for everyone to be listening attentively—chances are better that at least one student in each group is listening at any one time.

Staying true to the third rule may seem uncomfortable at first. It's typical during initial small-group experiences for individual students to ask questions or to make requests. When this occurs, I direct them first to check with their group and remind them that when all hands are raised, I'll come and discuss their problem or request. Responding in this way is not contrary to being a responsive and helpful teacher but instead motivates students to rely more on themselves. As I've observed students become more confident and independent, I've become more convinced that small-group work is an invaluable learning experience.

Individual Work

Even though I want to encourage communication among students, there are times when I ask students to work individually on assignments. Students' individual seatwork is important for helping me assess what they have and haven't yet learned. For me it's the rubber-hits-the-road time in terms of getting feedback about the effectiveness of my instruction. At these times, I'm clear with the students about why I'd like them to work by themselves. I often say, "Being able to see your work gives me a way to see if I was successful in teaching you, and what else I might need to do to be helpful." I keep the emphasis on their learning and I make myself available to help them.

I vary the assignments for individual work. Sometimes I ask students to practice a skill they were learning. Sometimes I pose problems that relate to a lesson I was teaching or an investigation that we were doing. At times I incorporate writing into their assignment, asking them to explain their reasoning or write about their learning.

For suggestions for individual work assignments incorporating writing and math, see "Starting Point 15: Incorporating Writing into Math Instruction" in Part 1 on page 73.

Choice Time: Math Menus

Math menus are one organizational structure for classroom instruction that offer students choices for learning investigations. A math menu is a list of options for students. I post the options on chart paper so the paper serves as sort of a class assignment pad for all students to see. Menu options pose problems, set up investigations, and suggest games that help students interact with one or more mathematical ideas that relate to the content we're studying.

Using menus has several advantages for students. It provides them with the opportunity to make choices, learn to manage their own time, and work on learning investigations at their own pace. Within a menu, students are able to make choices, both about the order in which they tackle the tasks and about which of the optional tasks, if any, they choose to do. Also, math menus provide general instructional advantages. When students are engaged with menu investigations, it's possible to work with individuals or a small group to meet their specific needs. Also, a menu can be used on days when you have to be absent, providing work that students can do with the supervision of a substitute teacher.

I incorporate menus into math instruction in two different ways. When working on individual assignments, students invariably complete their work at different times. Having a math menu of choices is especially useful when these students ask, "What do I do now?" At times I've prepared an extension investigation that specifically relates to the assignment they were doing, but some students complete these quickly while others are still working on the original assignment. Having the option of referring the students who are ready for more to a menu of choices keeps them productively engaged. It's a key instructional strategy I use to differentiate instruction.

Another way I use math menus is for the entire class period, giving all students in the class the opportunity to choose from the options. This is especially effective when we've been studying a particular topic. The menu choices offer additional ways for students to interact with the concepts and skills we were learning. Also, using menus in this way avoids giving the opportunity for making choices only to students who work more quickly. During these choice times, not all students will be involved with the same investigation. At times students work in pairs and at other times on their own, depending on the investigations.

Managing Math Menus

Teachers report different ways they manage the use of math menus. Some list the choices on the math menu; some also post directions for each investigation on a 12-by-18-inch sheet of construction paper. Other teachers prefer not to post directions for investigations but rather duplicate about half a dozen copies of each, mount them on poster board, and make them available for students to take to their seats. Either way, it's helpful to organize any special materials needed—tiles, number cubes, grid paper, and so on—so students have access to them. Other teachers set up stations, assigning different locations in the classroom for tasks and putting the directions and

> **Management Suggestion**
> I've found that it's helpful to mark each of the menu choices either I or P to designate whether it's an individual or partner investigation.
> —MSB

materials needed at each location. Whatever the organizational system, it's important to introduce each menu investigation to the entire class, and then have the directions available so students can refer to them for clarification.

Incorporating Math Menus into Instruction

To describe alternatives and give a range of possibilities, the following are scenarios of how teachers at different grade levels have incorporated math menus into their math teaching.

Donna's Sixth-Grade Class

In Donna's sixth-grade class, the menu serves as the overall curriculum organizer for all subjects. Each Monday, she posts a clean piece of chart paper and lists assignments, some new for the week and others carried over from the previous week. Also, she may add additional assignments to a menu during the week and cross off others as due dates pass. For math, students record in a "math lab" book that they create using construction paper for the cover and newsprint for the inside. Donna stores these in a class mailbox. Donna works with small groups while the other students work on menu tasks, and she schedules whole-group instruction as needed, to introduce new concepts, present new menu options, or discuss completed work.

Bonnie's Third-Grade Class

For instructions on how to make a spinner, see "Spinner Experiments" in Part 2 on page 171.

For more on the investigations mentioned here, see *Number Puzzle* in Part 3 on page 354 and *The 0–99 Chart* in Part 2 page 295.

Bonnie uses a similar system as Donna with her third graders, but uses the menu just for math. When she introduces a new menu, she typically spends that math period in whole-group instruction, giving instructions and teaching skills that the students need in order to do the tasks. For example, if an investigation calls for spinners, she'll teach how to make a spinner.

If Bonnie plans to have students make 0–99 number puzzles, she'll introduce coloring patterns on the 0–99 chart. During menu time, students work alone or with a partner, depending on the task. When they need help, they must ask three other people for help before asking the teacher. While menus are always available, Bonnie varies instruction by also teaching whole-class lessons.

Doris' Seventh- and Eighth-Grade Classes

Doris teaches seventh and eighth graders, five classes a day, each for a fifty-minute period. She organizes all her classes into groups of four and changes groups every two weeks. Menus help to take advantage of the time as students arrive to class—students can get right to work, picking up where they left off when interrupted by the end-of-the-period bell the day before. Sometimes Doris begins a class period by having students in their groups compare their homework assignments. As they are doing this, she circulates to keep track of who did and didn't complete the assignment. In this system, students who didn't complete the work, or neglected to do it, are able to be involved with the math as others in their group share and explain. At times Doris teaches whole-class lessons and provides problem-solving experiences for the entire class, but menus provide an ongoing structure that maximizes learning time.

Barbara's First-Grade Class

Barbara teaches first grade. She generally devotes three times a week to menu time, which she structures without written tasks. Barbara has established eight work stations in the room and has a box for each station that has all the materials needed for an investigation. She introduces each investigation to the entire class. On a given day, there may be one or two new investigations introduced to be included with the familiar ones. The children learn to distribute the materials, carrying the boxes designated to each station and returning them to storage at the end of the work period. Each station is set up to accommodate a fixed number of children, and children are free to work at a station as long as space is available. Whole-group instruction for various purposes (such as teaching a new investigation, introducing word problems, or making a class graph) occurs for short periods of time, two to four times weekly. These instructional periods may precede menu time on a given day or may use the entire math time. Barbara does small-group instruction during the menu time when a classroom aide is available to supervise the rest of the students.

Wrapping It Up

When considering organizational changes to your math instruction, it makes sense to start slowly, trying new ideas and ways of organizing the curriculum and the students within the structure of what you usually do. Rather than jump into a massive restructuring, ease into changes with moderation. And keep in mind that things rarely work as smoothly the first time as they do the second. The third time will be even more comfortable. The more you work with a new idea, the more opportunity you have to make it useful for you and for your students.

For a useful resource that helps with organizing choice time, see *How to Differentiate Your Math Instruction* (Dacey, Bamford Lynch, and Eston Salemi 2013), a Math Solutions resource that includes helpful videos.

Connecting to English Language Arts Instruction

Starting Point 21
Building a Teaching Bridge from Reading to Math

From my experience providing math professional learning to teachers for more than forty years, I've learned that elementary teachers are typically comfortable with the reading concepts and skills they have to teach and take delight in watching their students become competent readers. Their eyes light up when they find the perfect book for a particular student. But I don't as often meet elementary teachers with the same attitude toward or intuition about mathematics. They don't always see the potential in math instruction for the kind of involvement, excitement, and creativity that emerges when they are teaching reading. Following is a description of my experience in helping teachers change this.

A Professional Learning Experience

We know that students learn best when they connect new learning to their existing knowledge and skills. I think that the same holds true for teachers, and I was interested in helping a group of K–5 teachers build on the skills and strengths they demonstrate in teaching reading to improve their math teaching. My goal for a beginning investigation was to initiate a conversation about what teachers could apply from their teaching of reading to their teaching of mathematics.

"What do you think is important when teaching reading?" I asked the group. They seemed surprised, since I had come there to conduct two days of professional learning on teaching math.

"Did you mean about reading or about math?" Justin asked gently. I think he was trying to rescue me.

"About reading," I responded. "I'd like you to talk in small groups and list your ideas."

Lisa had a question. "Do you want us to talk only about reading, or about the full spectrum of English Language Arts?"

I answered, "For now, please focus on reading."

As the teachers talked in small groups, I posted a large sheet of chart paper and wrote at the top: *When teaching reading, we want our students to* . . . When I reconvened the teachers, I explained that I was going to collect their ideas on the posted chart paper. I gave two directions, "Look over your list and as a group identify which you think are the most important three or five items. Also, choose one person to report for your group." I've found this procedure useful for discussions with classes of students when I want to be sure to hear from all groups.

After giving them a few additional minutes, I brought them together as a whole group again and said, "We'll go around the room and each group will report just one idea from your list. Then we'll continue going around the room until I've recorded all of your ideas. If another group gives the idea you were planning on contributing, then choose another from your list. If all of your ideas have been reported, it's fine to pass." A partial list of their ideas follow.

When teaching reading, we want our students to . . .

read fluently

love reading

develop good word attack skills

comprehend what they read

*make predictions about what might come next in
a story*

retell a story in their own words

*identify what's important and what's not as important in what
they read*

*experience shared reading, guided reading, independent reading,
and read alouds*

Then, to shift the focus to math, I said, "Let's go back through your ideas and think about how each might apply to the context of teaching math instead of teaching reading." The resulting discussion was revealing. Some acknowledged that the focus on comprehension and thinking skills was prevalent in their language arts instruction but was missing in their math teaching. In discussing the relationship between fluency in reading and fluency in math, some admitted that although they saw comprehension as key to reading fluency, in math they often felt relieved when students could just compute accurately. One teacher commented, "Sometimes I know that the students really don't understand why they are borrowing or carrying, but I don't know what to do." The teachers also revealed that the confidence they felt in their ability to articulate what they were doing with reading instruction didn't exist in their math instruction.

I discussed with them an aspect of teaching reading that is different when we think about teaching math. In reading, there's one gate-keeper skill—decoding. It's the essential skill that gives readers access to the entire world of printed matter. However, there isn't a comparable gatekeeper skill for math. Children first learn to count and then to add and subtract small numbers. Then they learn about place value and working with larger numbers before moving on to multiplication and division. All of this early learning relates to whole numbers. Then students have to learn about fractions, decimals, percents, and so on. There isn't one gatekeeper skill that children can practice and perfect—they must build a succession of skills.

But there's one significant way that teaching reading and math are similar. When a child is learning to read, everybody knows that proficiency is all about bringing meaning to the printed page. For example, I can "read" texts in Spanish, since I've studied some Spanish, yet still not understand much of what I'm reading. Similarly, students aren't considered to be proficient readers if they can pronounce the words but don't understand the material. Comprehension is key to being a successful reader, and the same standard should hold true for math.

If students have memorized the math facts and can perform computational procedures, teachers often think of them as proficient. But we've seen over and over again how students can borrow, carry, bring down, or invert and multiply without understanding why the procedures work or how to apply them to problem-solving situations. The challenge is to help students develop meaning and make sense of what they do in math class.

I next asked teachers to identify teaching strategies they were comfortable using for teaching reading. I posted another sheet of chart paper, ruled it into two columns, and recorded their ideas in the left column. We then discussed how these strategies can relate to opportunities for math instruction, and I recorded these in the right column.

Teaching Strategies

In reading . . .	*In math . . .*
. . . we often ask students to make predictions about what might come next.	*. . . we can ask students to make estimates before solving problems.*
. . . writing and oral communication are important aspects of instruction.	*. . . having students write down and discuss their ideas can help their understanding.*
. . . we don't expect students' writing to be identical, even when writing about the same topic.	*. . . we can encourage different methods for reasoning, solving problems, and presenting solutions.*
. . . vocabulary instruction is integral.	*. . . we can use correct math vocabulary and also encourage students to do so.*
. . . read-aloud books provide students with common experiences from which they can learn.	*. . . we can use children's books to stimulate math thinking and problem solving.*
. . . we blend whole-class discussions, small-group instruction, and individualized reading and writing.	*. . . the same strategies can be appropriate and effective.*

Wrapping It Up

In our final discussion, the consensus among the teachers was clear. Just as with students, it helps to rely on our strengths to build up those areas where we need improvement. If teaching English Language Arts is one of your strengths, thinking about how it can apply to teaching math can be fruitful for you and for your students.

Starting Point 22
Teaching Math Vocabulary

Mathematics is sometimes described as its own language and the teaching of math as the teaching of a second language. There's a good deal of truth in thinking of math in this way. While many of the words that we use to describe mathematical ideas are familiar to us, their meanings in general usage are often very different from their mathematical meanings.

Thinking About the Mathematical Meanings of Words

Think about the terminology of *even* and *odd*. In common usage we talk about shares being *even* when each person has the same amount, or knitting stitches being even when they are consistently the same size. We even talk about having to *even* up the piles. In mathematics, however, we use *even* very specifically to describe integers that are divisible by two. An *even* number can be divided into two equal groups with no extras. While in common usage, *odd* describes something unusual or strange, in mathematics, *odd* describes whole numbers that aren't even; that is, they aren't divisible by two, or can't be divided into two equal groups without having a remainder.

In common usage, when we talk about things that *multiply*, such as animals or plants, we mean that they increase in number. When we *multiply* numbers in mathematics, however, we specifically mean that we are combining a certain number of equal-size groups. And sometimes the answer to a multiplication problem is less than one or both of the numbers multiplied—for example, $6 \times \frac{1}{2}$, which we can think of in one way as $\frac{1}{2} + \frac{1}{2} + \frac{1}{2} + \frac{1}{2} + \frac{1}{2} + \frac{1}{2}$, produces an answer of 3, which is less than 6.

Many examples exist of words whose unique meanings when used as mathematical terminology differ from their common meanings—*difference, product, factor, power, face, remainder, dividend, times, compass, expression, positive, negative, improper, rational, irrational, real*, and on and on. Even the word *half* has a common nonmathematical colloquial use when a child says, "Your half is bigger than my half." In mathematics, the important idea about halves of the same whole is that they are exactly the same amount or size or quantity!

Try This Now

Read the paragraph below. Then reread, thinking about the meanings of the italicized words in common usage and then about their mathematical meanings. How might you teach the common usage of these words in a language arts lesson? How might you teach the mathematical meanings of these same words?

> *Even if it rains tomorrow, our football team will face the opponent. The two teams are pretty even. One difference is that their team was last year's state champion. We think that the weather will be an important factor in the game's outcome.*

Learning mathematics as a second language isn't exactly analogous to learning a second language. When studying a new language, the contexts relate to things you already know about—for example, events or people in your life, feelings, perhaps navigating when traveling. You learn how to use the new language to name things, ask questions, and describe your thoughts. You already have understanding of the ideas you want to express, and learning the new language is about learning a new way to communicate these ideas.

However, the purpose of learning the language of mathematics is to be able to communicate about mathematical ideas and relationships, which aren't always familiar. And mathematical language by itself doesn't necessarily give students access to understanding. That is, I can use the word *multiple* to describe the relationship between two numbers like 12 and 3, or the word *polygon* to describe some two-dimensional shapes, or *equivalent* to describe the relationship between two fractions or expressions. But understanding the mathematical knowledge may not exist.

Understanding Relationships

When thinking about vocabulary instruction that helps students learn the language of mathematics, it's essential that students understand the mathematical ideas and relationships the vocabulary describes. Mathematical terminology by itself doesn't reveal the meaning of concepts, but rather it labels concepts and gives us a way to communicate about them. Once students have made sense of a mathematical idea or concept, then it's appropriate, and essential, to connect their knowledge to the standard mathematical language. And this calls for explicit and systematic teaching.

Also, it's important for teaching language in math classes to focus on words and phrases that relate to the mathematical content described in detail in standards—*equation*, *addend*, *multiply*, *decimals*, *integers*, and so on. But it's also important to focus on academic vocabulary that describes the processes that students engage in when interacting with mathematical ideas. When teaching vocabulary in either category, it's essential that knowledge of mathematical vocabulary is neither the end goal of mathematics instruction, nor the primary indicator of students' mathematical success.

A Vocabulary Lesson: Classifying Polygons

I visited a fifth-grade class to teach a lesson on defining and classifying polygons. The students had been studying geometry. They had learned about area and perimeter, explored angles and how to measure them, and more. Their experiences had been hands-on and engaging. While they had a good deal of experience with polygons in their investigations and had learned the names of many polygons—*triangles*, *quadrilaterals*, *hexagons*, and others—they hadn't yet defined polygons or thought about different ways to classify them. They were now ready to do so.

To prepare for the lesson, I drew shapes on eight 4-by-6-inch small cards, some polygons and some not.

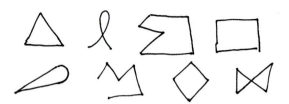

To begin the lesson, I drew a vertical line to divide the board into two columns and posted one shape in each column—the triangle in the first column and one shape that looked like a cursive "l" in the second. I didn't give the students any information about the shapes. And I didn't label the columns yet, but planned later to label the left column Polygons and the right column Not Polygons.

I explained to the class, "I drew six more shapes. We'll play a game with them. I'll post another shape and you'll give your opinion about whether I've placed it in the correct column—thumb up for agreement, thumb down for disagreement, thumb sideways for not being sure. Then I'll tell you where it belongs." This prepared students for how to respond when their classmates would post their own shapes a bit later. I repeated this step for the six remaining shapes.

After all of my shapes were posted in the correct columns, I asked students to think quietly for a moment about my system. Then I said, "Talk with your partner about your ideas. Then, together, agree on a shape to draw on a card to add to the chart." I had cut 5-by-8-inch index cards in half for them to use and distributed one to each pair as they talked.

When they had drawn their figures, I had each pair come up and post the shape they had drawn, as I had done, with the others responding with their thumbs. I gave feedback after each so that each shape wound up in the correct column. We continued until all of their shapes were sorted correctly.

I then labeled the columns *Polygons* and *Not Polygons*. I asked them what they thought were the characteristics of the shapes that were polygons, and I wrote their ideas on the board. Students' ideas included:

straight sides	*no curved sides*
no cross overs	*OK to be in and out*
like a fence	

Next to some of their ideas, I added standard mathematical vocabulary:

straight sides	*no curved sides*
no cross overs (no intersections)	*OK to be in and out (convex and concave)*
like a fence (closed, not open)	

If you're interested in seeing a version of this lesson on video, refer to *Supporting English Language Learners in Math Class: A Multimedia Professional Learning Resource, Grades K–5* (Bresser, Felux, Melanese, and Sphar 2009). The authors model how to teach the lesson in a class of students for whom English isn't their first language.

Then I asked the students each to write a definition of what they thought a polygon was. I left the shapes posted and used them later to introduce or reinforce additional vocabulary related to polygons—*triangle, quadrilateral, pentagon, hexagon, closed, convex, concave,* and *parallel.* In later lessons, students would write definitions of these terms and more.

Wrapping It Up

Instruction that is effective for teaching mathematics vocabulary can draw on practices that have been found helpful for teaching vocabulary as part of students' literacy instruction. Following are instructional strategies that address vocabulary instruction in the context of mathematics lessons.

Identify the vocabulary to be taught.
Identify the relevant terminology for all lessons.

Introduce vocabulary after developing understanding of the related mathematical ideas.
Vocabulary instruction must always follow students making sense of the ideas being taught.

Explain the vocabulary by connecting its meaning to students' learning experiences.
Keep explanations brief and directly connected to students' firsthand experiences. When vocabulary relates to mathematical symbols, point to the symbols when saying the words.

Have students pronounce the words.
It's valuable to have all of the students say a new word together several times when it is first introduced.

Write new vocabulary on a class Math Words chart.
Seeing words written is supportive for all students and essential for some students to be able to learn them.

Have students keep their own lists of math words.
Copying words from the chart provides students a first experience with writing them down. For use on their own assignments, students can refer to the math words either on the class Math Words chart or on their own lists.

Use the vocabulary regularly.
Be consistent and use new terminology as often as possible. Again, when vocabulary relates to mathematical symbols, point to the symbols as you say the words.

Encourage students to use math vocabulary in discussions and on assignments.
Prompt students to use new terminology when they present ideas or complete assignments.

For more on this topic, see "The Language of Math" in Part 4 on page 474.

Starting Point 23
Using Children's Literature to Teach Math

In my early years of teaching, my collection of children's books wasn't typically where I looked for help when planning math lessons. But that has changed. I now see children's books as wonderfully effective tools for teaching math, and I rely on them regularly for inspiration when planning lessons. They've become valuable assets for engaging students with mathematical concepts and sparking their imaginations in ways that textbooks or workbooks don't. I've found that connecting math to literature can boost confidence for children who love books but are wary of math. And students who already love math can learn to appreciate stories in an entirely new way.

Selecting Children's Books

One important aspect of incorporating children's books into math instruction is making good choices about the books to use. I consider these three questions before selecting a book to use as a read-aloud springboard for a math lesson:

CHOOSING A BOOK FOR A MATH LESSON

1. Is the book of high quality from a literary perspective?

2. Does the book present content that is mathematically sound and grade-level appropriate?

3. Is the book effective for helping students learn to think and reason mathematically?

I now have shelves full of children's books that I use over and over again for math lessons.

Math Lessons Using Literature

There's a huge variety of books available that provide many opportunities for teaching math lessons. And while the books and lesson goals differ, I follow the same guidelines when planning these lessons.

USING A CHILDREN'S BOOK IN A MATH LESSON

1. Read the book aloud. (At times, reread the book if it's appropriate to do so.)

2. Allow time for a classroom discussion of the book.

3. Introduce the math connection to the class and assign the math work to be done in class, typically an investigation, a problem, an exploration, or a game.

4. After students have had time to complete the assignment, lead a classroom discussion for students to present their work and listen and respond to one another's ideas.

5. If appropriate, assign homework based on the lesson.

While the goal after reading a book aloud to a class is to launch a math lesson, I first allow time for students to enjoy the book. As with any read-aloud experience, I want students to savor the text and examine the illustrations. Sometimes I'll reread all or part of the book, and I always provide the opportunity for a classroom discussion about it. Only then do I shift the students' attention to make the math connection. After the lesson, I make the book available for students to revisit on their own or to check out to take home and enjoy with their families.

Example Lesson: One Is a Snail, Ten Is a Crab

One book that I've read to many first and second graders, always to the delight of the children, is *One Is a Snail, Ten Is a Crab* by April Pulley Sayre and Jeff Sayre (2003). The book counts by groups of feet—1 is a snail, 2 is a person, 3 is a person and a snail, 4 is a dog, and so on, up to 10 is a crab. Then the book continues by multiples of 10 up to 100, which the illustration shows as 10 crabs and also as 100 snails. As I read the book, I encourage children to make predictions about which number comes next and how it could be represented. After reading the book, I engage children in writing riddles for numbers that weren't in the story, but using the characters introduced. For example, the number 12 could be represented as 12 snails, but could also be represented as four snails and one spider, or as three dogs, or two dogs and two people. I assign different numbers to different children, as a way to differentiate the lesson. Children decide on one way to represent their number, and then the others try to guess. The book is ideal for helping young students build their understanding about place value as they represent and solve addition problems with numbers up to 100.

Literature Connection
One Is a Snail, Ten Is a Crab has become one of the books I give as a gift to young children. It's a terrific way to give parents an idea of how they can enjoy reading time with their children that also supports their math learning.

— MSB

Example Lesson: How Big Is a Foot?

Another book that has been a long-time favorite for me is *How Big Is a Foot?* by Rolf Myller (1992). If you haven't yet discovered this book, it's a delight. I last read it to a third-grade class. The teacher was beginning a unit on measurement and asked if I would do something on length, specifically about using rulers to measure feet and inches. I brought two copies of the book with me, one with a 1962 publication date and the price of $.95 on the cover. The other was a more recent reprint, in a smaller size but with the same charming illustrations, and with a 1992 publication date and the price of $3.99 on the cover. I showed the children the two versions and wrote the two years and prices on the board.

Literature Connection
I was amazed to find my falling-apart 1962 version of *How Big Is a Foot?* by Rolf Myller (1992), which I probably bought when I was teaching and buying book-club books along with my students. It would be good to use the two copies as a math lesson in inflation for older students.

— MSB

    1962 $.95

    1992 $3.99

I asked two questions, "How many years later was the 1992 book published? How much more does the newer book cost?" I gave them time to think by themselves and then to talk with a partner before I led a classroom discussion. Then we talked about the different illustrations on the two covers. After that, I read the story.

The book is a tale about a King who wanted to give the Queen something very special for her birthday, something entirely new and unique. He thought and thought and decided on a bed. No one slept in beds then, the story explains (without any details about their sleeping protocols). The King called the royal carpenter. And, without giving away his secret to the Queen, he asked her to lie down on the floor wearing her pajamas and her crown (which she wore to bed regularly). The carpenter measured, using his feet, and decided the bed needed to be six feet long and three feet wide. Then he assigned the building project to his little apprentice, with "little" being the clue to what happened next. The apprentice built a bed that was six of his feet long and three of his feet wide. The illustration of the Queen trying out the bed, with her feet hanging over and the crown way above the pillow, was not a pretty picture. The apprentice wound up in jail where he had plenty of time to think.

I stopped reading at this point in the story and asked the children what advice they would give the apprentice. The students had ideas about how he should contact the King and ask for another chance and about how he might use a ruler or measuring tape. Dario suggested in a matter-of-fact tone, "Tell him to build a Queen-sized bed." After all who wanted had the chance to share an idea, I finished reading the story. The apprentice eventually figures out the problem, and all ends well.

I then introduced how to measure using a standard ruler. I posted a photo I had printed on $8\frac{1}{2}$-by-11-inch paper of my own foot with a ruler next to it. I talked with the students about how it was important to line up one end of what you're measuring with the end of the ruler, as I had done with my foot. I talked with them about what you might do if the length is in between two numbers, as was my foot. Then I had them work in pairs, selecting at least five things around the room to measure. It was an active lesson, even more so since it was the hour before lunch.

Example Lesson: How Strong Is It?

Older students as well benefit from being introduced to math ideas through children's books. Another of my favorites is *How Strong Is It?* by Ben Hillman (2008). The book uses clever trick photography to show more than twenty different examples of strength, with an explanatory column of text next to each. It shows a giant spider web stopping a jet plane, an elephant using its truck and tusks to hold up a log with four football players standing on it, a great white shark chomping through a 6-inch (15-centimeter) chunk of firewood, how Rapunzel's hair (or anyone's hair) is stronger than high-tech rope, and more. The book is ideal for investigations that engage students with measurement in both U.S. customary and metric units, place value, estimating, and solving problems with multidigit whole numbers.

When I paged through the book with a class of fifth graders, there were lots of oohs and aahs. The students were fascinated by the illustrations. Each of the photos lends itself to a lesson, and on this day I chose to use the photo of the elephant and the four football players. The accompanying text explains that an elephant can lift, using its tusks and trunk, more than 900 kilograms. I told the class that an average fifth grader weighs about 35 kilograms. (This information isn't in the book—I checked online to get it.) I wrote on the board:

An elephant can lift more than 900 kg.

A fifth grader weighs about 35 kg.

I asked the class, "Could an elephant lift everyone in the class with its trunk and tusks? What would we need to do in order to figure this out?" I asked the students to think for a moment by themselves and then asked them to talk with a partner. There were 27 students in the class, and the agreement was that we needed to multiply 27 times 35 to figure out if an elephant could lift all of them.

For this problem, I told the students that I'd like to see if we could figure out the answer without resorting to paper and pencil. "I'll record on the board to keep track of your thinking," I told them. The students had experienced solving problems like this. I recorded as they first suggested multiplying 27 times 30, and then 27 times 5, and then adding the partial products.

27 × 35

27 × 30

    20 × 30 = 600

    7 × 30 = 210

    600 + 210 = 810

27 × 5

    20 × 5 = 100

    7 × 5 = 35

    100 + 35 = 135

   810

+ 135

   945

Brett stated, "The elephant couldn't lift us all. We weigh more than 900 kilograms." Joey objected, "But an elephant can lift more than 900 kilograms." Brett defended his position. He said, "Yeah, but we don't know how much more." Mary, often a peacemaker, said, "If one of us was absent, then the elephant could probably lift the class."

I left it at that.

Wrapping It Up

I'm always on the lookout for children's books to add to my collection, and grateful to colleagues who continue to share their finds with me. Even with older students, I love how children's books provide vehicles for math lessons in unique ways. I especially love how the books stimulate and support conversations among students. It's gratifying to see this excitement for math.

In "Beginning Number Concepts" in Part 3 on page 337, I present examples for using children's books. For additional suggestions, not only for young children but also for older students, see the *Math Reads* collection of books published by Scholastic and the Math, Literature, and Nonfiction series published by Math Solutions. Most of my favorite ideas are in these resources. You can view titles from these links: mathsolutions.com and http://teacher.scholastic .com/products/ math-concepts-skills/ math-reads/ math-books-topics.htm.

Problem-Solving Investigations

Overview

Mathematical content is the focus of Part 2, connecting to classroom instruction through more than one hundred problem-solving investigations that are appropriate for different grades. These problem-solving investigations provide classroom-tested instructional ideas for engaging students with the mathematical content of the K–8 curriculum in whole-class lessons, with partners or small groups, and through individual assignments. The investigations also serve to deepen teachers' understanding of the mathematics to teach through modeling instructional experiences that engage students with the math they need to learn. I first share a three-phase structure that I've found to be useful when planning whole-class problem-solving investigations. Then, to illustrate this structure, I outline a sample lesson, one of my favorites, using this structure.

The investigations are grouped into five sections—Measurement, Data, Geometry, Patterns and Algebraic Thinking, and Number and Operations. Each of these sections is organized similarly and includes:

- an overview to the particular mathematical focus;

- sample whole-class lessons;

- additional investigations for whole-class lessons; and

- independent investigations (for partner or small groups, and also suitable or for choice time explorations).

All of the instructional ideas draw from my own teaching experiences over the years in different grade levels. Sometimes when I've revisited investigations from the book to present in a class, or after I've taught the activity again, I made notes in the margins of my own copy of the previous edition of the book. I've included these notes here as asides and reminders.

About the Mathematics Sections

Understanding the mathematics we have to teach is extremely important to teaching the mathematics effectively. To that end, the investigations in Part 2 have been enormously helpful for strengthening my own mathematical understandings. Sometimes I've explored the investigations with others in professional development settings, sometimes I've grappled with them on my own, and sometimes I've learned in classroom settings as students engaged with them.

To offer insights into the mathematics, I elaborate on some of the investigations with a section titled "About the Mathematics" (labeled with a *About the Mathematics* icon). I wrote these mathematical explanations in response to the many queries I've received over the years asking for math help with particular problems. In these sections, I describe how I thought about the mathematics when I explored the investigation and explain aspects of the underlying mathematics to help make the mathematics more accessible. These commentaries appeared in Part 4 of the previous edition of *About Teaching Mathematics*, but here I've included them immediately following the particular investigations they address.

When writing these commentaries, I was aware that there are dangers in offering answers and explanations—answers can put an end to thinking and other people's explanations can be hard to follow. However, I decided that there's even more danger in not understanding the underlying mathematics, especially as we strive to help students become mathematically proficient. Please keep in mind that my personal explanations model one way to think about the mathematics, not the only way to approach an investigation or arrive at a solution. And it's always best to try an investigation yourself before reading my findings.

Also, to benefit from my personal commentaries, merely reading them isn't sufficient. It's important that you think about the ideas and make sense of them for yourself. I learned when studying mathematics in college that it was always helpful to have paper and pencil nearby, to write notes or make sketches to explore an idea or keep track of my thinking. I've continued to do this whenever I read about mathematical ideas.

It's important to remember that we all learn in individual ways and on our own timetables. My comments reflect the particular way that I thought about the mathematics, not the only way or necessarily the best way to approach an investigation. All of us have encountered math problems we haven't yet solved and ideas we haven't yet learned. I believe that staying involved as a learner of mathematics has helped me become a better teacher of mathematics.

Planning Whole-Class Lessons with Problem-Solving Investigations

A Three-Phase Structure for Planning Lessons

I've found a three-phase structure useful for planning lessons with problem-solving investigations—*Introducing* for launching the investigation, *Exploring* for students to work independently, and *Summarizing* for a classroom discussion to share results and talk about the mathematics involved.

> ## A THREE-PHASE STRUCTURE FOR PROBLEM-SOLVING LESSONS
>
> Introducing
>
> Exploring
>
> Summarizing

At times, it's possible to manage all three stages of the lesson within one math period. But keep in mind that teaching a lesson should not necessarily imply a one-day experience. Investigations can extend for two, three, or more days so that all groups have adequate time to explore and can contribute to the summarizing.

Introducing

When introducing a problem-solving investigation, the goal is to help the students understand what they are to investigate and how they are to work. This is best done with the whole class so that everyone gets the same information. Sometimes I also prepare written directions either to post or distribute to groups. Also, depending on how much experience the students have had with problem-solving lessons, I may review the guidelines for working cooperatively in small groups.

When planning how to introduce an investigation, I rely on four teaching steps:

1. Present or review concepts. (Here I want to be sure that students have the prerequisites needed.)

2. Pose a part of the problem or a similar but smaller problem. (I choose an example that's accessible to the students and use it to provide an initial opportunity for them to work with their partners or groups.)

3. Present the investigation. (Also having written directions is supportive, especially for students who more easily process information when they see as well as hear it.)

4. Discuss the task to make sure students understand what they are to do. (It's helpful to have several students restate the directions.)

Exploring

Once the students understand what to do, the exploring part of the lesson begins. This is the time when students engage with the investigation, typically working cooperatively in pairs or small groups, but

---

Teaching Tip
When I taught middle school with a fixed time schedule for class periods, I often let students know that we'd return to an investigation the next day. Sometimes I'd have a direction on the board for students to return to work in their groups and at other times I'd begin the class period with a classroom discussion.
— MSB

For guidelines for working cooperatively in small groups, see "Starting Point 20: Four Structures for Organizing and Managing Classroom Instruction" in Part 1 on page 111.

While the students work, I circulate and focus on the following:

1. Observe the interaction, listening to how groups organize working together, the ideas they discuss, and the strategies they use. This is also the time to help any students who need additional support to be able to engage effectively with the investigation.

2. Offer assistance when needed, either when all members of a group raise their hands or if a group is not working productively.

3. Provide an extension to groups that finish more quickly than others.

A Closer Look: Offering Assistance to Students

When I'm offering assistance during the exploration stage, my goal is to give assistance that moves the group toward working independently. When groups are working well, I don't interrupt; rather, I listen and observe students to assess how they are thinking and learning. When groups are experiencing difficulty and are bogged down, I've found that their problems generally fall into two categories, each calling for a different type of assistance.

One category is difficulty with the investigation itself. The group may be stuck about what to do or is pursuing an incorrect line of thought. If students are stuck, I've found it helpful to ask students to restate what they know so far and then pose an example for them to solve. I may need to explain concepts again or model for them how they might proceed. Once they can restate the problem and do an example successfully, I have them return to work on their own. If students aren't stuck but are pursuing an erroneous idea or have made an error, then I point out a contradiction that illustrates their erroneous thinking or ask them how they arrived at a certain conclusion. I avoid telling answers but instead leave the group once the students are aware of their mistake.

However, the difficulty may fall into a second category that relates to the group interaction rather than with the problem itself. Groups bog down for different reasons. For instance, the group may lack the needed impetus to get started. This may be obvious because of lack of materials, such as paper, pencil, or manipulative materials. If this is the problem, it helps to join the group for a short time to get a sense of what's happening, suggest that someone do what's necessary to get started, and, when a student in the group accepts that responsibility, leave them to work on their own. Groups may also need help with focusing. You may hear questions like "What are we supposed to do?" or "Didn't the teacher say to do it this way?" In these instances, I offer the clarification needed.

Other problems with group interaction may arise. Sometimes, one person takes over and ignores the others' ideas. At times, a member of the group doesn't contribute or doesn't understand what the group is doing. In these kinds of situations, I point out to the group what I

Teaching Tip
I've found it helpful when I circulate to jot down notes about what might be useful for a later classroom discussion.
— MBB

Teaching Tip
During the exploration stage, it's helpful to have some extensions of the problem to offer groups who complete their work early. Also, I try and have something in mind for students who may not be ready for the content of the investigation.
— MBB

For help with giving students extensions, see suggestions for using math menus for choices in "Starting Point 20: Four Structures for Organizing and Managing Classroom Instruction" in Part 1 on page 111.

FYI
Thinking about how groups might experience difficulty with the investigation reminds me of the importance of interacting with the investigation myself, so that I'm aware of the math involved and have thought about misconceptions or erroneous thinking that might arise.
— MBB

observed and restate that the group's job is to work together. In these instances, it may be helpful to give the group more specific guidelines, such as:

- Make sure that everyone has an equal chance to talk. After you share an idea, wait until everyone else has offered a thought before you talk again.

- Find a way that everyone can contribute some part to the solution of the problem.

- We all need encouragement, so give feedback to each other when someone offers an idea that is helpful.

Summarizing

Summarizing an investigation is extremely important and should not be skipped or shortened for lack of time—it's crucial for students to reflect on their learning, hear from others, and connect others' experience to their ideas. To prepare for summarizing discussions, it's helpful to give groups or individual students time to write summary statements about their experience—patterns they noticed, conclusions they made, and/or what they learned in general. Sometimes I collect and read these in advance of a summarizing discussion and then select groups or students to report. Don't let the clock push the curriculum, but rather stay attuned to the learning needs of the students. Also, having students come together in a gathering place helps them focus.

Four goals are important when summarizing with the class:

1. Have pairs or groups review their work and think about what to report in a class discussion. If they haven't written summary statements to describe what they noticed and learned, ask them to do so now.

2. Initiate a classroom discussion. (First have groups report how they organized working together. Sometimes I ask groups to choose a spokesperson who will report to the class.)

3. Next have groups report their results or solutions, explaining their reasoning or strategies. (You may ask them to display their work, or you can record on the board as they report. Then solicit comments from others.)

4. Generalize from the solutions. (Generalizing a solution involves extending it to other situations not necessarily dependent on the specific limitations of the problem.)

A Closer Look: Discussion Questions When Summarizing

The following questions are useful for summarizing discussions.
For discussing how groups worked together:

- "How did you organize the work in your group?"

- "What problems did you encounter?"

- "Was your method of organizing effective, or can you think of a better way to have worked?"

> **Teaching Tip**
> It helps at times to ask each person in the group for an idea about what he or she can do to be helpful to the group.
> —MSB

> **FYI**
> I've included "About the Mathematics" sections for about one-third of the investigations in Part 2 in order to provide insights into the underlying mathematics. These are useful for thinking about what to anticipate and address when summarizing.
> —MSB

> **FYI**
> Summary statements are statements written by students about their experience with the investigation—patterns they notice, conclusions they made, and/or what they learned in general.
> —MSB

For discussing strategies, results, and solutions:

- "What math ideas or strategies did your group use to get started on the problem?"

- "What other ideas came up as you worked?"

- "How did you decide if your solution makes sense?"

- "How can you check your solution?"

For eliciting generalizations:

- "What patterns did you notice as you investigated?"

- "Can you think of another problem you've solved that this reminds you of?"

- "What summary statement can you make about the investigation?"

A Sample Lesson Using the Three-Phase Structure

For a specific example of a problem-solving investigation using the three-phase lesson planning structure, here I present one of my favorites—*The Consecutive Sums Problem*. I can't remember where or when I first encountered this problem, but it's long been a staple in my teaching repertoire. For many years I've presented this problem to teachers in professional development settings and to classes of students, mostly in grades 3 and up.

 Sample Lesson

The Consecutive Sums Problem

One reason I like this investigation is because the mathematical skills demanded are minimal—adding with sums to 25. The low computational demand allows for keeping the focus of the lesson on investigating patterns, making conjectures, testing theories, and representing and communicating ideas. Following is a description of how the three-phase structure for a problem-solving lesson can apply to *The Consecutive Sums Problem*.

The specific suggestions I give for using *The Consecutive Sums Problem* for a problem-solving investigation evolved from the many times I've taught this lesson in different settings. For any problem, I find it's always important to explore it first so that I have a thorough understanding of the mathematics involved. Then I'm better able to focus on the three-phase structure to facilitate the lesson successfully with students.

Introducing

1. **Present or review concepts.** First explain what consecutive numbers are so that students understand they are numbers that go in order, such as 1, 2, 3, 4 or 11, 12, 13. Each comes right after the other without skipping. Ask students for examples of sequences of three or four consecutive numbers. Ask them to explain why a sequence, such as 15, 16, 18, is not a sequence of consecutive numbers.

2. **Pose a part of the problem or a similar but smaller problem.** Ask, *Who can think of one way to write the number 9 as the sum of consecutive numbers?* The usual response is $4 + 5$. Record on the board, and underneath it write another equation:

   $9 = 4 + 5$

   $9 = 2 + 3 + 4$

   Ask the students to verify that it's true that $2 + 3 + 4$ adds to 9, and also that the numbers are consecutive. Tell the class that this shows that it's possible to write 9 as the sum of consecutive numbers in at least two different ways.

   If you think the students would benefit from another example, ask about 15, which can be represented as the sum of consecutive addends in three ways—$15 = 7 + 8$, $15 = 4 + 5 + 6$, and $15 = 1 + 2 + 3 + 4 + 5$.

For Younger Students
Finding consecutive addends for the sums from 1 to 15 may be more appropriate for younger students. A similar investigation for younger students is to figure out different ways to find numbers that add to 10. Here, without the constraint of the addends having to be consecutive, students gain experience thinking about combinations of 10. It's helpful for this investigation to give students interlocking cubes of different colors so that they can build trains of 10 cubes in different ways, and then represent their trains with appropriate equations. Using only two colors and asking students to find combinations of two addends limits the investigation, while using more colors can extend the investigation.

— MSB

When Observing
I find that noting groups' different ways of organizing to work together and displaying their work is helpful for preparing for a summarizing discussion. Then, when I ask groups to report in a later classroom discussion, I can call on specific groups to be sure a variety of approaches gets reported.

— MSB

3. **Present the investigation.** Ask the students, in their groups, to find all the ways to write each of the numbers from 1 to 25 as the sum of consecutive addends. Tell them that some of the sums are impossible and challenge them to see if they can find the pattern of those numbers. Direct them to look for other patterns as well, such as how many different sums there are for different numbers. Provide groups with large paper for recording. Ask them to write on the paper their group members' names, the equations, and also summary statements about the patterns they find.

4. **Discuss the task to make sure students understand what they are to do.** Ask for questions. Review the guidelines for group work if you think that's necessary.

Exploring

1. **Observe the interaction, listening to how groups organize working together, the ideas they discuss, and the strategies they use.** Notice how groups decide to work together. Some groups divide up the numbers so that one person does 1 to 6, the next does 7 through 12, and so on. In other groups, individuals work on whichever numbers they choose and then come together to record their findings. Some groups have one person do all the recording while others share that job among the members. Recording formats differ as well. Some students list the numbers from 1 to 25 and write the possibilities next to each. Other groups organize the numbers by how many different ways they found for each, so all those that could be written in only one way are in one column, those that could be written in two ways are in another, and so on. Some groups don't present their findings in an organized way. Sometimes each student in the group lists his or her ideas, or they collaborate on a paragraph of ideas. If they're working together, I don't intervene—they'll hear about options during the summarizing part of the investigation.

2. **Offer assistance when needed.** Sometimes a group will summon you to ask a procedural question, such as whether they should orient their recording paper the long way or the short way. Let them make those decisions for themselves and tell them they'll see later what other groups decided. Keep in mind that although deciding which way to orient the paper may seem like a minor decision to you, it isn't always so for students. Organizing work on paper is a skill students need to acquire, and group decisions can help them do so.

Groups sometimes make erroneous generalizations. For example, when they discover that it's impossible to write 2 and 4 as the sums of consecutive numbers, they may conclude that 6 would fit the pattern and also be impossible. In such a situation, confront them with a contradiction. Ask the group to consider $1 + 2 + 3$. When they realize that the sum of those numbers is 6, leave them to rethink their hasty generalization.

You may notice a group bogged down in a way related not to the problem itself but to some procedural issue. For example, the group isn't keeping a group record. Join that group and ask, *How can you keep track of what you're discovering?* (This way you find out if they understood your instructions about recoding on a group paper.) Then ask, *Who will get the paper for your group?* (This may prompt someone to do so.) Or ask, *What do you need to do in order to get started?*

Sometimes, a group has written all the sums it can find and calls you over to announce that they are finished. However, when you look at the recording, you see that the students haven't written any statements about patterns they've found. The usual response is that they can't think of any. Ask questions to probe their thinking:

> *How could you describe the pattern of numbers impossible to write as the sum of consecutive addends? (Write a summary statement.)*

> *What do you notice about all the numbers that had three possible ways?*

> *Which numbers had only one possible way?*

> *Which numbers don't have any possible ways?*

When the students have begun to consider some of your questions, leave them to write statements to summarize what they've noticed. If you feel they need more support, help them word one summary statement.

3. **Provide an extension to groups that finish more quickly than others.** If a group has completed work to your satisfaction, offer a challenge:

> *Can you find a way to predict how many ways 36 can be written as the sum of consecutive numbers?*

> *Investigate other sums as well.*

Summarizing

1. **Have pairs or groups review their work and think about what to report in a classroom discussion.** If they haven't written summary statements to describe what they noticed and learned, ask them to do so now.

2. **Initiate a classroom discussion.** First have groups report how they organized working together. Then ask groups about how they worked together:

> *How did your group organize to do the work?*

> *Did any other group organize in the same way? Who organized differently?*

> *Do you think you would change how your group worked if you extended the investigation to include sums up to 50?*

3. **Next have groups report their results or solutions, explaining their reasoning or strategies.** Ask groups how they approached finding ways to represent sums with consecutive addends.

If possible, have groups post their recording sheets so students

Teaching Tip
I've found it helpful to ask groups not only to think about what they'd like to report, but also to choose a spokesperson. Also, sometimes I focus on one particular aspect of the investigation. For example, sometimes I ask them to choose one of their summary statements to share. Then I ask the others to listen to see if they had the same or similar statement— this helps students know that I expect them to listen to each other's reports.
— MBB

can see how others organized their findings. Discuss any differences and similarities in solutions. Ask groups how they were sure they had found all the possible ways to write any particular number.

4. **Generalize from the solutions.** Ask students to report their summary statements. One way that I've found successful is to ask a group to report just one of their statements. Then others see if they made the same conclusion. Then I continue around the room, asking each group to report a summary statement that hadn't been presented yet. A group can pass if it doesn't have a new statement to report.

Another way to lead this part of the discussion is to pose questions for students to discuss:

Which sums were impossible to write with consecutive addends? Elicit different descriptions by encouraging students to explain in their own words: "Start with one, and multiply by two." "They're doubles." Point out that we call these numbers the "powers of 2."

What patterns did you notice for sums that you could write in two ways? Continue asking about sums that could be written in three ways and four ways.

What patterns did you notice for sums that could be written as the sum of two addends? Continue by asking about sums that could be written with three addends and four addends.

What do you notice about sums that are prime numbers?

Planning Lessons Using the Three-Phase Structure Template

I've found it helpful to refer to this template when I'm planning to introduce a problem-solving investigation, especially when it's the first time I'm teaching the lesson.

See Reproducible R.1 for a template you can print and use. Downloadable at mathsolutions.com/atm4theditionreproducibles

Introducing

1. Present or review concepts.

2. Pose a part of the problem or a similar but smaller problem.

3. Present the investigation.

4. Discuss the task to make sure students understand what they are to do.

Exploring

1. Observe the interaction, listening to how groups organize working together, the ideas they discuss, and the strategies they use.

2. Offer assistance when needed.

3. Provide an extension to groups that finish more quickly than others.

Summarizing

1. Have pairs or groups review their work and think about what to report in a classroom discussion. If they haven't written summary statements to describe what they noticed and learned, ask them to do so now.

2. Initiate a classroom discussion. First have groups report how they organized working together.

3. Next have groups report their results or solutions, explaining their reasoning or strategies.

4. Generalize from the solutions.

Problem-Solving Investigations: Measurement

About the Mathematics

This icon indicates that I've written a mathematical commentary for the investigation. I've written these explanations in response to queries from teachers asking for math help with particular problems. I encourage you to try the investigation first before reading my explanation.

— MSB

Why Teach Measurement?

Measurement is part of all of our daily lives. We measure out coffee, juice, and cereal for breakfast. We figure out how much time we have before leaving for school or work. We check the fuel gauge in our car to be sure we have enough gas. We watch our speed as we drive. We keep track of the time throughout the day. Back at home we measure for recipes when we cook. We figure out how much paper and ribbon we need to wrap a present. We check to see how long it is until our favorite evening TV show begins. When we measure, we are connecting mathematics to our environment. The ability to use measuring tools—rulers, measuring tapes, thermometers, measuring cups, scales, and the like—and to estimate with these tools are necessary skills for students to develop.

Measuring is the process of determining the dimensions or quantity of something. Measuring involves making comparisons between what is being measured and a suitable standard of measure. When developing understanding and skills relating to measurement, students must learn about the standard units that relate to the attributes of what they're measuring. They also must learn how to choose appropriate units of measurement and use measuring tools correctly. They need to understand that no matter how carefully done, measurements at best are approximate. Students need practice making estimates and learning to evaluate when measurements are "close enough." Estimating when measuring can help make the concept of rounding meaningful. Solving problems that involve measuring gives context to students' understanding of number and operations.

Instruction in measurement intersects with other topics in the elementary math curriculum. Measuring gives children practical applications for the computation skills they are learning. It also provides a way to tie basic geometric concepts to number concepts. In addition, measurement offers opportunities for interdisciplinary learning in social studies, geography, science, art, music, and more.

Stages in Learning About Measurement

When planning classroom measurement investigations, it's helpful to consider four stages in learning:

STAGES IN LEARNING ABOUT MEASUREMENT

1. Making comparisons between objects by matching.
2. Comparing objects with nonstandard units.
3. Comparing objects with standard units.
4. Choosing suitable units and tools for specific measurements.

---

1. Making comparisons between objects by matching.

Young students compare objects by matching, without the use of other tools of measurement. They order things by this method of comparison.

2. Comparing objects with nonstandard units.

Students benefit from first using a variety of objects for measuring—parts of the body, straws, paper clips, cubes, books, and whatever else is readily available.

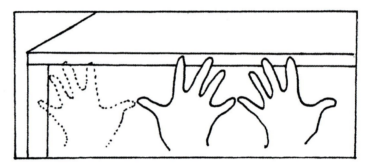

3. Comparing objects with standard units.

Standard units should emerge as an extension of nonstandard units, necessary for communicating about what we're measuring. It makes sense that students become comfortable with both the metric and English systems. We live in a "bilingual" measurement world and students need to be familiar with both measurement systems.

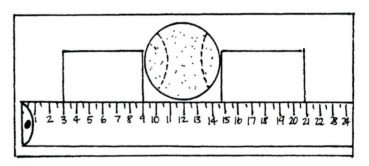

4. Choosing suitable units and measuring tools for specific measurements.

Students learn to select the appropriate standard units of measurement needed for specific applications and to choose measuring tools appropriate for the tasks at hand.

Mathematical Practices

The investigation and study of measurement support the development of the mathematical practices described in the Common Core and other standards documents for students in all grades. The mathematical practices should be connected to the content standards by engaging students in solving problems, reasoning, making conjectures, applying math to everyday life, using appropriate tools, communicating precisely, looking for patterns and structure, and looking for regularity in mathematical methods. The investigations in this section provide ways to make connections between practice and content standards.

Mathematical Content

It's helpful to understand which measurement concepts and skills are appropriate for different grade levels. In addition to the specifics listed below, students are expected to solve word problems that involve the measurements they are studying. Below are content designations that align with the Common Core and other standards documents.

Kindergarten: Describe and compare measureable attributes of objects and engage in investigations that call for direct comparison of two objects to see which has more or less, which is taller or shorter, and so on.

Grade 1: Measure lengths using nonstandard units and order three objects by their lengths. Tell and write time in hours and half hours.

Grade 2: Measure and estimate lengths using standard units. Tell and write time to the nearest five minutes and solve word problems involving money.

Grade 3: Measure and estimate liquid volumes and masses using standard units of grams, kilograms, and liters. Tell and write time to the nearest minute.

Grade 4: Understand the relative sizes of measurement units (e.g., 1 ft is 12 times as long as 1 inch, 100 cm equal 1 m) and solve problems involving measurement of time, liquid volumes, mass, money, area, perimeter, and angles.

Grade 5: Convert among different-sized units within standard measurement systems and solve problems involving volumes of solid figures.

Grade 6: Solve problems involving area, surface area, and volume.

Grade 7: Solve problems involving angle measures, area, surface area, and volume.

Grade 8: Solve problems involving volume of cylinders, cones, and spheres.

For the sample lessons, I used the Introducing/Exploring/ Summarizing model for problem-solving lessons, described on page 135.

Teaching Tip
Be sure to choose string that isn't stretchy—stretchy string can distort measurements. Also, ahead of time, cut lengths of string equal to your height that students then can trim to their own heights. This wastes bits of string but helps to avoid chaos.
— MSB

FYI
When you say that your height is equal to about three times your around-the-head measurement, there's often confusion about whether to write this ratio as 1:3 or 3:1. Actually both are correct, depending on whether you've representing head:height or height:head. Substituting the actual measurement values for head and height into the ratio shows where the smaller and larger numbers belong. For example, the ratios above represent head:height. My height is about 65 inches and the distance around my head is about 21 inches; therefore, head:height = 21:65 or head/height = $\frac{21}{65}$. These are close to 1:3 or $\frac{1}{3}$.
— MSB

For a discussion of how this investigation relates to learning about circles, see "Starting Point 2: Uncovering the Curriculum" in Part 1 on page 8.

Sample Whole-Class Lessons

Following are two sample lessons that describe, in detail, investigations designed to help students develop understanding and skills with measurement. The first suggestion engages students with nonstandard measurements and the second on standard measurements with a focus on the metric system. Each uses the Introducing/Exploring/Summarizing model for problem-solving lessons.

Sample Lesson

A Nonstandard Measuring Investigation (Body Ratios)

While measuring with nonstandard units is typically relegated to the early grades, investigations using nonstandard measurements to explore body ratios are appropriate for older students as well. When using these investigations with younger students, the focus is on introducing measuring; for older students, in addition to the measuring experiences, the investigations also provide a context for including the concept and representations of ratios.

Materials

string, enough for each student and the teacher to cut a piece equal to his or her height

Introducing

1. **Present or review concepts.** Ask the students to estimate how many times a piece of string equal to their height would wrap around their head as a headband. Then, to model for students how to cut their string, have a student assist you in cutting a piece of string equal in length to your height.

   Wrap your string around your head to demonstrate that your height is equal to about three times your around-the-head measurement. Explain, *My height is about three times as long as the distance around my head.* For older students, also use the language of ratio to describe this relationship, *Mathematically, we say that the ratio of my head to my height is 1 to 3.* Show how to record the ratio, using either or both of the two symbols shown:

$$\text{head} : \text{height} = 1 : 3 \qquad \frac{\text{head}}{\text{height}} = \frac{1}{3}$$

2. **Pose a part of the problem or a similar but smaller problem.**
   Ask, *What do you think the ratio is between the length of my foot and my height?* (Or, for younger students, ask, *How many of my foot lengths do you think equal my height?*) After students offer estimates, ask, *How could I find out?* Then use your height string to demonstrate, measuring the length of your foot and then folding it to see how many of your foot lengths equal your height. Your height should be about six or seven times your foot length. For older students, record: *foot:height = 1:6 and foot/height = $\frac{1}{6}$.*

To model another body ratio, show that your foot and forearm are just about the same length, a measurement that seems to surprise students. Record that as well: *foot:forearm = 1:1* and *foot/forearm = $\frac{1}{1}$* .

3. **Present the investigation.** Give the class directions. Explain, *First cut a piece of string equal to your height. Work in pairs and help each other do this. Then, working individually, use your height string to explore ratios on your body. Record at least ten ratios.* (Older students record as ratios. For younger students, model on the board how to record their ratios without the standard symbolism; for example, My height = 6 feet. Or: My height = 3 times around my head.) *Then, with your group or partner, compare the ratios you each found and see which are true for all of you.*

BODY RATIOS DIRECTIONS

1. Cut string equal to your height.

2. Find at least ten ratios on your body. Record.

3. Compare with your partner (or group).

---

4. **Discuss the task to make sure students understand what they are to do.** Ask for questions. Have students report the ratios they found. If appropriate, reinforce the standard notations for representing ratios.

Exploring

1. **Observe the interaction, listening to how groups organize working together, the ideas they discuss, and the strategies they use.** This is also the time to help any students who need additional support to be able to engage effectively with the investigation. Check how students are recording their ratios. Suggest other body ratios for students who are stuck.

2. **Offer assistance when needed.**

3. **Provide an extension to groups that finish more quickly than others.**

Summarizing

1. **Have pairs or groups review their work and think about what to report in a classroom discussion.** Ask them to write a summary statement to describe what patterns they noticed and what conclusions they made.

2. **Initiate a classroom discussion.** First have groups report how they organized working together.

3. **Next have groups report their findings.** List the common ratios on the board to see which were the same (or about the same) for everyone (or almost everyone).

4. **Generalize from the body ratios they found.** Ask, *Which ratios would be different for babies and why?*

FYI
All students in the class will be at least six "feet" tall. I often suggest that students announce at home how they can prove that they are six feet tall. They take their height string home to demonstrate and also explain that they're learning about measurement in math class. — MBB

Extensions
Suggestions for building on and extending students' experiences with *Body Ratios* can be found under "Independent Investigations." Useful investigations are *Longer, Shorter, or About the Same* (page 154), *Standing Broad Jumps* (page 158), *Are You a Square?* (page 154), *A Half-Size Me* (page 155), *Index Card Portrait* (page 155), and *Statue of Liberty Measurements* (page 155). These can be used with the whole class, as small group or partner investigations, or for choice time explorations (see also "Starting Point 20: Four Structures for Organizing and Managing Classroom Instruction" in Part 1 on page 111).

FYI
Babies' heads are proportionally larger than the adult ratio. That's why it's important to have babies wear hats in cold weather so they don't lose too much of their body heat. If any of your students have infant brothers or sisters, send a note home asking parents for help measuring the baby's height and head circumference. — MBB

Sample Lesson

Measuring with Standard Units (Introducing the Metric System)

This lesson introduces students to the metric system, focusing mainly on length. The investigation begins with students measuring classroom objects using Cuisenaire rods to find things that are 1 cm, 10 cm, and 1 m long. This provides students with concrete references for each of these metric measures of length. Students connect their experience to the standard units and their representations, and then have further measurement experiences using these units.

Materials

white and orange Cuisenaire rods, 1 of each per student
train of ten orange Cuisenaire rods taped on a table
string, enough for each student to cut off a 1-meter length
5-by-25-centimeter tagboard strips, 1 per student
12-by-18-inch construction paper for folders, 1 piece per student

Introducing

1. **Present or review concepts.** Show students a white and orange Cuisenaire rod and also demonstrate how to cut a length of string equal to ten orange Cuisenaire rods. Do not refer to the metric measures of the rods or the string.

2. **Pose a part of the problem or a similar but smaller problem.** Model finding one thing in the classroom that is as long as the white rod, the orange rod, and the string.

3. **Present the investigation.** Distribute a white rod and an orange rod to each student. Explain, *First you should cut a piece of string equal in length to ten orange rods. Then find and record at least five things that are the same length as each of these three lengths: the white rod, the orange rod, and the string.* Draw facsimiles of recording papers on the board for students to use as models.

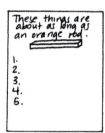

4. **Discuss the task to make sure students understand what they are to do.** Ask for questions. If you think it's needed, have the class observe as a student measures several objects with an orange rod. Repeat if needed with other students. Point out that it's OK for students to measure and record the same objects.

Exploring

1. **Observe the interaction, listening to how groups organize working together, the ideas they discuss, and the strategies they use.** Note those that may be useful for a later classroom discussion.

2. **Offer assistance when needed.**

3. **Provide an extension to groups that finish more quickly than others.**

Summarizing

1. **Have pairs or groups review their work and think about what to report in a classroom discussion about the objects they measured.** If they haven't written summary statements to describe what they noticed and learned, ask them to do so now.

2. **Initiate a classroom discussion.** First have groups report how they organized working together. Ask for any particular challenges when they were measuring.

3. **Next have groups report about the objects they measured.**

4. **Generalize from the investigation by connecting their experiences to the metric labels.** Tell the students that there are other names for the measuring tools they've been calling the white rod, the orange rod, and the string. They're also called 1 centimeter, 1 decimeter or 10 centimeters, and 1 meter or 10 decimeters or 100 centimeters. Write the following sentences on the board and have the students record them at the bottom of the appropriate recording sheets.

> *The white rod is 1 centimeter long. (1 cm)*
>
> *The orange rod is 10 centimeters or 1 decimeter long. (10 cm = 1 dm)*
>
> *The string is 1 meter or 10 decimeters or 100 centimeters long. (1 m = 10 dm = 100 cm)*

Also, ask students to find some measures on their bodies that match the three lengths so they'll always have a reference for those measurements with them. Record on a page like this:

Metric Body Measures

1 cm long _____
1 dm long _____
1 m long _____

Teaching Tip

Taping a train of ten orange rods on a table for students is useful for having students cut a 1-meter length of string. To avoid congestion, I tape two or three trains in different parts of the room.

— MBB

Extensions

Suggestions for building on and extending students' initial experiences measuring objects with the white rod, orange rod, and string can be found under "Independent Investigations." Useful investigations are *Practicing Measuring* (page 156), *Writing a Measurement Story* (page 156), and *Extending Metric Lengths to Volume and Capacity* (page 229). Students can add the work from these additional investigations to the folder they made. These can be used with the whole class, as small group or partner investigations, or for choice time explorations (see also "Starting Point 20: Four Structures for Organizing and Managing Classroom Instruction," in Part 2 on page 111).

Teaching Tip

When introducing new names for the measuring tools, it's helpful to relate their different names to the students' experience. For example, students may call their parents Mom and Dad, but some people call their parents by their first names or by Mr. and Mrs. These all are labels for the same people.

— MBB

See Reproducible R.1 for a template you can print and use for organizing the additional investigations into the three-phase lesson structure. Downloadable at mathsolutions.com/ atm4theditionreproducibles

Additional Investigations for Whole-Class Lessons

In this section I include suggestions for additional investigations that are suitable for whole-class lessons. In contrast to the following section of Independent Investigations, these ideas especially benefit from engaging the entire class with them, and then collecting and comparing the students' results. These aren't presented in the elaborated three-phase lesson structure but rather are general ideas that can be expanded into the three-phase structure.

Round Things

Materials
circular objects—plates, glasses, jar lids, etc.
ruler or other measuring sticks or tape
string for measuring circumferences
compasses (optional)

The Lesson
Choose a circular object and demonstrate measuring its diameter and circumference in several ways—measuring with string, using a measuring tape, and rolling the object on a piece of paper to mark the length of one rotation.

Draw a chart on the board:

Organize students into pairs and give the following directions:

1. Draw a chart as shown.

2. Choose a circular object and measure its diameter and its circumference.

3. Record your results on your chart.

4. Measure at least ten circular objects.

5. Review your measurements to look for patterns that describe the relationship between the diameter and circumference of each.

Lead a classroom discussion. At some point, focus students on looking at the result of dividing the circumference by the diameter for each circle they measured.

Connect the investigation to pi. Explain to students that when you divide the circumference of any circle by its diameter, the result is always a little more than 3. Actually, it's about 3.14, or $3\frac{1}{7}$, which is described as pi. Another way to say this is that pi is the ratio of the circumference to the diameter of a circle. This holds true for all circles, no matter how large or small. Write on the board:

pi (or π) ≈ 3.14 or $3\frac{1}{7}$ $\approx$ is a symbol for "about equal to"

The Perimeter Stays the Same

Materials
centimeter grid paper, 1 sheet per student ☐**R** See Reproducible R.2

The Lesson
Either on the board or a piece of chart paper, rule two columns and label them Greatest Area and Least Area. Then give the following directions:

1. Draw three different shapes on centimeter grid paper following three rules.

    Rule 1: Stay on the lines when you draw.

    Rule 2: You must be able to cut your shape out and have it stay all in one piece.

    Rule 3: Each shape must have a perimeter of 30 centimeters.

2. Record the area on each shape, labeled with *sq cm* or *cm²*.

3. Cut out the shape with the greatest area and the shape with the least area. Tape them in the correct columns.

Before students begin, model how to outline shapes on centimeter grid paper that follow the three rules. First outline a rectangle, as shown below on the left, with the length of 10 cm and the width of 5 cm. Verify that its perimeter is 30 cm by adding the lengths of the four sides (10 + 10 + 5 + 5). Record its area—A = 50 sq cm or 50 cm².

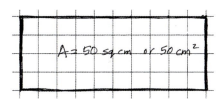
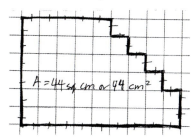

Then outline a shape that isn't a rectangle to illustrate that shapes don't have to be rectangles. Use the example shown above on the right. Model how to mark off the units in the perimeter as you count them. Then count the squares in the shape and record its area.

Posting their shapes presents a visual difference between shapes with the greatest area (which will have a more square-like shape) and those with the least area (which are typically longer and skinnier). After students have posted their shapes, ask them to examine what they notice. Then lead a discussion using the following questions:

What do you notice about the shapes with the greater areas?

What do you notice about the shapes with smaller areas?

Extension
Design a Garden. Pose the following problem:

If you had 100 feet of fencing, how would you design a rectangular garden with the greatest area possible?

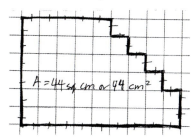

Teaching Tip
I've found it helpful to post the three rules as a reminder for students.
— MSB

Teaching Tip
I've found it useful to model drawing several correct shapes and several incorrect shapes as well to be sure that students understand the rules.
— MSB

Independent Investigations

Following are measurement investigations to use as individual assignments or for partner or small group work. These are also suitable for choice time explorations.

For more on using investigations with various instructional groups, see "Starting Point 20: Four Structures for Organizing and Managing Classroom Instruction" in Part 1 on page 111.

Longer, Shorter, or About the Same

You need: string

Cut a piece of string equal to a length on your body—for example, your hand span, foot length, or distance from elbow to fingertip.

Use the string to find things in the room that are longer, shorter, or about the same. Record your findings, writing the names of the objects you measure or drawing pictures, whichever is more appropriate.

Longer, Shorter, or About the Same can also serve as an extension (especially for younger students) to *A Nonstandard Measuring Investigation (Body Ratios)* on page 148.

> **Teaching Tip**
> After students have completed *Are You a Square?*, post a chart ruled into three columns titled "I am a square," "I am a tall rectangle," "I am a wide rectangle." Have students record in the correct column, either by writing their names or making a tally mark. Then have the students discuss the results.
> — MSB

Are You a Square?

You need: a length of string equal to your height

Use your height string to compare your height with your reach, both arms outstretched.

Decide if you are a square, a tall rectangle, or a wide rectangle. (Squares have equal heights and reaches, tall rectangles have heights that are longer than reaches, and wide rectangles have longer reaches than heights.)

Compare with your classmates.

Are You a Square? can also serve as an extension to *A Nonstandard Measuring Investigation (Body Ratios)* on page 148. Students can use their height strings from the lesson. If students don't have height strings, refer to page 148 for information about how to model for students how to cut their strings.

A Half-Size Me

You need: a length of string equal to your height

Fold your height string in half and cut a length of butcher paper equal to that measurement. This is the height of a half-size you.

Use your string to measure the length from the top of your head to your chin. Fold this length in half and measure down from the top of the paper. That shows where your chin will be.

Continue measuring this way, using string to find half the width of your face, half the height of your neck, half the width of your shoulders, half the length of your arms, and so on. The more measurements you take, the more accurate your drawing will be.

When you've drawn yourself, color the drawing to show how you're dressed today. Post your portrait.

Index Card Portrait

You need: a length of string equal to your height

Follow the procedure for *A Half-Size Me*, but this time fit your portrait on a 5-by-8-inch index card. To begin, fold your height string in half and see if it will fit. Then fold it in half so it's $\frac{1}{4}$ the original length, and test again. Continue until your height string is no longer than 8 inches. Do the same for all body measures.

Statue of Liberty Measurements

You need: a length of string equal to your height

The Statue of Liberty's nose, from bridge to tip, measures 4 feet, 6 inches. How could you use your string and your own body to estimate how long her right arm is, from shoulder to fingertip?

Extension

Other Measurements. Below are other dimensions that suggest similar investigations:

Heel to top of head: 111 feet, 1 inch
Width of eye: 2 feet, 6 inches
Width of mouth: 3 feet

A Half-Size Me, Index Card Portrait, and *Statue of Liberty Measurements* can also serve as extensions (especially for older students) to *A Nonstandard Measuring Investigation (Body Ratios)* on page 148. Students can use their height strings from the lesson. If students don't have height strings, refer to page 148 for information about how to model for students how to cut their strings.

FYI
The Statue of Liberty's right arm actually measures 42 feet. If students' answers are far off, ask them to surmise why the Statue of Liberty's proportions aren't the same as ours but instead are made so that she looks "right" from our viewing perspective, an artistic adjustment. For other dimensions, visit the website, nps.gov/stli/historyculture/statue-statistics.html.

— MSB

Practicing Measuring

You need: a ruler for measuring lengths

Copy the chart below onto a piece of paper.

		Estimate	Measurement	How Far Off ?
	Length of Hand			
	Length of Foot			
	Around your wrist			
	Around your head			
	Length of arm			

Measure after making each estimate (do this rather than making all the estimates first; each estimate can help with the next).

Writing a Measurement Story

Write a story titled "If I Were 1 Centimeter Tall."

Foot Measuring #1: Foot Cutout

You need: construction paper, 1 sheet

Trace your left foot (with your shoe off) on a piece of construction paper. Cut it out.

Record your name, shoe size, and the length of your foot in centimeters.

Compare your shoe size and foot length with your classmates. Do longer feet always have larger shoe sizes?

About the Mathematics

For insights on my mathematical findings in this investigation, see the About the Mathematics section following Foot Measuring #3.

Foot Measuring #2: Area and Perimeter

You need: your cutout foot (from *Foot Measuring #1*)
string
centimeter grid paper, 1 sheet [R] See Reproducible R.2

Trace around your cutout foot on centimeter grid paper.

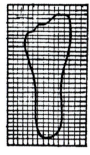

Figure out the area of your foot in square centimeters and record.

Cut a piece of string equal to the perimeter of your foot.

Measure the string in centimeters. Can you find someone with the same length perimeter? Are your foot areas about the same?

Extension

Half the Perimeter. Cut a piece of string half as long as the perimeter of your foot. Use it to make a foot shape on centimeter grid paper. Compare this area with the area of your foot. What do you notice? What do you think is happening?

About the Mathematics

For insights on my mathematical findings in this investigation, see the "About the Mathematics" section following *Foot Measuring #3*.

Foot Measuring #3: Squaring Up

You need: string and foot area (from *Foot Measuring #2*)
centimeter grid paper, 1 sheet [R] See Reproducible R.2

Tape the string that's equal to the perimeter of your foot to a piece of centimeter grid paper in the shape of a square.

Answer these questions:

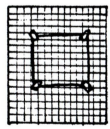

1. What is the area of the square?

2. How does this area compare with the area of your foot?

3. If the areas are different, why do you think this is so? If they are the same, why do you think this is so?

Extension

Giant Foot. Draw a giant foot that is about twice the size of yours. Compare the length and perimeter of this giant foot with the length and perimeter of your cutout foot.

About the Mathematics

I was mathematically flabbergasted the first time I encountered the foot measuring investigations that involve perimeters and areas. The foot I fashioned with a string half as long as my foot perimeter for the extension of *Foot Measuring #2* was surprisingly teeny. And as I followed the directions of *Foot Measuring #3* and formed the perimeter string into a square, I was thinking, "Well, this a much more efficient way to figure the area of my

---

Teaching Tip
Students' foot data (from *Foot Measuring #1* on the previous page) are useful for making class graphs. For younger students, a picture or bar graph of their foot lengths is appropriate. For older students, plotting their foot lengths and shoe sizes on a coordinate grid provides a way to look at the relationship between these two measures. — MBB

Teaching Tip
I always reinforce for students that the perimeter is measured in *centimeters* since it's a measure of length, but the area of their foot is measured in *square centimeters* since it's a measure of area. Also, I post the abbreviations, cm for length and sq cm or cm² for area. — MBB

FYI
"Twice the size" is a vague direction. This is intentional. Read the mathematical discussion that follows for information about this. — MBB

foot than dealing with all those bits and pieces of centimeter squares." But I was shocked when I found how far off the area of the square was from the area I'd calculated for my foot. Whoa, I thought, what did I do wrong? Why is the area of the square so much more than the area of my foot? And why was the area of the foot shape I made with the half length of my foot perimeter so much less? I recalculated the areas again, and the differences were still substantial.

The best way to describe myself at this time is that I was experiencing *disequilibrium*. I was confused because I thought that a shape with half the perimeter of the other should have an area half as much, and two shapes with the same-length perimeter should always have the same area. But the experiences with my measurements contradicted this belief.

It turned out that what I thought was wrong. I learned this from immersing myself in other investigations. I experimented with my perimeter string, first shaping it into a pencil-shaped rectangle, long and skinny. It had hardly any space inside at all, so now the area my foot perimeter string formed was very much less than the area of the square and of my foot. But when I shaped the string into a rectangle with more foot-like dimensions, the area was closer to the area of my foot. My understanding shifted. I no longer erroneously believed that shapes with the same-length perimeter had to have the same area. But don't just take my word for it—there's no substitute for firsthand experience, so if you haven't already done so, try some investigations for yourself.

Also, for further help in understanding why shapes with the same-length perimeter don't necessarily have the same area, try the investigation, *The Perimeter Stays the Same* on page 153.

A note about the *Giant Foot* extension (*Foot Measuring #3*): The problem doesn't specify whether the giant foot should be twice the area of yours or a foot that's twice as long and twice as wide as yours. The wording is intentionally vague, providing another opportunity to think about area and perimeter in relationship to each other. Enlarging a foot so that it's twice as long and twice as wide as yours gives it an area that's much more than twice as large! Making it just twice as long doubles the area, but makes for a very long, thin foot. The challenge is to make a foot that is the correct shape with an area twice as large. It's a bit tricky. It may help to try to draw a square with twice the area of another and see how the lengths of the sides compare.

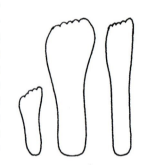

Standing Broad Jumps can also serve as an extension to A Nonstandard Measuring Investigation (Body Ratios) on page 148.

Teaching Tip

After students have completed *Standing Broad Jumps*, consider making a class graph of the broad jumps in foot lengths and ask students what they notice. Or give this as a special project for some students who can then present their representations to the class.

— MSB

Standing Broad Jumps

You need: a paper cut-out of your foot or a piece of string equal to your foot length

Work with a partner to figure out how many of your own foot lengths equal your standing broad jump. Take three trials and use the longest.

Compare your data with your partner, and with other classmates. Is there a general relationship between foot lengths and lengths of the standing broad jumps?

Book Measuring

You need: 5 books
          measuring tape or string
          scale

Choose five books. Label the books A, B, C, D, and E.

Order the books from largest to smallest in the ways listed below. For each, predict first before measuring. What did you notice? What relationships are there among the measures?

	1st	2nd	3rd	4th	5th
weight					
thickness					
height					
width					
size of cover					

Box Measuring

You need: centimeter grid paper, 1 sheet **R** See Reproducible R.2

If you take a piece of 20-by-20-centimeter grid paper and cut a square the same size from each corner, you can fold up what's left to make a box.

 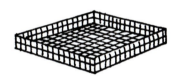

Make boxes from other pieces of 20-by-20-centimeter squared paper, each time varying the size square you cut from each corner. (Remember to cut the same size square from all four corners for each piece.) How many different-size boxes can you make using this method? Try it.

Now figure out the volume of each box. Which of these boxes holds the most?

About the Mathematics

By following the directions and cutting the same-size square from each corner, cutting only on the lines so that the squares you're removing measure a whole number of centimeters on a side, you can make nine different-size boxes. Cutting a 1-by-1-centimeter square from each corner and folding what remains results in a flat box that measures 18 centimeters by 18 centimeters by 1 centimeter. As pictured above, cutting a 2-by-2-centimeter square from each corner results in a box not quite as flat. The larger the square you cut from each corner, the taller the resulting box.

You can cut squares from each corner up to 9-by-9 centimeters. (If you try cutting 10-by-10-centimeter squares, you wind up with four separate pieces and no box at all!) The nine boxes nest nicely, but merely looking at them isn't sufficient for comparing their volumes. (Students generally figure out from this investigation that multiplying the three dimensions of a box gives its volume.)

The following table, which compares the volume of each box with the dimension of the square cut from each corner, shows that cutting a 3-by-3 square from each corner results in the box with the largest volume.

Side of corner square (cm)	Dimensions of box ($\ell \times w \times h$)	Volume of box (cm³)
1	18 × 18 × 1	324
2	16 × 16 × 2	512
3	14 × 14 × 3	588
4	12 × 12 × 4	576
5	10 × 10 × 5	500
6	8 × 8 × 6	384
7	6 × 6 × 7	252
8	4 × 4 × 8	128
9	2 × 2 × 9	36

Suppose, however, that you weren't restricted to cutting squares that measured a whole number of centimeters on a side. (You didn't think this was the end of the problem, did you?) If you cut a 3.5-by-3.5-centimeter square from each corner, for example, the resulting box would be 3.5 centimeters tall and have a 13-by-13-centimeter base. Its volume would be 591.5 cubic centimeters ($13 \times 13 \times 3.5 = 591.5$). This is larger than any of the boxes already cut.

You might want to investigate what size square to cut from each corner to get the box of maximum volume. You might also compare the surface areas of the boxes. Removing squares from each corner reduces the surface area left to form a box, but a box with less surface area can have a greater volume!

Your Height in Money

You need: nickels, at least 20
quarters, at least 20
ruler or other measuring stick or tape

Figure out which you would rather have: your height made of a row of quarters laid side-by-side or your height made as a stack of nickels? How much is each worth? Estimate first and then figure.

How Thick Is Paper?

You need: a book

Devise a way to figure out the thickness of a sheet of paper in the book you chose. Then do it. Compare your result with others' results.

Wraparound

You need: a strip of paper a few inches wide (adding machine tape
works well)
ruler or other measuring stick or tape

Make a measuring tape that, when wrapped around a tree or pole or
other circular object, tells you the diameter of that object.

If you're stumped about how
to proceed with this problem
of making a measuring tape
that tells you the diameter of a
circular object when wrapped
around it, it might help if
you first try the *Round Things*
investigation on page 152.

About the Mathematics

Here's an approach to *Wraparound* that makes sense to me. First, I made a
table similar to the one suggested for Round Things, with data organized
as shown below:

Diameter	Circumference
1	3.14
2	6.28
3	9.42
⋮	⋮

I then marked a tape in intervals of 3.14 inches, but labeled them to
match the related diameters; that is, I labeled the 3.14-inch mark 1, the
6.28-inch mark 2, and so on. (I could have made it a metric measure by
marking off intervals of 3.14 cm each.) Of course, since measurements are
never exact, my tape produced only approximations, but they were close
approximations.

How Long Is a Minute?

You need: a way to time one minute
a chart as shown below

Work with a partner. For each item on the chart, first guess how many
times you think you can do it in 1 minute. Record your guesses on
your chart.

Next, one of you times one minute as the other bounces a ball and
records the number of bounces. Then switch roles. Repeat for each of
the items.

	Guess	Count
Bounce a ball.		
Write your name.		
Say "six sick sheep."		
Count by three's to 30		

Teaching Tip
Draw the chart on the
board for students to copy
or reproduce for them
to use. Sometimes I've
had students brainstorm
additional things for timing
to add to the chart, and
asked students to choose
from their suggestions to
extend their chart.
— MBB

Did a minute seem long or short as you tried these activities? If
you sat quietly for one minute, do you think it would seem like a longer or shorter time than if you bounced a ball for one minute?

Ratio with Cuisenaire Rods

You need: Cuisenaire rods, 1 individual set

Measure across your desk using only light green rods.

Figure out how many rods it would take to measure the same distance if you used only red, only white, or only blue rods. Explain your reasoning.

Test by measuring with the rods.

Extension

Other Rods. Do the same for the other color rods as well.

Yarn Shapes

You need: yarn or string
         tiles, about 100

Cut a piece of yarn or string fifty centimeters long and tie the ends together so you have a loop.

Make a shape with your loop.

Predict how many tiles will fit inside your shape.

Fill your shape. Use ten tiles of each color to make counting easier. You may want to tape your loop in several places to hold it while you fill it.

Sketch your shape and record how many tiles filled it.

Repeat for four more shapes, making them as different from one another as you can.

Examine the shapes that held the most and least numbers of tiles. Write what you notice about these shapes.

It's useful to relate Yarn Shapes to the Foot Measuring investigations on pages 156–158. The more the yarn loop resembles a circle or square, the greater its area; the more it resembles a pencil or a straw, the less its area.

Perimeter with Cuisenaire Rods

You need: Cuisenaire rods, 1 red, 2 light green, and 1 purple
         centimeter grid paper, 1 sheet   R See Reproducible R.2

Arrange one red rod, two light green rods, and one purple rod into a shape on centimeter grid paper in such a way that when you trace around it, you draw only on the lines of the grid paper. Also, you must be able to cut out the outlined shape and have it remain in one piece. (Corners touching are not allowed.)

Make several different shapes in this way.

Trace and record the perimeter for each shape.

Experiment to find how to arrange the rods to get the longest perimeter and the shortest perimeter.

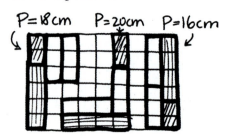

Double the Circumference

You need: small circular object to trace (jar lid, cup, etc.)
　　　　string
　　　　centimeter grid paper, 1 sheet **R** See Reproducible R.2

Trace around the circular object onto the centimeter grid paper.

Figure out the area in square centimeters and record it inside the circle.

Cut a piece of string equal to the circumference of this circle.

Cut another piece of string that's double the circumference of the circle and use it to form a new circle on the paper. Tape it in place.

Estimate and then figure out the area of the new circle.

Write a sentence that describes the relationship between the circumferences and areas of the two circles.

Estimate and then figure out the area of a circle with a circumference equal to half that of the original circle.

Extension

Double the Pizza. When the circumference of a pizza pan doubles, should the price double? Explain your reasoning.

About the Mathematics

If this problem had been called Double the Perimeter and asked you to investigate a square instead of a circle, it would have been easier to solve. You wouldn't need to find a square object to trace, but could draw any size square. To make the investigation easy, you could decide that the area of the square you'd draw would be 1 square unit. Then you wouldn't need string to measure its perimeter—its perimeter would be 4 units, 1 unit per side. Doubling the perimeter would be 8 units, and a square with a perimeter of 8 units would have 2 units per side. The area of the larger square would be four times that of the smaller. Halving the original perimeter to 2 units would produce a square that measured $\frac{1}{2}$ unit on a side with an area of $\frac{1}{4}$ square unit. Trying this for other size squares would show that doubling the perimeter consistently produces a square with an area that is four times as large and halving the perimeter consistently produces a square with an area that is one-fourth as large.

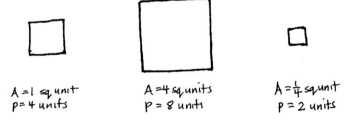

A = 1 sq. unit　　A = 4 sq. units　　A = ¼ sq. unit
P = 4 units　　　P = 8 units　　　P = 2 units

The examples you try may be convincing to you, but they're not enough for an acceptable proof. You also need a convincing argument. Algebra is a useful tool for proving that doubling the perimeter of a square always results in a square with an area that is four times as large. Suppose we call the side of the first square s. Its perimeter is $s + s + s + s$, or $4s$; its area is $s \times s$ or s^2. Doubling the perimeter to $8s$ results in a square with each of its four sides measuring $2s$. The area of this new square is $2s \times 2s$, or $4s^2$. And $4s^2$ is four times greater than s^2, no matter what s measures.

Try using algebra to prove that halving the perimeter produces a square with an area that is one-fourth as large.

What about circles? If you double the circumference of a circle, will the area of the new circle be four times as large? And if you halve it, will the area be one-fourth as large? Yes. As the investigation suggests, you can experiment to see that this seems to be so. And you may notice as you investigate that doubling the circumference of a circle doubles its radius. The area of a circle with a radius r is $\pi \times r^2$, or πr^2. For a radius of 3 inches, the area is $\pi \times 3^2$, or $\pi \times 9$, which is about 28.26 square inches. Double the radius to 6 inches and the area is $\pi \times 6^2$, or $\pi \times 36$, which is about 113.04 square inches. And 113.04 is four times as large as 28.26.

The area of a circle with a doubled radius of $2r$ is $\pi \times (2r)^2$, which is $\pi \times (2r \times 2r)$, which is p $4r^2$, or $4\pi r^2$. And $4\pi r^2$ is four times as large as πr^2. It's possible to use the same logic to verify that halving a circumference results in a circle with an area one-fourth as large.

A sticky part of this reasoning is to be convinced that doubling the circumference of a circle really does double its radius. The circumference of a circle is equal to p times the diameter. Since the diameter is the radius doubled, the circumference can be thought of as $2\pi r$. Doubling this circumference makes it $4\pi r$. This means that, for the larger circle, $4r$ is its diameter, so the radius is $2r$, which is twice the original radius of r.

If you find this explanation confusing, let this be a reminder about how difficult it can be to follow someone else's reasoning. You have to turn ideas around in your head to make sense of them in your own way. This reasoning works for me, and I've gotten clearer about it as I've worked to get it down in writing. It may help you to talk with a colleague about my thinking or to try writing down your own explanation.

The Area Stays the Same

You need: 5-by-8-inch index cards, 2 per student

centimeter grid paper, 1 sheet [R] See Reproducible R.2

Cut several squares that measure 5 centimeters on each side from a corner of one of the index cards. Use the centimeter grid paper to help you.

Use this shape to make other different shapes. You can do this by cutting the square on the diagonal into two triangles and putting them together in various ways so that the same length sides match or by cutting the square in other ways and arranging the pieces together.

Trace around the different shapes you make, cutting each from the index cards. You will need at least five shapes, including the 5-centimeter square. All of your shapes will have the same area.

Draw a line segment equal in length to the perimeter of each shape. Label each line segment with the shape.

Investigate how the perimeters compare. Write a statement about your findings.

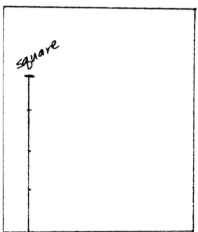

FYI
When drawing a line segment equal in length to the perimeter of a shape, you can use the actual shape. First trace along one side, then rotate the shape and trace along the next side, repeating until you've traced all sides and formed a line segment.

— MBB

About the Mathematics

This investigation is one of my favorites for several reasons. It's extremely versatile—I've had success with it in third through eighth grades. I like the fact that children create for themselves different-shape figures that all have the same area. I like using the shapes they make to introduce the terminology for polygons—*triangle, quadrilateral, pentagon, hexagon,* and so on. And comparing the perimeters of the figures they make themselves seems to offer convincing evidence to students that shapes with the same area can have different perimeters.

Problem-Solving Investigations: Data

About the Mathematics

This icon indicates that I've written a mathematical commentary for the investigation. I've written these explanations in response to queries from teachers asking for math help with particular problems. I encourage you to try the investigation first before reading my explanation.

— MSB

Why Teach Data?

Technological advances continue to make more statistical information available to us than ever before. On the Internet, in newspapers and magazines, on television, and from conversations, we are flooded with data that demand an increasing understanding of statistics for us to understand their use. What's the effectiveness of seat belts and why should we wear them? Is there a link between texting while driving and automobile accidents? What can you do to hedge against rising living costs? Which money market or retirement fund makes the most sense? What does a particular advertising claim really mean? Is the death penalty a deterrent to crimes of murder? How do you weigh the benefits of birth control pills against their dangers? Should a certain food dye be banned because it has caused cancer in rats under some conditions? What effect will the rate of population growth have on our lives? How should the increased number of older people in our society affect social decisions? For all of these questions, and many others, concepts relating to statistics and probability are integral for making decisions.

Statistics has never enjoyed a terrific reputation. It's been said that you can prove anything with statistics. To some, statistics and lies are often synonymous. Many people have been hardened against statistics by claims of politicians and advertisers. However, our society is increasingly making use of ideas found in statistics and probability. Students need to develop skills that enable them to live in this statistical society so they will not be misled or blinded by data. Without these skills, they will have an incomplete understanding of the world they live in.

Experiences with data provide real applications of arithmetic. When basic computational skills are used in a context, students have the opportunity to see the advantages and limitations of their calculations. Most everyday applications of arithmetic are statistical, done with variability in mind and with some degree of uncertainty—estimating costs, calculating the amount of wallpaper or floor covering needed, figuring time for trips or cooking. The simple arithmetic done is valuable only in the context of its application. To understand those applications, we need probability and statistics, and therefore, they are essential elements of students' basic number skills.

Studying about data also helps students develop critical thinking skills. In carrying out investigations in probability and statistics, students develop ways to cope with uncertainty as they search for the truth in a situation and learn to report it faithfully. Approaching situations statistically can make students face up to prejudices, think more consistently about arguments, and justify their thinking with numerical information. This approach has applications in all areas of life—social, political, and scientific.

Students' experiences with data in grades K–5 help build the foundations for their study of statistics and probability in grade 6 and up. Statistics is the science or study of data. Statistical studies require collecting, measuring, sorting, representing, analyzing, and interpreting information. The information is then used for predicting, drawing inferences, and making decisions. There's typically a degree of uncertainty with data that are collected. This means that statistics is most often concerned with using information in the face of uncertainty. Probability gives a way to measure uncertainty and is therefore essential to understanding statistical methods.

Stages in Learning About Data

The teaching of data should stem from real problems. A theoretical or abstract approach is not appropriate for the elementary grades. The approach should be based on investigations that draw on students' experiences and interests. Their intuition needs to be challenged. Once they sense what "should happen" in a situation, then it's timely for them to carry out an experiment to test their predictions. Not only will such experiments provide firsthand experience in collecting, organizing, and interpreting data, but they will also reinforce computational skills. Basic to learning about data are the following ideas:

STAGES IN LEARNING ABOUT DATA

1. Collecting Data

2. Organizing and Representing Data

3. Interpreting Data

4. Sampling

5. Assigning Probabilities

6. Making Inferences

---

1. Collecting Data

Students need experience gathering both categorical data and measurement data. Categorical data comes from sorting into categories and is appropriate for K–2 students. It's appropriate for students in grades 3 and up to generate measurement data from measuring various objects.

2. Organizing and Representing Data

Students need experience organizing data and representing them graphically in a variety of graphs, tables, and charts.

3. Interpreting Data

Students should learn to read graphs, making quick visual summaries as well as further interpretations and comparisons of data through finding means, medians, and modes.

4. Sampling

In real life, even though information is often needed about an entire population, it may be possible to sample only a part of the population. That information from the sample is then used to infer characteristics about the total population. Students need to learn the difference between random and nonrandom samples and the importance this difference makes in statistical studies.

For example, to determine the percentage of people in the general population who are left-handed, you would not poll only professional baseball players as a random sample. (Why not?)

5. Assigning Probabilities

Initial experiences with measuring uncertainty should be informal and should include discussion of whether a result is possible or likely, or whether outcomes are equally or not equally likely. Assigning probabilities gives further information for making a decision in the face of uncertainty. The probability of an event can be represented by a number from 0 to 1. For example, the probability of rolling a 4 when rolling a die is $\frac{1}{6}$. The probability of rolling an even number when rolling a die is $\frac{1}{6}$. The numerator of the fraction represents the number of outcomes you're interested in; the denominator represents the total number of possible outcomes.

6. Making Inferences

Students need to draw conclusions based on their interpretation of data, including moving from looking at data of single characteristics to looking at data that calls for investigating associations involving two variables.

Mathematical Practices

The investigation and study of data support the development of the mathematical practices described in the Common Core and other standards documents for students in all grades. The mathematical practices should be connected to the content standards by engaging students in solving problems, reasoning, making conjectures, applying math to everyday life, using appropriate tools, communicating precisely, looking for patterns and structure, and looking for regularity in mathematical methods. The investigations in this section provide ways to make connections between practice and content standards.

Mathematical Content

It's helpful to understand which data concepts and skills are appropriate for different grade levels. Below are content designations that align with the Common Core and other standards documents.

Kindergarten: Classify objects into categories; count the number in each category and sort the categories by how many there are in each.

Grade 1: Organize, represent, and interpret data with up to three categories; answer questions about the total number, how many in each category, and how many more or less are in one category than in another.

Grade 2: Draw picture graphs and bar graphs with up to four categories; solve addition, subtraction, and comparing problems using information from bar graphs; generate measurement data by measuring lengths and show in a line plot.

Grade 3: Draw scaled picture graphs and bar graphs; solve one- and two-step "how many more" and "how many less" problems from data; generate measurement data by measuring lengths and show in a line plot.

Grade 4: Represent and interpret data with line plots; solve problems involving addition and subtraction of fractions from the data.

Grade 5: Represent and interpret data about measuring volumes with line plots; solve problems involving operations with fractions from the data.

Grade 6: Develop understanding of statistical variability; summarize and describe distributions using dot plots, histograms, and box plots.

Grade 7: Use random sampling to draw inferences about a population; draw informal comparative inferences about two populations; understand that the probability of a chance event is a number between 0 and 1; approximate the probability of chance events; use organized lists, tables, tree diagrams, and simulation to find probabilities.

Grade 8: Construct and interpret scatter plots; know that straight lines are widely used to model relationship between two variables; interpret slope and intercept in problems involving measurement data; understand patterns of association between data from two categories.

Sample Whole-Class Lessons

Following are two sample lessons that describe, in detail, investigations that help students develop understanding and skills with data. The first suggestion engages students with spinner experiments and the second with graphing.

 **Sample Lesson**

Spinner Experiments

Spinner experiments provide a good beginning probability and statistics experience. They give students the opportunity to make individual predictions, collect data using a graph, and compare their individual results with a larger class sample. Younger students benefit from the practice of recording and analyzing information; older students can be challenged to extend the experiment into a more formal analysis of the probability involved. Making the spinners gives all students practice in following directions.

Materials

5-by-8-inch cards, 1 per student
paper clips, 1 per student
plastic straws, 1-inch length per student
half-inch grid paper for graphing, 1 sheet per group **R** See Reproducible R.3

Introducing

1. **Present or review concepts.** Use the following directions to demonstrate how to make a spinner, with the class following along step by step.

HOW TO MAKE A SPINNER THAT REALLY SPINS

1. Cut a 5-by-8-inch index card in half. Cut a circle, about 3 inches in diameter, from one half of the card. Divide and label it as shown.

2. Mark a dot in the center of the other piece of card. Draw a line from the dot to one corner of the card.

3. Bend up the outside of a paper clip. This part should point straight up when the paper clip is lying flat on the desk.

(continued)

For Younger Students
Young children may need more assistance making spinners. Have extra supplies on hand for mishaps.
— MSB

(continued from page 171)

4. Poke a hole in the center of the circle (be exact) and another hole in the dot on the card.

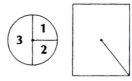

5. Push the bent end of the paper clip through the hole in the card. Tape the rest of the paper clip to the bottom of the card. Make sure the side of the card with the line is facing up.

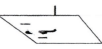

6. Put the $\frac{1}{4}$-inch length of plastic straw and then the spinner face on the paper clip.

7. Cover the tip of the paper clip with a piece of tape.

2. **Pose a part of the problem or a similar but smaller problem.** Ask, *When you spin the spinner, is any number more likely to come up than any other number? Why do you think so?* Or, if you prefer, ask, *When you spin the spinner, I think that 3 is more likely to come up than 1 or 2. Why do I think that?* After students have offered their ideas, explain the experiment. *You'll spin your spinner and keep track of what comes up on a graph recording sheet like this.* Demonstrate for the class. Cut a 3-by-11 recording sheet from half-inch grid paper; write the numbers 1, 2, and 3 in the bottom row; then spin several times, recording 1s, 2s, and 3s in the correct columns as they occur. After three or four spins, ask, *What do you think the entire graph might look like when one number reaches the top of the paper?*

3. **Present the investigation.** On the board, wall, or bulletin board, post labels for 1, 2, and 3 to indicate three sections. Explain, *Each of you will make a spinner, cut a graph recording sheet, and try the*

experiment. When one of the numbers reaches the top, you've completed the experiment. Post your record sheet in the correct section. If you complete the experiment while others are still spinning and recording, cut another record sheet and do it again.

4. **Discuss the task to make sure students understand what they are to do.** Ask for questions. Also, it's helpful to have a few students repeat the directions. If you think it would be helpful, post an abbreviated version of the directions:

DIRECTIONS FOR SPINNER EXPERIMENTS

1. Make a spinner.
2. Cut out a 3-by-11 record sheet.
3. Do the experiment and record.
4. Post your record sheet in the correct place.

Exploring

1. **Observe the students as they work.** Typically, there aren't major problems. Some students may need help making their spinners.

2. **Offer assistance when needed.**

3. **Provide an extension for students that finish more quickly than others.** Ask them to repeat the experiment and post their new results.

Summarizing

1. **Have pairs or groups review what has been posted and think about what to report in a classroom discussion.** Ask them to write summary statements to describe what conclusions they can make.

2. **Initiate a classroom discussion.** First have students report about their experience doing the experiment.

3. **Next have groups report their conclusions about the data posted.** Most likely, 3 reached the top of the graph recording sheets more often, but there will be instances of 1 or 2 reaching the top first. Ask, *What fraction of the recording sheets had 3 as the winner? What fraction had 2 as the winner? What fraction had 1 as the winner?*

4. **Generalize from the solutions.** Since the number 3 had the same amount of space on the spinner as the numbers 1 and 2 combined, ask the students how they might find out if the number 3 actually came up in half of all the spins. To find out, redistribute the graph record sheets to groups and have them figure out how many 1s, 2s, 3s came up in all. Since the graph record sheets have 10 blank squares in each column, it's easy to calculate the total number of 3s on sheets where 3 reached the top. But rather than do the calculation, have each group cut their graph recording sheets into columns and tape together separate trains for 1s, 2s, and 3s. Then you can lay them on the floor to compare.

Extensions
Suggestions for building on and extending students' experiences with spinners can be found under "Independent Investigations." Useful investigations are *Two-Person Spin* (page 184), *Design Your Own Spinner* (page 185), and *Got a Match?* (page 185). These can be used with the whole class, as small group or partner investigations, or for choice time explorations (see also "Starting Point 20: Four Structures for Organizing and Managing Classroom Instruction" in Part 1 on page 111).

About the Math
Although the number 3 is twice as likely to come up as either 1 or 2, there's no guarantee that 3 will come up exactly twice as often when you do the experiment. Very few of the graph recording sheets (if any) will actually reflect that result. The mathematical theory of probability says that the more times you spin a spinner, the closer the results will match the theoretical distribution.

— MSB

Graphing in the Classroom

Graphing is a way to present data in a concise and visual way that makes it possible to see relationships in the data more easily. In order to learn to interpret graphs and use them as problem-solving tools, students benefit from experience with making their own graphs. Making graphs requires collecting, sorting, and classifying data. Such experiences are appropriate at all grade levels. Rather than present one problem-solving lesson, this section provides ideas for graphing experiences for all grades.

Introducing Graphing: Three Main Types

In the early grades, graphing experiences best begin concretely. A pictorial representation of that relationship can be introduced at a later stage; still later, a symbolic graph could be made. The possibilities for things to graph should be taken from the interests of the children and can draw on experiences that occur in the classroom.

THREE MAIN TYPES OF GRAPHS

1. Real Graphs

2. Picture Graphs

3. Symbolic Graphs

REAL GRAPH

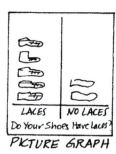
PICTURE GRAPH

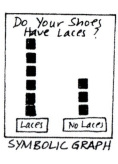
SYMBOLIC GRAPH

Real Graphs

Real graphs use actual objects to compare and build on students' understanding of more and less. For example, have each student take off one shoe and place it in one of two rows: with laces or without laces. This creates a concrete graph. Other possible topics for concrete graphs include:

Is your pencil dull or sharp?

Which paste jars need filling and which don't?

Are the bottoms of your shoes smooth or bumpy?

Picture graphs

Picture graphs use pictures or models to represent real objects. Students can draw pictures or they cut pictures from magazines. Examples include a rubbing of the bottom of their shoes, a picture of the cookie they like best, and a picture of a pet.

For a way to introduce students to sorting materials into categories and making real graphs, see *Junk Sorting* on page 178.

Symbolic Graphs

Symbolic graphs are the most abstract because they use symbols, such as a colored square or tally mark, to represent real things.

Interpreting Data on Graphs

An important aspect of a graphing investigation is the discussion and interpretation of the information. Progress made by students is directly related to the time spent on discussion. The following are the kinds of questions that can be asked about graphs, whether they are real, pictorial, or symbolic.

Which column has the least?

Which column has the most?

Are there more ___ or more ___?

Are there fewer ___or fewer ___?

How many more ___are there than ___?

How many fewer ___are there than ___?

How many are___ there altogether?

As students become familiar with graphs, they should be able to draw conclusions from the information without being prompted with questions.

Ideas for Graphs

Draw on your students' experiences for topics for class graphs. Suggestions appear below. Consider making graphs part of your morning routine by posting a graph before students arrive and having them record on it. These "attendance" graphs can be concrete, pictorial, or symbolic. They can ask for opinions, require factual reporting of information, or require some action before students record the information requested. After students become familiar with a variety of attendance graphs, have pairs prepare them for the class.

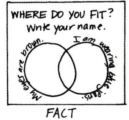

OPINION

FACT   PROCESSING

Discuss graphs in the following ways:

- Use the graphs to write equations that show the relationships reported. In the "What age would you like to be?" graph, you can write an addition equation to show the number of students who would like to be a different age than they are now; for example, $17 + 4 = 21$.

- Ask students to make generalizations from graphs. For example: *Most students in our class wish they were older.* Less than one-fourth of the students are happy with their present age.

For more on the "think, pair, share" routine, see "Starting Point 14: The Importance of Classroom Discussions" in Part 1 on page 67.

Teaching Tip
When posing questions to the class for discussion, I find it useful to use the "think, pair, share" routine: ask students to think by themselves first, then turn and talk with a neighbor, and finally participate in a classroom discussion.

— MSB

- Pose questions that can be answered from the graph for students to answer as an individual assignment, to answer in pairs or with a small group, or to discuss with the class. For example: *What percent of our class has brown eyes? What fraction of our class would like to be older?*
- Ask students to write questions for others to answer.

More Ideas

Following are ideas for other graphs.

1. Do you have a library card?
2. Is your Halloween costume scary or not scary?
3. How many scoops of rice do you think will fill the jar?
4. What time did you go to sleep last night?
5. At what age do you think you'll be a grownup?
6. About how many glasses of water do you drink each day?
7. What's your favorite TV show?
8. How many pencils are in your desk?
9. Which do you think there are more of on the U.S. flag—long red stripes, long white stripes, short red stripes, or short white stripes?
10. How many letters are in your first name?
11. Is your last name longer, shorter, or the same length as your first name?
12. Does your last name begin with a letter in the first half of the alphabet or the last half?
13. Do you have a middle name?
14. Are your earlobes hanging or attached?
15. What's your birthday month?
16. Who decides when you get your hair cut?
17. Do you have a younger brother or sister?
18. How much do you think this costs? (a can of juice, a bag of peas in the pod, a bowl of apples, etc.)
19. Are you left-handed or right-handed?
20. Do you have moons on any of your fingernails?
21. What color are your eyes?
22. How many sections do you think are in this orange?
23. What do you like to put on your hamburger?
24. What do you call your mother—Mother, Mom, Mommy, something else?
25. Do you like spinach?

26. How many cubes can you hold in one hand?

27. Have you ever visited another country?

28. How do you like to eat eggs—scrambled, hard-boiled, soft-boiled, fried, other, not at all?

29. If A = $0.01, B = $0.02, C = $0.03, and so on, how much is your first name worth?

30. Is your hair straight, curly, or wavy?

31. Which of these holidays do you like best—Thanksgiving, Halloween, or April Fool's Day?

32. How many televisions are in your house?

33. How many computers are in your house?

34. Do you like to ride a bicycle?

35. Do you think children should choose their own bedtime?

Additional Investigations for Whole-Class Lessons

See Reproducible R.1 for a template you can print and use for organizing the additional investigations into the three-phase lesson structure. Downloadable at mathsolutions.com/atm4theditionreproducibles

In this section I include suggestions for additional investigations that are suitable for whole-class lessons. In contrast to the following section of Independent Investigations, these ideas especially benefit from engaging the entire class with them, and then collecting and comparing the students' results. These aren't presented in the elaborated three-phase lesson structure but rather are general ideas that can be expanded into the three-phase structure.

Junk Sorting

Materials

collection of a dozen or more objects for each pair or group (keys, jar lids, fabric swatches, buttons, nuts and bolts, postcards, shells, polished rocks, etc.)

The Lesson

To introduce this investigation, choose one collection and gather the students so everyone can see the objects. Having the students sit in a circle with space in the middle for the objects works well. Ask them to talk with a partner about what they notice about the objects. Then ask a student to tell one thing he or she noticed. For jar lids, for example, a student may notice, "Some are white." Then ask two other students to sort the objects into two sets—in this case, the lids that are white and the lids that aren't white. Ask the students to line up the two sets to make a real graph. Repeat, asking for something else a student noticed about the lids, and again sort them into two lines. Continue until the students have exhausted all possibilities.

Then distribute a collection to each pair or group. After they've had time to inspect their collection, give the following directions:

1. Explore sorting your collection into two or three sets in several ways, lining up the objects each time.

2. Choose one way for others to look at. On a piece of paper, write down how you would label the characteristic of each set. Place the paper face down next to your arrangement.

3. Then you'll rotate around the room, trying to figure out how others sorted their materials. When you think you know, turn over their paper to check your prediction. Next sort the materials in a different way, writing the new characteristics under the old ones and again turning the paper face down. Move to another table.

4. When you've had the chance to look at several other collections, return to your collection and examine the different ways others sorted it.

After students have done this, initiate a classroom discussion for students to describe what they learned from seeing how others sorted their materials.

Teaching Tip
Sending home a note with a list of the kinds of materials you need for collections is one way to build a supply. It's also a chance to let families know about how you'll use the materials to engage their children in learning about data.
— MSB

For Older Students
While this is ideal for younger students, I've also done the investigation with older students. For a greater challenge, I ask them to sort their collections into four sets.
— MSB

Tiles in the Bag (Version 1)

Materials
small paper bag
tiles in colors, 10

The Lesson
Place ten tiles in a bag, some of two different colors. Tell the students that you've put ten tiles in the bag in two colors, but don't reveal how many of each color. Go around the class, asking individual students to draw out a tile without looking, note its color, and then replace it. (This is called taking a sample with replacement.) Have a student record the colors on the board. Here are two suggestions for recording:

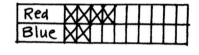

After ten draws, ask students to look at the information and decide whether they are willing to predict how many of each color are in the bag, or if they need more information. Have students confer in pairs and then share their opinions.

Repeat for ten more draws, and again have students think, discuss with a partner, and share. Repeat as many times as needed for most of the students to feel that they're ready to predict how many of each color tile is in the bag.

After students predict, reveal the contents of the bag and discuss how it relates to their prediction.

Extension
More Experiments. Try the same investigation with a different configuration of two colors. Or, for older students, try the investigation with ten tiles in three colors.

This is another time when the "think, pair, share" routine works well. For more on this routine, see "Starting Point 14: The Importance of Classroom Discussions" in Part 1 on page 67.

For Younger Students
A more appropriate question for younger students might be: Which color do you think there's more of in the bag? For this, I typically put in seven or eight of one color, and three or two of the other.

— MSB

Teaching Tip
For some students, this investigation is an exercise in guessing, with a smattering of intuition and a good deal of hopeful predicting. Others predict by drawing on ideas relating to ratio and proportion. Taking fifty or one hundred draws (if the students are interested) makes predicting easier and more valid.

— MSB

Tiles in the Bag (Version 2)

Materials
3 small paper bags filled with tiles in this way:
25 red, 5 blue
20 red, 10 blue
10 red, 20 blue

The Lesson
This investigation gives students the opportunity to experience why a greater sample size is more reliable for making a prediction. On the board, write:

25 red, 5 blue

20 red, 10 blue

10 red, 20 blue

Tell the class that these describe the contents of the three bags. Have a student choose one bag at random so that even you do not know its contents. Then, using the procedure described in Tiles in the Bag, Version 1, make 25 random samples with replacement. On the board, list the samples so that you have a record of what was drawn and the order of the samples.

Compute the percent of red tiles for each of these: the first 5 samples, the first 10 samples, the first 15 samples, the first 20 samples, all 25 samples.

Use these questions to lead a discussion:

Which bag do you think we used?

Which bag would you have chosen if you had based your decision on the first five samples? Ten? Fifteen? Twenty?

How many samples do you think you need to make an accurate prediction?

Then reveal the contents of the bag and revisit the discussion questions.

Sampling Bean Populations

Materials

white beans, 1 package
brown beans, 3 packages
paper bag to hold all the beans

Teaching Tip
Choose white and brown beans that are about the same size.
— MSB

The Lesson

Organize students into pairs or small groups. Mix the four packages of beans together in a paper bag. Go around the room and have each student take a small handful of beans and sort them into white and brown groups. Then ask the students in each pair or group to pool their samples and organize the beans into two rows, lining them up so they can make a visual comparison.

Write the following five choices on the board:

3 white and 1 brown

2 white and 2 brown

1 white and 3 brown

4 white

4 brown

Ask each group to use the information from sorting their bean samples to predict which of the choices is most likely if they were to take four beans from the bag with their eyes closed.

Have pairs or groups present their predictions and their reasoning to the class.

Return all the beans to the bag. Then have each student pick out, without looking, four beans. Have students record a tally mark next to the choice on the board that matches their sample. Discuss the results.

Divide the beans among the groups and have the students count the number of brown and white beans they have. Record their counts on the board and have them figure out the totals for each color of bean. Then lead a classroom discussion to have students compare these totals with the samples of handfuls and the samples of four beans.

The 1-2-3-4 Investigation

Materials

slips of paper, about 3-by-3 inches, each with the numbers 1, 2, 3, 4 as shown, 1 per student

1 2 3 4

The Lesson

The following item appeared in the San Francisco *Chronicle* newspaper: "Write the numbers 1, 2, 3, and 4 on a piece of paper. Ask somebody to circle any one of these numbers. Four out of five asked will circle the 3." Do not read this to the class yet, but organize an experiment to test this prediction.

1. Tell students that you're going to give them a slip of paper, face down. Ask them not to peek until you tell them what you want them to do. Then distribute one of the slips with 1 2 3 4 on them to each student.

2. Ask students, without revealing what they do or talking with anyone, to turn over their slip, circle one of the numbers, and turn the slip facedown.

3. Write the following question on the board and ask students to choose A or B. If they choose A, they should also select one of the four numbers on their slip.

4. Which do you think is true?

   A. The number ___ will be circled many more times than any other.

   B. All of the numbers will be circled about the same number of times.

5. In groups or pairs, ask students to discuss their ideas. Have students report to the class.

6. List the numbers 1, 2, 3, and 4 on the board. Have students tape their slips next to the number they circled to graph the class data.

7. Read the statement from the San Francisco *Chronicle*. Then discuss whether the class results match the newspaper prediction.

Extensions

For Homework. To see if the results would change with a larger sample, have each student take home three additional slips for others to circle a number. Have them predict how these additional samples will affect the graph. Then, the next day, have students post their slips on the graph. Discuss the results.

Other Versions. What if the numbers had been in a different order? What if the slips had the letters a, b, c, and d on them instead? What about other letters or shapes? Have interested students devise and carry out their own investigations.

Alphabetical Probability

Materials

a strip of adding machine tape with the letters of the alphabet written on it as shown. Roll up the strip and secure with a paper clip.

E T A O [N I] S R H L D C U [P F] M W Y [B G] V K [Q X] [J Z]

The Lesson

This investigation uses probability and statistics techniques to analyze the frequency of letters in the English language. The letters on the adding machine tape are in their order of usage in the English language. (Letters that are bracketed have the same frequency of occurrence.) Do not reveal the order until the end of the lesson. Follow these steps.

1. Have students decide, individually, what they think are the five most commonly used letters in the English language. Ask them to list their predictions and put a star next to the letter they think is the most common.

2. Ask students to share their individual predictions in small groups and decide on one group prediction.

3. Then have each student choose a sentence from a book and tally how many times each letter appears in the sentence. Have groups compile their individual results and put their results on a class chart. Find the totals for each letter and then list the letters of the alphabet in the order of frequency according to the students' findings.

4. Compare the class results with students' predictions and with the actual order of frequency in the English language.

Extensions

A Language Riddle. Write the following three sentences on the board and ask the students what is strange about them. *This is odd. Do you know why? Try and find out.* [None of them use an "e," the most common letter.]

A Language Challenge. Have students choose one of the five most common letters and write three sentences without using it.

Probability in Games. Investigate the games of Scrabble and Boggle to see how they used the information about frequency of letters.

Typewriter Keyboards. When Christopher L. Sholes invented the typewriter in 1867, he purposely scrambled the letters so typists couldn't type too quickly and jam the keyboard. (Your two most agile fingers rest on rarely used J and K, while your left pinky is used for A.) Have students design a keyboard that makes use of this mathematical investigation. Then compare their keyboard with the one pictured. This was patented by August Dvorak in 1936 to make better use of the frequency of letters.

FYI
There's a great deal of information online about typewriter history and the Dvorak keyboard. Doing an internet search for typewriter keyboard history provides lots of research options.
— MSB

For more on using investigations with various instructional groups, see "Starting Point 20: Four Structures for Organizing and Managing Classroom Instruction" in Part 1 on page 111.

Teaching Tip
Students need spinners for *Two-Person Spin* on this page, and *Design Your Own Spinner* and *Got a Match?* on the next page. If students haven't made spinners, show them how using the directions on page 171. Or post the directions for students to use to make their own independently.
— MSB

Teaching Tip
Post a class chart titled *Which Sum Won?* that's an enlarged version of the recording sheet. Have pairs color in a square to indicate which sum won when they tried the investigation. I like to leave the class chart up and have students try the investigation again when they have time available. The more data, the better to see what happens. Discuss with students that the sums of 2 and 3 come up less often because there are fewer ways to get them than the other sums since they depend on 1s and 2s, which have less space on the spinners.
— MSB

Two-Person Spin is ideal as an extension to the investigation *Spinner Experiments* on page 171.

Independent Investigations

Following are investigations to use as individual assignments or for partner or small group work. These are also suitable for choice time explorations.

Two-Person Spin

You need: spinner as shown below
half-inch grid paper **R** See Reproducible R.3

Work with a partner. You each need a spinner with the numbers 1, 2, and 3 on it, with the number 3 on half the spinner face, as shown.

Cut a 5-by-11 recording sheet from half-inch grid paper and write the numbers 2, 3, 4, 5, 6 in the bottom row. These numbers are the possible sums when you and your partner each spin your spinner and add the numbers that come up.

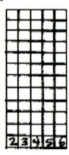

First, together predict which sum you think will come up most often when you spin your spinners and add the numbers.

Then you both spin your spinner. Add the numbers and write the sum in the correct column above the bottom row. Take turns recording the sums. Continue until one sum wins by reaching the top of your graph recording sheet.

Repeat and see if you get the same results. Also, compare your results with others who have tried the investigation.

Design Your Own Spinner

You need: spinner

half-inch grid paper, 1 sheet **R** See Reproducible R.3

In this investigation, you design your own spinner and test what happens when you spin and record the numbers that come up.

Cut out a graph recording sheet 11 squares high and as many squares wide as numbers on your spinner. On the bottom row, write the numbers on your spinner.

Paste your graph recording sheet to a blank sheet of 8-by-11-inch paper (see illustration).

Write a prediction about which number will reach the top first if you spin and record each number as it comes up.

Do the experiment, recording the numbers that come up on your graph recording sheet.

Write about the results: Which number reached the top first? How does the result compare with your prediction?

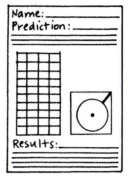

Design Your Own Spinner can also serve as an extension to the investigation *Spinner Experiments* on page 171.

Teaching Tip
Have students post their work for others to examine. I've found that students are interested in each other's spinners and results.
— MBB

Got a Match?

You need: spinner

half-inch grid paper **R** See Reproducible R.3

Work with a partner. First make identical spinners.

Spin your spinners and compare to see if the same number comes up on both.

Make a prediction: If you do this twenty-four times, on how many spins you think your results will match?

Draw two columns and label them Match and No Match. Then do the experiment, recording with a tally mark each time if the result is a match or not.

Write about how your outcome compares with your prediction.

About the Mathematics

This investigation invites two people to spin two identical spinners, predict how often the results will match, and then test the prediction by spinning and recording the matches that come up in twenty-four spins. No specific spinner is suggested, but let's consider the problem with the 1-2-3 spinner used in the investigation on page 182. My method for thinking about this spinner can be applied to any other spinner.

One complication with using the 1-2-3 spinner is that it's twice as likely that the number 3 will come up than either 1 or 2. In order to think about this problem, I need to figure out a way to compare equally likely outcomes. I can do this with the 1-2-3 spinner by imagining that it's divided

Teaching Tip
Sometimes I have pairs of students try the investigation with dice first. I give each student a 1–6 die and explain that they will roll them at the same time, see if they have a match or not, and record each roll with a tally mark in the correct column. I ask them to predict first what they think might happen and then roll the dice twenty-four times.
— MBB

into fourths, with the number 3 in two of the fourths. To be clear, I'll label them 3a and 3b. This gives four equally likely outcomes from spinning—1, 2, 3, and 3— and is the same as having three outcomes with the 3 twice as likely.

When I spin two spinners, I can get either Match or No Match, and I need to investigate how often each of these options occurs. To do so, I'll make a list of all the possibilities. Here's how I reason.

If a 1 comes up on the first spinner, there are four equally likely possibilities for what will come up on the second spinner—1, 2, 3a, or 3b. This means that a 1 on the first spinner produces either 1-1, 1-2, 1-3a, or 1-3b. This isn't so good for a match—only one out of four possibilities. The same holds true if a 2 comes up on the first spinner—2-1, 2-2, 2-3a, or 2-3b— only one more possible match. This is not looking good for matches. Maybe the 3s will help.

If I spin 3a on the first spinner, then the four possibilities after spinning the second spinner are 3a-1, 3a-2, 3a-3a, 3a-3b. Ah, things are looking up. Since 3a and 3b are the same number, this produces two matches. And the same is true if I spin 3b on the first spinner. There are two matches in the four possibilities—3b-1, 3b-2, 3b-3a, 3b-3b.

I count up the total number of ways the two spinners could match (1-1, 2-2, 3a-3a, 3a-3b, 3b-3a, 3b-3b)—there are six. Then I count up the total ways that the two spinners wouldn't match (1-2, 1-3a, 1-3b, 2-1, 2-3a, 2-3b, 3a-1, 3a-2, 3b-1, 3b-2)—there are ten. Of the sixteen possible ways, there is a $\frac{6}{16}$ chance of getting a match and $\frac{10}{16}$ chance of not getting a match.

Birthday Twins

If you ask people to tell you their birthdays (the month and the day), how many people do you think you'll have to ask before you find two people who are birthday twins?

Record your prediction: *I think I'll have to ask ___ people before finding birthday twins.*

Now try it and see. Take a poll. List each person's birthday. Stop when you get a match.

Record the outcome: *I asked ___ people before finding birthday twins.*

The Left-Handed Experiment

By taking a sample of some people in your school, can you determine approximately how many right-handed people there are for every left-handed person? Follow this procedure:

1. Find out how many people there are in your school.

2. Decide how many people you'll sample. Then ask this number of people, "Are you right-handed or left-handed?"

3. From this sample, figure out how many right-handed people there are for each left-handed person.

4. Now take a census to find out how many right-handed and left-handed people there actually are in the school. Visit each class and take a poll. Compile your results. How many right-handed people are there for each left-handed person in the entire school?

5. Compare the results of your sample with the census. Are they similar? Were you satisfied with your sampling procedure? If not, how would you improve the way you sampled? Write a report.

Extension

Investigate Other Topics. With a partner or small group, investigate other topics using the procedure outlined in *The Left-Handed Experiment.* Here are suggestions:

By sampling, determine approximately how many red-, blond-, brown-, and black-haired people there are in your school.

By sampling, decide how many people there are with each eye color.

Use sampling to determine the favorite TV show of students in your school.

The X-O Problem

You need: 3 small cards the same size, marked as follows:

> 1 with an X on both sides
> 1 with an O on both sides
> 1 with an X on one side and an O on the other side
> small paper bag

Put the three cards into the paper bag and play the following game.

Draw one card at random (without peeking) look at what's marked on just one side. Predict what you think is on the other side. Then turn the card over and check your prediction. You score a point if you predicted correctly.

Decide what would be a good strategy for predicting so that you would score the most points possible.

Test your strategy by playing the game thirty times. Keep track for each draw what you predicted and what was actually on the other side of the card. How many points did you score? Are you satisfied with your strategy?

Play again, trying another strategy if you like.

About the Mathematics

I found choosing a strategy for this problem perplexing. I first thought about the problem in a certain way, then decided I was wrong, and finally I decided on the strategy that would be most effective. I offer my experience to reinforce the concept that erroneous ideas are often opportunities that lead us to correct thinking.

My first idea was this: There are three cards—one with an X on both sides, one with an O on both sides, and one with an X on one side and an O on the other. OK, that means there are three Xs and three Os altogether. If I draw one card at random and look at what's marked on just one side, I "use up" one of the marks. So if I see an X, what's left are two Xs and three Os. And since there are more Os left, I'll predict that the other side of my card will be an O. If I see an O, then I'd predict the other side would have an X.

I tested my strategy by playing thirty times, as directed in the investigation, each time predicting the opposite of the mark that was showing. My prediction was correct less than half of the time. I played another thirty times, and the results were about the same. I wasn't satisfied.

I mulled over the situation. I talked with friends. I mulled some more. I was stuck, frustrated, and took a break from thinking about the problem. When I came back to it, I decided to try a different approach, one that had been suggested by a friend. Instead of focusing on the numbers of Xs and Os, her suggestion was to consider that two of the cards have the same mark on both sides—both X or both O—and only one card has a different mark on each side. When you draw one of the cards at random, she told me, there's a $\frac{1}{3}$ chance that you'll draw the card with an X on one side and an O on the other and a $\frac{2}{3}$ chance that you'll draw a card with the same mark on both sides. A probability of $\frac{2}{3}$ is twice as likely as a probability of $\frac{1}{3}$, so her advice was to predict the mark I saw.

I was skeptical, although I could see the logic of her approach. I just couldn't see why it was better than my initial idea. But I decided to try it by predicting, each time I drew, that the same mark I saw would be on the other side, assuming that two-thirds of the time I would draw a card with either X on both sides or O on both sides.

Again, I played thirty times, as directed in the activity, each time predicting the same mark as the one showing. My prediction was correct twenty-three times, more than two-thirds of the draws. I played another thirty times, and my prediction was correct eighteen times, less than two-thirds but more than half. Now I was satisfied that if I predicted what I saw I'd do better in the long run. When I compiled my data with the data others collected in their trials, I was even more convinced. Not only did I have a theoretical prediction that made sense, but the prediction was consistently supported by actual data. Case closed.

After doing this, I thought more about why my initial idea was wrong. I decided that thinking about the Xs and Os as separate entities didn't make sense since they weren't independent of the cards on which they were drawn. My idea would make sense if there were six cards, three marked X and three marked O, but my idea didn't relate to the game in this problem.

Also, I've observed teachers in professional development classes choosing strategies different from either of the two I tried. Some alternated predictions between X and O, not paying attention to what came up first, but sticking to an X, O, X, O pattern. One person tossed a coin each time, predicting X on heads and O on tails. Some predicted randomly, depending on a feeling for each draw, reasoning that it wouldn't make any difference because it was a game of chance. In these cases, while there were occasional short runs of success, overall results were dismal. Remember, the larger the sample, the more reliable the data to substantiate a prediction or theory.

The Two-Dice Sum Game

You need: counters, 11 per player
              1–6 dice, 2 per pair or group of students

This is a game for two or more players. Each player draws a number line from 2 to 12, with spaces between the numbers large enough so counters fit on the numbers.

Place your eleven counters on your number line in any arrangement. (You may put more than one counter on some numbers and none on others.)

Take turns rolling the dice. On each roll, every player removes one counter that's on the number that matches the sum of numbers that come up on the two dice. (If players have more than one counter on a sum, they may remove only one of them. If players don't have a counter on a sum, they don't do anything.) The winner is the first player to remove all eleven counters.

Decide on the best winning arrangement of counters on the number line. Explain your thinking.

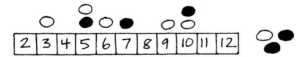

How Many Throws?

You need: 1–6 dice of two different colors, 1 per student
            individual charts as shown, 1 per student

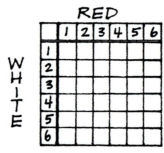

Work with a partner. One of you rolls the dice and makes a tally mark on the "How Many Throws?" chart for each throw. The other enters the sum that comes up in the correct space on the "White-Red" chart (unless it was already entered before). Notice that the colors are important. For example, red 3 and white 2 gives 5, red 2 and white 3 also gives 5, but you'd write the 5 in different boxes.

Throw the dice and record until you have filled in all but five of the sums on the "White-Red" chart.

Compare with others to see if you had similar blank sums.

About the Mathematics

My findings for this investigation are part of my commentary for the next investigation, *How Many Ways?* on page 191.

How Many Ways?

You need: chart, as shown

Complete the chart by filling in the possible outcomes for each sum when rolling two dice. Keep in mind, as in *How Many Throws?*, that 3, 1 is a different outcome from 1, 3.

Possible Totals	2	3	4	5	6	7	8	9	10	11	12
			2,2 3,1 1,3								
Total Ways			3								

After you complete the chart, add across the numbers in the bottom row (Total Ways). Did you get thirty-six? If not, there's a goof somewhere. Correct your work, asking for help if needed.

List the possible totals in order, from the sums with most possibilities to the sums with the fewest.

The probability of rolling a 7 is six chances out of the thirty-six possible outcomes. Mathematicians write this as $P(7) = \frac{6}{36}$ or $\frac{1}{6}$. Record the probability of rolling each of the other sums.

About the Mathematics

Following are my explanations for both the *How Many Throws?* investigation (page 190) and the previous investigation, *How Many Ways?*. The two investigations offer several ways to think about the probabilities that result from throwing two dice.

From experiences they've had playing games with dice, many people learn that when rolling two dice, it's less likely to get sums of 12 or 2 than sums of 6, 7, or 8. Also, some learn that in general it's less likely to get a sum by rolling a double; for example, it's less likely to get a sum of 8 from rolling two 4s than it is from rolling 5 and 3 or 6 and 2. Experience is an excellent teacher for building our intuition about probabilities. Collecting and analyzing data about rolling two dice as suggested in these activities helped me fully understand the probability involved.

In *How Many Throws?*, one of the charts presented is an addition table for adding the numbers 1 through 6 to get thirty-six sums. The investigation directs you to complete the chart by entering each sum as it comes up from throwing two dice and also to keep track of the number of throws it took to complete the entire chart. An important part of completing the chart is to use dice of different colors (red and white are suggested in the activity) or different sizes so that you can easily distinguish the dice and record sums correctly.

RED

	1	2	3	4	5	6
1	2	3	4	5	6	7
2	3	4	5	6	7	8
3	4	5	6	7	8	9
4	5	6	7	8	9	10
5	6	7	8	9	10	11
6	7	8	9	10	11	12

WHITE

Take the sum of 4, for example. You can get a sum of 4 by rolling 3 and 1 in two different ways—3 on the first die and 1 on the second die, or 1 on the first die and 3 on the second die. Each of these possibilities is represented by a different location on the addition table. Also, you can get a sum of 4 by rolling 2 on both dice. There's only one way for this to happen—2 on the first die and 2 on the second die—and therefore there's only one place on the chart to enter this sum. For the sum of 4, there are a total of three possible ways, with double 2s being half as likely as getting 3 and 1. Understanding this is the key to understanding the probabilities when throwing two dice.

When you complete the addition table, you've recorded all of the thirty-six equally likely outcomes possible when throwing two dice. Of these sums, you can count and see that the sum of 7 can be made in six different ways—more ways than any other sum, but not much more. The sums of 6 and 8 each come up in five different ways. The sums of 2 and 12 can each come up only one way either double 1s or double 6s. This is why it's more likely to roll sums of 6, 7, or 8 than 2 or 12. Of course, when throwing dice to complete the chart, you may roll sums of 2 or 12 several times each, but according to probability theory, in a large sample of rolls, 2 and 12 will each come up only about $\frac{1}{36}$ of the time, while the sum of 7 will come up $\frac{6}{36}$ (or $\frac{1}{6}$) of the time.

The probabilities of the sums are

$$P(2) = \frac{1}{36}$$

$$P(3) = \frac{2}{36}$$

$$P(4) = \frac{3}{36}$$

$$P(5) = \frac{4}{36}$$

$$P(6) = \frac{5}{36}$$

$$P(7) = \frac{6}{36}$$

$$P(8) = \frac{5}{36}$$

$$P(9) = \frac{4}{36}$$

$$P(10) = \frac{3}{36}$$

$$P(11) = \frac{2}{36}$$

$$P(12) = \frac{1}{36}$$

While 7 is your best bet when rolling two dice, a probability of $\frac{6}{36}$ means that you have only a $\frac{1}{6}$ chance of getting a sum of 7. These aren't very good odds, so take care when applying this knowledge.

The chart suggested for *How Many Ways?* is a different way of organizing the same information that appears on the addition table. Some people find it a clearer way to display what happens; others prefer the first way. One of the goals when studying mathematics is to learn to think flexibly, so it's a good exercise to try to make sense of both charts.

Possible Totals	2	3	4	5	6	7	8	9	10	11	12
	1,1	1,2 2,1	1,3 2,2 3,1	1,4 2,3 3,2 4,1	1,5 2,4 3,3 4,2 5,1	1,6 2,5 3,4 4,3 5,2 6,1	2,6 3,5 4,4 5,3 6,2	3,6 4,5 5,4 6,3	4,6 5,5 6,4	5,6 6,5	6,6
Total Ways	1	2	3	4	5	6	5	4	3	2	1

There are other ways of making sense and displaying the information about what happens when you roll two dice. For example, some people reason as follows: Suppose a 1 comes up on the first die. Then there are six possibilities for the second die—1, 2, 3, 4, 5, and 6. This accounts for six possible sums when a 1 comes up on the first die—2, 3, 4, 5, 6, and 7. If 2 comes up on the first die, again there are the same six possibilities for the second die—1, 2, 3, 4, 5, and 6. The possible sums with 2 on the first die are 3, 4, 5, 6, 7, and 8. Continuing in this way will identify the thirty-six possible sums. Below is a way to diagram this way of thinking, often called a tree diagram.

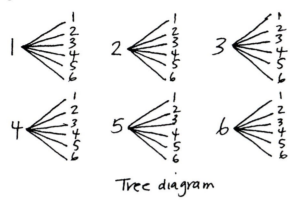

Tree diagram

To help students connect the tree diagram to the thirty-six possible sums, a friend said that she writes equations to show the six sums for each "tree." That is, on the first tree, she writes $1 + 1 = 2$ next to the first branch, $1 + 2 = 3$ next to the second branch, and so on to $1 + 6 = 7$ next to the bottom branch. Doing this for all the trees helps relate the sums to the addition table shown earlier on page 192.

How Many Rolls to Get a 1?

You need: 1–6 die

Roll a die until a 1 comes up. Record how many rolls it took. Do this five times.

Record your five results on the class chart.

HOW MANY ROLLS TO GET A 1?
Use tally marks to show your results.

1	11	21
2	12	22
3	13	23
4	14	24
5	15	25
6	16	26
7	17	27
8	18	28
9	19	29
10	20	more

Extension

How Many Rolls to Get a 6? Investigate how many rolls it takes to get a 6? Would the results be similar or different? How could you find out?

Teaching Tip

Teaching Tip
Create a class chart titled *How Many Rolls to Get a 1?* (as shown) for students to record their results. Then use the data for a classroom discussion. The data is useful for identifying the range, mean, mode, and median.

— MSB

Teaching Tip
After students have collected their individual data, lead a classroom discussion to see who set the record for the most rolls of two dice without getting doubles. One way to display class data is to list the numbers from 1 to 20 on the board and ask each student to come up and make a tally mark to indicate his or her greatest number of rolls before getting doubles. Add more numbers if someone rolled more than 20 times. If appropriate use the data to figure out the range, mean, mode, and median.

— MSB

What's the Record?

You need: 1–6 dice, 2 per student

Roll two dice until you get a double (two 1s, two 2s, and so on). As you roll, make tally marks to keep track of the how many times you roll before a double comes up. Record how many rolls it took. Repeat to collect more data.

Fair Game—Even and Odd Sums

You need: 1–6 dice, 2 per pair of students

Work with a partner. Take turns rolling the two dice. Player A scores a point if the sum is even. Player B scores a point if the sum is odd.

Is the game fair? If not, how could you make the game fair? Explain your reasoning.

Play the game again, this time figuring the product. Player A scores a point if the product is even. Player B scores a point if the product is odd.

Is the game fair? If not, how could you make the game fair? Explain your reasoning.

About the Mathematics

Two versions of this dice game are suggested. In the first, Player A scores a point if the sum is even and Player B scores a point if the sum is odd. There are eleven possible sums when rolling two dice—2, 3, 4, 5, 6, 7, 8, 9, 10, 11, and 12. Six of these sums are even and five of these sums are odd. But that's not enough information for deciding who has the advantage, because the sums aren't equally likely. You need to compare the combined probabilities for the even sums with the combined probabilities for the odd sums. For example, there is a $\frac{1}{36}$ chance of rolling a 2, a $\frac{3}{36}$ chance of rolling a 4, $\frac{5}{36}$ for 6, $\frac{5}{36}$ for 8, $\frac{3}{36}$ for 10, and $\frac{1}{36}$ for 12. Adding these results in a probability of $\frac{18}{36}$ for rolling an even sum. That's the same as $\frac{1}{2}$, leaving $\frac{1}{2}$ for rolling an odd sum. (You can check by adding the probabilities for the odd sums.) So this is a fair game.

Thinking about the products requires collecting new information about dice. I did this by creating a multiplication table that looked like the addition table suggested in *How Many Throws?* on page 190. The multiplication table not only reveals the possible products—1, 2, 3, 4, 5, 6, 8, 9, 10, 12, 15, 16, 18, 20, 24, 25, 30, and 36—but lets you count how often each product occurs. (Remember, you have to account for all thirty-six possible ways the dice can come up.)

But before listing and counting all the ways, I began to wonder if there was an easier way to think about the problem. (Mathematicians often—and gladly—spend more time seeking an "easier" way to solve a problem than it would take to do what's obvious but laborious.) I thought about what happens when you multiply even and odd numbers. If you multiply any number by an even number, the product will be even. That means that you get an even product from even x even, even x odd, and odd x even. The only time you get an odd product is when you multiply two odd numbers. So, hey, I'd rather have the even products. Forget the listing and counting of the thirty-six possibilities; I'm satisfied. Are you?

Tile Trading

You need: 2 paper bags (labeled A and B), 2 per student
        tiles, 15 red and 15 blue (or any two colors)

Place fifteen red tiles in Bag A and fifteen blue tiles in Bag B.

Without peeking, put one tile from A into B. Shake B.

Put one tile from B into A. Shake A.

Repeat, again moving one tile from A into B, and then from B into A.

If you continue until you have moved thirty tiles, predict how many of each you'll have in each bag after doing this:

A _____ red _____ blue

B _____ red _____ blue

Now do it. What was the outcome?

A _____ red _____ blue

B _____ red _____ blue

Try the experiment several more times. Discuss with others what you think "should happen." Note: You may want to move fewer tiles or more tiles.

Shake and Peek

You need: shake-and-peek box

Work with a partner. Shake the box, tilt so a marble falls into the corner, and record the color you see. Repeat many times. Stop when you and your partner feel you have a sufficient number of samples to predict what's in the box. (Hint: The box has ten beads.)

Teaching Tip
For Shake and Peek, you need to make several small boxes, each containing ten marbles of two colors, taped shut, with a corner cut out not large enough for a marble to fit through but large enough to be able to view its color. Do not reveal to the students how many of each color marble is in each box. I usually make several boxes with different combinations of colors, labeling them A, B, C, and so on. I use the same letter for boxes with duplicate combinations of marbles.

— MSB

Shake and Spill

You need: two-color counters, 6 per student

If you spill six two-color counters, there are seven possibilities of what might come up—6 red, 5 red and 1 yellow, 4 red and 2 yellow, 3 red and 3 yellow, 2 red and 4 yellow, 1 red and 5 yellow, 6 yellow. If you shake and spill the counters twenty-five times, do you think you'll get one result more often than the others? If so, what will it be? Why do you think that?

Try it, spilling the counters at least twenty-five times and keeping track of what comes up each time.

Extension

Other Numbers. Try the experiment with other numbers of counters.

About the Mathematics

In this problem, you investigate what to expect when you shake and spill six two-color counters. Here are seven possible outcomes from shaking and spilling six counters:

6 yellow — ○ ○ ○ ○ ○ ○
5 yellow, 1 red — ○ ○ ○ ○ ○ ●
4 yellow, 2 red — ○ ○ ○ ○ ● ●
3 yellow, 3 red — ○ ○ ○ ● ● ●
2 yellow, 4 red — ○ ○ ● ● ● ●
1 yellow, 5 red — ○ ● ● ● ● ●
6 red — ● ● ● ● ● ●

Shaking and spilling the six counters twenty-five times typically produces evidence that these outcomes are not equally likely. Six yellow or six red come up much less frequently than either three yellow and three red, or four of one color and two of the other.

To understand why this is so, it may help to think about what happens when you shake and spill just one counter. For each counter there are two possibilities—red or yellow—and a fifty-fifty chance for either to come up. The two possibilities are equally likely. With six counters, however, and an equal chance for each counter to come up yellow or red, it's rare for all six to come up the same color on the same spill. It's more likely that some of the six counters will come up yellow and some will come up red.

Does this mean that there's a fifty-fifty chance that you'll get three yellow and three red when you shake and spill six counters? No, it's not that simple.

If you're interested in learning about figuring the probabilities of three yellow and three red, all red, four yellow and two red, or any of the other possibilities, the "About the Mathematics" notes under *Two-Coin Toss* offers an explanation (see page 197). But to help set the stage for your thinking, first try the *Two-Coin Toss* investigation that follows.

Two-Coin Toss

You need: coins of two different denominations, 1 of each

Toss two coins together twenty-five times. After each toss, record what comes up—two heads, two tails, or one head and one tail. What do you think will result?

Prediction: two heads _____ two tails _____

one head/one tail _____

Outcome: two heads _____ two tails _____

one head/one tail _____

About the Mathematics

Two-Coin Toss is similar to doing *Shake and Spill* (page 196) with only two counters. That's because coins and two-color counters both have two equally likely possibilities—heads and tails, or red and yellow. You can say that there's a fifty-fifty chance a coin will come up heads, or that the probability of a coin coming up heads is $\frac{1}{2}$. The same is true for tails.

When tossing two coins, or two two-color counters, there are three possibilities:

two heads	two yellow
one head, one tail	one yellow, one red
two tails	two red

But these possibilities are not equally likely. That's because there's only one way of getting two of the same—both have to come up heads or yellow, or tails or red. But when one of each comes up—one head and one tail, or one yellow and one red, there are two different ways this can happen. To understand why this is so, think about tossing two different coins, a penny and a nickel, for example. For one head and one tail to come up, it either can be heads on the penny and tails on the nickel or vice versa. If you were tossing two pennies, unless they had different dates and you noted them, it wouldn't be obvious that there are two ways for one head and one tail to come up.

Mathematically, this translates to four equally likely outcomes when tossing two coins:

two heads

heads on Coin 1, tails on Coin 2

tails on Coin 1, heads on Coin 2

two tails

This means that there's a $\frac{1}{4}$ chance that both coins will come up heads, a $\frac{1}{4}$ chance that both will come up tails, and a ½ chance that one will come up heads and the other tails. (Note that the sum of the probabilities of all the equally likely possibilities for tossing two coins—$\frac{1}{4} + \frac{1}{4} + \frac{1}{2}$—adds to 1. The same holds true for tossing only one coin—$\frac{1}{2} + \frac{1}{2}$ adds to 1. The sum of the probabilities of all the equally likely possibilities always adds to 1.)

These probabilities don't imply that if you toss two coins four times, then both heads are sure to come up once, both tails once, and one of each twice. The probabilities are theoretical. They imply, but do not guarantee, that if you toss two coins many times, you can expect them to land with one head and one tail showing about twice as often as landing with

About the Math
In my experience, students know that if you toss just one coin, there are two possibilities—heads and tails. If you toss two coins, they typically think that there are possibilities—both heads, both tails, or one of each. However, with two coins, there are four equally likely possibilities. Read the "About the Mathematics" explanation to understand this.

—MBB

two heads showing or two tails showing, and that two heads or two tails should come up about the same number of times.

Let's go back to thinking about two-color counters. As I wrote earlier in my finings, *Two-Coin Toss* is similar to doing *Shake and Spill* (page 196) with only two counters. Shaking and spilling two counters is mathematically the same as tossing two coins—there are four equally likely outcomes. In order for this to make sense, it may help if you thought about labeling the two counters so you could tell one from the other, perhaps by writing a small 1 on both sides of one of them and a small 2 on both sides of the other. The four equally likely outcomes and the probability of each are:

two yellow ($\frac{1}{4}$)

yellow on Counter 1, red on Counter 2 ($\frac{1}{4}$)

red on Counter 1, yellow on Counter 2 ($\frac{1}{4}$)

two red ($\frac{1}{4}$)

Labeling helps you make an accurate count of what really is possible. Without labeling the counters 1 and 2, the two different ways that one of each color would come up would be indistinguishable, but it would still be a more likely possibility:

two yellow ($\frac{1}{4}$)

one yellow, one red ($\frac{2}{4}$, or $\frac{1}{2}$)

two red ($\frac{1}{4}$)

Now let's think about shaking and spilling three counters. Labeling them 1, 2, and 3 helps you list all of the equally likely possibilities:

three yellow

yellow on Counters 1 and 2, red on Counter 3

yellow on Counters 1 and 3, red on Counter 2

yellow on Counters 2 and 3, red on Counter 1

yellow on Counter 1, red on Counters 2 and 3

yellow on Counter 2, red on Counters 1 and 3

yellow on Counter 3, red on Counters 1 and 2

three red

There are eight equally likely possibilities, so each has a probability of $\frac{1}{8}$.

Ignoring which counters come up which color but instead looking at the number of counters that come up red or yellow, I could combine the possibilities into four categories, and also

combine the probabilities:

three yellow ($\frac{1}{8}$)

two yellow, one red ($\frac{3}{8}$)

one yellow, two red ($\frac{3}{8}$)

three red ($\frac{1}{8}$)

Adding the probabilities—$\frac{1}{8} + \frac{3}{8} + \frac{3}{8} + \frac{1}{8}$—produces 1, ensuring that I've taken into account all the possible outcomes.

You can continue in this way to analyze what happens when shaking and spilling four two-color counters, then five, and finally six. Here's how I analyzed the situation for six two-color counters:

six yellow ($\frac{1}{64}$)

five yellow, one red ($\frac{6}{64}$)

four yellow, two red ($\frac{15}{64}$)

three yellow, three red ($\frac{20}{64}$)

two yellow, four red ($\frac{15}{64}$)

one yellow, five red ($\frac{6}{64}$)

six red ($\frac{1}{64}$)

While it's more likely for three of each color to come up than any other possibility, the probability of getting three yellow and three red is $\frac{20}{64}$, which is closer to a probability of $\frac{1}{3}$ than it is to $\frac{1}{2}$.

If you follow my reasoning, congratulations (to both of us)! If not, then you may need more time, more experience, the help of a friend, or another way to look at the situation. We all learn in our own ways and on our own timetables.

One more mathematical connection that may help: Instead of writing lists of the possibilities for shaking and spilling different numbers of counters, I could arrange the possibilities in a way that produces interesting patterns. For two counters, for example, I could arrange the possibilities like this:

YY   YR   RR
      RY

For three counters, I put those with two yellows and one red in one column, and those with two reds and one yellow in another:

YYY   YYR   YRR   RRR
       YRY   RYR
       RYY   RRY

For four counters, I would arrange the possibilities like this:

YYYY   YYYR   YYRR   YRRR   RRRR
        YYRY   YRYR   RYRR
        YRYY   YRRY   RRYR
        RYYY   RYRY   RRRY
                RYYR
                RRYY

Now examine the number of entries in each column in relation to the probabilities for the possibilities. For two counters, the probabilities for each of the three columns are $\frac{1}{4}$, $\frac{2}{4}$, and $\frac{1}{4}$. For three counters, the probabilities for the columns are $\frac{1}{8}$, $\frac{3}{8}$, $\frac{3}{8}$, and $\frac{1}{8}$. For four counters, since there are sixteen possibilities altogether, the probabilities for the columns are $\frac{1}{16}$, $\frac{4}{16}$, $\frac{6}{16}$, $\frac{4}{16}$, and $\frac{1}{16}$. (Try it for five counters and see how the pattern extends.)

The arrangement of numbers below is what's called Pascal's Triangle:

The numbers in this pattern relate to the way I arranged the possibilities above and the numerators of their probabilities! For example, the numbers in the fourth row of Pascal's Triangle are the numerators of the combined probabilities for shaking and spilling three counters—$\frac{1}{8}, \frac{3}{8}, \frac{3}{8}, \frac{1}{8}$. For five counters, the numbers are 1, 5, 10, 10, 5, and 1. And if you extend Pascal's Triangle, the next row has the numbers 1, 6, 15, 20, 15, 6, and 1—the numerators of the probabilities for shaking and spilling six counters listed earlier. Connections like these help us see how mathematical ideas relate to one another. And while figuring the probabilities generates the numbers in Pascal's Triangle, you can also continue the pattern of numbers by adding any two adjacent numbers to get the number underneath. Try to figure out how extending Pascal's Triangle can help you think about what happens when you shake and spill more than six counters.

For a more detailed explanation of how to use *The Game of Pig* in the classroom, see *A Number Game: The Game of Pig* in Part 3 on page 366.

The Game of Pig

You need: 1–6 dice, 2 per pair of students

This is a game for two or more players. The goal of the game is to be the first to reach 100.

Players take turns. On a turn, you roll the dice as many times as you like, mentally keeping a running total of the sum. When you decide to stop rolling, record the total for that turn and add it to the total from previous turns.

The catch: If a 1 comes up on one of the dice, the player's turn automatically ends and the player scores 0 for that round. If 1s come up on both dice, not only does the turn end, but the player's total accumulated score so far returns to 0.

After becoming familiar with the game, write a strategy for winning.

Fair Game—Paper, Scissors, Rock

Play this game with a group of four: three players and one recorder. Decide who will record and who is Player A, Player B, and Player C.

All players make a fist and on the count of four, each player shows either:

> paper (by showing an open hand, face down)
>
> scissors (by showing two fingers)
>
> rock (by showing a fist)

Play the game twenty times with these rules:

Player A gets a point if all players show the same sign.

Player B gets a point if only two players show the same sign.

Player C gets a point if all players show different signs.

Tally the winning points:

Player	Tally	Total
A		
B		
C		

Is this game fair? Which player would you rather be? How could you make the game more fair?

About the Mathematics

This game of *Paper, Scissors, Rock* as described is not fair! One way to analyze why is first to account for all of the equally likely possibilities and then see which player has an advantage.

There are three possibilities for what each person shows on a turn—scissors, paper, or rock. A player could show the same sign over and over again, but to analyze the game, you need to think of them as three equally likely random choices.

To analyze the possibilities, I made a list using *p*, *s*, and *r* to stand for paper, scissors, and rock. I also labeled three columns *A*, *B*, and *C* to represent the three players. And I followed a pattern to help be sure that I've found all of the possibilities. I listed the following twenty-seven equally likely possibilities.

In these twenty-seven possibilities, the same sign comes up only three times, a probability of $\frac{3}{27}$. (I marked these with an asterisk.) Two players showing the same sign comes up eighteen times, a probability of $\frac{18}{27}$. All players showing different signs comes up six times, a probability of $\frac{6}{27}$. (I marked these with an exclamation point.) To be sure that I counted correctly, I added the three probabilities—$\frac{3}{27} + \frac{18}{27} + \frac{6}{27}$. The sum is 1, which indicates that I've accounted for all of the possibilities. To make the game fair, you either need to decide on new rules that give each person the same chance of winning or keep the rules as they are and change the number of points each person gets when his option comes up.

```
A  B  C
p  p  p   *
p  p  r
p  p  s
p  r  p
p  r  r
p  r  s   !
p  s  p
p  s  r   !
p  s  s
r  p  p
r  p  r
r  p  s   !
r  r  p
r  r  r   *
r  r  s
r  s  p   !
r  s  r
r  s  s
s  p  p
s  p  r   !
s  p  s
s  r  p   !
s  r  r
s  r  s
s  s  p
s  s  r
s  s  s   *
```

Teaching Tip
After students have tried
the investigation, lead a
classroom discussion. Before
the discussion, it's helpful
to have students write
summary statements about
what they noticed. See page
137 for information about
using summary statements.

— MSB

The Popcorn Problem

You need: cubes, 1 each of six colors
          paper bag

A popcorn company found that sales improved when prizes were put in the popcorn boxes. They decided to include a felt-tip pen in every box and to use pens in six different colors. The company bought equal numbers of pens in each color and were careful when shipping popcorn to stores to send boxes with the same number of each color pen. When you buy a box, you have an equal chance of finding any one of the six colors of pens inside.

About how many boxes of popcorn do you need to buy to have a good chance of getting a complete set of six different-colored pens? Write about your reasoning.

Try the following investigation to simulate the situation: Put six different-colored cubes to represent the pens into a bag. Reach into the bag and, without looking, draw a cube. Note its color and replace it.

Continue until you have drawn out one of each color, keeping track of the number of draws you make. (How many draws do you think will be needed?)

Repeat the investigation. Then compile results from other class members.

Extension

A Second Experiment. Repeat the simulation, this time putting sixty cubes in the sack, ten each of six colors. Compare the results with the first simulation.

Problem-Solving Investigations: Geometry

(continued)

> **About the Mathematics**
>
> This icon indicates that I've written a mathematical commentary for the investigation. I've written these explanations in response to queries from teachers asking for math help with particular problems. I encourage you to try the investigation first before reading my explanation.
>
> — MSB

(continued from page 203)

Why Teach Geometry?

In the elementary grades, instruction in geometry provides for the development of the concepts of shape, size, symmetry, congruence, and similarity in both two-dimensional and three-dimensional spaces. Experiences begin with familiar objects and utilize a wide variety of concrete materials to develop appropriate vocabulary and to build understanding. In middle school instruction, more formal generalizations in geometric relationships are emphasized. The investigations in this section are designed to provide problem-solving experiences in geometry that help students develop understanding of geometric properties and relationships.

Young children have many geometric experiences before entering school. They spend a great deal of time exploring, playing, and building with shapes. In their play experiences, children encounter relationships among shapes naturally. They sort and re-sort objects in a variety of ways. They make discoveries about how some blocks fit together and others don't. They learn about shapes that roll, slide, or do neither.

These initial investigations should be nurtured and extended in students' school learning of mathematics. In their classroom experiences, students should have opportunities to explore shapes and the relationships among them. They benefit from problem-solving investigations that lead them to notice patterns and structures in shapes and to develop reasoning processes in spatial contexts. They need experiences that relate geometry to ideas in measurement, number, and patterns. Through these kinds of investigations, students grasp how mathematics adds to their understanding of the world.

Although elementary mathematics instruction has always included geometry, the major emphasis in elementary mathematics has always been on number and operations. This sometimes results in geometry being perceived as less important. Also, many teachers remember geometry as a high school subject that dealt mainly with formal proofs and complicated terminology.

However, geometry is a significant branch of mathematics, the one most visible in the physical world. Developing spatial ability has applications in everyday life, a fact that any adult encounters when having to figure quantities for wallpaper, floor covering, paint, fabric, lawn needs, or a myriad of other home projects. Geometric concepts and relationships are also essential to many branches of industry, the building trades, interior design, architecture, as well as other work situations. Geometry is an integral and vibrant part of mathematics instruction.

Stages in Learning About Geometry

When planning classroom geometry investigations, it's helpful to consider four stages in learning:

> **STAGES IN LEARNING GEOMETRY**
>
> 1. Recognizing shapes in real-world objects.
> 2. Noticing properties of shapes.
> 3. Describing shapes by their properties.
> 4. Categorizing shapes.

1. **Recognizing shapes in real-world objects.**

   Students first see shapes in the contexts of objects in their worlds—a rectangle looks like a door, a circle looks like a plate, a triangle looks like a cracker, the checkerboard has squares on it, and so on. These contexts define their initial engagement, not the properties of the shapes themselves.

2. **Noticing properties of shapes.**

   Young students first notice the number of sides shapes have, for example that rectangles and squares have four sides and triangles have three sides. Later they expand these ideas and become aware of other components of shapes—some rectangles are long and thin, a shape with three sides but is "upside down" (with the point at the bottom instead of at the top) is still a triangle.

3. **Describing shapes by their properties.**

   Through instructional experiences, students begin to use the properties of shapes to describe and categorize them. For example, they focus on the lengths of sides of shapes, and think about rectangles as having opposite sides the same length while squares have all four sides the same length. Or they focus on the angles of shapes to describe rectangles and squares as having four right angles, but learn that a triangle can't have all right angles.

4. **Categorizing shapes.**

   At this stage, students see relationships among different categories of shapes and learn to describe them. For example, polygons are all closed figures with straight sides; quadrilaterals are polygons that share the same characteristic of having four sides; squares and rectangles are quadrilaterals (and, therefore, polygons) and share the same characteristic of having four right angles; squares are special kinds of rectangles because they have four sides of equal length. These more abstract ideas about geometric shapes give students access to higher-level geometry.

Mathematical Practices

The investigation and study of geometry support the development of the mathematical practices described in the Common Core and other standards documents for students in all grades. The mathematical practices should be connected to the content standards by engaging students in solving problems, reasoning, making conjectures, applying math to everyday life, using appropriate tools, communicating precisely, looking for patterns and structure, and looking for regularity in mathematical methods. The investigations in this section provide ways to make connections between practice and content standards.

Mathematical Content

It's helpful to understand which geometry concepts and skills are appropriate for different grade levels. Below are content designations that align with the Common Core and other standards documents.

Kindergarten: Identify and describe shapes in their environment using their names and positions (above, below, in front of, etc.); compare shapes according to their sizes, similarities, and differences; build shapes with materials.

Grade 1: Reason with shapes and their attributes by building and drawing shapes with different attributes; compose shapes from other shapes; partition circles and rectangles into two and four equal shares.

Grade 2: Continue to reason with shapes and their attributes, now recognizing and drawing shapes with defined attributes (e.g., number of sides or angles); identify triangles, quadrilaterals, pentagons, hexagons, and cubes; partition circles and rectangles into two, three, and four equal shares and use terminology of halves, thirds, and fourths.

Grade 3: Continue to reason with shapes and their attributes, now learning that shapes in different categories may share properties (e.g., rectangles and parallelograms have four sides); partition shapes into parts with equal areas and express a part as a fraction of the whole.

Grade 4: Draw and identify lines and angles, and classify shapes by properties of their lines and angles; recognize figures with lines of symmetry.

Grade 5: Graph points on the coordinate plane to solve real-world and mathematical problems; classify two-dimensional figures into categories based on their properties.

Grade 6: Solve real-world and mathematical problems involving area, surface area, and volume.

Grade 7: Draw, construct, and describe geometrical figures; describe the relationships between them; solve real-life and mathematical problems involving angle measure, area, surface area, and volume.

Grade 8: Understand congruence and similarity using physical models, transparencies, or geometry software; understand and apply the Pythagorean theorem; solve real-world and mathematical problems involving volume of cylinders, cones, and spheres.

Sample Whole-Class Lessons

The following two sample lessons describe, in detail, hands-on investigations that help students develop understanding and skills with geometry. The first lesson engages students with pentominoes, which are shapes made from arranging five squares; the second lesson, investigating shapes made from arranging four triangles, works for students in grades 1 and up. Each uses the Introducing/Exploring/Summarizing model for problem-solving lessons.

 **Sample Lesson**

Pentominoes

This hands-on geometry investigation engages students in searching for possible arrangements of five squares, a geometric visualization task. Students also face the challenge of deciding when they've found all possible arrangements, which requires the use of logical reasoning.

Materials

square tiles (about 1 inch on a side), 5 per student
one-inch grid paper ruled into squares the same size as the tiles, 2 sheets per small group of students **R** See Reproducible R.4

Introducing

1. **Present or review concepts.** Three points are important here. First, explain and demonstrate the rule for making shapes with square tiles: One whole side of each square must touch at least one whole side of another. Draw the following examples on the board to illustrate:

Second, explain how to decide if two shapes are the same or different. Draw the following shapes on the board:

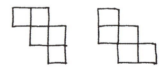

To demonstrate how to decide if two shapes like these are the same or different, first draw each on grid paper and cut them out. (This also models for the students how to record and cut their shapes.) Demonstrate how you can flip and rotate the two shapes until they fit exactly one on top of the other. Explain that when two shapes are exactly the same size and shape, they are called *congruent* and are considered to be the same.

Finally, discuss the word *pentomino*. Show the students a domino or draw a picture of a domino on the board. Point out that it's made of two squares. Explain that a pentomino is a five-square version of a domino. If students are familiar with pentagons, point

For the sample lessons, I used the Introducing/Exploring/Summarizing model for problem-solving lessons, described on page 135.

FYI
I've found that students who struggle numerically often experience success with this spatial investigation. This gives me the opportunity to reinforce for the class that there are many different aspects to mathematics, and we all differ in how we respond to them.
— MBB

Vocabulary Suggestion
If you don't have a chart posted for math vocabulary, this is a good time to begin a Math Words chart. List congruent and pentomino. Use this terminology whenever there's an opportunity.
— MBB

out that *pent* indicates that pentagons have five sides, just as pentominos are made from five squares.

2. **Pose a part of the problem or a similar but smaller problem.** Ask students, *Suppose you were trying to find all the different arrangements of three squares instead of five squares, following the rule that one whole side of each square has to match at least one whole side of another. What shapes are possible?* Have students try this. There are only two possible shapes and they're called *triominoes*: ⬚⬚⬚ and ⬚⬚.

   Have them use tiles to make all the different arrangements of four squares. (There are five possible *tetrominoes*.)

3. **Present the investigation.** Ask pairs or groups to find all of the different ways to arrange five squares into pentominoes. Direct them to use the tiles to make shapes, draw them on the grid paper, and cut them out. Remind them to use the flip-and-rotate test to be sure that each of their shapes is different.

4. **Discuss the task to make sure students understand what they are to do.** Ask a few students to explain to the class what they are to do. Then ask for questions.

Exploring

1. **Observe the interaction, listening to how groups organize working together, the ideas they discuss, and the strategies they use.**

2. **Offer assistance when needed.** Two situations typically arise during the investigation. You may notice that some students have cut out congruent shapes but think they are different. In that case, comment that you notice that some of their shapes are congruent, and leave them to find them.

   The second situation arises when students feel they have found all the possible shapes and ask if they have them all. I typically respond that we'll talk about this together when all groups are ready and I encourage them to look for a way to analyze their arrangements to see if they have all that are possible. At times, to encourage groups who haven't found them all, I'll tell them that there still are more, but I don't tell how many. Or, if a group has cut out more than twelve shapes and thinks they're all different, I tell them that their set includes at least one pair of congruent shapes.

3. **Provide an extension to groups that finish more quickly than others.**

Summarizing

1. **Have pairs or groups review their work and think about what to report in a classroom discussion.** If they haven't written summary statements to describe what they noticed and learned, ask them to do so now.

2. **Initiate a classroom discussion.** First have groups report how they organized working together. Ask students to report how they found different shapes and decided who would cut out the pieces.

Teaching Tip
One question I'm asked regularly by teachers is whether to reveal to the students the number of possible shapes. (There are twelve pentominoes.) As a general rule, I don't reveal this until after groups have grappled with the investigation and we've had a whole-class discussion. My reason is to keep the focus on the investigation, not on racing for a correct answer.
— MBB

Extensions
Suggestions for building on and extending students' experiences with pentominoes can be found under "Independent Investigations" on page 222. When teaching this whole-class lesson, a particularly good investigation to offer groups who finish more quickly than others is *Pentomino One-Difference Loop* (page 240), which is easy to explain and doesn't require any additional materials. Other extensions include *Making Topless Boxes* (page 240), *The Pentomino Game* (page 240), and *Milk Carton Geometry* (page 240), which you can use with the whole class, as small-group or partner investigations, or as a choice time exploration. (See "Starting Point 20: Four Structures for Organizing and Managing Classroom Instruction" in Part 1 on page 111.)

3. **Have groups report their results or solutions, explaining their reasoning or strategies.** Ask a pair or group to choose one of their pentominoes and post it on the board. Then ask a second pair or group to post a different pentomino. Continue around the room, having pairs or groups post a different pentomino (or pass if they don't have a different pentomino to offer). Continue until all twelve pentominoes have been posted, or until no one has a different pentomino to post. If some pentominoes are missing, give students the chance to investigate further.

4. **Generalize from the solutions.** Review the meaning of congruence.

Sample Lesson

The Four-Triangle Problem

This problem is an extremely versatile investigation that I've taught to classes of first graders and on up to middle school. The investigation helps students explore geometric concepts, learn geometric vocabulary in context, and develop spatial reasoning skills. Since the four triangles used in the investigation come from cutting squares on the diagonal, leaving one of the square's right angles intact in each triangle, they all are right triangles. Also, all of the triangles are the same size, making them congruent right triangles. It's possible to arrange four congruent right triangles into a larger right triangle, five noncongruent quadrilaterals, two noncongruent pentagons, and six noncongruent hexagons.

Materials

3-inch squares of construction paper in two colors, about 150 of each color works for a class of 24 students
18-by-24-inch newsprint, 1 sheet per pair of students
6-by-9-inch newsprint, several sheets per student (optional)

Introducing

1. **Present or review concepts.** Begin by showing students how to cut one of the 3-inch squares in half on the diagonal to make two triangles. Point out that each triangle has a square corner. For older students, introduce or reinforce the standard terminology: a square corner is a *right angle* and a triangle with a right angle is a *right triangle*.

2. **Pose a part of the problem or a similar but smaller problem.** Ask each student to cut a square as you did and explore different ways to put the triangles together, following the rule that two edges the same size must be matched. Have them tape the triangles together or paste them onto 6-by-9-inch newsprint and then cut out the shape. Post an example of each of the three possible shapes—square, triangle, and parallelogram.

3. **Present the investigation.** Working in pairs, students each take a different color square, cut it into two right triangles, and then together arrange their four triangles into a shape following the same rule of matching edges that are the same length. Have them either tape each four-triangle shape they make or paste it on newsprint that you've cut into 6-by-9-inch pieces and cut it out.

4. **Discuss the task to make sure students understand what they are to do.**

Exploring

1. **Observe the interaction, listening to how groups organize working together, the ideas they discuss, and the strategies they use.** Circulate to be sure that all students are successful making one four-triangle shape.

2. **Offer assistance when needed.** Sometimes students feel they have found all the possible shapes. When this occurs, I do a quick count and, if there are fewer than fourteen, I tell them to keep looking for more. I don't reveal how many there are but just encourage them to keep exploring. Also, if I notice that students have made two shapes that are the same, I point this out by placing one on top of the other to show they are the same.

3. **Provide an extension to groups that finish more quickly than others.** When groups have found all the shapes while others are still working, I ask them to sort their shapes by the numbers of sides they have. To explain, I choose one of their shapes and model how to count the sides.

Summarizing

1. **Have pairs or groups review their work and think about what to report in a classroom discussion.** If they haven't written summary statements to describe what they noticed and learned, ask them to do so now.

2. **Initiate a classroom discussion.** First have groups report how they organized working together.

3. **Have groups report their results.** To do this, ask a pair or group to choose one of their four triangle shapes and post it on the board. Then ask a second pair or group to post a different shape. Continue around the room, having pairs or groups post a different shape (or pass if they don't have a different shape to contribute). Continue until all fourteen shapes have been posted, or until no one has a different shape to post.

On chart paper, list the numbers 3, 4, 5, and 6 and tell the class that you'd like to sort their shapes depending on the number of sides they have. Choose one of the posted shapes and demonstrate counting its sides. Tape or paste it on the chart paper next to the correct number. Have students move the other shapes, calling on students to come up and move one at a time. (See the illustration that follows for all of the shapes sorted.)

Vocabulary Suggestion
Add square, triangle, and parallelogram to the Math Words chart and make a sketch of each. Use this terminology whenever there's an opportunity. —MSB

Extensions
To build on and extend students' experiences with this investigation, try the whole-class lesson *Rotating Shapes* on page 238. See "Independent Investigations" for other extensions, which you can use with the whole class, as small-group or partner investigations, or as a choice time exploration. (See also "Starting Point 20: Four Structures for Organizing and Managing Classroom Instruction" in Part 1 on page 111.)

4. Generalize from the solutions. Finally, introduce the geometric vocabulary. Title the chart Polygons and write *triangle*, *quadrilateral*, *pentagon*, and *hexagon* next to the numbers. Add the new vocabulary to the Math Words chart.

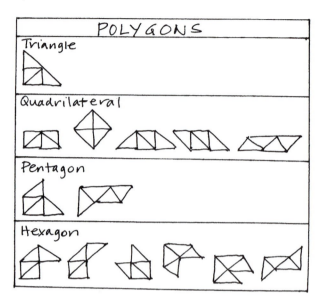

Additional Investigations for Whole-Class Lessons

In this section I include suggestions for additional investigations that are suitable for whole-class lessons. In contrast to the "Independent Investigations" section that follows on page 222, these ideas especially lend themselves to whole-class engagement and to the collection and comparison of the groups' results. These additional investigations aren't presented in the three-phase Introducing/Exploring/Summarizing lesson structure but rather are general ideas.

Introductory Investigations with Pattern Blocks

Materials
pattern blocks, 1 set per group of 4–6 students
9-by-12-inch construction paper, 1 per student

The Lesson
The following suggestions are useful for giving students the opportunity to become familiar with pattern blocks, satisfy their curiosity about the material, and prepare them for other pattern block investigations. Distribute pattern blocks and ask students to explore with them and see how many different shapes and colors there are. After a few minutes, interrupt them and ask, *What did you notice about the pattern blocks?* Introduce the correct terminology for each piece: *triangle*, *square*, both *parallelogram* and *rhombus*, *trapezoid*, and *hexagon*.

Then engage them with the following investigations.

1. Make a floor, covering as large an area as you'd like. Try it using blocks that are different kinds. Then see if you can do it using only one kind of block. Will all blocks work?

2. Make a straight road using only one kind of block. Can you do this with each different block? Which of your roads can you make turn a corner?

3. Make a design with the pattern blocks on a piece of construction paper. Trace around the outside of your design with a marker. List how many of each block you used. Exchange papers with classmates to see if you can fit the proper pieces into each other's designs.

4. Try building a larger triangle using only green triangles. Try building a larger square using only orange squares. Try the same with each of the other pieces. Which work and which do not?

5. Try building a shape exactly the same as (congruent to) the yellow hexagon using only green triangles. Try this with each of the other pieces. Which work and which do not?

6. If the area of the green triangle has the value of 1 unit, find the value of the area of the blue, red, and yellow pieces. Do the same with the area of the blue diamond as 1 unit, and then again with the red and yellow pieces as 1 unit.

7. Compare the areas of the orange and white pieces. Convince a friend of your comparison.

See Reproducible R.1 for a template you can print and use for organizing the additional investigations into the three-phase lesson structure. Downloadable at mathsolutions.com/ atm4theditionreproducibles

Vocabulary Suggestion
If you don't have a chart posted for math vocabulary, this is a good time to begin a Math Words chart. If you have a chart, list the new terminology and make a sketch for each. Use the words regularly as students explore the pattern blocks.
— MSB

Teaching Tip
Introducing pattern blocks reminds me of how important it is to provide students time to explore materials. Without time to satisfy their curiosity, it's hard for them to focus on tasks without being distracted. I've learned that exploring time is time well spent.
— MSB

Teaching Tip
Either give students the directions one by one and allow time for them to explore, or post the directions and allow students to go at their own pace. I've done both, depending on the class. If students can work well independently, I find giving them the list works well.
— MSB

Teaching Tip
Suggestions 6 and 7 are only suitable for older students who have had experience figuring areas of shapes.
— MSB

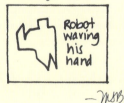
The Tangram Puzzle

Materials
6-inch squares of construction paper, 1 per student

The Lesson
The tangram puzzle is a square cut into seven pieces. The directions that follow show how to cut the square into two pairs of congruent triangles, one middle-size triangle, one square, and one parallelogram. Distribute 6-inch squares of construction paper to students and have them follow along as you demonstrate how they can cut their own puzzles.

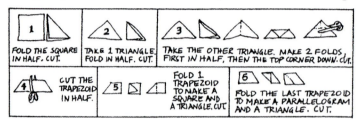

When students all have their seven pieces cut, continue as follows:
1. Ask students to arrange three triangles—the pair of small triangles and the middle-size triangle—into a square. Draw a chart as shown and sketch the shape.

2. Then ask them to arrange the same triangles into a triangle, a rectangle, a trapezoid, and a parallelogram. As students find shapes, sketch them on the chart.

3. Continue with arranging five pieces of the tangram puzzle (all but the two large triangles) to make the same shapes.

4. Repeat with all seven pieces.

Extensions
Tangram Areas and Perimeters. Use the two small congruent triangles to compare the areas of the square, the parallelogram, and the middle-size triangle. Then compare their perimeters.

Using All Seven. Find the thirteen different convex shapes you can make with the seven Tangram pieces.

Making Squares. You can show a square with just one tangram piece or arrange all seven into a square. What about making a square using two, three, four, five, or six pieces? One of those is impossible. Which is it, and why isn't it possible?

About the Mathematics

Extension 1: Tangram Areas and Perimeters
This investigation offers another way to look at the mathematical ideas in the measurement investigations of *Square Up* on page 236, *Double the*

Circumference on page 163, and *The Area Stays the Same* on page 165. The tangram pieces allow you to think about how area and perimeter relate by comparing shapes instead of resorting to standard units of measurement.

To compare the areas of the square, parallelogram, and middle-size triangle, rearrange the two small triangles to make each shape. The areas of these three shapes are the same. Then match their edges to compare their perimeters. The parallelogram and middle-size triangle have the same-length perimeters, but the perimeter of the square is shorter. This is because the same amount of area is squashed together more compactly in a square, requiring less perimeter. If you rearranged the same area into a long, skinny rectangle, you'd need a longer "fence" to surround it and the perimeter would therefore be longer. If you made a circle of the same area, however, the circle's circumference would be shorter than even the square's perimeter—the circle is the most economical shape for minimizing the distance around.

Extension 2: Using All Seven

This investigation asks you to use all seven pieces of the tangram to make different convex shapes. A convex shape is one with all of its interior angles measuring less than 180 degrees. Shapes with at least one interior angle greater than 180 degrees are called concave. Students have told me that concave shapes are easy to spot, saying, "They go in and out," or "They have dents."

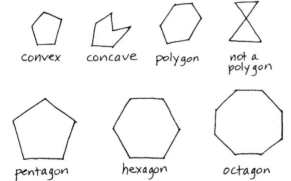

The shapes you build with the tangram pieces are all polygons. A polygon is a closed shape (which means it encloses an interior region the way a fence encloses a yard) made of connecting straight line segments. Sometimes a polygon is defined as a "simple closed curve." This seems contradictory, as the sides of a polygon are all straight line segments, but the definition has been in common use for quite some time. The "simple" part of the definition is important. It means that the line segments enclose one contiguous interior region that isn't divided into smaller regions. One way to think about this is to think of the corners where line segments meet—the vertices—as fence posts. Only two segments of the fence can touch each fencepost.

The directions for this extension could have asked you to use the seven tangram pieces to investigate convex polygons, instead of convex shapes. It's hard to decide when to use standard mathematical terminology or more common language. A good pedagogical approach is to use both—common language to provide access to an idea and correct terminology to help learners extend their mathematical vocabulary.

One more comment about the convex polygons you search for in this investigation. Polygons are categorized by the number of sides they have—triangle, quadrilateral, pentagon, hexagon, heptagon, octagon, and so on. Any shape with four sides—a square, a parallelogram, a rectangle, and so on—is a quadrilateral. When a polygon has all identical sides and angles, it's called a regular polygon. A square is a regular polygon and so is an equilateral triangle. When we see pictures of pentagons, hexagons, and octagons, typically they've been drawn as regular polygons.

The convex shapes you make in this investigation, except for the square, aren't regular polygons. The rectangle shown below, for example, was made from the seven tangram pieces, but it isn't a regular quadrilateral because its sides aren't all the same length. A regular quadrilateral has to be a square.

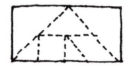

When doing this investigation, be sure to name the different polygons you make.

Extension 3: Making Squares

I know it isn't possible to form a square from six tangram pieces. I can't remember where I heard this, but my own experience experimenting with the tangram pieces convinced me that it's true. However, for a long time I wasn't able to explain why. (It's not enough to assert that I tried really hard to make a square from six pieces and couldn't—a proof calls for a convincing argument.) I was stymied. I don't mean to imply that I spent a lot of waking hours thinking about why I couldn't arrange six tangram pieces into a square, but I remained intrigued and wondered about it whenever I taught a lesson using the tangram puzzle.

I once raised this question at our annual retreat of Math Solutions instructors. I formed a panel of four people who had a good deal of mathematical expertise, experience, and confidence but who hadn't yet thought about this particular problem and asked them to think about it together, out loud, while the rest of us observed. My idea was that it would be interesting not only to learn about why a square can't be formed from six tangram pieces but also to have the chance to see mathematical thinkers in action.

We observed the four people rummaging for ways to approach the problem. They cut tangram pieces; they moved pieces about; they exchanged ideas; at times, one person would retreat into private thoughts and then reemerge to share discoveries; others would build on these ideas, as interested in how the others thought as they were in their own ideas. The group functioned in the way I want groups of students in the classroom to function.

Because of this experience I finally learned why making a six-piece square isn't possible. I offer my understanding knowing that it's hard to follow someone else's reasoning but hoping that my explanation will be useful to you and, perhaps, get you interested in this problem if you haven't been up to now.

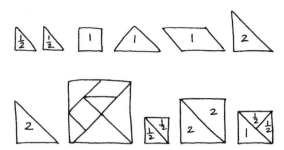

Think about the small square tangram piece as having an area of 1 square unit. As you may have learned from the first extension investigation, the parallelogram and middle-size triangle have the same area—also 1 square unit. The two small triangles that together form the square, parallelogram, and middle-size triangle each have an area of $\frac{1}{2}$ square unit. Since the large triangles can be made from a square and two small triangles, they each have an area of 2 square units. Using these values, the square formed by all seven tangram pieces has an area of 8 square units. (Check to make sure you are with me this far; this information will be important a bit later.)

Now think about making a square with 2, 3, 4, 5, 6, and 7 tangram pieces. First, you can make a square with two pieces by using the two small triangles. This square is the same size as the small square tangram piece and therefore has an area of 1 square unit. And because you can find the area of a square by multiplying the length of a side by itself, it measures 1 unit on a side. If you use the two large triangles to make a square, however, each side measures 2 units (it's equal in length to two sides of a square), and its area is 4 square units. (Use your tangram pieces to check that this is so.) This also makes sense because $2 \times 2 = 4$.

What about using three pieces to make a square? The chart on page 218 shows how to use two small triangles and the middle-size triangle to make a square. Its area is 2 square units. Each of its sides is equal in length to the long side of the small triangle, which is its hypotenuse. This is more than 1 unit but less than 2 units. How much is that, exactly? Although two is a small number that's generally easy for computations, in this situation it's easier to figure the length of a side for squares with larger but more cooperative areas. For a square with an area of 49 square units, for example, the sides are 7 units (since $7 \times 7 = 49$). For a square with an area of 64 square units, the sides are 8 units. In these examples, 49 and 64 are square numbers. (Take 49 or 64 pennies and you could arrange either number into a square array.) And 7 and 8 are the square roots of 49 and 64. We could say that the sides of those two squares are, respectively, $\sqrt{49}$ and $\sqrt{64}$. Finding the square root of 2 isn't so friendly, so we could use a calculator, pressing 2 and then the square root key (my calculator displays 1.4142135, which makes sense because it's in between 1 and 2). Or we could just say that the side is long.

Another way to figure the length of this side is to recall the Pythagorean theorem, which states that for a right triangle (and all of the tangram triangles are right triangles because they all have a right angle), the hypotenuse (the long side) is equal to the square root of the sum of the squares of the other two sides. The theorem is often written as $a^2 + b^2 = c^2$. The illustration of a right triangle with sides that measure 3 and 4 and a hypotenuse that measures 5, and showing the sides squared, may help you see how the Pythagorean theorem makes sense. And the theorem can be a helpful clue for understanding this problem. To use the Pythagorean theorem to figure the length of the hypotenuse of the small tangram triangle, I use the information that the shorter sides are each 1 unit, the same as the length of the side of the small square. The hypotenuse is the square root of $1^2 + 1^2$, which is $\sqrt{2}$. Then I use my calculator as I did earlier to get that messy number of 1.4142135.

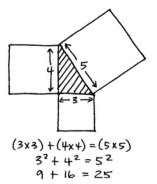

$$(3 \times 3) + (4 \times 4) = (5 \times 5)$$
$$3^2 + 4^2 = 5^2$$
$$9 + 16 = 25$$

Another clue is that if you examine the sides of all the tangram pieces, they either are 1 unit, twice that (2 units), $\sqrt{2}$ units, or twice that ($2\sqrt{2}$ units). (Again, use your tangram pieces to make sense of this information.)

four pieces

On to making a square with four pieces. Ah, that's possible. First I make a two-piece square using the two large triangles and then I replace one of the triangles with three pieces—the two small triangles and the square. The resulting four-piece square still has an area of 4 square units and measures 2 units on a side.

A five-piece square can be made from the five small pieces. It's the same size as the four-piece square—4 square units—and its sides measure 2 units. I already know

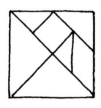

five pieces

about the seven-piece square. That's the square made from all seven tangram pieces. Its area is 8 square units and each of its sides is the length of the long side (the hypotenuse) of the large tangram triangle piece. This is the same as twice the hypotenuse of the small triangle, which measures $\sqrt{2}$. So each side of the seven-piece square measures $\sqrt{2} + \sqrt{2}$, which can also be written as $2\sqrt{2}$.

seven pieces

For a square to be formed from six pieces, one piece of the tangram puzzle has to be eliminated. The choices are to eliminate either one of the small triangles, $\frac{1}{2}$ square unit; the square, parallelogram, or middle-size triangle, 1 square unit; or a large triangle, 2 square units. So the area of a six-piece square would measure either $7\frac{1}{2}$ square units, 7 square units, or 6 square units. The side of a six-piece square, therefore, would have to measure either $\sqrt{7\frac{1}{2}}$, $\sqrt{7}$, or $\sqrt{6}$. However, there aren't any tangram pieces with sides any of those lengths or combinations of those lengths. All we have are sides of lengths 1, 2, $\sqrt{2}$, and $2\sqrt{2}$, so it isn't possible to form a square with six tangram pieces.

Convinced? If not, give it time. Remember that I thought about this problem for a long time—years—before finally making sense of it for myself. Try again when you're interested and rested. And don't forget the tangram pieces; they contain many of the clues to thinking about this problem.

Investigations with Four Toothpicks

Materials
flat toothpicks, about 80 per pair or small group
toothpick dot paper, 1 sheet [R] See Reproducible R.5

The Lesson
Ask pairs or groups to work together and investigate all the different ways to arrange four toothpicks following two rules:

1. Each toothpick must touch the end of at least one other.

2. Place toothpicks end to end or to make square corners.

These are OK.   These are not OK.

Explain that if a shape can be rotated or flipped to look like another shape, both shapes are the same. It's helpful to draw the shape in question on a piece of paper, flip it, and hold it up to a window to see it from the other side to tell if it's the same as another shape.

These are the same.

Ask students to record their shapes on the toothpick dot paper.

When they find all sixteen shapes, they cut their dot paper to make a set of cards.

Extensions
The Toothpick Game. This game is suitable for partners or a small group. Students each need their cards and four toothpicks. One student chooses a starting card, makes the shape with the toothpicks, and deals the remaining cards to the other players. (Discard extras so each player has the same number of cards.) Players place their cards face up so all are visible. In turn, each plays a card that shows a pattern that can be made from changing the position of exactly one toothpick on the pattern shown. Players help each other with moves and discuss patterns. Players pass if they can't play. The winner is the first player to play all of his or her cards.

The Put-in-Order Problem. Working with a partner or small group, students arrange the cards so that each pattern can be made from the previous pattern by changing the position of just one toothpick.

Teaching Tip
Tell students that there are sixteen possible shapes. Encourage students to check with one another as they search for shapes.
— MSB

Management Suggestion
Give each student a paper clip to keep their cards together. I've found it helpful for students to write their initials on the back of each of their cards. This helps return cards to their owners.
— MSB

Introductory Investigations with Geoboards

Materials
geoboards, 1 per student
rubber bands, about 6 per student

The Lesson
The following suggestions are useful for helping students become familiar with geoboards, satisfy their curiosity about the material, and prepare them for other geoboard investigations.

Tell the class that they'll have the chance to use geoboards to learn about geometry. Distribute a geoboard and rubber bands to each student and ask them to explore making shapes by stretching rubber bands around the geoboard pegs. After a few minutes, interrupt them and ask what they noticed.

Then engage students with the following investigations:

1. Ask students to stretch rubber bands to make numerals. Check with your partner and see if you made them the same way.

2. Ask them to make their initials, and then make other letters.

3. Ask them to make a shape of something that can fly. After they each have done this, have students show the class what they made and discuss. For example: "Joe made a rocket. Did anyone else make a rocket? How are the rockets alike? How are they different?"

4. Ask students to use just one rubber band to make a shape that touches four pegs with one peg inside. It helps to describe this as making a fence that has four fence posts and one tree inside the fence. Have students check with their partners to see that they both did this correctly. Have students show their shapes and see how many different solutions they found. Continue with similar instructions: make a shape that touches five pegs with zero inside; make a fence with five fenceposts and two trees inside, and so on.

5. Ask students to use one rubber band to make a shape that is not a square but that looks the same no matter which side the geoboard rests on. Have students share their shapes and see how many different solutions they found.

Sorting Shapes on the Geoboard

Materials
geoboards, 1 per student
rubber bands, 1 per student

The Lesson
Distribute a geoboard and rubber bands to each student and direct them to make a shape using one rubber band. Ask eight to twelve students to prop their geoboards on the tray beneath the board. Then sort them into two groups, moving them into separate groups on the tray. (See suggestions that follow for ways to sort them.) Don't reveal to the class the characteristics you used, but have the students discuss in pairs or small groups how you sorted them. When groups think they know, they don't reveal their idea but they bring up another geoboard shape and add it to the group where they think it belongs. Then, give feedback about whether they put their shape in the correct group, according to your system. After a while, have someone describe how the shapes were sorted. Repeat, sorting into three or more groups.

> ### SUGGESTIONS FOR SORTING GEOBOARD SHAPES
>
> do or do not have at least one right angle
>
> touch a corner peg on the geoboard or not
>
> have zero, one, two, . . . pegs inside
>
> have three, four, five, . . . sides
>
> are or are not symmetrical
>
> are a closed figure or not

Extension
Your Turn. Have groups brainstorm different ways to sort shapes and choose one to try with the class. The group sorts the shapes and the rest of the class, teacher included, tries to guess.

It's important that students have had the opportunity to explore geoboards before you introduce this investigation. See *Introductory Investigations with Geoboards* on page 220.

FYI
This is one of my favorite activities. Students enjoy the guessing and trying to "read my mind." I can change the characteristics to work for younger or older students. I also can use the discussions to model using geometric terminology.   —MSB

Independent Investigations

Following are geometry investigations, which you can use as individual assignments, as small-group or partner investigations, or as a choice-time exploration.

For more on using investigations with various instructional groups, see "Starting Point 20: Four Structures for Organizing and Managing Classroom Instruction" in Part 1 on page 111.

No-Lift Letters

It's possible to draw this shape without lifting your pencil and without retracing any line.

Try it. Then investigate the alphabet. Which uppercase letters can you write without lifting your pencil and without retracing any line? Record.

Extensions

A Pattern of Odd Vertices. You can tell if you can draw a letter without lifting your pencil or retracing a line by looking at the points where line segments meet or end (the vertices) and seeing how many of these points have an odd number of line segments meeting there (odd vertices).

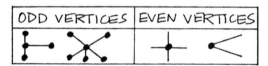

Count the odd vertices for all the letters than can be written without lifting your pencil or retracing. What pattern do you notice?

LETTER	B	C	D	
ODD VERTICES	0	2	0	

Lowercase Letters. Investigate the patterns with lowercase letters.

Letters with Rotational Symmetry. Some letters have rotational symmetry. That means they are the same when turned upside down. Make a list of these.

About the Mathematics

The house shape shown in *No-Lift Letters* is one that fascinated me as a young child. Once I realized that I could draw the house without lifting my pencil or retracing a line if I drew it in a certain way, I practiced and practiced until I could do it correctly every time. Then I experimented with other shapes.

Much later, from doing an investigation like *A Pattern of Odd Vertices*, experimenting convinced me that the only shapes that could be drawn this way were those with zero or two odd vertices. Now I had a way to predict before I tried whether it was possible to draw a shape without lifting the pencil or retracing any line.

It was even later that I began to understand why it was possible to draw shapes with zero or two odd vertices without lifting the pencil or retracing any line. It seemed so strange that this was a rule that worked. Then I engaged in a different kind of investigating, trying to understand why shapes with one, three, or more odd vertices didn't work. I came to see that an odd vertex was a dead end to be avoided, so zero odd vertices was best. Two odd vertices are OK because they provide places to begin and end. More than two odd vertices are trouble. And I haven't yet figured out how to draw a shape with just one odd vertex; maybe it's not possible.

My personal passage through this investigation shows how the same mathematical experiences can be appreciated in different ways at different ages. I returned to this problem over and over again for years. The discovery about odd and even vertices wouldn't have interested me as a young child trying to master how to draw a shape without lifting my pencil or retracing any line. Later, however, learning the rule was exciting to me, like uncovering a secret. But it wasn't until even later that I became interested in why the rule made sense. And perhaps there's still more to think about with this investigation—it wouldn't surprise me.

I sometimes hear teachers worry that students have done an investigation in a previous year and therefore will no longer be interested. That hasn't been the case for me. I've found that students often enjoy returning to things they've previously learned. I've also found that revisiting investigations offers students the opportunity to see a situation in new ways and to bring to it their new maturity, experience, and learning.

Area and Perimeter

You need: *Area and Perimeter* Shapes, **R** See Reproducible R.7
duplicated on tagboard

Cut out the shapes on the *Area and Perimeter* sheet.

Order the pieces according to their areas.

Compare the perimeters of the pieces.

Write summary statements to describe what you discovered.

Extensions

Sorting by Shape. Compare the areas and perimeters of each of the triangles, then the squares, then the rectangles, and finally the parallelograms. Write statements that describe what you discovered.

Similar Shapes. Similar shapes have the same shape but are different sizes. You can informally test to see if two shapes are similar by "sighting" with one. Here's how. Place the large square on the table. Stand up so you're looking down on it. Hold the small square in one hand, close one eye, and move the square up and down until it exactly covers the larger square. Because it can cover it exactly, they are similar. Will all squares be similar? Test the triangles, parallelograms, and rectangles the same way. Which are similar and which are not?

Other Shapes. All of the pieces on the sheet fit perfectly into a rectangle. Could all of them be arranged into a triangle? A square? A parallelogram? Find ways to arrange them into other shapes.

Square Partitioning

Draw nine squares on a sheet of paper and number them as shown.

Divide each square into the number of smaller square regions written beside it. Examples:

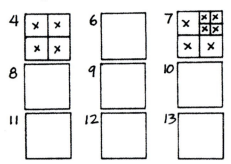

Extensions

There's More Than One Way to Cut a Square. Find all the different ways you can partition a square into a given number of smaller squares.

What's Wrong with Five? Notice that five was omitted. How come?

Going Further. Continue the investigation for larger numbers.

About the Mathematics

This investigation demonstrates how rummaging around and getting immersed in a problem can reveal useful patterns that aren't obvious at first. At least that's what happened to me. For example, from fiddling with this investigation, I discovered a tried-and-true system for partitioning squares into any number of smaller squares in this sequence—4, 7, 10, 13, 16, 19, and so on—with the numbers continuing to increase by three. When you divide a square into four equal-size squares, the change from one square to four squares represents an increase of three squares, so the system is to divide any existing square into four equal-size squares. All of the numbers in the sequence are one more than a multiple of three.

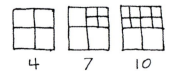

The next one that seemed easy to do was to partition a square into nine smaller squares, making a 3-by-3 array. Once I had nine squares, I could divide any square using the system I had discovered before and get three more squares. So this took care of 9, 12, 15, 18, 21, and so on. Or I could divide any of the nine squares into nine more squares, which added eight more squares, to solve the problem for 17, 25, 33, 41, 49, and so on.

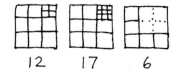

But I was getting ahead of the problem with these large number solutions. What about partitioning a square into six, eight, or eleven squares? I stumbled into six from erasing some lines from the nine-square. And I found eight and eleven from dividing a square into a 5-by-5 array and then erasing some interior lines.

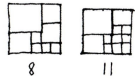

8   11

But enough. The fun in a problem like this is the discovering—if you like that sort of thing. I do. Once I have systems, I'm no longer interested, although at times I become delighted all over again when someone gives me a completely new way to look at a problem I thought I completely understood.

The lesson is—be mathematically curious. It's a key to becoming mathematically competent.

So what's the story with five? It's not possible to partition a square into five smaller squares, a reminder that not every mathematical problem has a solution.

Penticubes

You need: interlocking cubes (Snap or Multilink cubes),
about 50 per student

This investigation extends the pentomino investigation (see page 208) into three dimensions. Penticubes are three-dimensional shapes made from five cubes each. See how many you can construct.

Extensions

Penticube Jackets. Using paper ruled into squares the same size as the faces of the cubes, cut a jacket to fit a penticube. (Jackets are nets that fold to cover exactly all faces of the penticube.)

More Penticube Jackets. Take one penticube and find different possible jackets. (Is the number of possible jackets the same for each penticube?)

Surface Area. Compare the surface area of different penticubes. What do you notice about the shapes of penticubes with different surface areas?

Penticube Riddles. On grid paper, draw three views of a penticube— top, bottom, and side. Staple the drawings to a paper bag that holds the actual penticube. Others try to build the shape from the drawings and check their construction with the structure in the bag.

Perspective Drawing. Use isometric dot paper to draw penticubes.

 See Reproducible R.10

Building Rectangular Solids. Put together several of the same or different penticubes to make rectangular solids. Investigate which dimensions of rectangular solids are possible to build.

The Banquet Table Problem

You need: tiles, 24 per student

centimeter or half-inch grid paper $\boxed{R}$ See Reproducibles R.2 and R.3

A banquet hall has a huge collection of small square tables that fit together to make larger, rectangular tables. Arrange tiles to find the different numbers of people that can be seated if twelve small tables are arranged into a larger rectangular table. Sides of small square table have to match.

Do the same if twenty-four are used.

Record on squared paper.

Extensions

The 100-Table Problem. If one hundred small square tables are arranged into a large rectangular table, find the most and least numbers of people that can be seated.

Banquet Cost. If the banquet hall charges by the number of square tables used, what's the least expensive way to seat sixteen people? Fifty people? Sixty? One hundred? Any number?

About the Mathematics

This problem uses the context of arranging tables for a banquet to explore the ideas of area and perimeter. Different arrangements of twelve square tables all have the same area but have different perimeters and, therefore, can seat different numbers of people. For example, putting all twelve tables in one row to make a long, thin table seats the most people—twelve on each side and one at each end for a total of twenty-six. Arranging the tables into a 6-by-2 rectangle results in seating for sixteen people—six on each side and two at each end. A 4-by-3 arrangement seats fourteen people—four on each side and three on each end. These are the only rectangular arrangements that I had in mind when I wrote the problem. However, students have found ways to arrange the tables in other ways, leaving holes in the center.

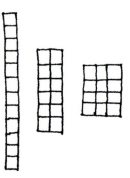

From time to time, students interpret a problem in a different way from the one intended. It's difficult to give precise directions all the time. My first impulse when a student built a table with a "hole" was to clarify that this wasn't what I meant, that I had meant only "filled-in" rectangles. I was locked into the goal I had for the lesson, for students to see the relationship between the number of small tables and the pairs of factors of that number. (For 12, the pairs of factors are 1×12, 2×6, and 3×4.) I wanted them to see that long, thin tables had longer perimeters than did more square-like tables.

When a student suggested a banquet table with a hole, and then others argued about whether or not people could sit inside the hole, I felt that I was losing mathematical control over the lesson.

I relaxed, however, and decided to see the diversion not as a potential disaster but as a way for students to follow their curiosity. The students continued to search for all possible tables and record their findings. Later, in a classroom discussion about the banquet tables made from twelve, twenty-four, and one hundred small tables, I asked them to consider just those tables that were filled-in rectangles.

This focused us on looking at the mathematics I felt was important. For additional activities that also address area, perimeter, and relationships between them, see *Square Up* (page 236) and *The Area Stays the Same* (page 165). Also, *Spaghetti and Meatballs for All!* (1997), a children's book I wrote, uses the context of a family reunion to show how rearranging tables can affect seating.

Literature Connection
Spaghetti and Meatballs for All! presents a variation on the problem. Mr. and Mrs. Comfort set eight tables with four at each for thirty-two people, but as guests arrive with their own ideas for seating, they rearrange the tables in different arrangements. The story guides students to think about the mathematical confusion caused. —*MSB*

Interior Regions

Which uppercase letters have interior regions? That means if you built a fence in the shape of that letter, it would keep your dog inside.

Record on a chart as shown.

About the Mathematics

It's generally easy for students to sort the letters into those that do and don't have interior regions, so there's not much to discuss about this investigation. But in the spirit of looking for connections among activities, I revisited this investigation after writing the discussion for *Extension 2: Using All Seven,* from *The Tangram Puzzle,* page 215, which had made me wonder whether any uppercase letters were polygons. (If you aren't sure what a polygon is, read the explanation for *Using All Seven* on page 215.) The only letter formed only by straight line segments that enclose an interior region is A, but it has extra "tails," a feature that eliminates it from the polygon classification. Some of the letters that don't have interior regions would be polygons if their two dangling line segments were joined. For example, L and V would become triangles; M and W would become pentagons, actually concave pentagons. (Again, read the *Using All Seven* explanation if you're not sure what makes a shape concave.)

Straight or Curved?

Which uppercase letters have only straight line segments? Which have only curves? Which have both? Record like this:

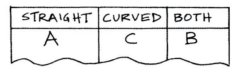

STRAIGHT	CURVED	BOTH
A	C	B

Then put your results on a Venn diagram, like this:

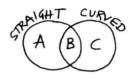

About the Mathematics

Deciding which of the uppercase letters have only straight line segments, curves, or both is another easy sorting investigation. Converting the chart to a Venn diagram, however, may be something new. A Venn diagram is a clever way to display sets of information when there is information that belongs in more than one set. (Venn diagrams are named for John Venn, a British mathematician [1834–1923], who worked in statistics, probability, and logic.)

If this investigation is your class's first experience with a Venn diagram, it may help to use cutout letters and two circles of different-colored yarn. First form the two circles so that they don't overlap, then designate one for letters with straight line segments and one for letters with curves. The problem of where to put letters that have both straight line segments and curves comes up fairly quickly. Ask the students for suggestions. Some may suggest a third yarn enclosure, but that doesn't solve the problem of a letter such as B belonging in all three sets. Some students may suggest making three Bs; you can counter that you have only one of each letter and push them to think of an easier way than cutting out more.

If no one suggests overlapping the circles, then tell them about Venn's idea. Draw a Venn diagram as shown above, write B in the intersection, and have them verify that it's in both the yarn circle for letters with straight line segments and the yarn circle for letters with curves. While ideas like making three Bs might work, Venn diagrams have become accepted convention for displaying information like this, so students should become familiar with how they work.

Geometry Building

You need: a set of about 10–15 objects (blocks, toothpicks, squares, etc.), 1 set per student
barrier (from books or binders) so each person has a working space that no one else can see

Work with a partner. One of you builds a structure using some or all of the materials and then describes it, step by step, so your partner can build it. Your partner can ask questions at any time. Finally, lift your barriers to see if the structures you built are the same.

Switch roles and try it again so everyone has the chance to be the describer. Discuss the language used, focusing on what was useful and what was not.

Teaching Tip
This Geometry Building experience is especially valuable for English language learners, and also for all students with limited language skills.
— MBB

Extending Metric Lengths to Volume and Capacity

You need: heavy paper or tagboard

Construct a 10-centimeter cube from heavy paper or tagboard. Notice that your cube is about half of a half-gallon milk carton. This means a 10-cm cube holds about the same as 1 quart (1 qt).

Hint: Here are two shapes that fold up into a cube.

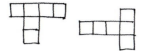

Teaching Tip
To prepare for this investigation, it's useful to have a plastic 10-centimeter cubic container, so you can demonstrate that it holds about the same as a quart. Also, bring in a quart and half-gallon empty milk carton.

— MBB

Pool Hall Math

You need: centimeter grid paper, 1 sheet **R** See Reproducible R.2

For this investigation, a pool table is a rectangle (or a square, since squares are also rectangles) with any dimensions. The ball always starts at the lower left corner. It moves by going to the opposite corner of each square it enters and keeps moving until it reaches a corner. Examples:

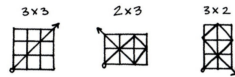

If the ball goes through *every* square on the table, then that pool table is *interesting*. If the ball doesn't go through every square, the table is *boring*. Find ten interesting and ten boring pool tables. Record their dimensions.

See if you can find a pattern for predicting whether a pool table is interesting or boring before you test it

Extensions

Exit Corners. Examine where the ball leaves each pool table. Some go out at A; others at B or C. Find ten different pool tables for each exit corner. Can you find a way to predict the exit corner?

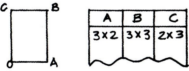

Paths. The ball takes different paths on different tables. Find all the different patterns for the paths the balls take.

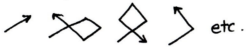

etc.

About the Math
A 10-cm cube holds 1 liter by metric measure. If packed with cubic centimeters (white Cuisenaire rods), it would hold one thousand of them (1000 cc or 1000 c³). Also, if you filled this liter container with water, that much water would weigh 1 kilogram (1 kg). Metric measures all relate to each other in a tidy fashion. After students have made their cubes and compared them to milk cartons, introduce the metric measures for the cubes they made.

— MBB

This investigation serves as an extension to the sample whole-class lesson *Measuring with Standard Units (Introducing the Metric System)* on page 150.

That's Just Half the Story

You need: small rectangular mirror

Some letters have mirror symmetry. That means when you place the mirror on them, you can see the whole letter—half on your paper and half in the mirror.

Investigate which letters work this way. Also, investigate which letters work by placing the mirror in more than one way.

Record the uppercase letters on a chart as shown. Draw dotted lines to show where you placed the mirror.

These work one way.	These work more than one way.	These do not have mirror symmetry.
A	X	F

About the Mathematics

This is the first of several activities that use the uppercase alphabet letters for geometric investigations. *That's Just Half the Story* investigates which of the letters have mirror symmetry, also called *line symmetry*. Some teachers make cutout block letters available, and students fold them to test for symmetry instead of using mirrors. This works well.

The letters that work only one way have exactly one line of symmetry—A, B, C, D, E, K, M, T, U, V, W, and Y.

Some letters have more than one line of symmetry—H, I, O, and X.

And some letters have zero lines of symmetry—F, G, J, L, N, P, Q, R, S, Z.

It's also possible for a shape to have an infinite number of lines of symmetry. If the O is formed as a perfect circle, for example, as long as a fold goes through the center of the circle, the two halves will match. Any line that goes through the center of a circle is a line of symmetry.

When students do this investigation, they're often surprised and unsettled to find that N, S, and Z do not have lines of symmetry. I think this is because the letters appear to have a kind of balance that letters like F and G, for example, don't have. While N, S, and Z don't have mirror symmetry, they have *rotational symmetry*. This means that if you imagine each as a cutout letter attached to a surface with a pin through its center, you can rotate the letter 180 degrees so that it's upside down and it will look the same. Notice that the letters that have more than one line of symmetry also have rotational symmetry.

A note about rotational symmetry: Shapes can have rotational symmetry at other than 180 degrees. A square, for example, has rotational symmetry at 90 degrees, and an equilateral triangle has rotational symmetry at 120 degrees.

More Geoboard Investigations

You need: geoboard
          rubber bands, 2

Try the following geoboard investigations:

1. Make a shape that touches five pegs. (Think of the rubber band as a fence, and the pegs it touches as fenceposts.) Then try shapes that touch six and four pegs.

2. Make a shape that has three pegs inside. (That means if the shape is a fence, the pegs inside are trees inside the fence.)

3. Make a shape that has ten pegs outside it, not touching the rubber band. (Think of them as trees growing outside the fence.)

4. Make a shape that has five fenceposts with three trees inside. Then try six fenceposts with two trees inside and three fenceposts with two trees inside. A challenge: Are there any combinations of fenceposts and trees that are not possible?

5. Use two rubber bands. Use each to make a line segment so the two line segments touch a total of nine pegs.

6. Repeat number 5 again, this time finding different ways to make the line segments (a) parallel, (b) intersecting, (c) perpendicular, and (d) the same length.

a line segment

7. Make a triangle with one square corner and no two sides the same length.

8. Make a four-sided polygon with no parallel sides.

9. Make a four-sided polygon with all sides different lengths.

10. Make a four-sided polygon with no square corners but with opposite sides parallel. (What is this polygon called?)

11. Make a four-sided polygon that is not a square, not a rectangle, not a parallelogram, and not a trapezoid.

12. Make two shapes that have the same shape but are different sizes and are not squares.

Teaching Tip
This investigation and several that follow call for using geoboards, a time-honored manipulative for helping students develop understanding of a range of geometric ideas. I strongly advise engaging students with Introductory Investigations with Geoboard on page 220 and Sorting Shapes on the Geoboard on page 221 before they try any of the additional geoboard investigations in this section.

— MBB

Management Suggestion
One way I've done this is duplicated the twelve investigations for each group and directed the students to work through them in order, in pairs or small groups. The procedure I've used is for them each to find a solution to the same problem, compare results and discuss similarities and differences, and then continue with the next direction.

— MBB

Area on the Geoboard

You need: geoboard
            rubber bands, at least 6
            Area on the Geoboard Recording Sheet  See Reproducible R.6

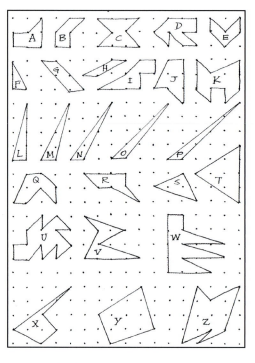

Find the area of each shape.

About the mathematics

If you can figure the area of the twenty-six shapes on the Reproducible R.6, you can probably figure the area of any shape on a geoboard. To do so, there are a few techniques that are useful.

One is to get good at spotting halves of squares. In Shape A, for instance, there are two whole squares and half of another; its area is $2\frac{1}{2}$ square units. In Shape B, there is one square intact topped by a parallelogram that is formed from two half-squares. Keep an eye out for those halves and you'll do fine with Shapes A through E. You can also confirm these areas by using small paper squares the size of square units, cutting them in half, and fitting them together to make all of the shapes from A to E.

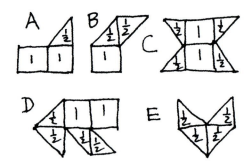

The next shapes get tricky. You can continue to use small paper squares, cutting them to fit the odd-looking shapes and adding up the bits and pieces. One problem with this approach is that measurement is never exact, and the lack of precision will be frustrating. Trust me, it's better to use your head than paper and scissors, at least for these problems.

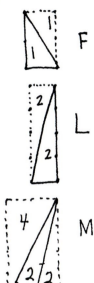

Here's my advice. Think about rectangles. They're the easiest to figure because you have to count only whole squares. Look at Shape F. It's not a rectangle, I realize, so I make it into one. The rectangle I draw has 2 square units; F is half of it; therefore, F is worth 1 square unit. (OK, if you'd like, verify this by the paper-and-scissors method.)

Look at L. If I "rectangulate" it, the rectangle will have an area of 4 square units, so the area of L is 2 square units.

Nice work, you say, but you took the easy ones. What about M? Or N? Or O or P?

My advice is this: Relax and rectangulate. My additional advice is that it's always easier to figure out what's outside the shape but inside your rectangle. Look at what happens when I draw a rectangle to enclose M. Its area is 8 square units. The triangle on the right side is the same as L and, therefore, has an area of 2 square units. The triangle on the left is half of the rectangle, so its area is 4 square units. Subtract these two areas from the whole rectangle, and you're left with 2 square units for M.

If you do N, O, and P the same way, you'll find that they each have an area of 2 square units. Does it seem peculiar that L, M, N, O, and P all have the same area? It made sense to me once I noticed that they all have the same length base and the same height (which is the perpendicular distance from the base to the opposite vertex). Also, I know that you can figure the area of a triangle by multiplying the base times the height and dividing by two ($A = bh/2$). Looking at the illustration of rectangulating L helps show this; the area of the rectangle can be found by multiplying its base times its height ($A = bh$), and the triangle is half as big. Because L, M, N, O, and P all have the same base and height, their areas are also all the same.

With these techniques—rectangulate, figure out what's outside the shape but inside the rectangle, then subtract—I can figure the area of all the shapes on the page. Following are the answers (all in square units) so that you can check the answers you get.

A = $2\frac{1}{2}$	L, M, N, O, P = 2
B = 2	Q = $3\frac{1}{2}$
C = 4	R = 3
D = 4	S = $2\frac{1}{2}$
E = 2	T = 6
F = 1	U = $6\frac{1}{2}$
G = 2	V = $4\frac{1}{2}$
H = 1	W = 8
I = $3\frac{1}{2}$	X = 4
J = $3\frac{1}{2}$	Y = 9
K = $5\frac{1}{2}$	Z = $8\frac{1}{2}$

Geoboard Line Segments

You need: geoboard
          rubber band

Find the next-to-the-longest line segment you can make on the geoboard.

Explain why you're sure your answer is correct.

Extension

How Many. How many different-length line segments are there on the geoboard? Find a way to record them and order them from shortest to longest.

About the Mathematics

There are fourteen different-length line segments you can make on the geoboard by stretching rubber bands so that pegs of the geoboard are the end points of the segments. Four of them are parallel to the sides of the geoboard, measuring 1, 2, 3, and 4 units. Then there are four that are on the diagonal from one side or corner to the opposite side or corner.

Students often think that the diagonal line segments are also 1, 2, 3, and 4 units, but that's not correct. A line segment from a peg to the next diagonal peg is longer than a line segment from a peg to the peg directly above or below it. You can use a ruler or string to test that this is so. Or you can think about the Pythagorean theorem, since the diagonal is the hypotenuse of the right triangle. (You can read about the Pythagorean theorem in the explanation about *Extension 3: Making Squares of The Tangram Puzzle* on page 216.)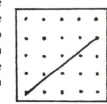

In addition to these eight line segments, there are six more, not parallel to any of the eight I described so far. The line segment that goes from one of the bottom corner pegs to the opposite top corner peg is the longest on the geoboard. The next-to-the-longest line segment goes from one bottom corner peg to the peg just under the opposite top corner peg. I think this is correct because the diagonal line segments are all hypotenuses of right triangles, and this particular one is the hypotenuse of a right triangle whose sides measure 4 units and 3 units. Use the Pythagorean theorem to calculate that this hypotenuse is 5 units, longer than the longest segment that is parallel to the sides of the geoboard. No other right triangle, except for one with both sides 4 units, has sides this large.

Teaching Tip
Point out to students that they can form squares on the diagonal, without sides parallel to the sides of the geoboard.
— MBB

Management Suggestion
To compile students' work, I ask students to choose one of their shapes, copy it onto large geoboard dot paper, cut it out, and post it. I ask them to post only shapes that haven't already been posted.
— MBB

Areas of Four on the Geoboard

You need: geoboard
          rubber band
          small geoboard dot paper, several sheets **R** See Reproducible R.11
          large geoboard dot paper, 1 sheet **R** See Reproducible R.12

The square made by stretching a rubber band around four pegs with no pegs inside has an area of 1 square unit. Find other shapes with an area of 4 square units.

Record them on small geoboard dot paper.

Pick's Theorem

You need: geoboard
rubber band

There's a function called Pick's theorem (named after the mathematician who discovered it) that enables you to find the area of any shape on the geoboard from the number of pegs on the perimeter of the shape (P) and the number of pegs inside the shape (I). The following sequence of activities suggests a way to investigate this theorem.

1. The square with an area of 1 has four pegs on its perimeter and zero pegs inside. Investigate other shapes with four pegs on the perimeter and zero pegs inside. Compare their areas. What about shapes with four pegs on the perimeter and one peg inside? Two pegs inside? Three? Four? Five? Any number? Write a formula that describes the relationship.

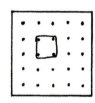

   Remember: P = pegs on the perimeter
   I = pegs inside
   A = area of the shape

P	I	A
4	0	1
4	1	
4	2	
4	3	
4	4	
:	:	

2. Do the same investigation for shapes with other numbers of pegs on the perimeter.

P	I	A
3	0	
3	1	
3	2	
3	3	
:	:	

P	I	A
5	0	
5	1	
5	2	
5	3	
:	:	

P	I	A
6	0	
6	1	
6	2	
6	3	
:	:	

3. Now investigate patterns for the areas of shapes when the number of inside pegs stays constant and the number of pegs on the perimeter varies. For example:

P	I	A
3	0	
4	0	
5	0	
6	0	
7	0	
:	:	

P	I	A
3	1	
4	1	
5	1	
6	1	
7	1	
:	:	

P	I	A
3	2	
4	2	
5	2	
6	2	
7	2	
:	:	

etc.

4. Finally, can you find a master formula that allows you to figure the area (A) for any combination of pegs on the perimeter (P) and pegs inside (I)? That's Pick's theorem.

   Just to check your formula:

P=8 I=2 A=?

P=6 I=1 A=?

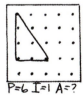

P=9 I=5 A=?

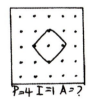

P=4 I=1 A=?

Shape Construction on the Geoboard

You need: geoboard
rubber band
small geoboard dot paper, **R** See Reproducible R.11
several sheets

Construct shapes that fit each of the following. Record on geoboard dot paper. See if you can find more than one solution for any of these?

1. a rectangle with area of 2 square units

2. a triangle with area of 2 square units

3. a triangle with area of 3 square units

4. a parallelogram with area of 3 square units

5. a hexagon with area of 4 square units

6. a rectangle and square with the same area (Which has the smaller perimeter?)

Geoboard Square Search

You need: geoboard
rubber bands, at least 7
small geoboard dot paper **R** See Reproducible R.11

Find all the different-size squares you can make on the geoboard (Hint: There are more than four.) Record on geoboard dot paper.

Geoboard Triangle Search

You need: geoboard
rubber bands, at least 7
small geoboard dot paper **R** See Reproducible R.11

Find triangles with areas of 5 and 7 square units. Record on geoboard dot paper.

Square Up

You need: geoboard
rubber band
Unifix cubes or game markers with holes in them,
12 each of two colors

This game is for two players. Each player takes twelve cubes in one color.

Players take turns putting one cube of their color on an empty peg on the geoboard.

When you think four of your cubes mark the corners of a square, say, "Square up."

Then your partner says, "Prove it."

Stretch a rubber band around the pegs you've marked to prove it's a square.

Teaching Tip
Point out to students that they can form squares on the diagonal, without sides parallel to the sides of the geoboard.
—MSB

Mirror Cards

You need: 3-by-5-inch index cards, 3
small piece of yarn or string
small mirror
hole punch

Follow the directions to make mirror cards:

1. Cut two of the index cards in half.

2. Punch holes in the same corner of the four half cards and in the card that wasn't cut. Put the stack of cut cards on top and tie all five cards together with a piece of yarn. Write your name on the back of each card.

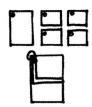

On the bottom half of the uncut card, make a design.

Put a mirror anywhere on the design, and draw on the first half card what you see both on your design and in the mirror.

Flip that half card up. Move the mirror and draw what you see now on the second half card.

Continue until you've drawn five designs in addition to your original one.

Try to solve others' cards, using the mirror to figure out where the creator placed it to get the design drawn. Write your name on the back of the uncut card to show you've solved the set. If you have trouble solving one, talk with the person who drew it.

The Fold-and-Cut Investigation

You need: paper
scissors

Fold a piece of paper in half. Cut out a small shape on the fold.

Try to draw what the paper will look like when you unfold it.

Then unfold and compare.

Do this at least five times.

Note: Try deciding on a shape first and then cutting to see if you get it.

Extension

Fold Twice. Try the same investigation, but fold the paper twice before cutting.

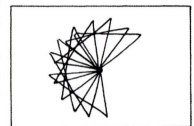

Rotating Shapes

You need: a four-triangle shape
         5-by-8-inch card
         12-by-18-inch drawing paper

Choose a four-triangle shape, trace it on a 5-by-8-inch index card, and cut it out.

Then draw a dot near the middle of a 12-by-18-inch sheet of drawing paper.

Place a corner of your shape on the dot and trace it. Then rotate the shape, keeping the same corner on the dot, and trace again.

Continue rotating and tracing.

Teaching Tip
This investigation extends The Four-Triangle Problem, page 210. However, students can make designs like this using other shapes as well.
— MSB

Hexagon Fill-in Puzzle

You need: pattern blocks, 1 set
        Hexagon Fill-in Puzzle **R** See Reproducible R.8

Six blocks will fill the hexagon shape with as few pieces as possible—three yellow hexagons and three blue parallelograms. (Try it.) To fill the hexagon shape with the most number of pattern blocks as possible, you would use twenty-four green triangles.

Explore the following:

1. Can you find ways to fill the hexagon shape with each number of blocks from 6 to 24 (7, 8, 9, 10, etc.)? Record.

2. For each of the numbers possible, find different ways to fill the shape. Record. (A different way means a different collection of blocks, not a different arrangement of the same blocks.)

Teaching Tip
This investigation and the two that follow call for using pattern blocks, a time-honored manipulative for helping students develop understanding of a range of geometric ideas. I strongly advise engaging students with pattern blocks before they try these investigations.

— MSB

To provide students with initial pattern block experiences, see *Introductory Investigations with Pattern Blocks* on page 213.

Hexiamonds

You need: green triangles from the pattern blocks, 6 per student
        pattern block triangle paper, 1 sheet **R** See Reproducible R.9

Hexiamonds are shapes made from six equilateral triangles arranged so that each triangle touches at least one other. Whole sides must touch.

Use the green triangles to find all the different (noncongruent) hexiamonds. Cut them out of the triangle paper to verify that they are different.

Record your solutions.

Explain how you know you have found all the solutions.

Angles with Pattern Blocks and Hinged Mirrors

You need: pattern blocks, 1 set
pair of rectangular hinged mirrors
5-by-8-inch index card with a dot and line on it,
as shown below

The size of an angle is a measure of rotation, and degrees are used to measure angles.

Follow the steps to figure out how many degrees there are in the angles formed by the corners of each pattern block. Use the following procedure:

1. Place a corner of a block in the hinged mirrors.

2. Close the mirrors so the corner nestles snugly.

3. Use pattern blocks to build the design made by the pattern block on the table and also what you see in the mirrors.

4. Sketch or trace the design.

5. Figure the degrees in the corner of the pattern block nestled into the mirrors by dividing 360 degrees by the number of blocks in the design. Label on your drawing to show the number of degrees in the nestled angle.

Construct other-size angles using the pattern blocks, hinged mirrors, and the index card. Experiment with the following suggestions:

1. Use combinations of pattern blocks. For example, the orange square and blue parallelogram can be put together to make an angle that is 90 degrees plus 60 degrees.

2. Use the hinged mirrors and the index card. For example, place the hinged mirrors so you see five dots and a pentagon. Trace along the base of the hinged mirrors to draw the angle created. Divide 360 degrees by five to figure the size of the angle traced. Label the angle.

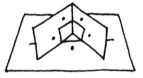

Extension

Impossible Angles. What size angles cannot be constructed using pattern blocks and hinged mirrors?

Making Topless Boxes

You need: 12 cut-out pentominoes, 1 set

Sort the pentominoes into two sets, those that will fold into a box and those that will not. For example, the pentomino that looks like the Red Cross symbol will fold into a topless box and the middle square will be the bottom, opposite the open side.

For each of the other pentominoes, follow three steps:
1. Predict whether or not you think it will fold into a box.
2. If you think it will, mark with an X the square that you think will be the bottom.
3. Fold to test your prediction.

Extensions

Milk Carton Geometry. Save school milk cartons. (Rinse them well!) Cut off their tops so they are topless boxes. Then try to cut them so they lie flat in the different pentomino shapes.

Factory Box Problem. Someone in a factory bought lots of cardboard that measured 5 squares by 4 squares and wanted to cut each sheet into four pieces so each piece would fold into a topless box. How could the sheet be cut?

The Pentomino Game

You need: 12 cut-out pentominoes, 1 set
one-inch grid paper R See Reproducible R.4

Cut a game board from grid paper that is a 5-by-12 squares. Be sure the squares on the game board match the size of the squares on your pentominoes. Try to fit all twelve pentominoes on the game board.

To play with a partner, take turns placing a pentomino on the board. The object is to be the last player to play a piece, making it impossible for your opponent to fit in another. In this game, you do not have to place all of the pentominoes, just until one player is blocked

Pentomino One-Difference Loop

You need: a set of 12 cut-out pentominoes

Place the pentomino that looks like the Red Cross symbol on the desk. Next to it, place another pentomino that could be made by moving only one square in the Red Cross shape. Continue with another that could be made by moving only one square in your second shape. Continue placing pentominoes and see if you can make a continuous loop.

Problem-Solving Investigations: Patterns and Algebraic Thinking

About the Mathematics

This icon indicates that I've written a mathematical commentary for the investigation. I've written these explanations in response to queries from teachers asking for math help with particular problems. I encourage you to try the investigation first before reading my explanation.

— MSB

Why Teach Patterns and Algebraic Thinking?

Students' experiences with patterns and algebraic thinking in grades K–5 build a ramp for their more formal study of expressions, equations, and functions in middle school. Essential for developing students' algebraic thinking are experiences with creating, recognizing, and extending patterns. This extends to describing patterns verbally and representing them symbolically in several ways—numerically on tables (often called T-charts), algebraically using equations with variables, and geometrically on coordinate graphs. Functions evolve from the investigation of patterns and make it possible to predict results beyond the information at hand. Functions are useful for solving problems in mathematics and in many other fields of study—including science and economics.

In kindergarten through grade 5, the primary focus on patterns and algebraic thinking is to help develop the meanings of operations and the relationships among them. However, it's also beneficial to include instructional experiences that help prepare students for the middle school focus on formulating algebraic equations, examining patterns and relationships numerically and visually on coordinate graphs, and learning about functions. This section suggests ways to provide these experiences.

Stages in Learning About Patterns and Algebraic Thinking

In kindergarten through grade 2, investigating numerical patterns builds on and supports the instructional focus on developing meanings for addition and subtraction. In grade 3, investigating numerical patterns helps build understanding of the meaning and properties of multiplication and division. In grades 4 and 5, students' work with patterns extends to generating, analyzing, and representing patterns from rules and identifying their features, in preparation for a focus on expressions, equations, and functions in middle school.

> ### STAGES IN LEARNING ABOUT PATTERNS, FUNCTIONS, AND ALGEBRAIC THINKING
>
> 1. Introducing Patterns
> 2. Describing Patterns Verbally
> 3. Introducing Functions
> 4. Representing Patterns Numerically, Algebraically, and Geometrically
> 5. Learning the Uses of Variables

1. Introducing Patterns

Looking for patterns is natural for young children, and early experiences should focus on recognizing regularity, identifying the same pattern in different forms, and using patterns to make predictions.

For example, beneficial are experiences of introducing a repeating pattern like *clap, snap, clap, snap, clap, snap, . . .* and having children join in. Next students can represent the pattern with materials—by making a train of interlocking red-blue-red-blue-red-blue cubes, for example. And then can also represent the pattern with letters, in this case *ababab . . .* , and predict what comes later in the sequence. In this pattern, for example, the twelfth element will be *snap, blue,* or *b.* It helps to progress from easy patterns to more complicated ones:

clap, clap, snap, clap, clap, snap, clap, clap, snap, . . .

□ □ △ □ □ △ □ □ △ □ □ △ . . .

a a b a a b a a b a a b . . .

Number sequences, like *2, 4, 6, 8, . . .* and *1, 2, 4, 8, 16, . . . ,* also provide patterns for students to investigate. Growth patterns like these are recursive patterns; that is, each number is found from the previous number by repeating some process. Experiences with growth patterns provides a foundation for students' later study of functions.

What comes next ?
1, 4, 7, 10, 13, 16, . . .
0, 2, 6, 14, 30, 62, . . .
2, 12, 22, 32, 42, 52, . . .

2. Describing Patterns Verbally

An important step for students is to describe patterns like these verbally. With both repeating and or growth patterns, students benefit from examining the patterns, extending them, and then verbally describing how they determine subsequent terms. For example, for a repeating pattern like aabaab . . . , a student might explain, "They go in threes with two the same and then one different, or It starts with two, then has one, then goes back to the two, then one again." For a growth pattern like 1, 2, 4, 8, 16, . . . , a student might explain, "You add each number to itself," or "You double each number to get the next," or "Each one is two times the one before."

3. Introducing Functions

Functions describe situations where one quantity determines another. Younger children extend their investigations of patterns to beginning experiences with functions by exploring number patterns that describe relationships that exist in the real world. For example, have a child come to the front of the room and point out that we see two eyes. Then have another child join the first and determine that we now see four eyes. Continue with this pattern of relating the number of children with the number of eyes—one child has two eyes, two children have four eyes, three children have six eyes, and so on. The number of eyes is a function of the number of children. Children can record the eyes pattern and then predict beyond the information they have recorded.

Other patterns to investigate with young children in this same way include fingers, thumbs, toes, noses, the number of points on any number of five-pointed stars, the amount of money for any number of nickels or dimes, the number of children needed to turn any number of jump ropes, and so on.

Asking students to look for patterns in the relationships between two sets of numbers is valuable preparation to develop their understanding of functions. For example, we know that one tricycle has three wheels and two tricycles have six wheels. How many wheels do three tricycles have? Four tricycles? How about *n* tricycles? The number of wheels is a function of the number of tricycles. This means that since each tricycle has three wheels, we can use the rule of multiplying the number of tricycles by three to determine the number of wheels for any number of tricycles.

Older students are introduced more formally to the concept and standard notation of functions, by producing a set of ordered pairs, such as in the tricycle-and-wheels example of (1, 3), (2, 6), (3, 9), (..., ...) (one tricycle and three wheels, two tricycles and six wheels, and so on). Note that the order of the numbers in each pair is significant—(3, 1) would mean that for three tricycles there is one wheel, and that's not true. Also, for any number of tricycles, there is only one correct number of wheels; it's not possible to have a different pair of numbers beginning with 1, 2, 3, or any other number.

4. Representing Patterns Numerically, Algebraically, and Geometrically

An important goal of mathematics instruction is for students to learn to represent patterns in three forms:

1. Numerically in a table

2. Algebraically in an equation

3. Geometrically on a coordinate graph

Numerically in a Table

For the tricycle example, using T to represent tricycles and W for wheels, you can represent the function in a table, often called a T-chart. You can think of T as the *input* and W as the *output*.

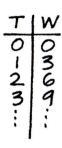

Algebraically in an Equation

The relationship between tricycles and wheels can also be represented in an algebraic equation using T and W as variables: $T \times 3 = W$. Because the number of wheels depends on the number of tricycles, mathematicians often refer to W, the quantity of wheels, as the dependent variable, determined by a rule that is applied to T, the independent variable.

Geometrically on a Coordinate Graph

Graphing a function calls for using the ordered pairs to place points on a coordinate graph. The standard way is to start where the two heavy lines (the axes) meet. This point is called the *origin*. Use the first number in each pair to count over to the right from the origin, use the second number to count up, and place a dot. Young children can learn this system of placing points without much difficulty. Notice that the dots for the tricycles-and-wheels function are in a straight line, indicating that it is a linear function.

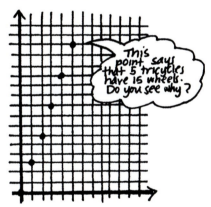

5. ## Learning the Uses of Variables

Representing patterns algebraically calls for the use of variables, as T and W were used to represent the function about tricycles and wheels. However, variables serve other purposes as well. Young children typically first learn about using variables as placeholders for unknown numbers. For example, beginning in grade 1, the Common Core content standards for mathematics calls for students to solve one- and two-step addition and subtraction word problems using equations with a symbol for the unknown number to represent the problem (NGA Center and CCSSO 2010). In these situations, variables represent missing numbers—specific, nonvarying numbers that can be determined by solving the equation.

Later, students learn that variables can be used not only for specific unknown quantities but also for a wide range of values.

Equations that use variables in this way can generalize arithmetic properties. For example, $o + 0 = o$ is true for any value of o because we know that adding zero to a quantity results in the same quantity. Zero is called the *additive identity*. Similarly, $n \times 1 = n$ for any value of n; the number one is the *multiplicative identity*. Other examples of using variables to describe arithmetic properties include $a + a = 2a$, $o \times 0 = 0$, and $x + y = y + x$. Each of these equations is true for any values of a, o, x, or y.

Variables are also used in formulas; for example, $A = lw$, with A, l, and w representing varying quantities of area, length, and width.

Mathematical Practices

The investigation and study of patterns and algebraic thinking support the development of the mathematical practices described in the Common Core and other standards documents for students in all grades. The mathematical practices should be connected to the content standards by engaging students in solving problems, reasoning, making conjectures, applying math to everyday life, using appropriate tools, communicating precisely, looking for patterns and structure, and looking for regularity in mathematical methods. The investigations in this section provide ways to make connections between practice and content standards.

Mathematical Content

It's helpful to understand which concepts and skills relating to patterns and algebraic thinking are appropriate for different grade levels. Experiences in grades K–3 help prepare students for the explicit expectations about patterns leading to functions that begin in grade 4. Including these experiences, while not demanded by the Common Core, is appropriate and supported by the Common Core recommendation that teachers teach topics that lead, as a byproduct, to other Common Core topics. Also, a focus on building algebraic thinking is essential for helping students engage in the mathematical practices (NGA Center and CCSSO 2010). Below are content designations that align with the Common Core and other standards documents.

Kindergarten: Understand addition and subtraction.

Grade 1: Represent and solve problems involving addition and subtraction; understand and apply properties of operations and the relationship between addition and subtraction; work with addition and subtraction equations.

Grade 2: Represent and solve problems involving addition and subtraction; work with equal groups of objects to gain foundations for multiplication.

Grade 3: Identify arithmetic patterns in the addition and multiplication tables and explain them using properties of operations.

Grade 4: Generate and analyze patterns that follow given rules.

Grade 5: Analyze patterns and relationship, including forming ordered pairs from corresponding terms from two patterns.

Grade 6: Apply and extend previous understandings of arithmetic to algebraic expressions; use variables to represent numbers and write equations when solving problems, and analyze relationships using tables and graphs.

Grade 7: Use variables to represent quantities and construct equations to solve problems.

Grade 8: Understand that a function is a rule that assigns to each input exactly one output; compare properties of functions algebraically, graphically, numerically in tables, or by verbal descriptions.

Sample Whole-Class Lessons

The following two sample lessons describe, in detail, investigations to help students develop understanding and skills with patterns and algebraic thinking. The first suggestion uses a children's book, *Two of Everything*, as the springboard for an investigation that is appropriate for students in grades K and up. The second suggestion presents a problem situation for students to investigate and represent in a T-chart, describe verbally, make a coordinate graph, and, if appropriate, write an equation. Each uses the Introducing/Exploring/Summarizing model for problem-solving lessons.

For the sample lessons, I used the Introducing/Exploring/Summarizing model for problem-solving lessons described in Part 1 on page 135.

Sample Lesson

Two of Everything

This lesson is based on a delightful children's book, *Two of Everything*, which tells the story about a magical brass pot that doubles whatever is put into it. Finding the pot is a wonderful discovery for Mr. Haktak. But a problem arises when his wife, Mrs. Haktak, trips and falls into the pot and then emerges as two Mrs. Haktaks! The story delights students in all grades. It provides a context for examining a growth pattern which, depending on the grade level, students can describe verbally, record on a T-chart, graph on a coordinate plane, and represent with an equation.

Materials

Two of Everything by Lily Toy Hong (Albert Whitman and Company, 1993)
interlocking cubes, at least 10 each of two or three colors per student (for K–2 classes)

Introducing

1. **Present or review concepts.** Read the book aloud to the class.

2. **Pose a part of the problem or a similar but smaller problem.** Draw a T-chart on the board and label the columns In and Out. Write 5 about halfway down the In column, leaving room to write *1, 2, 3,* and *4* above it.

Ask, *If we put five coins into the pot, how many coins would come out?* Record *10* in the right column next to the *5*. Repeat for four coins and possibly also three coins to be sure students understand the pattern and how to record.

In	Out
3	6
4	8
5	10

3. **Present the investigation.** Students work in pairs to make a T-chart and complete it for putting one to ten coins into the pot. Then they write about what the magic pot is doing. If appropriate, ask students to write an equation to describe the pattern ($O = I + I$ or $O = I \times 2$) and also graph the pairs on a coordinate grid.

4. **Discuss the task to make sure students understand what they are to do.** Have a few students restate the task.

Exploring

1. **Observe the interaction, listening to how groups organize working together, the ideas they discuss, and the strategies they use.**

2. **Offer assistance when needed.** If students have difficulty writing about the pattern, have them tell you aloud what they notice, and then encourage them to write what they said on their paper.

3. **Provide an extension to groups that finish more quickly than others.** Ask students to make up their own rules for the magic pot. Either let them decide on their own rules, or ask them to investigate an "add 3" pattern where the pot always gave back three more of whatever was put into it. Ask students to make a T-chart and, if appropriate, write an equation and graph the pairs on a coordinate grid.

Summarizing

1. **Have pairs or groups review their work and think about what to report in a classroom discussion.** If they haven't written summary statements to describe what they noticed and learned, ask them to do so now.

2. **Initiate a classroom discussion.** First have groups report how they organized working together.

3. **Next have groups report their results or solutions, explaining their reasoning or strategies.**

4. **Generalize from the solutions.** Have students discuss how they describe and represent the pattern. Some students think of doubling as adding a number to itself, and others relate doubling to multiplying by 2. Some write the equation in different ways; for example, $I + I = O$, $O = I + I$, $y = x \times 2$, or $2x = y$. If students made graphs, discuss the pattern of the points, that they go in a straight line and each point is one over to the right and two up from the previous point.

For Younger Students
In K–1 classes, I've found it helpful to draw a pot and list numbers in the In and Out columns on the sides, as shown. Also, it's possible to change the rule for the pot and revisit the experience. Here's what it looked like when we put cubes into the magic pot and the rule was to add 2.

In
1 cube
2 cubes
3 cubes
4 cubes

Out
3 cubes
4 cubes
5 cubes
6 cubes

—MBB

For a PDF of the *Two of Everything* lesson from *Lessons for Algebraic Thinking, Grades 3–5* (Wickett, Kharas, and Burns 2002) go to mathsolutions.com/documents/0941355489_CH1.pdf. The chapter describes in detail how the lesson evolved in one class. For information about the Lessons for Algebraic Thinking series for grades K–2, 3–5, and 6–8, visit mathsolutions.com.

Painting Towers

This sample lesson models the kinds of investigations in the rest of this section. Each presents a problem situation for students to investigate, describe verbally, represent in a T-chart and on a coordinate graph, and, if appropriate, write an equation. After students understand the directions, as introduced through *Painting Towers*, you can present the other problems for students to investigate.

Materials

interlocking cubes, 10 for each pair or small group
centimeter grid paper for graphing, R See Reproducible R.2
1 per students

Introducing

1. **Present or review concepts.** Explain, "This is a problem about figuring out how many squares you'll have to paint on a tower." Show the class one cube and explain, "Suppose the tower is only one cube tall. There are five squares to paint—four on the sides and the top. We don't paint the bottom." Draw a T-chart on the board and label the columns Cubes and Squares. Record *1* under Cubes and *5* under Squares.

Cubes	Squares
1	5

2. **Pose a part of the problem or a similar but smaller problem.** Add another cube so the tower is two cubes tall. Write a *2* in the Cubes column. Ask students how many squares they'd have to paint on a tower that is two cubes tall. Write a *9* in the Squares column since there are nine squares to paint, eight on the sides and again the one on top.

Cubes	Squares
1	5
2	9

> **Teaching Tip**
> Use the "think, pair, share" routine described on page 68 to have students think about how many squares to paint for a tower that is two cubes tall.
>
> — MSB

3. **Present the investigation.** Explain, "For this investigation, you're going to continue with a tower that is three cubes tall, then four cubes, and so on, recording on the T-chart. Continue until you can describe the pattern and figure out how many squares you'd need to paint if the tower is ninety-nine cubes tall. Write about the pattern, write an equation to describe it, and make a graph." It may be helpful to duplicate and distribute a copy of the problem to each group.

PAINTING TOWERS

Suppose you build a tower of interlocking cubes that is ninety-nine cubes tall. And suppose you paint every square on all four sides of the tower, as well as the top. (You don't have to paint the base of the tower.) How many squares do you have to paint? What's the relationship between the height of the tower and the number of squares to paint?

With a cubical tower that is only one cube high, there are five squares to paint—four sides and a top.	With a cubical tower that is two cubes high, there are twenty squares.	How many squares for a cubical tower three cubes high? Four? Make a chart.
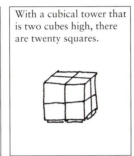 Don't count the bottom.	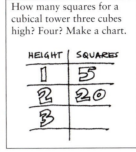	HEIGHT | SQUARES 1 | 5 2 | 20 3 |

For Younger Students
When teaching younger students, assign only the first two directions—continuing the pattern on the T-chart and describing the pattern in words.
—MSB

4. **Discuss the task to make sure that students understand what they are to do.** Have a few students restate the task.

Exploring

1. **Observe the interaction, listening to how groups organize working together, the ideas they discuss, and the strategies they use.**

2. **Offer assistance when needed.** If students have difficulty writing about the pattern, have them tell you aloud what they notice, and encourage them to write what they said on their paper.

3. **Provide an extension to groups that finish more quickly than others.** (See *More Painting Towers* on page 254 for a related problem about cubical towers.)

Summarizing

1. **Have pairs or groups review their work and think about what to report in a classroom discussion.** If they haven't written summary statements to describe what they noticed and learned, ask them to do so now.

2. **Initiate a classroom discussion.** First have groups report how they organized working together.

3. **Have groups report their results or solutions, explaining their reasoning or strategies.** Have students discuss how they describe the pattern.

4. **Generalize from the solutions.** Students typically notice and describe the pattern that the number of squares to be painted increases by 4 each time—5, 9, 13, 17, and so on. If students made graphs, discuss the pattern of the points, that they go in a straight line and each point is one over to the right and four up from the previous point. Figuring out the equation is more difficult for students, and

Extensions
For additional suggestions regarding building on and extending students' experiences, see "Independent Investigations" on page 253. You can use these investigations with the whole class, as small-group or partner investigations, or as a choice time exploration. (See also "Starting Point 20: Four Structures for Organizing and Managing Classroom Instruction" in Part 1 on page 111.)

not something that is essential, especially for younger students. It requires thinking about each pair of numbers in the T-chart and thinking about a way that 1 relates to 5, 2 to 9, 3 to 14, and so on. One way to represent the equation, using the variables s for squares and h for the tower's height, $s = h \times 4 + 1$. This is because towers have four sides, so the squares on the sides of the tower will be 4 times its height, and the "plus 1" represents the top of the tower.

Additional Investigations for Whole-Class Lessons or Independent Work

The suggestions in this section are structured similarly to *Painted Cubes* and are suitable either for whole-class lessons or independent work. If you choose to use some or all of the suggestions as whole-class lessons, note that they aren't presented in the elaborated three-phase lesson structure but rather are general ideas that you can expand into the three-phase plan.

If you choose to use them as individual assignments or for partner or small group work, it's important that students understand the general directions for *Painting Towers* and follow the same routine for these. It may help to write the directions for the routine on the board or a chart for students to have as a reference for these investigations.

If you choose to use any of these suggestions as whole-class lessons, see Reproducible R.1 for a template you can print and use for organizing the additional investigations into the three-phase lesson structure. Downloadable at mathsolutions.com/atm4theditionreproducibles

For more on using investigations with various instructional groups, see "Starting Point 20: Four Structures for Organizing and Managing Classroom Instruction" in Part 1 on page 111.

PATTERN INVESTIGATION

1. Continue the table started until you have the number 10 in the In column.

2. Describe the pattern.

3. Make a graph and describe the pattern made by the points.

4. If you can, represent the pattern with an equation.

Paper Folding

Suppose you fold a piece of paper in half, and then in half again, and again, until you make six folds. When you open it up, how many sections will there be?

With one fold, you will have two sections.	With two folds, you will have four sections.	Make a chart. Continue the folding. Look for a pattern.
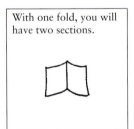	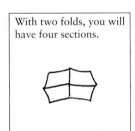	FOLDS / SECTIONS 1 / 2 2 / 4

Dot Connecting

Suppose you draw ten dots on a circle. If you draw lines connecting every dot to every other dot, how many lines will you draw?

With just one dot, there will be zero lines.	With two dots, you can draw one line.	How many lines will you draw for three dots? Four? Make a chart.
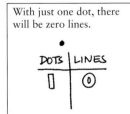 DOTS / LINES 1 / 0	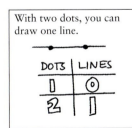 DOTS / LINES 1 / 0 2 / 1	

More Painting Towers

You need: interlocking cubes (Snap or Multilink), about 125 per pair

Suppose you build a cubical tower that is ninety-nine cubes tall. And suppose, as you did for *Painting Towers*, you have to paint every square on the four sides and the top of the tower. (You don't have to paint the base of the tower.) How many squares do you have to paint?

With a cubical tower that is only one cube high, there are five squares to paint—four sides and a top.

Don't count the bottom.

With a cubical tower that is two cubes high, there are twenty squares.

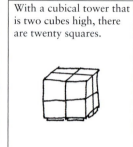

How many squares for a cubical tower three cubes high? Four? Make a chart.

HEIGHT	SQUARES
1	5
2	20
3	

Paper Tearing

Suppose you tear a piece of paper in half and give half to someone else. Then each of you tears your piece in half and passes half on to someone else. How many people will have a piece of paper after ten rounds of tearing like this?

With one tear, there will be pieces for two people.

After the second round of tears, there will be pieces for four people.

Continue tearing the paper. Record on a chart. Look for patterns.

TEARS	PIECES
1	2
2	4
3	

The Diagonal Problem

If you have a twelve-sided polygon (a dodecagon), how many diagonals can you draw? Remember that diagonals connect the corners of shapes.

A triangle has three sides and no diagonals.

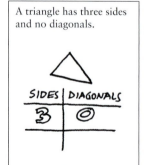

SIDES	DIAGONALS
3	0

A four-sided figure (a quadrilateral) has two diagonals.

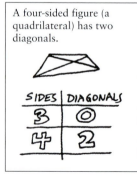

SIDES	DIAGONALS
3	0
4	2

What about a pentagon? A hexagon? And so on?

SIDES	DIAGONALS
3	0
4	2
5	

Points Dividing a Line

If you put twenty points on a line segment, how many sections can you count?

With one point, you will have two sections. 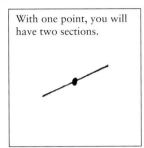	With two points, there will be three sections. 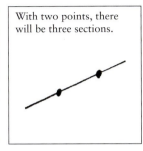	Continue making points and counting sections. POINTS | SECTIONS 1 | 2 2 | 3

The Ice-Cream-Cone Problem

If an ice-cream shop sells thirty-one different flavors of ice cream, how many different double-dip cones can they make? Hint: Use different-colored interlocking cubes for flavors and build the cones.

If the shop has only one flavor, there will be only one possible double-dip cone.	With two flavors, there are three combinations for double-dip cones. 	How many double dips are possible with three flavors? Four? Make a chart and look for patterns. FLAVORS | DOUBLE DIPS 1 | 1 2 | 3

Extensions

Order of the Flavors. If you count vanilla on top and pistachio on the bottom as different from pistachio on the top and vanilla on the bottom, how will your result change?

Triple-Dip Cones. Try the same problem for triple-dip cones.

Squares from Squares

If you build larger and larger squares from small squares, how many squares will you need to build one that measures 12 on a side?

For a square with sides of 1 unit, you need one square.	For a square with sides of 2 units, you need four squares.	For a square with sides of 3 units, you need nine squares.	Continue the pattern. LENGTH OF SIDE | SQUARES 1 | 1 2 | 4 3 | 9

More Squares from Squares

If you build squares as in *Squares from Squares*, what will be the length of the perimeter of a square that is 12 on a side?

For a square with sides of 1 unit, the perimeter is 4.	For a square with sides of 2 units, the perimeter is 8.	For a square with sides of 3 units, the perimeter is 12.	Continue the pattern.
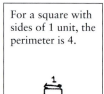	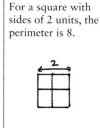	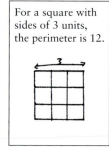	LENGTH OF SIDE / PERIMETER 1 — 4 2 — 8 3 — 12

Rod Stamping

Imagine the white Cuisenaire rod is a rubber stamp that stamps 1-centimeter squares. How many stamps would it take to cover each of the other rods? What is the pattern?

The white rod takes six stamps.	The red rod takes ten stamps.	Continue the pattern.
 (DON'T FORGET THE BOTTOM)	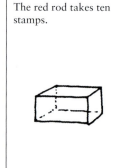	ROD / STAMPS 1 white — 6 2 red — 10 3 green 4 purple 5 yellow 6 dark gr. 7 black 8 brown 9 blue 10 orange

More Rod Stamping

Suppose you take rods of one color and pretend to glue them together as the picture shows. Figure out how many stamps are needed for each and look for the pattern.

The purple rod (as a sample) takes eighteen stamps.	Two purple rods glued take twenty-eight stamps.	Continue the pattern.
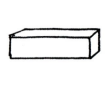	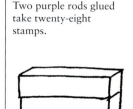	RODS / STAMPS 1 — 18 2 — 28 3 —

Extension

Gluing Rods Together. Suppose you glue the rods together, offsetting each 1 centimeter, as the picture shows. Make a chart of the stamps needed and look for the pattern.

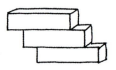

About the Math
To check where the 18 comes from with one purple rod, it's important to know that it takes four stamps to stamp each of the four sides (16) plus two more to stamp the top and bottom.   —MSB

A Row of Triangles

If you line up one hundred equilateral triangles (like the green triangles from the pattern blocks) in a row, what will the perimeter measure? (You may think of this as a long banquet table made from individual triangular tables. How many people can be seated?)

With one triangle, the perimeter is 3 units.	With two triangles, the perimeter is 4 units.	With three triangles, the perimeter is 5 units.	Continue the pattern.

TRI-ANGLES	PERI-METER
1	3
2	4
3	5

A Row of Squares

If you line up one hundred squares in a row, what will the perimeter measure? (As in *A Row of Triangles*, you may think of this as a long banquet table made from individual square tables. How many people can be seated?)

With one square, the perimeter is 4 units.	With two squares, the perimeter is 6 units.	With three squares, the perimeter is 8 units.	Continue the pattern.

SQUARES	PERI-METER
1	4
2	6
3	8
4	

A Row of Hexagons

If you line up one hundred regular hexagons in a row, what will the perimeter measure?

With one hexagon, the perimeter is 6 units.	With two hexagons, the perimeter is 10 units.	With three hexagons, the perimeter is 14 units.	Continue the pattern.

HEXA-GONS	PERI-METER
1	6
2	10
3	14
4	

Note: There's a way to figure out the pattern for a row of any regular polygon. Try it if you're interested.

A Row of Pentagons

If you line up one hundred regular pentagons in a row, what will the perimeter measure?

With one pentagon, the perimeter is 5 units.	With two pentagons, the perimeter is 8 units.	With three pentagons, the perimeter is 11 units.	Continue the pattern.
			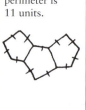

Interlocking Trains

If you make trains ten cubes long using two colors of interlocking cubes, how many different arrangements can you make? (Note: The order of the colors matters. For example, for a train that is three cubes long, red-red-blue and red-blue-red each count as a different arrangement.)

A train that is one cube long has two arrangements.	A train that is two cubes long has four arrangements.	How many arrangements would there be for trains that are three cubes long? Four? Make a chart.
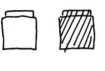	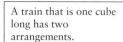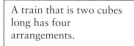	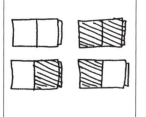

Toothpick Building

If you continue the pattern shown to build a row of one hundred triangles, how many toothpicks will you need?

For one triangle, you need three toothpicks.	For two triangles, you need five toothpicks.	How many do you need for three triangles? Four? Five? Make a chart.
	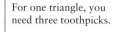	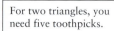

Extension

More Shapes. Try the problem for rows of squares, pentagons, and hexagons.

The Handshake Problem

Suppose everyone in this room shakes hands with every other person in the room. How many handshakes will that be?

With only one person in the room, there will be no handshake. 	With two people, there will be one handshake. 

How many handshakes will there be with three people? Four? Continue the chart.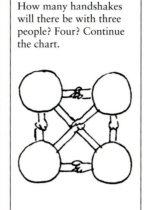

About the Mathematics

This is a problem that has generated a fair amount of mail from readers. I include this long-winded explanation as an example of how to approach, in general, the other investigations in this section. Typically I've included the investigations with discussions at the beginning of the sections. However, I've included it here at the end to offer a collection of ideas for you to experience before you read through and think about my ideas.

Typically, letters I receive about *The Handshake Problem* do not request help with figuring out the number of handshakes for successive numbers of people. That seems to be something that readers are able to do from acting it out, making a drawing, or using some other strategy. Here's the table completed for up to ten people:

PEOPLE	HAND-SHAKES
1	0
2	1
3	3
4	6
5	10
6	15
7	21
8	28
9	36
10	45

People usually include in their letter their discoveries about how to continue the table by following the pattern in the Handshakes column. The number of handshakes increases each time by one more than the previous increase—from 0 to 1 is 1 more, from 1 to 3 is 2 more, from 3 to 6 is 3 more, from 6 to 10 is 4 more, and so on. Continuing the pattern, there are 9 more handshakes for 10 people than there were for 9 people ($45 - 36 = 9$), so the number of handshakes for 11 people would be 10 more than for 10 people. Since $45 + 10 = 55$, if 11 people were each to shake hands with everyone else, there would be 55 handshakes in all.

Three questions are asked most frequently in the letters I receive:

1. Why do handshakes generate this pattern?
2. How can you figure out how many handshakes there will be for a large number of people, say one hundred or more, without making a long table?
3. What's the formula for this pattern?

In a way, all three questions are the same. The answer to Question 1 is the rationale for the pattern of handshakes. This rationale can be applied to any number of people to answer Question 2. And a rationale can often be expressed as an algebraic formula, which would answer Question 3.

A rationale first. Suppose you are one of the people in the room. With how many other people will you shake hands? This depends, of course, on the number of people in the room and therefore changes for different numbers of people. What stays the same, however, is that you'll shake hands with everyone in the room except yourself. That means that the number of handshakes for you will be one less than the number of people in the room. The same is true for everyone else in the room: each person in the room shakes hands with one less than the total number of people.

If there were five people in the room, for example, each of the five people will do four handshakes. You can try this by drawing five people in a circle and drawing hands connecting each person to every other person. Every person shakes hands with four others. And if five people each do four handshakes, I reasoned, that makes twenty handshakes altogether. Right?

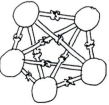

Wrong! Look at the table on the previous page. According to the table, for five people, there are ten handshakes, not twenty.

When I first encountered this problem, it took me a while to figure out where the glitch was in my thinking. Then I had a lucky realization—a mathematical "Aha!" Counting all twenty handshakes was twice as many as there should be because I was counting each handshake twice. For example, if you were in the room, then I counted shaking hands with you as one handshake. But I also counted your shaking hands with me as one handshake. This is double trouble.

So I refined my rationale. First I reasoned that each person shakes hands with one less than the total number of people. Then I figured out how many handshakes that makes altogether (by multiplying the number of handshakes each person makes by the number of people). Finally, I cut the number in half.

I tried my refined rationale for another number. For six people, for example, each person shakes hands with five others. That makes thirty handshakes, which is twice as many as there really are, since each handshake has been counted twice. Half of thirty is fifteen. Check the chart! Also, try my rationale for other numbers to be sure it holds true.

Now I can answer Question 2. Suppose there are one hundred people in the room. Each person shakes hands with ninety-nine others. If one hundred people do this, it seems that there would be 9,900 handshakes, but that's double the correct answer of 4,950 handshakes.

To answer Question 3, I need to translate my rationale to an algebraic equation. The number of people varies from room to room, and therefore we need to use a variable to represent it. Also, the number of handshakes depends on the number of people, so we need to use a variable to represent it as well. How about p for people and h for handshakes? Each person in the room shakes hands with one less than the total number of people, so each person makes $p - 1$ handshakes. With p people altogether, that makes p times $p - 1$ handshakes, which we can write in algebraic shorthand as $p(p - 1)$. But that's twice as many handshakes as we need, so I have take half of $p(p - 1)$, or divide $p(p - 1)$ by 2 to get the number of handshakes. Here are two ways to write a formula that works:

$$h = \tfrac{1}{2} p(p-1)$$
$$h = \frac{p(p-1)}{2}$$

If you followed this, great. If you didn't, maybe you'd like another way to think about the problem. Here's another rationale. (Remember, there's usually more than one way to think about any math problem.) Well, it's not a totally different rationale. Go back to the way I began thinking about the problem, supposing that you're one of the people in the room, and figuring out that you'll shake hands with one less than the number of people in the room. So you do $p - 1$ handshakes.

Now suppose that I'm also in the room and I have to shake hands with everyone else. But I already shook hands with you. To avoid that double trouble later, I won't shake hands with you again and will, instead, shake hands with everyone else except you. This means I do $p - 2$ handshakes. Now the third person shakes with everyone else except for you and me—$p - 3$ handshakes.

Continue thinking in this way and then add up the handshakes. For five people in a room, for example, you shake hands with the four others. Then I go around the room, skipping you and shaking hands with the three others. Then the third person skips both you and me and shakes hands with the two others. The fourth skips you, me, and the third person and shakes hands with the only other person in the room—the fifth person. The fifth person then doesn't have to do any more handshaking since he (or she) already shook hands with you, me, and the other two people. Total the handshakes—four for you, three for me, two for the third person, and one for the fourth person—$4 + 3 + 2 + 1 = 10$. Yup, it works.

Try it for six people. The first does 5 handshakes; the second does 4; the third, 3 handshakes; the fourth, 2 handshakes; the fifth, 1 handshake; the sixth is finished. Add $5 + 4 + 3 + 2 + 1$ and you get 15.

This method will also work for 100 people—$99 + 98 + 97 + 96 + 95 + 94 + 93 + \ldots + 1$. Bleh. If I had to do this much adding, I might as well just finish the table and have the answers for all of the numbers up to 100.

A friend told me another way to think about the problem, however, that also led to a viable formula. Suppose everyone shook hands with everyone else, including shaking hands with themselves. For five people, that would be five handshakes per person, which is five times five, or twenty-five handshakes. For six people, this reasoning means six handshakes per person, which is six times six, or thirty-six handshakes. For any number of people (p), it's p times p or p^2 handshakes.

Ridiculous, I protested. That's way too many handshakes, and people don't shake hands with themselves.

OK, my friend said, let's subtract the extras. Take out one handshake per person to eliminate the self-handshakes. For five people, that means subtracting five handshakes; for six people, that means subtracting six handshakes; for p people, that means subtracting p handshakes. So now we're down to $p^2 + p$.

No way, I protested again. For five people, that's $25 - 5$, or twenty handshakes; for six people, it's $36 - 6$, or thirty handshakes. These numbers are twice as big as they should be.

Ah, my friend said, I counted each handshake twice, as you did before. So I'll just take half of $p^2 - p$ and I'll have the right answer. I used this logic to write two versions of the formula:

$$h = \tfrac{1}{2}(p^2 - p)$$
$$h = \frac{p^2 - p}{2}$$

I tried the formulas for several other numbers. Bingo!
Now I had four options for formulas:

$$h = \tfrac{1}{2} p(p-1)$$
$$h = \frac{p(p-1)}{2}$$
$$h = \tfrac{1}{2}(p^2 - p)$$
$$h = \frac{p^2 - p}{2}$$

If you recall how to work with algebraic expressions, you can verify that these four options are really all the same.

Two last thoughts. The first one is a mathematical connection: *Dot Connecting* is mathematically identical to *The Handshake Problem*. Take a look. The sketches I made for *Dot Connecting* are just like the sketches I made for figuring out handshakes of people in a room, except they have just lines, not little hands. Ten lines connect five dots on a circle, for example, just as there are ten handshakes for five people in the room.

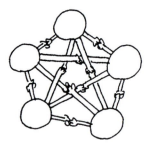 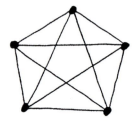

My last suggestion is to use the pairs of numbers on the table—(1, 0), (2, 1), (3, 3), (4, 6), and so on—to mark points on a coordinate graph. Look at the example about tricycles and wheels on page 245 if you need a reminder about how to do this. The points on page 245 go in a straight line, but the points for *The Handshake Problem* go in a curve. When you have $p \times p$, or p^2, in a formula, it's called a quadratic equation and makes a curve that's called a parabola. If this is a new idea for you, remember that learning something invariably leads to learning something new. Keep your mind open to learning about parabolas and other curves that come from graphing formulas. It may open a whole new aspect of math for you.

Problem-Solving Investigations: Number and Operations

About the Mathematics

This icon indicates that I've written a mathematical commentary for the investigation. I've written these explanations in response to queries from teachers asking for math help with particular problems. I encourage you to try the investigation first before reading my explanation.

— MSB

For suggestions for developing students' computation skills while also focusing on their number sense and ability to solve problems, see Part 3, "Teaching Arithmetic," on page 301.

Why Teach Numbers and Operations?

In the elementary grades, numbers and operations is the major focus of mathematics instruction, with an emphasis on arithmetic and students developing computational skills. While number and operations is the focus for this section, the emphasis here is on exploring numbers and numerical relationships through a broad variety of investigations. With a focus on understanding and using numbers, these investigations support and extend students' learning of arithmetic.

The investigations in the "Number and Operations" section relate to numerical investigations that help build students' understanding of properties of numbers and their number sense. Additional suggestions are included in Part 3 for number and operations that specifically address arithmetic understandings and procedures.

Numbers are used to describe quantities, compare quantities, identify specific objects in collections, and measure. In the elementary grades, students learn to make sense of the various ways numbers are used. They need to develop a sense of number that enables them to recognize relationships between quantities; to use the operations of addition, subtraction, multiplication, and division to obtain numerical information; to understand how the operations are related to one another; to be able to approximate and estimate when appropriate; and to apply their understandings to problem situations. Instruction should emphasize the development of students' number sense, help them see relationships among numbers, and encourage them to examine the properties of numbers. It's important for students to investigate the use of numbers in many situations so that they develop the confidence and flexibility to apply their understanding in new situations.

The investigations in this section require that students investigate numbers and apply them to problem situations. These problem situations differ from traditional word problems for which specific computation skills are used to get single answers. The focus here is on using numbers and numerical relationships in problems for which there are often a variety of solutions or a variety of possible ways to arrive at a solution.

Stages in Learning About Number and Operations

Basic to learning about number and operations are the following ideas:

> ### STAGES IN LEARNING ABOUT NUMBER AND OPERATIONS
> 1. Understanding the meanings of operations.
> 2. Understanding our base ten place-value system.
> 3. Understanding properties of arithmetic.
> 4. Understanding relationships between operations.

1. Understanding the meanings of operations.
Students develop understanding of the meanings of the four operations—addition, subtraction, multiplication, and division—by learning how the operations relate to a variety of contextual situations.

2. Understanding our base ten place-value system.

Our place-value system is an efficient use of only ten digits—0, 1, 2, 3, 4, 5, 6, 7, 8, and 9—to represent any quantity. Students need to learn that the value of a digit in a number depends on its place, and that the value of the places are units of ten—hundreds, thousands, ten-thousands, and so on.

3. Understanding the properties of arithmetic.

Students need to develop understanding of the commutative and associative properties of addition and multiplication, and also of the distributive property of multiplication over addition. Instruction should introduce these concepts in problem-solving settings rather than present their definitions abstractly.

4. Understanding the relationships between operations.

In students' early learning, the meaning of addition is typically separate from the meaning of subtraction. Students build relationships between addition and subtraction over time and come to understand subtraction as reversing the actions involved in addition and as finding an unknown addend. Likewise, the meaning of multiplication is initially separate from the meaning of division, and students gradually perceive relationships between division and multiplication analogous to those between addition and subtraction.

Mathematical Practices

The investigation and study of numbers and operations support the development of the mathematical practices described in the Common Core and other standards documents for students in all grades. The mathematical practices should be connected to the content standards by engaging students in solving problems, reasoning, making conjectures, applying math to everyday life, using appropriate tools, communicating precisely, looking for patterns and structure, and looking for regularity in mathematical methods. The investigations in this section provide ways to make connections between practice and content standards.

Mathematical Content

It's helpful to understand which numbers and operations concepts and skills are appropriate for different grade levels. Below are content designations that align with the Common Core and other standards documents.

Kindergarten: Compare numbers; understand addition and subtraction.

Grade 1: Represent problems involving addition and subtraction; understand and apply properties of operations and the relationship between addition and subtraction; work with addition and subtraction equations.

Grade 2: Represent and solve problems involving addition and subtraction; work with equal groups to gain foundations for multiplication.

Grade 3: Represent and solve problems involving multiplication and division; understand properties of operations and the relationship between them.

Grade 4: Use the four operations with whole numbers to solve problems; gain familiarity with factors and multiples; generalize and analyze patterns.

Grade 5: Write and interpret numerical expressions; analyze patterns and relationships

Grades 6–8: Build on ideas developed in K–5 in order to understand the rational numbers as a number system and to build understanding of the properties of operations on whole numbers and fractions.

Sample Whole-Class Lessons

The following lessons describe, in detail, investigations that engage students with number and operations as they look for numerical patterns. The first suggestion, *Number Sums*, is appropriate for students once they can write addition expressions for sums up to ten. The second, *Palindromes*, is appropriate for students who can add multi-digit numbers. Both investigations use the Introducing/Exploring/Summarizing model for problem-solving lessons.

> For the sample lessons, I used the Introducing/Exploring/Summarizing model for problem-solving lessons, described on page 135.

 Sample Lesson

Number Sums

The prerequisite for this investigation is that students can write addition expressions for sums up to ten. Although practice of basic addition facts is provided, the emphasis of the investigation is on finding all the ways to represent sums, looking for patterns, and making conjectures.

Materials

none are essential, but it may help younger students to have access to interlocking cubes in different colors

Introducing

1. **Present or review concepts.** Review with the students that there are different ways to write sums of numbers using addends 1, 2, 3, and so on. Use the number three as an example, showing the students the three ways to write three as a sum using addends greater than or equal to one. Record on the board:

   1 + 1 + 1

   2 + 1

   1 + 2

2. **Pose a part of the problem or a similar but smaller problem.** Ask the students to help you write all the ways to write addition expressions for the sum of four. Then go around the room asking each pair to report an expression that's different from what's recorded. If they don't have another, they just say, "Pass."

   Remind students that if the addends are in a different order, the expression is counted as a different way. Record the seven ways on the board:

   1 + 1 + 1 + 1

   1 + 1 + 2

   1 + 2 + 1

   2 + 1 + 1

   1 + 3

   3 + 1

   2 + 2

3. **Present the investigation.** Explain that the task is to find all the ways to write sums of the number five.

> **Teaching Tip**
> Sometimes students suggest expressions that use zero as an addend. When this happens, I acknowledge the suggestion and reiterate that for this investigation, we're using only addends that are 1 and greater.
> — MSB

> **Teaching Tip**
> It helps to use the "think, pair, share" routine (see page 68) and give students the chance to think first and then talk with a partner before you engage them in a classroom discussion.
> — MSB

> **Teaching Tip**
> If someone offers an expression that's already on the board, I acknowledge the suggestion by writing it next to the one it matches so the student can see that it's a duplicate. Then I erase it and explain that we need to record just one of each different expression.
> — MSB

4. Discuss the task to make sure students understand what they are to do. Ask for questions. Have a few students restate the task.

Exploring

1. **Observe the interaction, listening to how groups organize working together, the ideas they discuss, and the strategies they use.**

2. **Offer assistance when needed.** As you circulate, look for duplicates on the students' lists, most often from having the same addends in a different order. In these instances, tell the students that there's a duplicate and give them the challenge of finding it.

   Circulate and observe. If students call you over to announce that they've finished, do a quick count to see if they've found all fifteen ways. If they haven't, tell them that there are more (without telling them how many they're missing) and ask them to continue their search. Also, if you notice students repeated any expressions, give them this information but leave them the task of finding the repeats.

3. **Provide an extension to groups that finish more quickly than others.** If a group has found all fifteen different expressions while others are still working, suggest that they try the same investigation for the sum of six.

Summarizing

1. **Have pairs or groups review their work and think about what to report in a classroom discussion.** If they haven't written summary statements to describe what they noticed and learned, ask them to do so now.

2. **Initiate a classroom discussion.** First have groups report how they organized working together.

3. **Have groups report their results or solutions, explaining their reasoning or strategies.** Ask how they decided when they had found all expressions.

4. **Generalize from the solutions.** With the students, look at the pattern in the number of ways there are to write addition expressions for sums of three, four, and five. Ask the students to predict how many ways there are to write expressions for the sum of six. Assign the problem of finding the different ways to write sums of six to groups that did not get started on it during the exploration. Have the other students continue trying to figure out the pattern so they can predict how many expressions there are for sums of seven and eight.

Number	How many sums?
3	3
4	7
5	15
6	⋮
⋮	⋮

For Younger Students
This investigation is especially useful for engaging younger students in thinking about different combinations of addends. It also gives children informal experience thinking about commutativity and associativity.
— MSB

This problem asks students to find all the possible ways to represent small numbers as the sum of addends. When I listed the seven ways to write four as the sum of addends, I used an orderly approach to be sure to account for all the possible ways. I started by using all ones as addends, then listed the different combinations with twos, and then listed combinations with threes. My system isn't the only useful approach, but it works for me. I used the same system to find the fifteen possible combinations for the number five:

$$1 + 1 + 1 + 1$$
$$1 + 1 + 1 + 2$$
$$1 + 1 + 2 + 1$$
$$1 + 2 + 1 + 1$$
$$2 + 1 + 1 + 1$$
$$1 + 2 + 2$$
$$2 + 1 + 2$$
$$2 + 2 + 1$$
$$1 + 1 + 3$$
$$1 + 3 + 1$$
$$3 + 1 + 1$$
$$1 + 4$$
$$4 + 1$$
$$2 + 3$$
$$3 + 2$$

When I do this problem with young students, however, I typically find that they don't use an orderly approach but merely rummage to find different combinations. I sometimes show a class how I think about making a list to account for all the possibilities, but I do so with a light touch and don't push them to solve the problem my way. Besides, students' rummaging is valuable. While the addition may be trivial for older students, the investigation can still be interesting for them, especially if the focus is on predicting how many ways there are to write sums for greater numbers. As shown on the chart above, the numbers of ways to write sums for 3, 4, and 5 are 3, 7, and 15. The numbers of ways are all odd. They're also each 1 less than a power of 2. (The powers of 2 are 1, 2, 4, 8, 16, and so on, the numbers that are so useful for *King Arthur's Problem* on page 287.) Using this information, my prediction is that for the number 6 there are 31 possible sums (because 31 is 1 less than 32, the power of 2 that follows 16); for the number 7 there are 63 possible sums; for 8 there are 127.

My predictions also make sense if I evaluate the existing data another way. Look at the differences between 3, 7, and 15, the numbers of sums for 3, 4, and 5. The difference between 3 and 7 is 4; the difference between 7 and 15 is 8. These differences—4 and 8—are powers of 2. In a logical progression, the difference between 15 and the next number should be 16, the next power of 2. That would make the number 31, which is consistent with the prediction I made. The difference between 31 and 63 is 32, the next power of 2; and the difference between 127 and 63 is 64.

I didn't include in the problem thinking of all the ways to write sums for the number two. Maybe I should have, but it didn't seem interesting, since there's only one way to write two as a sum—1 + 1. But if I add that information to the table, I can see that it preserves the patterns I used for predicting, since one is one less than a power of two.

Number	How Many Sums?
2	1
3	3
4	7
5	15
6	31
7	63
8	127
⋮	⋮

A teacher suggested to me that an easier problem for children would be to consider the different combinations of addends for each number without worrying about the reversals, so that $2 + 1$ and $1 + 2$ would be considered the same since they use the same addends. For the number three, then, there would be only two possibilities:

$$1 + 1 + 1$$
$$1 + 2$$

In this version of the problem, the number four has four possibilities:

$$1 + 1 + 1 + 1$$
$$1 + 1 + 2$$
$$1 + 3$$
$$2 + 2$$

The number five has six possibilities:

$$1 + 1 + 1 + 1 + 1$$
$$1 + 1 + 1 + 2$$
$$1 + 2 + 2$$
$$1 + 1 + 3$$
$$1 + 4$$
$$2 + 3$$

Make a table of this information and predict the number of sums for six, seven, and eight. Both versions of the problem are fine, and you may think of another. What's important is that the problem engages students in looking for patterns and making conjectures.

Palindromes

This investigation engages students in looking for numerical patterns that emerge from adding numbers in a particular way.

Materials

large 0–99 chart, 1 per student [R] See Reproducible R.32
Palindrome Recording Sheet, 1 per student [R] See Reproducible R.33
crayons, colored pencils, or markers

Introducing

1. **Present or review concepts.** A palindrome is a number that reads the same forward and backward, such as 44, 252, or 8,008. A number that is not a palindrome, such as 13, can be changed into a palindrome by using a particular procedure: You reverse the digits and add. Demonstrate on the board how to do this. Since it takes one addition, 13 is a one-step palindrome.

$$\begin{array}{r} 13 \\ \oplus\ 31 \\ \hline 44 \end{array}$$

   Some numbers take more than one addition. Demonstrate with 67, which is a two-step palindrome.

$$\begin{array}{r} 68 \\ \oplus\ 86 \\ \hline 154 \\ \oplus\ 451 \\ \hline 605 \\ \oplus\ 506 \\ \hline 1111 \end{array}$$

2. **Pose a part of the problem or a similar but smaller problem.** Have the students try to change 48 into a palindrome. As they work, do it on the board so they can check their work. Then show the class how to record the results for 13, 68, and 48 on the Palindrome Recording Sheet.

3. **Present the investigation.** Each pair or group is to investigate all the numbers from zero to 99. First they should decide how to share the work. Everyone is to keep individual records on the chart as demonstrated. Also, each student is to record on a 0–99 chart, coloring the numbers that are already palindromes with one color, coloring in one-step palindromes with another color, and so on. As a group, they should agree on the colors to use. Direct them to look for patterns on both charts. Also, tell them not to tackle 98 and 89 unless they are ready for a serious bout with addition. (Each number takes twenty-four steps with a resulting palindrome of 8,813,200,023,188!)

> **About the Math**
> A colleague pointed out that the digits in each of the resulting palindromes in my examples were the same—44 and 1111. But that's not always the case. The number 67, for example, is a two-step palindrome that results in 484.
>
> — MBB

4. **Discuss the task to make sure students understand what they are to do.** To make sure students understand what they are to do, ask for questions. If you think it would be helpful, review the process of reversing and adding, and then recording, for another number, like 75, which is a two-step palindrome.

Exploring

1. **Observe the interaction, listening to how groups organize working together, the ideas they discuss, and the strategies they use.** Note those that may be useful for a later class discussion.

2. **Offer assistance when needed.** Problems do not generally arise during this exploration. Several class periods may be required for all pairs or groups to finish their work. Before beginning work on the second day, it may be useful to have a brief discussion about their progress so that students can hear from others about organizational tips, problems, and so on.

3. **Provide an extension to groups that finish more quickly than others.** Offer two suggestions to these groups. Either they can be computationally bold and tackle 89 or 98. Or they can investigation numbers greater than 99.

Summarizing

1. **Have pairs or groups review their work and think about what to report in a classroom discussion about how they investigated the numbers.**

2. **Initiate a classroom discussion.** First have groups report how they organized working together. Ask questions such as, How did you share the work? Was your system a good one? Did you change your system during the investigation? What do you think would be the best way for others to tackle this investigation?

3. **Have groups report their results or solutions, explaining their reasoning or strategies.**

4. **Generalize from the solutions.** Ask about patterns that emerged on charts. Start a chart of the students' discoveries. For example, some notice that when the sum of the digits of a number is less than ten, the number is always a one-step palindrome. Others notice that all resulting palindromes are multiples of eleven. Have the class look for other patterns such as these.

When Observing
I've found that groups sometimes start by dividing up the numbers and working individually, but then shift to collaborating in a different way as they begin to notice patterns, such as which numbers are one-step palindromes.

— MSB

Teaching Tip
I often ask students how they decided to color the one-digit numbers on the top row of the 0-99 chart. There's no right answer to this. Hearing one another's ideas gives students information about the decision-making process of other groups.

— MSB

Additional Investigations for Whole-Class Lessons

In this section I include suggestions for additional investigations that are suitable for whole-class lessons. In contrast to the following "Independent Investigations" section, these ideas especially benefit from engaging the entire class with them, and then collecting and comparing the students' results. These aren't presented in the elaborated three-phase lesson structure but rather are general ideas that can be expanded into the three-phase structure.

See Reproducible R.1 for a template you can print and use for organizing the additional investigations into the three-phase lesson structure. Downloadable from mathsolutions.com/atm4theditionreproducibles

Investigations with Raisins

Materials

$\frac{1}{2}$-oz boxes of raisins, 1 per student

$1\frac{1}{2}$-oz boxes of raisins, for *Extension 1: More Raisins*, 1 per small group of students

The Lesson

Organize the students into pairs or groups and follow these directions:

1. Show students a $\frac{1}{2}$-oz box of raisins. Have the students guess how many raisins it contains.

2. Distribute the boxes. Each student opens a box, counts the raisins that are visible, and makes an estimate of how many raisins are in the entire box. (Be sure to remind them not to remove any raisins yet.) They then discuss their estimates in their groups, decide on a group estimate, and report it in writing, explaining their reasoning.

3. Each student counts the raisins in his or her box, arranging them on paper so it's easy to see how many there are. Record the counts on the board.

4. Based on the information recorded on the board, students predict what one number might be a good estimate for how many raisins typically are in a box. Have them record individually and explain their reasoning, discuss their ideas with a partner, and finally report to the class.

5. Students figure how many raisins there are altogether in their group's boxes. They record and explain how they figured. Finally, they can eat their raisins if they wish, but have them save the boxes for the extensions. Also, save the information you recorded about their actual counts.

> **Teaching Tip**
> To focus more directly on place value, sometimes I give more specific direction to students about how to arrange their raisins, telling them to put the raisins into groups of ten.
> — MSB

Extensions

More Raisins. Give each pair or group a $1\frac{1}{2}$-oz box of raisins. Have them estimate how many raisins are in it and explain in writing how they did it. Have groups report to the class.

Sharing More Raisins. Have pairs or groups count the raisins in the larger box and then figure out how to share them equally. They write about how they solved this problem.

The second extension, *Sharing More Raisins*, is especially useful for introducing students to division; also see "Introducing Division" in Part 3 on page 387.

Coin Riddles

Materials
dimes, 4
pennies, 2

The Lesson
Hide the coins from view and present the clues below to the class in the sequence given.

After each clue, have groups discuss what they know for sure. Also, ask them if they have sufficient information to guess the coins you have or if they need another clue.

When they are sure they know, reveal the coins so they can check their solution. If they guessed incorrectly, talk with them about how their thinking was erroneous.

Clues

Clue 1: I have six coins.

Clue 2: I have only dimes and pennies.

Clue 3: I have at least two pennies.

Clue 4: I have more dimes than pennies.

For younger students

For younger students, one-clue riddles are more accessible. Here are three options.

Two-Coin Riddle. I have two coins worth eleven cents.

Three-Coin Riddle. I have three coins worth twenty-seven cents.

Four-Coin Riddle. I have four coins worth twenty-two cents.

For Younger Students
When teaching younger students, I've found that it's important to provide them coins to use for figuring out answers to coin riddles.
— MSB

The Border Problem

Materials
10-by-10 squares cut from centimeter grid paper,
1 per student   **R** See Reproducible R.2
5-by-5 squares cut from centimeter grid paper,
1 per student   **R** See Reproducible R.2

The Lesson
Ask students to figure out, without counting them one by one, how many squares there are in the border of a 10-by-10 grid. Record all the different ways reported by translating their verbal explanations to arithmetic notation. For example, a student might explain that they added four tens since there are ten squares on each side of the border, but then subtracted four because the corners were counted twice. I'd represent that as $(4 \times 10) - 4$.

Then have students test their methods on figuring out how many squares are in the border of a 5-by-5 grid.

Show the class a larger square grid, one for which they don't know the number of squares on a side. Ask them to describe how they would go about figuring the number of squares in its border. Show how to translate one of their methods into an algebraic formula. Have students work together to translate all their methods into formulas.

The Game of Poison

Materials
small objects, 13 per pair of students

The Lesson
The Game of Poison is a game for two people. Players place thirteen objects on the table and take turns. On a turn, a player may remove one object or two objects. Play continues until all objects have been taken. The last object to be removed is considered to be the poison, and whoever gets stuck taking the last object loses.

Extensions
Change the Number of Objects. Add one more object to the pile and play again. Try playing with other numbers of objects.

Change the Number a Player Can Remove. Change the rules so it's possible to remove one, two, three, or some other number of objects on a turn.

Make the Poison a Treat. Play the game so the person who removes the last object wins. How does this affect your strategies?

Odd Number Wins. Play the game so that players can remove one, two, or three of the objects. Whoever has an odd number of counters when all have been picked up is the winner.

Decision Making

Materials
1–6 die

See Race for 20 on page 292 for a related game. Also, *Race for 20* includes an "About the Mathematics" discussion that talks a bit about *The Game of Poison*.

The Lesson
Teach the game to the class by asking each student to set up a blank addition problem as shown, making boxes large enough so they can write a numeral in each.

Roll the die five times. Each time, call out the number that comes up and give students time to write the number in one of the five boxes. Once they write the number down, they cannot change its position. The goal is to place the numbers to produce the largest sum possible.

Play the game several times until you're sure all the students understand it.

Then assign the group task. Groups are to write one procedure that the entire group will follow in playing the game as a team. They may write this decision-making strategy any way they like, as long as it is clear to all group members and accounts for all possible rolls.

When groups have completed their procedures, play five rounds of the game. See if any group's strategy produces more wins than any other.

Have groups post their procedures to compare the different ways the procedures were written and the different strategies the groups used.

Riddles with Tiles

Materials
tiles (red, blue, yellow, green), about 5 of each color per student
small paper bag

The Lesson
To prepare for the lesson, put four yellow, four green, and four blue tiles into the paper bag. Tell students that you've put color tiles into the bag, but don't reveal any information about how many or what colors. Then read the clues, one by one, giving the students a chance to use their tiles to make a combination that might be in the bag.

> *Clue 1:* I have twelve tiles.
>
> *Clue 2:* I used three colors.
>
> *Clue 3:* There are no red tiles.
>
> *Clue 4:* There are the same number of green and blue tiles.
>
> *Clue 5:* I have four yellow tiles.

Extension
Riddle 2. Put four blue and two yellow tiles into the bag. Then present these clues:

> *Clue 1:* There are fewer than ten tiles.
>
> *Clue 2:* I used two colors.
>
> *Clue 3:* I have no green or red tiles.
>
> *Clue 4:* I have twice as many blue tiles as yellow tiles.
>
> *Clue 5:* I have two yellow tiles.

Teaching Tip
Sometimes I give students the first three clues at the same time. This typically results in animated discussions about what they know so far and what they're not sure about.

— MBB

Teaching Tip
After students are comfortable solving riddles, have them work in pairs to make up their own riddles for others to solve.

— MBB

Independent Investigations

The following investigations with number and operations, can be used as individual assignments, as small-group or partner investigations, or as a choice time exploration.

For more on using investigations with various instructional groups, see "Starting Point 20: Four Structures for Organizing and Managing Classroom Instruction" in Part 1 on page 111.

Making Change

Find all the ways to make change for $0.50.
Easier version: Find all the ways to make change for a quarter.
Harder version: Find all the ways to make change for $1.00.

About the Mathematics

Using the context of money, this problem calls for making a list of all possible ways and, in that way, it's similar to *Number Sums* (see page 267). The investigations are also similar in that both involve thinking about different addition combinations. I approached solving this investigation the same way I did for *Number Sums*, making a list in an orderly fashion that would exhaust all the possibilities for making change for $0.25, $0.50, and $1.00.

Instead of making a list, actually, I made a chart, writing the coins at the top and using each line for a different combination, indicating how many of each coin I would use. For $0.25, for example, I made the following chart, which produced twelve ways to make change:

10¢	5¢	1¢
2	1	0
2	0	5
1	3	0
1	2	5
1	1	10
1	0	15
0	5	0
0	4	5
0	3	10
0	2	15
0	1	20
0	0	25

Teaching Tip
Organizing the chart in an orderly way made it easier for me to decide when I had listed all of the possible ways. Many students don't naturally approach this problem in an organized way, so I try and model an example for them and explain the benefits the order provides.
— MSB

I've learned to look for patterns when I tackle a problem. In examining the chart above, I noticed a 2-4-6 pattern in the dimes column. There are two ways to use a dime twice, four ways to use a dime once, and six ways not to use a dime at all. This isn't a great discovery, but one that gave me some comfort that there was some order to what I was doing.

For $0.50, here's part of the chart I made; this chart has an additional column to account for quarters as well as dimes, nickels, and pennies:

25¢	10¢	5¢	1¢
2	0	0	0
1	2	1	0
1	2	0	5
1	1	3	0
1	1	2	5
1	1	1	10
1	1	0	15
1	0	5	0
1	0	4	5
1	0	3	10
⋮	⋮	⋮	⋮

I found forty-nine ways to make change for $0.50. The 2-4-6 pattern emerged again in the dimes column when one quarter was used, and also a 1-3-5-7-9-11 pattern in the dimes column when no quarters were used. Hmmm.

On to making change for $1.00: I knew that there would be many more ways to make change for $1.00, and I wondered if there was a way to find them other than starting another chart. Making such an elaborate list was going to be pretty exhausting.

I decided to use what I knew about making change for $0.50. I added a first column to the chart for using a 50-cent coin, using a different-colored pen to keep my previous work intact. Then I thought: If I added a 50-cent coin to each of the forty-nine ways for $0.50, each would then be worth $1.00, and that makes forty-nine ways. Also, I could make $1.00 using only two 50-cent coins, so now I had fifty ways which, I think, took care of all possibilities using one or two 50-cent coins. Now I had to figure out the ways to make change for $1.00 without using any 50¢ coins.

I thought that if I used the chart I'd made for making change for $0.50 and doubled the quantities for each coin, the amount on each line would double from $0.50 to $1.00. That would give another forty-nine ways, bringing my total up to ninety-nine ways. I wondered if doubling would take care of every other possibility, however. I realized that the ways I had considered so far used four quarters once and two quarters twenty-four times, but I hadn't considered any possibilities using one or three quarters. Oops. I went back to construct those.

It wasn't hard to figure that there were twelve ways with three quarters: I reasoned that because three quarters makes 75¢, I need 25¢ more, and I learned earlier that there are 12 ways to make change for 25¢. So if I added three quarters to each of those 12 ways, I'd have 12 new ways to make change for $1.00. That changed my total from 99 to 111 ways.

Now I thought that all I had to do was figure the ways using one quarter. With one quarter, I need 75¢ more. Maybe I can use the chart for $0.25 again, this time tripling the quantities for each coin so that the amount on each line would triple from $0.25 to $0.75. That would produce 12 more ways to make change for $1.00 using one quarter, bringing the total to 123.

Was this saving time? Should I just have made the list to begin with? How did I know whether I had accounted for all the possible ways? I didn't feel right about this number 123. I don't know why, but I felt there were other possibilities. I took a break. I fixed a cup of tea and a snack. I phoned a friend (about something completely unrelated). I went out and did an errand.

Then it came to me. I was thinking that there were only 12 ways to make change for $1.00 using one quarter, but that couldn't be right. That would be the same as saying that there were twelve ways to make change for $0.75 if I used only dimes, nickels, and pennies. But there were twelve ways to make change for $0.25 with dimes, nickels, and pennies, so there should be lots more ways to make change for $0.75 with these same coins. I went back to work, this time making a chart for the ways to make change for $0.75 with dimes, nickels, and pennies. I found seventy-two ways! (And 72 is the sum of $2 + 4 + 6 + 8 + 10 + 12 + 14 + 16$, an extension of the 2-4-6 pattern I had noticed earlier.)

My chart included those 12 ways from tripling the quantities in my old chart for $0.25, so I eliminated that step, went back to the previous total of 111 and added on the new 72 ways, to get a total of 183.

At this point I was sorry that I had ever included this investigation in the book and even sorrier that I had committed to offering solutions. Now I had heaps of paper on my desk and an answer of 183, in which I had little confidence. I decided that I needed to give the problem a fresh look, but this was not the time. I took another break and didn't return to the problem for several days.

When I returned to the problem, rested, I took a new approach. To make change for $1.00, I thought, I could use two 50-cent coins—that was one way. Or if I used one 50-cent coin, then my former logic made sense that there were 49 ways to make $0.50 with quarters, dimes, nickels, and pennies—adding the 50-cent coin to the ways I already had would bring each total to $1.00. So now I had fifty ways so far, as I had before. So far, so good.

OK, I eliminated the 50-cent coins and thought about what happened with quarters. I could make $1.00 with four quarters, three quarters, two quarters, one quarter, or no quarters.

Four quarters is easy—there's only one way.

For three quarters you need $0.25 more to make $1.00, and there are twelve ways to make that.

For two quarters, you need $0.50 more, and there are forty-nine ways to make that. But I couldn't count the ways on my list of forty-nine that already used one or two quarters, because those ways used three and four quarters total, which I had already counted earlier. This eliminated thirteen possibilities and left me with thirty-six more ways.

For one quarter, I needed $0.75 more. Let's see, the answer to that was somewhere in my heap of papers. (I hadn't thrown out anything.) There it was—using only dimes, nickels, and pennies, there were seventy-two ways to make $0.75.

There was only zero quarters left. How many ways could I make change for $1.00 with only dimes, nickels, and pennies? I started a chart. A 1-3-5-7 . . . pattern emerged for using ten dimes, then nine dimes, then eight, and so on down to zero dimes. That is, with ten dimes there was one way, with nine dimes there were three ways, with eight dimes there were five ways, and so on down to with one dime there were 19 ways and with zero dimes there were 21 ways. (That's the pattern of odd numbers from 1 to 21.) I didn't write all of the possibilities. Instead I figured out the number of ways by adding the odd numbers from 1 through 21 and got 121. Boy, I love patterns. So I went with 121 ways to make $1.00 using only dimes, nickels, and pennies.

What was my total this time? I had to add 50, 1, 12, 36, 72, and 121, which gave a total of 292. I hope this is right. But please write if you have a quarrel with my answer or my reasoning. I'd like to hear from you. Really. (I'll save my papers.)

How Many Sums?

If you add two or more of these numbers, find all the different possible sums you can get.

19   21   15   17   13

About the mathematics

Egad, I thought, another problem of finding all the different possible sums. But this time there are only five possible addends, so it should be easier.

I began by making a list of the possible combinations using two addends. I found ten:

19 + 21
19 + 15
19 + 17
19 + 13
21 + 15
21 + 17
21 + 13
15 + 17
15 + 13
17 + 13

I knew that I *didn't* need to reverse these combinations—I was interested in different sums and reversals would produce the same set of sums. Hey, I then thought, this is like *The Handshake Problem* (see page 259). If five people shake hands with each other, there will be ten handshakes altogether. It's also like *Dot Connecting* (see page 253). With five dots, I can draw ten lines connecting each one to every other one. (Keep an eye out for connections like these. They help build your mathematical intuition.)

I was feeling pleased with myself, but only for a moment. What if I was allowed to use the numbers more than once? Then I'd have to include 19 + 19, for example, and the other sums with both addends the same. But what did the problem call for?

I read it again. It wasn't clear. I could go either way. Well, it's my book, I thought. Which way was I thinking? I couldn't remember. (After all, I wrote the previous editions of the book quite a while ago.) But I could remember why I included the problem. It gives practice with addition in a way that also calls for looking for patterns. Both versions do that. So there really are two problems here, one in which you use each number only once and one in which you can use each number as many times as you'd like.

I opted to continue the way I started and went on to make a list of the possible combinations of three addends, using each number only once in each combination. Again, I found ten.

$$19 + 21 + 15$$
$$19 + 21 + 17$$
$$19 + 21 + 13$$
$$19 + 15 + 17$$
$$19 + 15 + 13$$
$$19 + 17 + 13$$
$$21 + 15 + 17$$
$$21 + 15 + 13$$
$$21 + 17 + 13$$
$$15 + 17 + 13$$

For possible combinations of four addends, I found five ways.

$$19 + 21 + 15 + 17$$
$$19 + 21 + 15 + 13$$
$$19 + 21 + 17 + 13$$
$$19 + 15 + 17 + 13$$
$$21 + 15 + 17 + 13$$

For five addends, there's just one way:

$$19 + 21 + 5 + 17 + 13$$

All in all, there were twenty-six combinations of addends. But I wasn't done, because the problem asked for different possible *sums*, not different possible combinations of *addends*.

I returned to the ten combinations with two addends and figured the sums:

$$19 + 21 = 40$$
$$19 + 15 = 34$$
$$19 + 17 = 36$$
$$19 + 13 = 32$$
$$21 + 15 = 36$$
$$21 + 17 = 38$$
$$21 + 13 = 34$$
$$15 + 17 = 32$$
$$15 + 13 = 28$$
$$17 + 13 = 30$$

The sums were all even, which makes sense, because whenever you add two odd numbers, the sum is even. And there were duplicate sums. I looked again at the numbers and realized that they were consecutive odd numbers—13, 15, 17, 19, and 21. If I added the first and the last, the sum would have to be the same as if I added the second and the fourth because I would be increasing one addend by two and decreasing the other addend by two. So there's more to discuss with students than merely calculating sums—there's also seeing relationships among pairs of addends.

For two addends, there were ten possible combinations, but only seven different sums. That's because 19 + 13 = 15 + 17; 19 + 15 = 21 + 13; and 19 + 17 = 21 + 15.

To think about the sums with three addends, I tried using this information to see which would be eliminated. First of all, I knew that all the sums would be odd, since adding three odd numbers always produces an odd number. That guaranteed that there wouldn't be any matches with the first set of sums, which were all even. But again there were duplicates in this set, which left me with seven different sums, making fourteen altogether so far.

The combinations with four and five addends produced unique sums, which added five more. The grand total: twenty possible sums.

I'm done—unless I want to do the other version of the problem and use the numbers more than once. Well, not right now. Maybe later.

Change from a $10.00 Bill

If you spend $1.85 and pay with a $10.00 bill, you get $8.15 in change. Notice that the digits in your change are the same as the digits in the amount you spent. Try to find all the other amounts you could spend and get change with the same digits. Explain why you think you've found all of the possibilities.

About the Mathematics

I found eleven solutions for the amount I could spend and get change with the same digits: $0.95, $1.85, $2.75, $3.65, $4.55, $5.00, $5.45, $6.35, $7.25, $8.15, and $9.05. The first one in the list has given people trouble because of the 0 in the dollar place.

Then I began to look at the amounts to see what I noticed, and then what that made me wonder about. Except for $5.00, which has the same in change as what was spent, all of the amounts ended in 5. Also, the sum of the two digits preceding 5, such as 1 + 8 in $1.85, always added to 9. So there is some structure here that emerged, which is what I next wondered about.

Full confession: I don't have a way to discuss this and present my ideas. Well, I should amend that. I don't have a way yet to discuss this and present my ideas. I'm still thinking. You're on your own.

Multiplication Possibilities

Find as many ways as you can to fill in this problem so the arithmetic is correct.

About the Mathematics

I used to view this as a ho-hum problem, just a twist on providing students with multiplication practice. Using trial and error to test different numbers certainly does support practice, but this investigation can also help develop students' number sense and logical reasoning skills.

The first thing I wondered about was how to get a 6 in the ones place of the answer. In order for that to happen, the product of the one-digit multiplier and the ones digit in the three-digit top number had to end in a 6. I wondered about which pairs of numbers made this possible. I started a list with 1 × 6. Then I thought about 2 as a factor, and came up with 2 × 3. For 3, 3 × 2 was obvious. For 4, I came up with 4 × 4, which made me realize that I was being fairly narrow with 1, 2, and 3, thinking only about how to get to a product of 6. I had skipped over 2 × 8. And if 6 and 16 are possible products that end in 6, so are 26, 36, 46, 56, 66, 76, 86, and 96. Now I began to think of ways to reach those products with two single-digit factors. My list evolved:

$$1 \times 6$$
$$2 \times 3$$
$$2 \times 8$$
$$3 \times 2$$
$$4 \times 4$$
$$4 \times 9$$

I skipped over 5. I knew that 5 times any number ends in either 5 or 0, so it wouldn't be a possibility. I continued.

$$6 \times 1$$
$$6 \times 6$$
$$7 \times 8$$
$$8 \times 2$$
$$8 \times 7$$
$$9 \times 4$$

I couldn't think of any others, but a dozen was a good start. OK, I thought, now what do I do?

I'm a just-get-started kind of problem solver, happy to try something and think about it afterward. I put a 1 in the box to use as the multiplier. Aha, that works if I use 966 as the top number. I put a check next to 1 × 6 on my list.

I then tried 2 as the multiplier. Ah, I thought, this works if I use half of 966 as the top number. (Do you see why that makes sense?) Since 966 is even, that's possible. Now I had two possibilities. I put a check next to 2 × 3.

Next on the list was 2 × 8. Well, if I used 2 as the one-digit multiplier, I already knew the answer—483—so 2 × 8 wouldn't work. I crossed it off my list. But what if I used 8 for the one-digit multiplier and the 2 in the ones place on top? What times 8 equals 966? Here's where knowing how multiplication and division relates helps. Dividing 966 by 8 gives 120.75, and that won't fit in the three boxes for the top number, so 8 can't possibly be a multiplier. I crossed off 8 × 2 and 8 × 7. My list now looked like the illustration to the right.

$$1 \times 6 \quad \checkmark$$
$$2 \times 3 \quad \checkmark$$
$$\cancel{2 \times 8}$$
$$3 \times 2$$
$$4 \times 4$$
$$4 \times 9$$
$$6 \times 1$$
$$6 \times 6$$
$$7 \times 8$$
$$\cancel{8 \times 2}$$
$$\cancel{8 \times 7}$$
$$9 \times 4$$

Now I started to wise up. I knew that 1 and 2 were possible single-digit multipliers; I knew that 8 was impossible; the only other numbers I needed to test were 3, 4, 5, 6, 7, and 9. I didn't really have to make that list after all. I could have merely tried those numbers, using what I know about the relationship between multiplication and division.

Also, I could use what I knew about divisibility. A number is divisible by 3 if its digits add to a multiple of 3. I added $9 + 6 + 6$ and got 21; since 21 is a multiple of 3, I knew that 3 would work. And I knew that 6 would also work, because even numbers that are divisible by 3 are also divisible by 6.

I did the divisions and found what I think are the only possibilities—966×1, 483×2, 322×3, 161×6, 138×7. (Where's the answer book to check my work?)

I began to wonder what other problems like this one would be good for students to try. That got me thinking more about the 966 problem. Judging by all the thinking it sparked for me, it seems that 966 was a good choice of number. What other factors would produce a product of 966? How could I think about that? I identified the prime factors of 966—2, 3, 7, and 23.

Then I rearranged and combined the factors in different ways, applying the commutative and associative properties. I came up with other problems—$(2 \times 3 \times 7) \times 23$, or 42×23; $(2 \times 7) 3 (3 \times 23)$, which is the same as 14×69; and 21×46. None fit the three-digit times one-digit format, but all produced the answer of 966. Who ever thought that I'd get so involved with 966?

So, what other numbers would be good to use in a problem like this to replace 966 and spark thinking? Here are three I tried that you might be interested in tinkering with. Or you can make up some of your own.

The Postage Stamp Investigation

You can combine different denominations of stamps to get the proper postage for a letter or package. In this investigation, you figure out the postage amounts that can be made when you are restricted to using only certain stamps.

To begin, if stamps came only in 3¢ and 5¢ denominations, what amounts of postage would be impossible to make? Is there a largest impossible amount? Explain your answers.

Do the same investigation if there were only 5¢ and 8¢ stamps. Then continue with other combinations of two denominations of stamps. For each, investigate the following:

1. How many impossible amounts are there?

2. Is there a largest impossible amount? If so, what is it?

Write an explanation for each of your answers.

About the Mathematics

The arithmetic calculations required in this problem aren't particularly challenging, which makes it accessible to some primary students as well as to upper-elementary students. And the patterns that emerge are interesting to students of all ages. I offer here how I thought about the problem of the possible postage to make with 3¢ and 5¢ stamps, and then with 5¢ and 8¢ stamps. I leave it to you to think about what happens with stamps of other denominations.

If I use only 3¢ stamps on an envelope, then the possible postage amounts are multiples of 3—3¢, 6¢, 9¢, 12¢, 15¢, and so on. Using only 5¢ stamps produces postage amounts that are multiples of 5—5¢, 10¢, 15¢, 20¢, 25¢, and so on. Combining both denominations produces other possible amounts. For example, one 3¢ stamp and one 5¢ stamp makes 8¢; two 3¢ stamps and one 5¢ stamp makes 11¢; three 3¢ stamps and one 5¢ stamp makes 14¢. These begin a pattern that increases by 3¢ each time and results in all new totals—8¢, 11¢, 14¢, 17¢, 20¢. Oops, there's a repeat, caused because it uses five 3¢ stamps, which is the same as three 5¢ stamps. So there will be some new amounts and some repeats from using one 5¢ stamp with different numbers of 3¢ stamps.

It seems way too complicated to figure out all of the possible amounts. Maybe it would be easier to think about the amounts that aren't possible. Maybe there's a pattern there that would give a tidy solution.

OK, I know from a bit of testing that it's not possible to use the stamps to make the amounts of 1¢, 2¢, 4¢, or 7¢. What is the next impossible number?

I listed the amounts from 1¢ to 25¢ and decided to try which I could make. After 7¢, all the amounts were possible, so I concluded that 1¢, 2¢, 4¢, and 7¢ were the only impossible amounts. The way I did my figuring was first to use trial and error to find solutions for all of the sums from 8¢ to 17¢. The next number, 18¢, was 10¢ more than 8¢, an amount I had already solved, which meant I could do 18¢ with two more 5¢ stamps. And 19¢ was 10¢ more than 9¢, another amount for which I had solution. Every subsequent number would be 10¢ more than something I had already done, which meant adding on two more 5¢ stamps to a previous solution. Actually, I could have done even less arithmetic and stopped once I found three consecutive numbers in a row with solutions—8¢, 9¢, and 10¢. Then all I had to do was add a 3¢ stamp on to 8¢ to make 11¢, then 3¢ to 9¢, and so on, to make every subsequent amount. But adding 10 seems so friendly.

There are four impossible amounts using 3¢ and 5¢ stamps, and the largest is 7¢. Done.

Well, not really done. Next the problem asks me to use only 5¢ and 8¢ stamps. Hoo-hah, this was harder. I was looking for a consecutive string of five numbers with solutions so I could apply the same logic, this time adding a 5¢ stamp to make all subsequent amounts. I finally found a string—28¢, 29¢, 30¢, 31¢, and 32¢. There were fourteen impossible amounts, all smaller— 1¢, 2¢, 3¢, 4¢, 6¢, 7¢, 9¢, 11¢, 12¢, 14¢, 17¢, 19¢, 22¢, and 27¢, with 27¢ being the largest impossible amount.

The problem suggests also investigating what happens with other combinations of stamps. I fiddled with some and was intrigued by the differences when both stamps were even or odd, or when there was one of each. The problem can get complex. But the beauty of it is that the only skill you need to get started is addition, and adding gets you pretty far. In a classroom, some students won't progress beyond adding to find solutions while others will search for patterns to reveal what's happening. There's something here for everyone.

	3¢	5¢
1	—	—
2	—		
3	1	0
4	—	—
5	0	1
6	2	0
7	—		
8	1	1
9	3	0
10	0	2
11	2	1
12	4	0
13	1	2
14	3	1
15)8		3
16	2	2
17	4	1
18	1	3
19	3	2
20	0	4
21	2	3
22	4	2
23	1	4
24	3	5
25)8	5	5/2

Arrow Arithmetic

You need: large 0–99 chart **R** See Reproducible R.32

Look at the starter hints below, using the 0–99 chart for reference. Then solve the others.

Starter hints: $18 \rightarrow = 19$ $18 \leftarrow = 17$ $18 \uparrow = 8$ $18 \downarrow = 28$

How about these? $18 \nearrow = ?$ $18 \nwarrow = ?$ $14 \swarrow \rightarrow \rightarrow = ?$
$76 \searrow \uparrow \uparrow = ?$

True or false? $16 \downarrow \downarrow \rightarrow \rightarrow = 38$
$24 \rightarrow \swarrow \nearrow \downarrow = 34$
$61 \uparrow \nearrow \rightarrow = 42$
$24 \uparrow \uparrow \uparrow \uparrow \nwarrow = 67$
$83 \searrow \searrow \searrow = 22$

Make up problems for others to solve.

Extension

Going off the Chart. How would you solve these? $9 \rightarrow = ?$ $7 \uparrow = ?$
$70 \leftarrow = ?$

For information about when to use the 0–99 chart and when to use the 1–100 chart, read "0–99 Chart versus 1–100 Chart" in "Questions Teachers Ask," page 464.

About the Mathematics

In this investigation, each arrow tells you to move one square on a 0–99 chart in the direction that the arrow is pointing. I like this investigation and have had success with it in classes from the primary grades through middle school. Students generally delight in figuring out what the arrows mean. Doing this investigation with students has taught me not to take for granted that the patterns that seem so obvious to me on the 0–99 chart are also obvious to students. Some students, even older ones, need to refer to the chart to check predictions, if not actually to arrive at answers. But I've found that when they are given time to experience the investigation, students make numerical discoveries that serve them beyond the arrow problems.

Young students typically continue to use the 0–99 chart as a reference for finding answers. Older students, however, either visualize the chart or translate the arrows to arithmetic calculations—an arrow pointing right results in adding one to the starting number; an arrow pointing down results in adding ten; an arrow pointing diagonally down to the right results in adding eleven; and so on. Thinking arithmetically helps students develop strategies for adding and subtracting eleven and nine, which is good practice for developing their mental arithmetic ability.

Teachers sometimes ask me why I use the 0–99 chart instead of the 1–100 chart. The investigation works equally well with either version, but on the 0–99 chart all of the numbers in the same decade, the twenties or thirties, for example, are on the same line. But this is a small preference, not a biggie. Take your pick of charts.

We're used to having one right answer to most math problems, and the extensions offer the refreshing possibility for different interpretations. For 9 →, for example, I've heard three different answers from students, each of which made sense according to how each reasoned.

1. The answer is 10, because → means add 1, and 9 + 1 = 10.

2. The answer is 0, because I think how the chart would look pasted on a cylinder, like a can of vegetables or soup. If you go one space to the right, you'll be back at the beginning of the same row.

3. You can't tell for sure, so I don't think there's an answer.

4. All of these answers show reasonable mathematical thinking. The system of arrows suggested in this problem isn't one that has been established as a conventional part of mathematics. Different answers to potentially ambiguous situations can exist as long as they're justified.

King Arthur's Problem

This is a fictionalized historical problem. King Arthur wanted to decide who was most fit to marry his daughter. He chose the following method. When all his knights were seated at the Round Table, he entered the room, pointed to one knight, and said, "You live." The next knight wasn't so fortunate. "You die," said King Arthur, and chopped off his head. To the third knight, he said, "You live," and to the fourth, he said, "You die," and chopped off his head. He continued doing this around the circle, chopping off the head of every other knight, until just one was left. The remaining knight got to marry the daughter but, as the legend goes, he was never quite the same again.

The problem is to figure out where you should sit in order to live. Do this for different numbers of knights. Find a pattern so you can predict where to sit no matter how many people are seated in the circle.

About the Mathematics

The way I made sense of this problem was to investigate first where the safe seat would be if there were only two knights, then try for three knights, four knights, five, and so on. For example, for five knights, here's what I did:

I wrote the numerals 1 through 5 in a circle.

I put my pencil on the 1 and said, "You live."

I then moved my pencil to the 2, said, "You die," and crossed it out.

I moved to the 3 and said, "You live."

I then moved my pencil to the 4, said, "You die," and crossed it out.

I next moved my pencil to the 5 and said, "You live."

I then moved to the 1, said, "You die," and crossed it out. Only the 3 and 5 were left.

I moved to the 3 and said, "You live."

I moved to the 5, said, "You die," and crossed it out.

The 3 was left, so it was the safe seat with five knights.

I recorded my findings on a table, hoping to find a pattern that would allow me to stop figuring for every different number of knights and, instead, find a way to predict where the safe seat would be for any number of knights. Below is the table up through twenty knights.

Number of Knights	Safe Seat
1	1
2	1
3	3
4	1
5	3
6	5
7	7
8	1
9	3
10	5
11	7
12	9
13	11
14	13
15	15
16	1
17	3
18	5
19	7
20	9

A confession here: I didn't actually apply the method I described above to all twenty numbers. I started looking for patterns after ten knights. I noticed that Seat 1 was the safe seat when there were one, two, four, and eight knights. I recognized the pattern of these numbers, that each was the double of the previous one. (These numbers are the powers of two.) That discovery led me to predict that with sixteen knights, Seat 1 would again be the safe one. I tried sixteen and found that I was correct.

I also noticed that even-numbered seats were never safe. This makes sense because the live-die pattern alternates the same way even and odd numbers do. Knights in the even-numbered seats get killed in the first pass around the circle.

And I noticed that the odd-numbered safe seats followed a predictable pattern—1, 3, 5, 7, and so on—until the next power of two. After sixteen knights, Seat 1 would again be safe when there were thirty-two knights, and the safe seat numbers after sixteen knights would go 3, 5, 7, 9, and so on up to when there are thirty-one knights. At that point, right before Seat 1 again became the safe seat, Seat 31 would be the safe seat.

OK, this is all interesting, but the power of patterns is that they allow you to predict beyond the information you currently have. What if there were 50 knights at the table? How would I figure out the safe seat without writing the numerals in a circle and applying my crossing-out method? Here's how I thought about this. I know that Seat 1 is safe for 32 knights, and the next time that Seat 1 will be safe is for 64 knights. The safe seats for

33 to 63 knights will be consecutive odd numbers—3, 5, 7, 9, . . . , 63. So, where will 50 hit? If you start with 32 (when the safe seat is 1) and count to 50, you count 19 numbers. (Check this out for yourself. I know that the difference between 32 and 50 is only 18, but I have to count both 32 and 50.) So the safe seat for 50 knights is the nineteenth consecutive odd number. The tenth consecutive odd number is 19, the twentieth consecutive odd number is 39 (see a pattern?), so the nineteenth consecutive odd number is 37. It's my bet that 37 is the safe seat for 50 knights. I checked my prediction by making a partial table, from 50 up to 64, where I knew 1 would be the safe seat again. If Seat 63 was safe for 63 knights, I'd be satisfied.

Number of Knights	Safe Seat
50	37
51	39
52	41
53	43
54	45
55	47
56	49
57	51
58	53
59	55
60	57
61	59
62	61
63	63
64	1

Hurray!

OK, now what if there are 100 knights at the table? Again, I start with what I know, that after 64 knights, the next time that Seat 1 is safe is for 128 knights. I also know that from 64 through 127 knights, the safe seat numbers will go in consecutive odd numbers—3, 5, 7, 9, . . . , 127. All I need to figure out is how many consecutive odd numbers there will be to get from 64 to 100. The difference between 64 and 100 is 36, but I have to count both 64 and 100, so I need to find the 37th consecutive odd number. I remember that the 10th odd number is 19 (1 less than twice 10) and the 20th odd number is 39 (1 less than twice 20). I try a few smaller examples to check this pattern. The 3rd odd number, 5, is 1 less than twice 3; the 4th odd number, 7, is 1 less than twice 4. So I'm comfortable figuring that the 37th odd number is 1 less than twice 37, or 73. So Seat 73 is the safe seat for 100 knights.

More people have written to me about *King Arthur's Problem* than any other problem in *About Teaching Mathematics*. Some write short desperate pleas for help. Others write longer letters, often explaining in their own words what I have just offered. Both long-letter writers and short-letter writers have made the same request—What's the formula?

Sorry, but it isn't possible to reduce every math problem to a formula that you can use to get the answer you want. Well, I could concoct a formula for King Arthur. Let me see. Let n represent the number of knights. Let s be the safe seat. Let p be the power of two that is closest to but less than n. Then, the number of consecutive odd numbers to count would be $n - p + 1$, and to figure out what the safe seat number is would be $2(n - p + 1) - 1$. Mush the variables and you get $s = 2n - 2p + 2 - 1$, or $s = 2n - 2p + 1$. So, if you like formulas, there you go.

But here's what I know. I may not—and probably won't—remember the formula, but I know that I'll always be able to figure out how to solve the problem. And that's what counts in mathematical thinking.

The Prison Problem

A jail had one hundred cells in it, all in a long row. The warden was feeling very jolly one night and told his assistant that he wanted to give all the prisoners a wonderful surprise. While they were sleeping, he wanted the assistant to unlock all the cells. This should be done, he told the assistant, by putting the key in each lock and turning it once.

Following the order, the assistant unlocked all the cells and then came back to report that the job was done. Meanwhile, however, the warden had second thoughts. "Maybe I shouldn't let all the prisoners go free," he said. "Go back and leave the first cell open, but lock the second one, by putting the key in and turning it once. Then leave the third open, but lock the fourth, and continue in this way for the entire row."

The assistant wasn't very surprised at this request. The warden often changed his mind. After finishing this task, the assistant returned, and again the warden had other thoughts. "Here's what I really want you to do," he said. "Go back down the row. Leave the first two cells as they are, and put your key in the third cell and turn it once. Then leave the fourth and fifth cells alone and turn the key in the sixth. Continue down the row this way."

The assistant again did as instructed. Fortunately, the prisoners were still asleep. As a matter of fact, the assistant was getting pretty sleepy, but there was no chance for rest yet. The warden changed his mind again, and the assistant had to go back again and turn the lock in the fourth cell and in every fourth cell down the row.

This continued all through the night, next turning the lock in every fifth cell, and then in every sixth, and on and on, until on the last trip, the assistant just had to turn the key in the hundredth cell.

When the prisoners finally woke up, which ones could walk out of their cells?

About the Mathematics

This problem has generated almost as much mail as *King Arthur's Problem*. When I first began to investigate it, I decided to solve a related but smaller problem. This technique often helps with math problems. Instead of thinking about a jail with one hundred cells, suppose the jail had only ten cells. What could I learn?

I wrote the numbers from *1* to *10* in a row to represent the cells. I followed the warden's first order, unlocked them all, and wrote *U* (for unlocked) under each number.

I then followed the warden's second order, left the first cell unlocked, locked the second, left the third unlocked, and so on. I wrote *Us* and *Ls* to indicate what I had done.

	1	2	3	4	5	6	7	8	9	10
	U	U	U	U	U	U	U	U	U	U
	U	L	U	L	U	L	U	L	U	L

I continued following the warden's orders until I had to turn the key just in the tenth cell, keeping track as I went.

	1	2	3	4	5	6	7	8	9	10
Unlock	U	U	U	U	U	U	U	U	U	U
Leave 1	U	L	U	L	U	L	U	L	U	L
Leave 2	U	L	L	L	U	U	U	L	L	L
Leave 3	U	L	L	U	U	U	U	U	L	L
Leave 4	U	L	L	U	L	U	U	U	L	U
Leave 5	U	L	L	U	L	L	U	U	L	U
Leave 6	U	L	L	U	L	L	L	U	L	U
Leave 7	U	L	L	U	L	L	L	L	L	U
Leave 8	U	L	L	U	L	L	L	L	U	U
Leave 9	U	L	L	U	L	L	L	L	U	L

Boy, this was tedious. Clearly I had to do some fast thinking. I certainly didn't want to do this for one hundred cells. What could I learn from what I had done so far?

For ten cells, the ones that remained unlocked after all I did were Cells 1, 4, and 9. But would they stay unlocked for the rest of the time if we did this for one hundred cells? Well, I knew that Cell 1 would for sure. It was unlocked the first time around, was skipped ever since, and would continue to be skipped no matter how many cells there were. And since I was now up to skipping the first ten cells before turning the lock in any of them, all of the cells from 1 through 9 would now remain untouched.

Now I began to rummage in my mind. One clue: What I was doing by following the warden's orders was a kind of jailhouse version of skip-counting. Skip-counting is related to multiplication. The answer must have something to do with multiplication. Another clue: The numbers of the unlocked cells—1, 4, and 9—are square numbers. What do I know about square numbers and multiplication?

OK, 1, 4, and 9 are square numbers because $1 = 1 \times 1$, $4 = 2 \times 2$, and $9 = 3 \times 3$. There's a tie to multiplication. I also know that square numbers are the only numbers that have an odd number of factors. All other numbers have pairs of factors. Think about 12, for example. Its factor pairs are 1×12, 2×6, and 3×4; 12 has six factors—1, 2, 3, 4, 6, and 12. Each factor is paired with a different number to make 12. But with square numbers, you can multiply a number by itself, so one of its factors has itself as a partner, resulting in an odd number of factors. Think about 16, for example. Its factor pairs are 1×16, 2×8, and 4×4, so 16 (a square number) has five factors—1, 2, 4, 8, and 16.

What does this have to do with the locking-unlocking pattern? With the skip-counting method, each cell will have its lock turned once for each of its factors as it comes up in the warden's screwy system. For numbers that are not square, which all have an even number of factors, the lock will be turned an even number of times. It started locked, and after an even number of turns, it will again be locked. The only way it could be left unlocked would be if the lock were turned an odd number of times, which can happen for only the square numbers. For me, the problem was resolved.

Race for 20

Play with a partner. Players take turns counting one or two numbers. The first player starts and counts either "One" or "One, two." The second player continues with the next number and counts on either one or two more numbers. The winner is the player who says, "Twenty."

Extensions

Change the Winning Number. Instead of *Race for 20*, play *Race for 21* or *Race for 32* or any other number.

Change How Many Numbers a Player Can Count. Change the rule so it's possible to count on one, two, or three numbers. Then try it counting on one, two, three, or four numbers.

About the Mathematics

I included this two-player game in *The Hate Mathematics! Book*, which I wrote in 1975! The game was part of my teaching repertoire then, and continues to be part of my teaching repertoire now. The game is easy to teach and learn. I've introduced it to students in all grade levels since the only prerequisite is that students can count to twenty. That makes it accessible to young students, but the game also engages and intrigues older students. I've also used it successfully with teacher and parent groups, most recently to help bring meaning to the Common Core content and practice standards. More about that in a bit.

As the directions explain, players take turns counting, each starting where the other left off and following the rule of saying either one or two numbers. The first player can begin either with, "One," or "One, two." The second player continues with one or two numbers. If the first player says, "One, two," then the second player could say, "Three," or "Three, four." And so on. That's it. The game really isn't a race since the goal isn't to count fast. Rather, the goal is to count smart.

In a way, the game has some of the attributes of a game that's a successful app. It's easy to learn to play, it's engaging, there are various versions, and its level of difficulty can be increased.

When I present a new investigation to students, I often ask, "What do you notice?" This is to encourage them to develop the habit of examining what they're doing to look for patterns or structure that help them make sense of what they're experiencing. (This relates especially to practice standard 1, Make sense of problems and persevere in solving them, and practice standard 7, Look for and make use of structure.) I find it useful to write on the board what students notice so students can benefit from each other's thinking. After they've had some experience, I ask, "What conjectures can you make about how to win the game?" (This relates especially to practice standard 3, Construct viable arguments and critique the reasoning of others.)

I typically model the game by asking for a volunteer to come up and play the game with me. "Before you volunteer," I advise the students, "be sure it will be OK with you to lose. I've been playing this game for many, many years, and you haven't. You might win, but don't count on it." (Oops, an accidental pun. Sorry.) I've been making this statement since I taught the game in a first grade class and the boy I chose to play against burst into tears when I reached twenty. So now I prepare students. Plus I also set up the goal that figuring out how to win so they can beat me is an accomplishment to strive for.

When two players have the same knowledge, *Race for 20* is no longer a very interesting game to play, just as *Tic-Tac-Toe* becomes no longer interesting. But with *Race for 20*, it's possible to change the challenge of the game. It can become *Race for 21* or *Race for 32* or *Race for 10*—whatever number you'd like. Also, the basic rule can change so that instead of having to count one or two numbers, a player has to count one, two, or three numbers. Or one, two, three, or four numbers. Or even count only one number. Each version alters the challenge. For any version, it's possible to "notice" and "make conjectures" that lead to a winning strategy.

Although I know how to win when playing *Race for 20*, I don't tell students what I know. They can demonstrate success by playing against me and winning consistently. Winning becomes proof of their success. Plus, if I tell them how to win, the game no longer holds any promise of interest. But I'll reveal here what I know so that I can demonstrate the thinking that the game can stimulate and also give you access to the other versions.

After playing the game several times, students notice (even young students) that the player who lands on seventeen can win. That's because if the other player counts on one number and says, "Eighteen," then the winning play is to count on two numbers, "Nineteen, twenty." And if the other player counts on two numbers and says, "Eighteen, nineteen," then the winning play is to count on one number, "Twenty." So this becomes an early "I notice" statement: *I notice that it's important to land on seventeen.* Students often feel cheerfully secure with this knowledge.

Then the challenge is: How can you be sure to land on seventeen? That would be the same as playing *Race for 17* instead of *Race for 20*. And if you try that game a few times, you'll find that the player who lands on fourteen can win. (Test this out to be sure it makes sense.) So another "I notice" statement that's useful *Race for 20* is: *I notice that it's important to land on fourteen, and then to land on seventeen.*

This is fine progress. But then the challenge becomes: How can I be sure to land on fourteen? That would be the same as playing *Race for 14* instead of *Race for 17* or *Race for 20*. When you play *Race for 14*, the strategy is to land on eleven. (Again, test this out to be sure it makes sense.)

Let's look for a pattern than leads to figuring out the structure of the game. To win, it's best to land on 17, 14, and 11, and if we continue that pattern, it's best to land on 17, 14, 11, 8, 5, and 2. In this pattern, the difference between successive numbers in the sequence is 3.

I realized after thinking about that pattern, that if I say, "Two," I'm on my way to a sure victory. And to ensure that I say, "Two," I want to go first and begin, "One, two." Then the game is essentially over. Next I want to say, "Five." If my opponent says, "Three," then I'll say, "Four, five." If my opponent says, "Three, four," then I'll say, "Five." There's no stopping me on the path to winning.

I know that if I definitely want to win, then I should go first. But that's not always the case. What if my opponent opts to go first? Then I have to hope he or she doesn't know the strategy and gives me the chance as we take turns counting to land on one of the essential numbers—5, 8, 11, 14, or 17. Usually I get that chance.

But why are these numbers so important? I pondered this for a while and then turned to *The Game of Poison* (see page 275). Both games are versions of a class of games called Nim. If you play *Race for 20* with twenty objects, instead of counting, and each player takes turns removing one or two objects, and the player who removes the last object is the winner, the game is more or less the same as *The Game of Poison*. In *The Game of Poison*, the player who removes the last object loses (that's the "poison"), but the structure of the games are the same. (Think about practice standard 7.) Playing *Race for 13* with the same rules as for the original *Race for 20* has the same structure as *The Game of Poison* but more closely mirrors it, and the same strategy for winning holds, except that the goal in *Race for 13* is to say, "Thirteen," and the goal in *The Game of Poison* is to avoid the thirteenth object.

Thinking about the two games together made *Race for 20* easier for me to analyze because I could manipulate objects. I literally could get my hands on the game in a way that helped reveal a structure. But first I thought about *Race for 20*. I realized that the one thing I could control when playing the game is to decide on each turn whether to count one number or two numbers. What I could also control is that when I play after my opponent, I can make a choice of one or two numbers to ensure that we count three numbers together. That is, if my opponent counts on one number and I next count on two numbers, we advance three numbers. And if my opponent counts on two numbers and I next count on one number, again we advance three numbers. So after we each take a turn, we get three numbers closer to twenty. I put out twenty objects and investigated what happens if I removed clumps of three. I realized that the same holds true when playing *The Game of Poison*. If my opponent removes one object, I can remove two, and vice versa, so I can control us removing three objects when we each take a turn playing.

Next I grouped the twenty objects into threes and wound up with six groups of three and two extras.

I set the two aside and realized that I wanted it to be my opponents turn to play when we were down to one group of three, which means we had removed seventeen objects—a number that usually isn't terribly useful but is extremely, extremely important in the *Race for 20* version, as I had learned earlier). I wanted to be the player to remove the seventeenth object, which is the same as saying, "Seventeen." To make that happen, I also want to be the player who removes the fourteenth, eleventh, eighth, fifth, and second objects.

What about the two extra objects? I tacked them on to the beginning of my thinking. If I want to remove the second object, then I want to go first. Otherwise, I have to hope that I get the opportunity to remove the fifth, eighth, eleventh, fourteenth, and, definitely, the seventeenth. This is the same in the *Race for 20* counting game as saying "Two" or "Five" or "Eight" or "Eleven" or "Fourteen" or, definitely, "Seventeen."

It all relates to multiples of 3 and 20 being equal to six groups of three plus two extra. Now, what happens if the game changes to one of the other versions, like *Race for 21*? Then I have to rethink the entire situation. I have to think about whether it's better to go first or second, and which numbers I want to land on. Thinking about this became doable to me. I relied on the same structure and regularity (again, think about practice standards 7 and 8) and looked at multiples of 3. I can think of 21 as seven groups of three. To be ensured of saying "Twenty-one," the sequence of numbers also to say go down by threes—18, 15, 12, 9, 6, and 3. There aren't any extras, as there were the two extras in *Race for 20*. To be sure I say, "Three" and am on my way to winning, I want my opponent to go first and say either, "One," or "One, two." Either way, I can land on three.

If your head is spinning a bit right now, so is mine. It's hard to follow someone else's reasoning. Don't forget that *Race for 20* is a game, to be played for enjoyment, as well as analyzed to make sense. And that's true for all of mathematics. Ideally math is to be investigated, as well as analyzed to make sense of what we're investigating. Enjoy first, then look for structure and regularity to make sense.

Number Bracelets

Explain this rule for making a number bracelet: Choose any two numbers from 0 to 9, add them, and record just the digit that appears in the ones placed in the sum. Continue following this rule to get a string of numbers until the first two numbers you chose appear again.

Demonstrate by starting with 8 and 9. Add them to get 17, but just record the digit in the ones place, the 7. Then add the last two numbers—the 9 and the 7—and record 6, the ones place of their sum. Continue until you get back to where you started: 8, 9, 7, 6, 3, 9, 2, 1, 3, 4, 7, 1, 8, 9, 7, . . .

When you begin with 8 and 9, there are twelve numbers in the series before 8 and 9 come up again.

Answer these questions:

1. How many different possible pairs of numbers can you use to start?

2. What's the shortest bracelet you can find?

3. What's the longest bracelet?

4. Investigate the odd and even patterns in all your bracelets.

The 0–99 Chart

You need: small 0–99 charts, 1 sheet [R] See Reproducible R.34
crayon, colored pencil, or marker

Follow these directions to color each of the 0–99 charts:

1. Color all the even numbers.

2. Color all the numbers with digits that add to eight.

3. Color the numbers with digits that differ by one.

4. Color all the numbers with a 4 in them.

5. Color the multiples of three.

6. Color the numbers with both digits the same.

For information about when to use the 0–99 chart and when to use the 1–100 chart, read "0–99 Chart versus 1–100 Chart" in "Questions Teachers Ask," page 464.

Pascal's Triangle

Figure out how to extend this pattern to include additional rows. Look for patterns in rows and diagonals.

```
            1
          1   1
        1   2   1
      1   3   3   1
    1   4   6   4   1
  1   5  10  10   5   1
```

Extension

Who was Pascal? Do research to find out who Pascal was.

Addition Table Investigations

You need: addition chart (see below; see also **R** See Reproducible R.35)

+	1	2	3	4	5	6	7	8	9	10
1	2	3	4	5	6	7	8	9	10	11
2	3	4	5	6	7	8	9	10	11	12
3	4	5	6	7	8	9	10	11	12	13
4	5	6	7	8	9	10	11	12	13	14
5	6	7	8	9	10	11	12	13	14	15
6	7	8	9	10	11	12	13	14	15	16
7	8	9	10	11	12	13	14	15	16	17
8	9	10	11	12	13	14	15	16	17	18
9	10	11	12	13	14	15	16	17	18	19
10	11	12	13	14	15	16	17	18	19	20

Describe general rules or shortcut methods to find the following:

1. The sum of any three horizontally adjacent numbers.

2. The sum of any three vertically adjacent numbers.

3. The sum of any 2-by-2 array of numbers.

4. The sum of any 3-by-3 array of numbers.

5. The sum of any 10-by-10 array of numbers.

6. The sum of any cross of five numbers.

7. The sum of any three diagonally adjacent numbers.

8. The sum of any four diagonally adjacent numbers.

9. The sum of any five diagonally adjacent numbers.

Invent at least three other problems like these and describe rules for them.

Where Does 100 Land?

If you write the counting numbers in rows with seven numbers in each, in which column will 100 land? In which row?

```
1  2  3  4  5  6  7
8  9  10 11 12 13 14
15 16 17 ···
```

Repeat with writing numbers in rows with six numbers in each. What's the location of 100 in this array?

```
1  2  3  4  5  6
7  8  9  10 11 12
13 14 15 16 ···
```

Write arrays with other length rows. Find a way to predict in which row and column 100 will land for any array of numbers.

Extension

From Column to Column. For each array, if you add a number from the second column to a number from the third column, in which column will the sum land?

On Which Day of the Week Were You Born?

Follow these directions to find out on which day of the week you were born:

1. Write down the last two digits of the year in which you were born. Call this number *A*.

2. Divide that number (*A*) by four, and drop the remainder if there is one. This answer, without the remainder, is *B*.

3. Find the number of the month in which you were born from the Month Table below. This number is *C*.

4. On what day of the month were you born? This number is *D*.

5. Add the numbers from the first four steps: $A + B + C + D$.

6. Divide the sum from Step 5 by the number seven. What's the remainder from that division? (It should be a number from zero to six.) Find this remainder in the Day Table. That tells you what day of the week you were born on. (This method works for any day in the twenty-first century.)

Month Table			Day Table	
January	1 (or 0 in leap year)		Sunday	2
February	4 (or 3 in leap year)		Monday	3
March	4		Tuesday	4
April	0		Wednesday	5
May	2		Thursday	6
June	5		Friday	0
July	0		Saturday	1
August	3			
September	6			
October	1			
November	4			
December	6			

About the Math
To figure out the day of the week for days in the twentieth century, you have to use different Day Table numbers: Sunday–1, Monday–2, Tuesday–3, Wednesday–4, Thursday–5, Friday–6, and Saturday–0.

—MSB

Sally and the Peanuts

On the way home from school, Sally McCrackin likes to eat peanuts. One day, just as she was reaching into her sack, a hideous, laughing creature jumped into her path, identified itself as a pig eyes, and grabbed her sack. It stole half of her peanuts plus two more. A bit shaken, Sally continued toward home. Before she had a chance to eat even one peanut, another horrid creature jumped into her path and also stole half of her peanuts plus two more. Upset, she continued on. (What else could she do?) But before she had a chance to eat even one peanut, another of these tricksters jumped out and did the very same thing—took half her peanuts plus two more.

Now there were only two peanuts left in Sally's sack. She was so despairing that she sat down and began to sob. The three little pig eyes reappeared, feeling some sense of remorse, and told her they would return all her peanuts to her if she told them how many she had altogether when she started.

How many peanuts had been in Sally's sack?

Extension

Other Sally and the Peanuts Problems. Suppose Sally had been left with three peanuts? Or there had been four nasty pig eyes that left her with just two peanuts? Can you find a way to predict how many peanuts Sally had in her sack to start with regardless of how many she was left with or regardless of how many pig eyes stole peanuts from her?

Number Sorting

You need: 30 cards or slips of paper, numbered 1 to 30

Sort the numbers in these ways:

1. into two groups

2. into three groups

3. into four groups

Record how you did this as shown in the example. Trade your paper with a classmate. Each of you tries to figure the rule the other used for sorting.

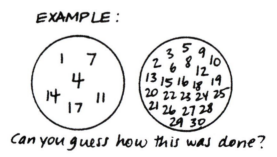

A Mathematical Tug-of-War

Use the information given to figure out who will win the third round in a tug-of-war.

Round 1: On one side are four acrobats, each of equal strength. On the other side are five neighborhood grandmas, each of equal strength. The result is dead even.

Round 2: On one side is Ivan, a dog. Ivan is pitted against two of the grandmas and one acrobat. Again, it's a draw.

Round 3: Ivan and three of the grandmas are on one side and the four acrobats are on the other.

Who will win the third round?
Write an explanation of your reasoning.

Digit Place

Play with a partner. Each player picks a three-digit number with no two digits the same. Take turns guessing each other's numbers. Each time someone guesses, the other person tells how many digits in the guess are correct and how many of the correct digits are in the correct place. A chart is useful for keeping track of the information.

Guess	D	P
293	0	0
356	1	1
296	0	0
⋮	⋮	⋮

Teaching Arithmetic

Overview

Arithmetic—the topic of uppermost concern for teachers, parents, and administrators—is the focus of Part 3. As one of the time-honored "three Rs," arithmetic instruction receives the largest share of attention and concern of all the topics in the elementary mathematics curriculum. It still reigns as the high-stakes math topic. The rationale for this is obvious: Arithmetic skills are necessary life tools that people use regularly every day. A person who isn't able to do arithmetic is handicapped in many situations.

Part 3 addresses arithmetic instruction in the elementary mathematics curriculum and builds on three essential aspects of arithmetic: computation, problem solving, and number sense. I think of these as the legs of a three-legged stool and weave these aspects into the specific classroom suggestions I provide for developing students' understanding and skills, keeping in mind the importance of balance between procedures and understanding.

The instructional suggestions in Part 3 embrace the idea that well-rounded instruction in arithmetic should be organized so that it

- introduces arithmetic concepts to students in real-world contexts;
- develops number sense and understanding of relationships among the operations;
- integrates arithmetic with the other strands of the mathematics curriculum;
- builds on students' own ways of thinking and language for describing their thinking;
- relies heavily on estimating and mental computation; and
- encourages students to use multiple strategies for arithmetic calculations.

The instructional suggestions in Part 3 are organized into nine sections—Beginning Number Concepts, Place Value, Addition and Subtraction, Introducing Multiplication, Introducing Division, Extending Multiplication and Division, Fractions, Decimals, and Percents. Each section is organized similarly and includes:

- an overview of the topic;
- suggestions for whole-class instruction;
- additional instructional suggestions (suitable for whole-class, partner, or small-group experiences and also choice time investigations); and
- suggestions for assessing students' understanding.

The ideas presented are designed to serve as models for classroom instruction that build students' understanding, confidence, and competence in arithmetic. All of the instructional ideas draw from my teaching experiences over the years in different grade levels. Sometimes when I've revisited investigations from *About Teaching Mathematics* to present in a class, or after I've taught the activity again, I made notes in the margins of my own copy of the previous edition of this resource. I've included these notes here as asides and reminders.

Arithmetic: The Three-Legged Stool

About the Three-Legged Stool

While the importance of arithmetic hasn't diminished over time, the criteria for evaluating students' proficiency with arithmetic and the methods for teaching arithmetic have shifted and broadened. Computation skills are only one aspect of arithmetic competence. Instruction in arithmetic must also develop the conceptual understanding that supports students' number sense and help students develop the ability to reason numerically to solve problems. Computation, problem solving, and number sense are three essential aspects of arithmetic instruction, just as three legs are needed for a stool to be sturdy and balanced. The goal of arithmetic instruction is for students to demonstrate competence and confidence with each.

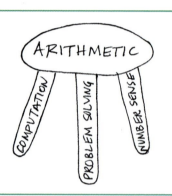

ESSENTIAL ASPECTS OF ARITHMETIC INSTRUCTION

- Computation
- Problem Solving
- Number Sense

Computation

Students with computational proficiency can calculate accurately and efficiently. Accuracy and efficiency do not necessarily mean that a student will use the same procedure for all problems, or that all students will use the same method for any one problem. Different methods are appropriate for different numbers, and students should learn multiple ways to reason numerically.

Mental Computation

Computing mentally is an important computational skill, often shortchanged in school. This may be, in part, because figuring in their heads doesn't produce written evidence or lead to assignments that students can take home. Also, standardized tests, which exert enormous influence on determining what's taught, don't measure students' ability to calculate in their heads. However, to be proficient with computation, students should be able to do a good deal of computing mentally without resorting to paper and pencil. When asked to figure 50 percent of a number, or to multiply a number by ten or one hundred, for example, a student's first impulse should be to think about the problem mentally, not to reach for pencil and paper.

Along with computing mentally to figure out exact answers, another numerical skill that's often shortchanged is estimation. Before calculating, students should be encouraged to estimate answers to help them justify if the answers they figure out are reasonable. Also, for problem situations, it's important that students know when an estimate will suffice (or even been more appropriate) and when an exact answer is necessary.

Memorization has a role in computation. Calculating both mentally and with paper and pencil requires having basic number facts committed to memory. However, when building students' understanding, memorization should follow, not lead, instruction. The emphasis of learning in mathematics must always be on thinking, reasoning, and making sense.

Paper and Pencil Computation

When problems are too complex or unwieldy to solve mentally, it's appropriate for students to figure out answers with the help of paper and pencil. This does not imply, however, that students necessarily use a specific procedure. While students may use paper and pencil to apply an algorithm they've learned, they also may use paper and pencil as tools to keep track of their reasoning and to provide a record of their thinking.

Look at the two examples provided here from fifth graders I interviewed. Both students used paper and pencil to figure out the answer to 5000 − 328, both got the correct answer of 4672, and both of them took about the same amount of time to complete the work.

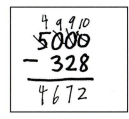

Alexa, grade 5

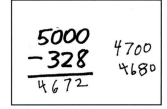

Jesús, grade 5

The example on the left shows how Alexa used paper and pencil to apply the algorithm she had learned. As she worked, Alexa clearly explained the steps she used, demonstrating her procedural proficiency. The example on the right shows how Jesús used paper and pencil to keep track of his thinking. Jesús didn't explain as he worked and I didn't interrupt him. I watched as he thought for a moment and then wrote 4700 to the right of the problem, thought again and then wrote 4680 underneath 4700, and finally wrote the answer of 4672. When I asked him how he reasoned, Jesús explained each step:

First I did 5000 minus 300, and that's 4700.

Then I took away 20 more and that left 4680.

And then I subtracted 8 and got the answer 4672.

The explanation that Jesús gave showed his ability to decompose 328 into its place value parts—three hundred, twenty, and eight. While his procedure is unusual, it indicates that Jesús was able to apply his understanding of place value. I'm not sure that I would have understood how Jesús had reasoned if he hadn't explained, which is why I find interviewing students so useful.

I tried Jesús' method for other problems. Although it's not a conventional algorithm, I find it surprisingly efficient.

Why has pencil-and-paper arithmetic computation become the mainstay of elementary arithmetic instruction? One way to

For more about the benefits of interviewing, see "Starting Point 16: The Benefits of One-on-One Interviews" in Part 1 on page 79.

understand this is to recognize that the ability to perform calculations has long been seen as essential for being successful in math. This practice has been in place long before calculators and computers removed the drudgery from computation, when there was no way to arrive at arithmetic answers other than doing calculations by hand. Because of the present availability of calculators and computers, however, the challenge is even greater to teach students to think and reason, so that they don't rely on answers without evaluating their accuracy and appropriateness.

With or without calculators and computers, however, learning to do paper-and-pencil arithmetic and practicing on isolated examples have never ensured that students learned to use these skills when needed. This deficiency is obvious to teachers when word problems are assigned and students repeatedly ask, "Do I need to add or subtract?" Arithmetic practice in isolation does not lead students to notice when they make a division error, such as omitting a zero in the quotient and thus producing an answer that is ten times too small.

However, it's still important for students to learn procedures for arithmetic. Arithmetic skills are necessary life tools. Doing arithmetic mentally demands an understanding of place value, mastery of basic facts, and the ability to estimate. Using calculators and computers successfully and evaluating the answers they produce require an understanding of the necessary arithmetic processes and the ability to identify if solutions are reasonable. Being able to use paper and pencil for arithmetic problems too complex to solve mentally is important.

For additional information about reasoning, see "Starting Point 5: Reasoning: A Perspective on Arithmetic" in Part 1 on page 26.

Problem Solving

While being able to compute accurately and efficiently is essential, both mentally and with paper and pencil, it's also essential that students learn to apply computation skills to problem-solving situations. It makes no sense to say that a student can do arithmetic but can't apply it in contexts.

You would never say that a person who can play only scales on the piano knows how to make music. You wouldn't assume that a person who can catch a football knows how to play the game. You wouldn't make the judgment that a person who can saw a board knows how to build a bookcase. The rudiments are necessary, but it makes no sense to learn them as ends in themselves.

The motivation for learning skills in life is their eventual use. Students who practice scales have heard music. Students who practice catching and throwing a football have seen football games. In school, however, students are too often expected to practice arithmetic skills without any sort of mathematical bookcase to build. No wonder so many students aren't motivated to develop their proficiency. What sense does it make? Instead of seeing arithmetic procedures as useful tools that save work, students often see them as making work, with a sole purpose of completing pages of exercises.

If students are able to read a story aloud but can't tell what the story is about, we wouldn't say that they were proficient readers. Comprehension is essential. Similarly, a student who can perform addition, subtraction, multiplication, or division calculations but can neither

For more on problem solving, see "Starting Point 8: Word Problems: Developing Understanding of Arithmetic Operations" in Part 1 on page 36.

explain why the procedures work nor apply them to problems has not demonstrated proficiency. Our definition of proficiency must include being able to apply skills to problem-solving contexts.

Routine and Nonroutine Problems

Word problems have long been traditional in mathematics instruction. They present situations for students to translate into arithmetic operations and then figure the answers. These are often referred to as "routine" problems.

Students should also have experience solving "nonroutine" problems. These problems require reasoning beyond translating situations to arithmetic operations. They may have more than one solution and/or more than one way to arrive at a solution. In the following problems, compare the "routine" version versus the nonroutine version. What do you notice?

For more about nonroutine problems, see "Starting Point 9: From Word Problems to Problem Solving: A Broader View" in Part 1 on page 41.

ROUTINE VERSUS NONROUTINE PROBLEMS

Dart Board Problem

Version 1: Routine

The center region on a dart board is worth 100 points; the next ring is worth 50 points; the next, 25 points; and the outermost, 10 points. Betty throws three darts in the outermost ring, one in the next ring, and two in the ring next to the center. What score does she earn?

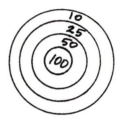

Version 2: Nonroutine

Betty throws six darts and earns a score of 150. Where might her darts have landed? Or Betty throws six darts and each lands in a ring. What are the possible scores Betty can earn?

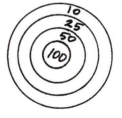

FYI
To stimulate my thinking about routine versus nonroutine problems, I've found it helpful to read routine problems and think about how to shift them into nonroutine problems. That's what I did with the *Dart Board* problem.

— MSB

For help with nonroutine problems, I often refer to two Math Solutions resources— *Good Questions for Math Teaching, Grades K–6* (Sullivan and Lilburn 2002) and *Good Questions for Math Teaching, Grades 5–8* (Schuster and Anderson 2005). Learn more at mathsolutions.com.

Number Sense

Number sense relies on strong conceptual understanding and encompasses a wide range of abilities, including being able to make reasonable estimates, think and reason flexibly, make sound numerical judgments, and see numbers as useful. Students with number sense have good numerical intuition. When applying computation skills to solve problems, they can judge if solutions are reasonable. Should they forget a procedure or part of a procedure, students with number sense can reason their way to a solution. They see numbers as tools, not barriers. They're curious about numbers and comfortable with them.

Students with number sense can solve the routine dartboard problem mentioned in the previous section by calculating mentally. They might jot down the number of points that Betty earned in each of the rings—30 in the outermost ring, 25 in the next one, and 100 in the ring next to the center. But they wouldn't need to line up the numbers and add the standard way. Rather, they could add 30 and 25 mentally to get 55 and then add on 100 for an answer of 155, or add 100 plus 30 first to get 130 and then add on 25 more to get 155. Even with a routine problem, there may be different routes to figuring out the answer.

Putting It All Together

It's possible that any given arithmetic lesson might focus on just one or two legs of the stool, but it's important to keep in mind that computation, problem solving, and number sense are not discrete and separate topics. Developing number sense depends on learning to compute. Solving problems also depends on computation. Deciding whether an answer makes sense, an important aspect of problem solving, draws on students' number sense. The stool stands because its legs are bound together by the seat of the stool. A plan for arithmetic instruction must incorporate attention to each leg so that students have a firm and well-balanced base on which to rest their understanding of number and operations.

Teaching What to Do (Procedures) Versus Teaching What to Do and Why (Procedures and Understanding)

Teaching *what to do* in mathematics—specifically arithmetic—is widespread practice. There's nothing inherently or necessarily wrong in teaching for *what to do* understanding. It's important to realize, however, that teaching procedures and teaching procedures in relation to their meaning are two very different approaches to teaching arithmetic.

Justifications for Teaching What to Do (Procedures)

Think about your own elementary and high school mathematics learning. Can you remember being taught long division, or how to find the area of a circle, or how to multiply algebraic expressions such as $(x + 3)(2x - 5)$ and not understanding why they worked? Think back on mathematics courses you have taken. Have you ever had the experience of passing a course, perhaps even with a good grade, yet feeling you did not really understand what you were taught? Check your students' mathematics textbooks for instances of teaching by procedural approaches—what do you find?

Teaching for *what to do* understanding is common to many students' experiences with arithmetic. Students are taught to learn rules and apply them—to add the ones first and then the tens, to borrow when subtracting, to put a zero in the second line when multiplying, to start from the left when doing long division, to multiply across the numerators and denominators to figure out the product of two fractions, to divide the numerators and denominators of fractions by the same number to simplify them, to line up the decimal points before adding, to count up the decimal places to see where to place the decimal point in the answer to a decimal multiplication problem. A blatant example of teaching for *what to do* understanding is the two-line rhyme for division of fractions:

Yours is not to reason why;
just invert and multiply.

Why is the practice of teaching the procedures of mathematics often detached from the meaning and applications of those procedures? In order to analyze the limits of this practice, it's important to understand the justifications that have been given to support an emphasis on teaching procedures. Here are some of the most common ones.

JUSTIFICATIONS FOR TEACHING WHAT TO DO (PROCEDURES)

1. Learning what to do is usually easier than learning what to do and why.
2. Textbooks often emphasize the learning of procedures.
3. The pressure of tests looms.
4. It's difficult to assess whether students understand the why of arithmetic.
5. Some teachers don't understand the difference between teaching procedures and teaching reasoning in arithmetic.

Reasons in addition to these five could be cited as well. Parental pressure often affects what teachers teach. Changing a habit is in itself difficult, especially without consistent support. Also, students make demands—many teachers have had the experience of explaining the meaning behind a procedure only to have the students listen, wait patiently, and finally say, "If you'll just show me how to do it, I'll do it."

Justification 1: Learning what to do is usually easier than learning what to do and why.

Actually, learning what to do is sometimes much easier. Take the example of learning how to divide fractions. The standard algorithm is to turn the fraction on the right-hand side upside down and then multiply across the tops and bottoms. This rule is simpler to learn (and to teach) than the principle that division is the inverse of multiplication, or that dividing by a number is the same as multiplying by its multiplicative inverse, which in the case of dividing by a fraction means multiplying by its reciprocal. If the goal of the mathematics instruction is to prepare students to produce a page of correct answers, teaching the appropriate procedures will meet this goal more quickly and easily.

Justification 2: Textbooks often emphasize the learning of procedures.

The basic goal of textbooks and workbooks too often is on helping students write correct answers, rather than teaching them to think and understand. This may sound harsh. After all, no textbook publishers or authors say or even suggest that they don't care if students think as long as they get the answers on the pages correct. Teachers' guides urge instructors to teach for the underlying understanding and often provide additional suggestions for doing so. But the reality exists, implicitly or explicitly: Students will show their understanding by being able to complete the work on the pages. Writing correct answers is the primary goal of teaching what to do; thinking, understanding, and seeing relationships are the primary goals of teaching what to do and why.

Justification 3: The pressure of tests looms.

Standardized tests are another reality. Teachers are accountable for students' performance and—in some communities—test scores are made public. For the most part, these tests evaluate students' proficiency with mathematical procedures. The procedures themselves are more quickly and efficiently learned by focusing specifically on how to do them. The fact that students continue to do poorly on test items that require more than rote learning does not seem to be a compelling enough reason to change the current emphasis on procedural mathematics.

Justification 4: It's difficult to assess whether students understand the *why* of arithmetic.

It isn't possible to perceive how students are thinking merely from the paper-and-pencil work they submit. Consider, for example, what the red group did in solving 19×21 (see Scenario 1 on page 315). Those students successfully performed the algorithm for multiplication but could only explain what they had done by resorting to rules they had learned. Judging their computational work alone wouldn't have revealed this important information.

Justification 5: Some teachers don't understand the difference between teaching procedures and teaching reasoning in arithmetic.

Many teachers don't feel competent or comfortable with mathematics. Although proficient with the computational algorithms, they themselves were probably taught these algorithms without learning the underlying reasoning behind them. It's been shown that teachers generally teach as they were taught. Besides, teachers cannot teach what they do not truly understand. These circumstances seriously hinder the effort to offer students a thinking mathematics curriculum.

Justifications for Teaching What to Do and Why (Procedures and Understanding)

In contrast to the list of justifications for teaching procedures, following are some of the reasons for teaching arithmetic in the context of meaning and application, of teaching the *why* as well as the *what* to do in mathematics. These reasons, too, are important to consider.

> ### JUSTIFICATIONS FOR TEACHING WHAT TO DO AND WHY (PROCEDURES AND UNDERSTANDING)
>
> 1. When you understand why, your understanding and skills can be applied more easily to new tasks.
>
> 2. Learning the meaning in arithmetic procedures makes them easier to remember.
>
> 3. Learning to reason is a goal effective in itself and leads to the continued support of learning.

Justification 1: When you understand why, your understanding and skills can be applied more easily to new tasks.

Teaching how to add, subtract, multiply, and divide decimals from the procedural approach focuses primarily on the various rules for what to do with the decimal points in each of the operations. When you add and subtract, you line up the decimal points; when you multiply, you count up the decimal places to figure where the decimal point goes in the answer; when you divide, you move decimal points when they appear in the divisor but not when they don't appear. Should you forget the rule for one particular operation, a rule from another has no bearing.

If, however, you learn why the rules for each of the operations make sense—if you learn to reason with decimals as well as to compute with them—then you can understand which answers are sensible in any situation. When multiplying decimals—for example, 15.3×2.1—students often learn to ignore the decimal points, do the multiplication and multiply 153×27, and then "count up" the decimal places in the original problem and insert the decimal point in the answer. For this example, 153×27 is 3213, and because each number in the problem had one digit after the decimal point, the answer would need to have two digits after the decimal point, which makes it 32.13. Counting decimal places in this way isn't necessary when students consider that they're multiplying a number that's a little more than fifteen by a number that's a little more than two, which means the answer has to be a little more than thirty. Then the only logical place to insert the decimal point is so the answer is 32.13. Instruction should guide students to think in this way.

It's more important that students develop the kind of understanding that allows them to apply their learning to the new and different situations they will be sure to meet than that they develop the ability to follow rules. This requires they understand why as well as knowing how. It's not an either-or situation—both are necessary. Knowing only the rules for figuring percents is not sufficient for choosing the best savings or money market account, the type of mortgage that makes most sense, or the best way to finance a new car. These decisions require understanding and judgments that extend beyond algorithmic thinking.

Justification 2: Learning the meaning in arithmetic procedures makes them easier to remember.

When you understand the reasons behind rules, you don't have to keep a large number of unrelated rules in your memory. A common error students make when adding fractions is to add the numerators and denominators—for example, they erroneously figure out that $\frac{1}{2} + \frac{1}{3} = \frac{2}{5}$. They are applying a procedure that's totally inappropriate in this instance and without thinking about the result. However, much of mathematics requires looking for the sense in the situation, not merely following a rule. It doesn't make sense to start with $\frac{1}{2}$, add to it, and wind up with an answer, $\frac{2}{5}$, that's less than the amount you started with. Yet many students don't notice this inconsistency or even think about looking for it.

Arithmetic instruction is often organized into bite-sized pieces, often seen as making curriculum goals more manageable. However, this practice masks a pedagogical risk. Teaching students in bite-sized pieces does not necessarily help them learn anything other than bite-sized skills. Some students make connections between the individual pieces. However, students who have difficulty usually have to repeat their experience with the pieces, as if a second go-around, or a third, will produce eventual success. Such instruction hasn't ever worked and never will.

Breaking the learning of mathematics into tiny pieces is like giving students a heap of graham cracker crumbs and wondering why they have no concept of the whole graham cracker. It's an attempt to simplify learning that may seem to be in the interest of students. But, in fact, it's counterproductive and in conflict with what's known about how students do learn. It's wrong to think that students can't deal with meaning and complexity.

Justification 3: Learning to reason is a goal effective in itself and leads to the continued support of learning.

All of us (hopefully) have experienced the joy of accomplishment that comes from figuring something out in order to produce a satisfying result. When students are taught to make sense out of mathematics, they receive support for seeing connections between ideas. Their connections can lead them to further learning in ways that do not occur when learning is approached as a series of unconnected events.

In his essay, "Nature Closely Observed," David Hawkins describes the distinction ancient Greeks made in their language between what they called arithmetic and what they called logistic. He writes:

> Arithmetic was the investigation of the world of numbers; logistic was a set of rules, to be memorized, for doing rote sums, differences, products, quotients. Arithmetic was a kind of science, always fresh

and open to endless investigation. Logistic was a dull art, needed for bookkeeping and other such practices, which you could learn by rote. If you understood something of arithmetic, you could easily master the rules of logistic; if you forgot those rules, you could reinvent them. What we mainly try to teach in all those early years of schooling is logistic, not arithmetic. We drag, not lead, and the efficiency of learning is scandalously low. (1983, 71)

The true measure of the failure of teaching only *what to do* is the feeling of mathematical incompetence and negativity toward mathematics experienced by so many otherwise highly educated people. This rejection of mathematics, sadly so common, is a clear indication that something is very wrong. It's not possible to appreciate something you don't truly understand, and the charge to teachers is a crucial one—to teach mathematics so that students are encouraged to make sense out of all they learn to do.

The Role of Algorithms

What should be the role of algorithms in teaching and learning arithmetic? First, a definition: Algorithms are systematic procedures that provide reliable and efficient ways to find accurate answers to computation problems and, therefore, simplify potentially difficult calculations. It's important for students to understand that algorithms are procedures that have been invented to carry out calculations that are done repeatedly. It's also important for them to learn how algorithms are based in the structure and logic of our number system.

Here's a typical problem that students are expected to solve with the standard subtraction algorithm:

$$\begin{array}{r} 31 \\ -16 \\ \hline \end{array}$$

It's not uncommon for students to arrive at the incorrect answer of twenty-five. They've "learned" to subtract, but when confronted with a problem that requires regrouping, students will frequently just take the smaller from the larger—a procedure they have been practicing in appropriate situations. They follow a rule they've learned but apply it to the wrong situation.

Students need to understand that one particular algorithm may be no better or more efficient than another, and that many methods, including ones they invent themselves, are equally valid. A major risk of instruction that emphasizes the teaching of specific algorithms is the risk of interfering with students' learning to make sense of numbers. When learning algorithms, students often focus on learning sequences of steps to carry out procedures, rather than on thinking and reasoning to make sense of numerical situations. Teachers know that it's common for students, when using standard algorithms, to make calculation errors and not even notice when they reach absurd solutions. Also, students sometimes reach for paper and pencil to solve problems that they should be able to do easily in their heads.

Suzanne H. Chapin and Arthur Johnson address the role of algorithms *Math Matters*:

> In the best of circumstances, algorithms free up some of our mental capacity so that we can focus on interpreting and understanding a solution in the context of a problem. In the worst of circumstances, algorithms are used when a task could be done mentally or are applied by rote with little understanding for the bigger mathematical picture—why the calculation is important and how the answer will be used. (2006, 43)

Sometimes rules for algorithms may not make sense to follow yet students are asked not to veer from the prescribed procedure. For example, it's common for first and second graders to learn to add two-place numbers. Initial problems typically don't require regrouping and are typically presented vertically:

$$\begin{array}{r} 34 \\ +21 \\ \hline \end{array}$$

The standard procedure taught is first to add the ones and then to add the tens. When teachers notice students adding the numbers from left to right, adding the digits in the tens place first, they often redirect the student to add the ones first instead. Why? It certainly makes no difference which digits you add first to arrive at the correct sum.

The teaching rationale, however, is that if students learn correctly in this simpler example, they more easily transfer their learning to the next, more complex task of adding when regrouping is necessary. It seems as if the decision is made in the interest of supporting the students' learning. However, teaching what to do in this instance is mainly to make students' arithmetic pursuits easier a few pages farther on in the book.

What do students perceive from being taught the rule of adding the ones first? Many merely learn to add the numbers on the right first, and then the numbers on the left, without thinking that first they are adding ones and then tens. To some students, a page of such problems looks much like a page of one-digit addition placed vertically, except that some of the numbers have been shoved together.

There's a danger in this instructional approach, even for those students who learn rules well. Such instruction teaches a student that it's OK for something not to make sense, that it's not necessary to understand what you're expected to do. This message is counterproductive to having students approach mathematics with the goal of understanding concepts and skills.

Other students, however, notice that they can do the exercises either way and get the same answer, but they know that they are supposed to add the right-hand column first. If they ask why, what might the teacher say? (What would you say?) The response most likely will be a "This is the way we do it" answer or "This will make your life easier later" answer. There isn't any other reason.

Lacking in this instructional approach is support for students who are trying to make sense out of the procedure. The most obvious message to students is that arithmetic requires that you follow rules.

It would be a bleak and joyless arithmetic picture if young students imagined all the rules they would have to face in the school years that stretched ahead! Fortunately for us, most students don't take this future view of life; hopefully, those that do will be forgiving.

Teaching Arithmetic: Scenarios from the Classroom

Much of what I've learned about teaching has come from talking with colleagues about their classroom teaching experiences. The following classroom scenarios help illustrate the importance of an instructional balance of procedures and understanding.

Scenario 1: Fourth Graders Solve 19 × 21

Sandra Nye, who taught in West Babylon, New York, asked her fourth graders to figure out the answer to 19 × 21. She wrote the problem on the board:

$$\begin{array}{r} 19 \\ \times 21 \\ \hline \end{array}$$

This was in early December when Sandra was preparing to begin a unit on multiplication. She knew her students had had some experience with multiplication in third grade. She put them into groups of four or five students and asked each group to choose a recorder to write down everything the group did. As the students worked, Sandra circulated, reading what they were producing and making notes on their papers to push them further or to ask them to clarify their thoughts. Her goal was to get insights into the students' thinking, rather than merely to test their ability to do the computation. Following are the dialogues between Sandra and each group as they occurred.

The Red Group

Students: *First we ×'s one times nine. Next we ×'s the one by the one. Then we go down a line and put a zero under the nine. Next we ×'s the two by the nine and the two by the one. Now that we have two answers (one on top and one on bottom) we add them and get an answer of 399.*

$$\begin{array}{r} 19 \\ \times 21 \\ \hline 19 \\ 380 \\ \hline 399 \end{array}$$

Sandra: *Why did you go down a line? What do the two answers mean? Why did you add them?*

Students: *We changed lines because the rules are to change lines and the rules are also to put a zero in the beginning of the second line. The rules are that way because there is no way to get 399 with 380 on* the same line as 19. We found this out in third grade. We added them because that's the way we were taught and it gives a sensible answer.

Sandra: *Now, can you explain each of the numbers in your answer?*

Students: *The 19 means that one times 19 equals 19. The 38 means that two times 19 equals 38. (Remember it's a rule to put a zero on the second line.) The 399 means 19 plus 380 equals 399. That's how we did this problem.*

Sandra: *Why is it a rule to put a zero on the second line? What's the purpose of the rule?*

Students: *Nobody in our group can remember why we put the zero on the second line. We told you above that it is a rule to put the zero on the second line.*

The Blue Group

Students: *This is how we solved our problem. First we times 19 × 21 and we got 389 and we found out it was wrong. The teacher put some answers on the board and told us they were wrong. The answers were 57; 3,819; and 389. Then about 5 minutes later we found out the real answer is 399. We added 21 × 19 times. We proved it by making a 21 × 19 rectangle. That is the way you set it up because any time you're timesing two-digit numbers, first you put down the first answer and then you put down a 0 on the next line before you multiply.*

$$\begin{array}{r} 19 \\ \times\,21 \\ \hline 19 \\ 380 \\ \hline 399 \end{array}$$

Sandra: *How do you get the first answer? What does it mean?*

Students: *You get the first answer by timesing 1 × 19. It means that you have the first part done.*

Sandra: *Why do you "put down a 0" on the next line? What does the number on that line show?*

Students: *So it makes the number bigger. That line should be the larger number.*

Sandra: *Why should that line be bigger?*

Students: *So you get a reasonable answer.*

Sandra: *What does 380 show? What numbers do you multiply to get 380?*

Students: *It shows 38 with a 0 on the end. You multiply 19 × 20 to get 380.*

Sandra: *Where is the 20?*

Students: *The 20 is the 21 without the one because you times the one already.*

The Purple Group

Students: *We wrote it this way:*

$$
\begin{array}{r}
19 \\
\times\, 21 \\
\hline
19 \\
38 \\
\hline
57
\end{array}
$$

Then we found out that we left out the zero in the second number.

Sandra: *How do you know there should have been a zero in the answer? And how did you realize that your first answer was wrong?*

Students: *There should be a zero in the second number because when you multiply with tens you put a zero in the ones place because you are not working with the ones. We realized that the answer should be much bigger than 57 because if you put 21 down 19 times it wouldn't add up to 57. It would be much bigger.*

Next we wrote down 19 21 times. Then we crossed off two 19s at a time, and put down 38. Then we crossed off two 38s at a time, and put down 76. Next we crossed off two 76s at a time, and we put down 152. It looked like this when we finished.

$$
\begin{array}{r}
152 \\
152 \\
+\ 95 \\
\hline
399
\end{array}
$$

Finally we put it like this and it was right.

$$
\begin{array}{r}
19 \\
\times\, 21 \\
\hline
19 \\
380 \\
\hline
399
\end{array}
$$

Sandra: *How did you decide to write it this way?*

Students: *We figured out the answer with addition and then we figured it out this way.*

About the Arithmetic

If merely given a quiz on which they were asked to do the computation, the red group would most likely have gotten it correct. They demonstrated procedural understanding of the algorithm for multiplying 19 × 21. Yet in both their explanation and their responses to Sandra's questions, the students consistently resorted to following the rules they had learned without being able to explain why. For example, when asked to explain where the partial product of 380 came from, they resorted to the rule that dictates adding a zero on the second line in two-place multiplication: " . . . 2 times 19 equals 38. (Remember, it's a rule to put a zero on the second line.)"

The other two groups were able to relate multiplication to addition and to verify their answers that way. The blue group seemed to be farthest along in making sense out of the partial products. When urged to explain where the 380 came from, they wrote that it was the result of multiplying 19 × 20: "*You multiply 19 × 20 to get 380. . . . The 20 is the 21 without the one because you times the one already.*" Although these students' understanding was incomplete as shown in their written work, their reasoning indicated a "what to do and why" understanding beyond rules learned by rote. The purple group, however, could justify the final algorithm as reasonable only because it worked to produce the correct answer.

Scenario 2: Fifth Graders Solve 47 × 23

Sandra tried a different experiment with her class the next year, again in December. This was a class of fifth graders. Sandra gave them an assignment to complete individually, as a formative assessment to guide her instruction: "Figure out the answer to 47 × 23. When you think you have the correct answer, explain why you think your answer is reasonable."

About a third of the students did the computation accurately, with the only difference that three wrote a zero in the second partial product and five did not, as shown below. Following are their actual explanations, with their misspellings, of why their answers were reasonable.

Correct Answers

$$\begin{array}{r} 47 \\ \times 23 \\ \hline 141 \\ 940 \\ \hline 1{,}081 \end{array}$$

My answer was reasonable because I added 141 and 940.

I think my answer is reasonable because I worked it out carefully.

My answer is reasonable because it is right multiplying and adding.

$$\begin{array}{r} 47 \\ \times 23 \\ \hline 141 \\ 94 \\ \hline 1{,}081 \end{array}$$

My answer is reasonable because I checked it.

I think it's reasonable because I added the right numbers and timed the right numbers.

I think my answer is reasonable because I took my time and check it.

I think my answer is reasonable because if you estimated 47 it would become 50 and if you estimated 23 it would become 20. 20 × 50 = 1,000 and 1,000 is close to 1,081.

I think my answer is reasonable because twenty-three is almost twenty, and forty-seven is about fifty and fifty times twenty is 1,000. My answer is about 1,000.

Incorrect Answers

The incorrect answers students gave varied, as did their explanations.
Following are eight incorrect responses.

47
×23

141
840

981

*My answer is
reasonable because I
know how to mutply
this way.*

47
×23

141
940

1,161

*My answer is
reasonable because I
know my times tabels
and I was paying
attention.*

47
×23

141
94

1,135

*I think my answer is
reasonable because I
understud the problem.*

47
× 23

141
614

755

*My answer is OK
because if you to take
the four and the two
and times it you would
get eight and the 755
and rounded it you
would get 800.*

47
×23

134
1480

1,614

*Its reasonbal because
I did what Im saposto
do.*

47
×23

141
1210

1,351

*cause I worked it out
four times*

47
×23

141
8,140

8,281

*I think my answer is
reasonable because I
did the problem step by
step and this is what I
cam out with 8,281.*

47
×23

141
×00

1,083

*My answer is
reasonable because
141 × 23 is 1,083.*

About the Arithmetic

Most of the students, whether their answers were right or wrong,
struggled with explanations in the context of the procedures, rather
than in the meaning of the operation. Only three students tried to justify their answers by referring to the numerical quantities.

Scenario 3: A Study with Fourth, Fifth, and Sixth Graders

In *School Science and Mathematics*, Thomas C. O'Brien and Shirley A. Casey (1983) reported the results of a study they conducted with fourth-, fifth-, and sixth-grade students. The students were asked to complete the following computations using paper and pencil:

$1.6 \times 3 =$ _____

$16 \times 3 =$ _____

$60 \times 1 =$ _____

$13 \times 16 =$ _____

$3 \times 60 =$ _____

Then the students were asked to write a story problem for 6×3.

The Answers

The five computations yielded success rates of 82 percent in grade 4, 75 percent in grade 5, and 97 percent in grade 6. The story problems, however, yielded different results. Of the fourth graders, only 25 percent wrote a story problem that was multiplicative in context. For the fifth graders, the figure was 15 percent, and for the sixth graders, it was 69 percent. More than half of the nonmultiplicative responses involved stories that described $6 + 3$, not 6×3, even though many of these stories ended with the statement $6 \times 3 = 18$. What did these students understand about multiplication?

About the Arithmetic

A student who is able to perform paper-and-pencil computations for the operations shows procedural understanding, knowing what to do in a situation. This does not necessarily mean that the student understands the why of that procedure—why it works, why it makes sense, why it's useful to problem situations. Knowing what to do and why means understanding the arithmetic procedure in relation to its meaning and application.

Scenario 4: Third Graders Learn Division

Dee Uyeda's third graders in Mill Valley, California, learned about division through a problem-solving approach. Working sometimes individually and sometimes in pairs and small groups, the students were asked to find solutions to division problems and to explain how they reasoned. They worked on problems with remainders along with problems without remainders.

Sharing Cubes: An Individual Assignment

Dee asked students to figure out how to share seventeen cubes equally among four students, describe their method, and then use the cubes to test their solution. The explanations they wrote revealed various approaches that helped Dee plan subsequent lessons. For example, Verity wrote: *Each kid gets 4 cubes and 1 goes to the classroom. I figerd it out by 4 plus 4 is 8 and 8 plus 8 = 16.* (Several other students also used addition to solve the problem.)

Joel wrote: *First I just gave one of the cubes to the good will. Then I devided 16 cubes. Because I know that 4 × 4 = 16 so 4 kids each get 4 cubes.* (Joel used what he knew about multiplication, a strategy also used by others.)

Jenee first drew seventeen cubes in a vertical line, then counted to divide them into four parts, and then wrote her explanation: *They each get 4 cubes and there will be one left over.*

Rebecca wrote: *I'm going to draw pictures of 17 cubes and four baskets. I put one cube at a time in the basket. Each basket gets four cubes if you want it to be even. Since you have sixteen cubes in all the baskets, the extra cube can go to someone.*

Elliot wrote: *I'm going to do it in 2's. I will count 8 2's and have 1 left. Each student would get 4 cubes.*

Lisa decided to use a calculator. In her explanation, she wrote about her limited understanding of decimals: *We each get 4. And put one in the box. How I did it: On the calculator, I pressed 17 ÷ 4 = that didn't work. Then I pressed 17 ÷ 2 = 8.5. .5 is a half. Two halfs is a whole. That is 8 + 9. Half of 8 is 4. And there is one left over.*

Dividing Money: Group Problems

Some of the division problems Dee gave to the students involved money. Dee asked students to share $5.00 equally among four students. All groups correctly solved this problem and their solutions were similar. For example, Michelle, Michael, Timothy, and Alana's group wrote: *Each person gets $1.25. We think this because if each person got a dollar there would be one dollar left. And there are four quarters in a dollar. So everybody gets a $1.25.*

As groups finished their work, Dee gave them the problem of sharing $0.50 equally among four students. Students found this problem more challenging. The numbers were more difficult for them and they had to decide what to do with the remainder. The same groups as above wrote: *We think each person gets 12¢ and there would be 2¢ left over that they could not split up, but they could buy bubble gum with the two cents and split the gum. We think this because we have to share the last two cents.*

Relating Division to Classroom Situations, a Group Problem

Whenever possible, Dee used classroom situations to pose problems. For example, the students counted and found there were 163 pencils in the class supply. They were given the problem of figuring out how many pencils each student would receive if they divided the pencils equally among them. Laura, Teddy, and Grace's group drew twenty-seven circles, one for each student, and used tally marks to distribute the 163 pencils. They wrote: *Everybody would get 6 and there would be 1 left over. We figured this out by drawing 27 circles. Grace put talley marks in them while Teddy and Laura counted. We proved it by adding 27 six times and adding one.*

Kendra, Bryce, and Marina's group wrote: *We think that each student will get 6 pencils and there will be 1 left over. We think this because we made a circle for each kid and gave them each five pencils. We added it up. It came to 135 so we took 135 from 163 and there*

For a more complete description of how to present this problem, see "Division Sharing Problems" in Part 3 on page 390.

were 28 left. *There are 27 kids in the class so each kid gets one more and there is one left.*

After students solved problems, they presented their results and methods to the class and discussed the different methods used. After discussing each problem, Dee showed the students the standard notation for representing division, $17 \div 4$, $4)\overline{17}$ and $\frac{17}{4}$, for example. With more experience, the students began to use the standard symbols in their own writing.

Scenario 5: Seventh and Eighth Graders Work with Percents

I remember as a beginning teacher teaching my eighth-grade students how to solve the three standard types of percent problems. It wasn't my finest hour. As an alternative, when Cathy Humphreys taught percents to her seventh and eighth graders in San Jose, California, she organized a unit around a series of problem-solving situations that called for applying percents. As Cathy described in *A Collection of Math Lessons, Grades 6–8* (Burns and Humphreys 1990), her students worked in small groups and presented their answers and methods to the class. For all problems, Cathy kept the emphasis on students' making sense of the situation and justifying the methods they used for their calculations. One such problem was the following:

> *A school has 500 students. If a school bus holds 75 students, is there enough room on one bus for all the school's left-handed students?*

Cathy gave the class the information that about 12 percent of Americans are left-handed. First, she collected information from the students about how many were right- and left-handed, and helped them to compare their class data with the national statistic. Then Cathy organized the class into pairs (and one group of three since there was an odd number of students) to solve the problem. Their written work showed a variety of approaches and explanations.

Martin and Tony wrote: *There will be 60 left-handed students on the bus. Out of 100 12% would be 12 people. Since 500 is 5 × more than 100 you times 12 × 5 = 60.*

Marshal and Kiet wrote: *Yes, there are enough seats to hold all of the left-handed people because 10% of 500 is 50 people, 2% of 500 is 10 people, so 50 plus 10 is 60 people, and each bus holds 75 people.*

Liz and Audrey wrote: *To get the answer we multiplied 500 students by 12% and got 60 people and the bus can hold 75 people so there is enough room.*

Khalil and Gina wrote: (These students took a completely different approach.) *We think you can because 75 is 15% of 500. We only have to put 12% on of the left-handed people.*

Jon and Phi wrote: (These boys took an inappropriate approach, dividing five hundred by twelve, but still arrived at a correct answer.) *After we did the problem we got 41.66 and it kept on going on so we rounded it off to 42 students. We then subtracted 75 into 42 and got 33. After we got 33 seats we knew all the left-handed people could get on the bus.*

FYI
Even though their reasoning was erroneous, the students who used division arrived at the correct conclusion. Correct answers can hide a lack of understanding—a reason for being sure to have students explain their thinking.
— MSB

Raymond, Paula, and Stephanie wrote: (This group also used division, dividing twelve by five hundred. They also got the correct answer.) *Yes, 12 ÷ 500 = 0.024 so out of 500 students 24 of them are left handed so the bus can hold all the left-handed people.*

This lesson occurred near the beginning of the unit, and Cathy knew to expect this sort of confusion. As stated in the *Mathematics Model Curriculum Guide* (California State Department of Education 1987, 14): "We must recognize that partially grasped ideas and periods of confusion are a natural part of the process of developing understanding."

Cathy led a classroom discussion during which students presented their methods and the class discussed them. She kept the focus of the discussion on making sense of the procedures presented. From many experiences during the unit with problems such as this one, students began to formulate their own understanding of how to work with percents. Teachers often fear that if they don't teach the standard procedures for percent problems, students won't learn to solve these types of problems. The reverse may be a greater worry, however. Teaching the standard procedures for percent problems can result in students being unprepared to reason with percents to solve problems.

Encouraging multiple strategies for computing requires a total commitment to making thinking and reasoning the cornerstone of mathematics instruction. It requires teachers to be curious about students' ideas, to take delight in their thinking, and to encourage them, at all times, to make sense of mathematics.

Relating Arithmetic to Real Life

The real-life situations people face that call for using arithmetic generally require that they do the following:

1. Choose the operation (or operations) needed.

2. Choose the numbers to use.

3. Perform the calculation—with a calculator, using paper and pencil, or figuring mentally.

4. Evaluate the reasonableness of the answer and decide what to do as a result.

Most daily math problems that adults face require reasoning that goes beyond mere computation. In real-life problems, all the needed information is rarely provided in one tidy package—often the data have to be collected, frequently from a variety of sources. There's rarely only one possible method or strategy for real-life problems—usually there are several viable ways to solve them. Often, there's no one solution that's the right or best one—life has no answer book. Consider the following problems.

A Real-Life Arithmetic Problem: The Thanksgiving Turkey

One example of a real-life arithmetic problem arises annually at Thanksgiving time—the preparation of the traditional turkey. For the cook, the responsibility is a real and important one, calling for roasting a turkey that will be deliciously succulent, large enough to feed all the guests with enough leftovers for the following days, and ready to serve at the time planned for dinner.

One problem for the cook to solve is: *What time should I get up in the morning to start the preparations so the turkey will be ready on time?* Although this may not seem to be an arithmetic problem, it is. The cook also needs to make other decisions about tasks that also require applying arithmetic skills.

First of all, what information do you have? You'd like dinner to be served at 5 P.M.; the turkey you have purchased weighs 17 pounds, 8 ounces; according to the cookbook, it takes 15 to 18 minutes a pound for the turkey to roast (the longer time is for a turkey that has been stuffed). You know you plan to stuff the turkey. How much time do you estimate the turkey will need to be in the oven? How close do you need to be in this estimate?

Of course, you need to take the turkey out of the oven long enough before 5 P.M. to make the gravy and let the turkey cool before it is carved. And, of course, it will take time in the morning to make the stuffing and truss the bird, something that every cookbook cautions never to do the night before. Perhaps you purchased packaged bread cubes for stuffing instead of planning to use leftover bread. This can save time but also may require another arithmetic decision. Each package provides enough to stuff a 12-pound bird. What do you do? Use one package and stretch it? Use two packages and cook the extra in a casserole? Use a package and a half and wrestle with some more arithmetic to adjust the recipe accordingly? How much time will all this take? And once you have made all your estimates, you then have to decide what time you really do need to get up in the morning to make it all happen on schedule.

When solving problems such as this in real life, you call on all the resources you have: knowledge, previous experience, intuition. You need to analyze, predict, make decisions, evaluate. And there are always factors of variability—how your oven behaves, how long this particular turkey will actually take to cook, how close your estimate is to the time it will take you to truss the bird. Students benefit from problems that reflect the spirit and intent of the Thanksgiving turkey problem.

A Real-Life Arithmetic Problem: Raising a Dog

Many children lobby their parents to get a dog. I read an article that suggested a real-life problem for students: How much would it cost to raise a medium-sized dog to the age of eleven? Solving this problem calls for attention in several phases:

1. *Decide what information is needed and where to collect it.* What are the costs that most likely will be encountered? What other costs are possible? How can you find out how much food, veterinarian care, licenses, and so on, will cost?

2. *Choose the numerical information to use.* Which of the amounts are reasonable to use? How can you predict possible changes in these costs over the eleven years? (Uncertainty and variability are always elements of problems in real life.)

3. *Do the necessary calculations.*

4. *Use judgment to interpret the results and make decisions about a possible solution.*

A problem like this is wonderfully suited for small groups of students. Working together gives students the opportunity to draw on the resources of other students, expand their individual views, and have the support needed for solving a complex problem. After completing the first phase, groups can compare decisions they made about what information is needed and decide if they have included all that is important. Similarly, they later can compare the information they collected and their final solutions.

There's no correct or absolutely verifiable answer to a problem such as this. However, a family trying to decide if they would like to add a dog to their household would benefit from having some sense of the potential cost. Exact accuracy is not possible, or necessary. Who can predict if your dog is going to gnaw on a leg of the dining room table or do some other damage that calls for repairs to be made? How can you predict how often the family will take a vacation and need to board the dog? What about unpredictable medical needs? There's value for students in tackling problems for which solutions will always be somewhat uncertain, and it will be important for them to defend the reasonableness of their solutions.

Other Examples of Real-Life Arithmetic Problems: Classroom or School Situations

A ready source for problems like the above dog-raising problem can be found by scouring class or school situations. Here are some possibilities:

- How much will it cost to have a class party?
- How many cars will be needed for a class field trip?
- What needs to be done to plan a school dance?
- What's a fair way to organize the scheduling of the school's computer lab?
- How can we divide our class into two fair teams for a track-and-field event?
- How many Friday the 13ths can occur in one year?
- What's a fair allowance for a student in your grade level?
- How can we figure out how many buttons are on all our clothes or how many pockets we have altogether?
- How can we find out how many dogs live in our town?
- According to the newspaper shopping information, which is the most economical supermarket for buying groceries for a family of four?

In order to function in our complex and changing society, people need to be able to solve a wide variety of problems. Preparing students to become effective problem solvers requires broadening the typical classroom applications of arithmetic. The challenge is to provide motivating problems that spark students' natural curiosity and allow them to learn and use skills in situations that simulate the way arithmetic is really used in life.

Beginning Number Concepts

About Beginning Number Concepts

Mathematics instruction in the early grades should make numbers an integral part of students' classroom experiences. Students need many opportunities to identify quantities, see relationships among numbers, and learn about the operations of addition and subtraction. When developing beginning number concepts, students benefit from explorations with concrete materials and with experiences relating numbers to problem situations. They also benefit from talking about their ideas and listening to the reasoning of other students.

Mathematical Practices

Developing understanding and skills with beginning number concepts support the mathematical practices described in the Common Core and other standards documents for students in all grades. The mathematical practices should be connected to the content standards by engaging students in solving problems, reasoning, making conjectures, applying math to everyday life, using appropriate tools, communicating precisely, looking for patterns and structure, and looking for regularity in mathematical methods. The investigations in this section provide ways to make connections between practice and content standards.

Mathematical Content

Instruction in the early grades focuses on concepts, skills, and problem solving related to addition and subtraction. The content in this section is appropriate primarily for students in kindergarten and also can support students in grade 1. Below are content designations that align with the Common Core and other standards documents.

> *Kindergarten:* Know number names and the counting sequence; count to tell the number of objects; compare numbers; understand addition and subtraction; gain foundations for place value with numbers 11 to 19.

> *Grade 1:* Represent and solve problems involving addition and subtraction within 20; understand and apply properties of operations and the relationship between addition and subtraction; work with addition and subtraction equations; understand place value and use place value to add and subtract within 100.

Whole-Class Instruction

The following suggestions for whole-class instruction introduce students to important and basic beginning number concepts. They are organized into five categories: creating math moments, playing number games, introducing addition and subtraction with word problems, a problem-solving lesson, and using children's literature.

Creating Math Moments

Relating numerical problem solving to everyday classroom situations helps students relate math to a setting that's real to them and see the usefulness of mathematics. Whenever possible during the day, create math moments that engage students with problem-solving opportunities. It's important not only for students to give answers but also to explain their reasoning.

Taking Daily Attendance

After ascertaining how many students are absent, ask the students to figure how many are present.

Organizing Students in Pairs

When students need partners for a class activity or are lining up in pairs, ask them first to figure out if everyone in the class will have a partner or if there will be an extra person. This provides students with informal experience thinking about odd and even numbers. Also, if appropriate, ask them to figure how many pairs there will be.

Collecting Permission Slips

After some students have returned their field trip permission slips, ask the students to figure out how many more slips still need to be returned.

Creating Recording Booklets

For particular projects, students can make their own booklets by folding 12-by-18-inch newsprint in half and making a cover from construction paper. Ask them first to figure out how many sheets they need so they'll have twelve pages to write on. (Decide first if students are to write on right-hand pages only or on both sides of the paper.)

Sharing Scissors

Ask students to figure out how many pairs of scissors are needed if each child shares a pair with a partner.

Guessing the Prices of Snacks

Show the students a can of juice, a box of crackers, a bag of apples, or some item with which they're familiar. Ask them to guess how much the item costs. After each guess, give a clue by telling whether the item costs more or less than the amount that was guessed.

How Many Dice

If each pair of students needs one die for a math investigation, have them figure out how many dice are needed in all.

A Number Game: Red + Black

Math games engage students' interest and provide a relaxed setting in which they can think about number relationships. The two-person card game *Red + Black* provides students valuable experience with representing ten as the sum of two addends.

Materials

a deck of 20 cards per pair of students—10 red and 10 black, 1 (or ace) to 10 of each color

Teaching the Rules of the Game

Explain that for this two-player game, each pair needs a deck of twenty cards, ten red and ten black, 1 (or ace) to 10 of each color. They also need one recording sheet to share. Model how to fold a piece of newsprint or copy paper into eight sections, as shown. Have each student fold a paper. They can use it to play the game twice, first recording on one side and then on the other.

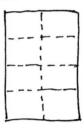

Teach the rules of the game by selecting two students to play while the rest of the class watches. Read each rule and have the pair you chose follow the directions.

RED + BLACK: RULES OF THE GAME

You need: a deck of 20 cards—10 red and 10 black, 1 (or ace) to 10 of each

Play with a partner. Follow these rules.

1. One student mixes the cards by placing them facedown and stirring them.

2. The same student deals all the cards, giving ten to each person.

3. Students each count the number of red cards and black cards they have.

4. Each student records an addition expression on the paper, first writing the number of red cards and then the number of black cards.

5. Continue, changing who mixes and deals the cards each time, until the recording sheet is full.

When you get to step four, it's helpful to draw a sample recording sheet on the board and introduce or reinforce the standard way to record addition: 4 + 6, for example.

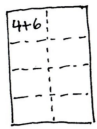

Have students play another round or two until you are confident that they all understand how to play. Then distribute cards and have the students play in pairs.

Circulate to be sure students are playing correctly. If a pair completes two games quickly, give them additional paper to fold into another recording sheet and play again.

Discuss the Game

After all students have played at least one game, lead a classroom discussion. Use this opportunity to introduce or reinforce the language—*add, addend, addition, plus*. Ask questions such as:

Which addition problem came up most often on your paper?

How many times did four (or any number) come up as an addend?

Which addition problem do you think came up more times in our entire class?

Extension

Make a Class Graph. Across the bottom of the board or bulletin board, prepare a class graph by posting eleven addition expressions to show all the possibilities of red plus black—0 + 10, 1 + 9, 2 + 8 . . . , 10 + 0. Then have pairs cut apart one of their recording sheets and post each section above the matching expression. Ask questions related to the graph:

How many times did 5 + 5 come up? 2 + 8? (Repeat for other combinations.)

Which came up most? How many more times did 1 + 9 come up than 0 + 10? (Choose two adjacent expressions so it's easier to compare.)

A Number Game: Empty the Bowl

This two-person game provides the opportunity to develop the take-away meaning of subtraction while also supporting addition and students' number sense.

Materials

cubes or tiles, 20 per pair of students
a small bowl, 1 per pair of students (plastic 8-ounce containers from cottage cheese, yogurt, etc.)
1–6 dice, 1 per student

Teaching the Rules of the Game

Show students the materials that they need to play the game, explaining that each pair needs a bowl with twenty cubes (or tiles). Demonstrate by having the class count with you as you place twenty cubes into a bowl. Also, it helps to talk about how to roll the die appropriately, so that it stays on their desk.

Explain that when you roll the die, the number that comes up tells how many cubes to remove from the bowl. One player rolls the die and records the number that comes up, and the other player removes the cubes. Select a student to be your partner and demonstrate a few rolls. Each time you roll, write on the board the number that comes up; then the student removes the cubes. After you've listed a few rolls and removed some of the cubes, ask, *How many rolls in all do you think it will take to empty the bowl?* Allow all students who have ideas to share them with the class. Then continue until the bowl is empty. Be sure to point out that you don't have to go out exactly; that is, for example, if two cubes are left in the bowl and you roll a three, it's OK to remove the two cubes and empty the bowl.

EMPTY THE BOWL: RULES OF THE GAME

You need: a bowl
   cubes or tiles, 20 per pair of students
   a die

Play with a partner. Follow these rules.

1. One student rolls the die and writes down the number that came up.

2. The student who rolled the die removes the number of tiles that came up on the die.

3. Continue until the bowl is empty.

4. Switch jobs and play again.

Play another game or a few more until you're confident that the students understand how to play. Then distribute the materials to pairs of students. Tell them that when they complete a game, they should play again. (Save the rolls you listed on the board for when you summarize their experience.) Allow time so that students play three to five games, or more if they're interested.

Discuss the Game

After all students have played at least three to five games, lead a classroom discussion. Use the questions that follow to probe their thinking about what they've learned from playing the game so far, asking questions such as:

What do you think is the most number of rolls it could possibly take to empty the bowl?

Why couldn't the bowl be emptied in just one roll?

Why couldn't the bowl be emptied in two rolls?

What do you think is the fewest number of rolls you would need to empty the bowl?

Although some students may not be able to answer these questions, raising the issues sets the stage for the kind of thinking you would like them to do. Also, their responses give you information about what individual students understand.

Extension
Make a Class Graph. On the board, list the numbers from 1 to 20, and write tally marks to indicate how many rolls it took you to empty the bowl in each demonstration game. To give the students experience with collecting statistical data and the opportunity to think more about what happens when they play *Empty the Bowl*, ask the students to count how many rolls it took for each of their games. Have students report and make tally marks as you did for the demonstration games. Have students discuss what they notice. You may wish to ask questions to spark their thinking:

What was the greatest number of rolls it took to empty the bowl?

What was the fewest numbers of rolls it took?

What would you predict about how many rolls it would take if you played again?

Introducing Addition and Subtraction with Word Problems
When students learn about the operations of addition and subtraction, it's helpful for them to see the relationship between these operations and also to connect them to the world around them. Word problems accustom students to looking at groups of people or objects, help them see the actions of joining and separating, and give students experiences figuring out sums and differences. It's useful for students to act out stories that involve addition and subtraction, either by pretending or using concrete materials to represent situations.

Acting Out Word Problems
Present word problems for which the students pretend to be animals, people, or things. For example:

_____, _____, _____, *and* _____ *are clowns at the circus.* _____, _____, *and* _____ *are more clowns who also come to perform at the circus. How many clowns are in the circus?*

_____, _____, *and* _____ *are birds sitting in a tree.* _____ *and* _____ *flew away. How many birds are left in the tree?*

_____ *put four books on the reading table.* _____ *put two more books on the table. How many books are on the table altogether?*

_____, _____, _____, *and* _____ *are standing near the door.* _____ *and* _____ *are sitting at their desks. How many more students are standing than sitting?*

Teaching Tip
After students are familiar with playing Empty the Bowl, make it a choice activity for partners.
— MBB

FYI
When students make predictions, I've experienced that some students refer to the data collected while others merely guess or express what they hope will happen.
— MBB

Beginning Number Concepts **333**

Once the students are comfortable acting out stories, model how to record stories symbolically. Writing the addition and subtraction equations that match the problem situations helps students see how symbols can be used to represent the stories. When students understand how to connect stories and symbols, have them write equations to describe other stories.

Modeling Word Problems with Cubes

Instead of acting out story problems, students can use interlocking cubes, such as Snap, Multilink, or Unifix cubes, to represent the people, objects, or animals in the stories. It helps to define work spaces for the students with construction paper, tagboard, or prepared counting boards on which you've drawn trees, oceans, corrals, and so on, to correspond to the story contexts you plan to use. Following are examples of stories for students to model with cubes:

There were four ladybugs and three ants in the grass. How many were there altogether?

We gave our rat six kibbles. He ate four of them. How many kibbles were left?

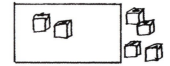

There were eight horses in the pasture. Six were brown and the rest were white. How many white horses were there?

Seven cars were in the supermarket parking lot. Three more cars arrived. How many cars were in the parking lot altogether?

A Problem-Solving Lesson: Making Necklaces

While routine word problems can serve to introduce students to the language and symbolization of addition and subtraction, nonroutine numerical problems provide opportunities for students to organize and stretch their thinking. Nonroutine problems contribute to building students' number sense and strengthening their ability to deal with new situations. A sample problem-solving investigation, *Making Necklaces*, follows and supports students' learning about numbers. Students look for patterns, estimate, add, graph, and compare volume. *Making Necklaces* engages students with both repeating and growth patterns, both of which are important to their numerical understanding and algebraic thinking.

For this sample lesson, I used the Introducing/Exploring/Summarizing model for problem-solving lessons, described in Part 2 on page 135.

Materials

pint jar of macaroni, dyed from being placed in a mixture of rubbing alcohol and red food coloring, then drained and dried
pint jar of macaroni that hasn't been dyed
string long enough to make a necklace that will slide over a child's head, one end dipped in glue to make it easier for students to string the macaroni, 1 per student

For help with introducing repeating and growth patterns, see "Introducing Patterns" in Part 2 on page 242.

Introducing

1. **Present or review concepts.** Talk with the children about what a necklace is and tell them that they'll be making necklaces following a math pattern.

2. **Pose a part of the problem or a similar but smaller problem.** This step is only necessary if you feel that the students need reinforcement with patterns. If so, talk about a necklace that is in an ABABAB . . . pattern, alternating red and white macaroni.

3. **Present the investigation.** Tell the students that they'll make a macaroni necklace following a particular pattern. Model for the class how to make a necklace using the following pattern: one red, one white, two reds, one white, three reds, one white, and so on, ending with six red and one white. Explain the pattern as you make the necklace. Show how to tie the ends of the string.

Show the students the materials you prepared for making necklaces and ask the following questions:

Do you think I've brought enough macaroni?

Will you need more red macaroni or more white macaroni for your necklace? Why do you think that?

When you've all made your necklaces, will we have more red macaroni left over, more white macaroni left over, or about the same of each?

How would you describe the pattern you'll be using?

4. **Discuss the task to make sure students understand what they are to do.** Have several students describe how they will make their necklaces. Then distribute string and macaroni for students to make their own necklaces. Make your sample available for students to refer to.

Exploring

1. **Observe the students as they work.** Circulate to be sure students are following the pattern you described for their necklaces.

2. **Offer assistance when needed,** especially with tying the knots.

3. **Provide an extension to students who finish more quickly than others.** Ask them to make another necklace as a gift for someone at home.

Summarizing

After the students have made their necklaces, collect the leftover macaroni in their original jars. Again ask the questions you asked before the students made their necklaces when you introduced the investigation. Have the students compare the amounts of the remaining macaroni.

Extension

Making a Graph and More Necklaces. On another day, tell the students that they'll have the chance to make another necklace using the same macaroni pattern, but with a color other than red. Have them record on a class graph to indicate whether they would like to use yellow, blue, green, orange, or purple. The students can either sign their names or post colored squares on which they've written their names.

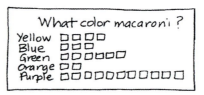

Discuss the graph using questions like these:

> *Which color was chosen most?*
>
> *Which color was chosen least?*
>
> *How many students chose yellow? Blue?* (Ask for each color.)
>
> *How many more students chose yellow than blue? Purple than orange?* (Ask for other colors, choosing those that are adjacent on the graph so students can more easily compare the amounts.)

Then discuss how much of each color macaroni the class will need. Use the jar of red macaroni as a reference. The students' responses will reveal whether they can relate information from a graph to the practical problem of deciding on quantities of macaroni to dye.

Finally, dye the macaroni using food coloring and alcohol, showing the students how to mix colors to get green, orange, and purple. Tell them they'll be able to make their necklaces the next day when the dyed macaroni has dried. Also tell them that in the meantime, they are to figure out how many white and how many colored macaroni they each need. You may want to prepare a sheet (see below) on which they can record their solutions and thinking. The next day, have students make their new necklaces.

Using Children's Literature

Children's literature is a valuable resource for math lessons. Children's books capture students' imaginations and interests and are effective for stimulating mathematical thinking and reasoning. The following suggestions model the kinds of investigations that can be initiated from simple counting books. For each, first read the book aloud, allowing time for the students to enjoy the text and illustrations. Then post the problem suggested.

Rooster's Off to See the World

Rooster's Off to See the World, by Eric Carle (1991), tells the story of a rooster who decided one day that he wanted to travel. Strikingly illustrated with colorful collages, the book describes how the rooster was joined by two cats, three frogs, four turtles, and five fish. A problem arose, however, when night fell and the animals realized that no plans had been made for food or shelter. They all became hungry, cold, and afraid and decided to return home.

Pose the problem: *How many animals altogether set out to see the world?* Ask students to show how they figure out the answer and explain their reasoning. Students who have difficulty writing can dictate their explanations.

One Gorilla

One Gorilla, by Atsuko Morozumi (1996), received the New York Times Best Illustrated Students' Book Award. This counting book begins, "Here is a list of things I love." The list includes one gorilla, two butterflies, three budgerigars, four squirrels, and on up, to ten cats. The gorilla appears on each page, and students take delight in the illustrations. This book suggests an extended version of the problem presented for *Rooster's Off to See the World*.

Pose the problem: *How many things altogether did the author love?* For students who find the numbers too difficult, suggest the alternative problem of figuring out how many things the author loved that could fly. This simplifies the problem to adding 2 + 3 + 9, the numbers of butterflies, budgerigars, and birds.

Note: Many other students' books also suggest this same problem, including *1 Hunter* by Pat Hutchins (1982) and *The Midnight Farm* by Reeve Lindbergh (1987). Although the mathematical thinking required for all these books is similar, the change in context makes each a new problem for the students. Engaging students with these problems over time gives you the opportunity to assess their progress.

Ten Black Dots

Donald Crews (1986) begins *Ten Black Dots* with a question: "What can you do with ten black dots?" He answers the question by incorporating black dots into colorful illustrations of everyday objects, beginning with one dot and continuing up to ten dots. Simple rhymes accompany the graphics. The book begins:

> One black dot can make a sun
> or a moon when day is done.
> Two dots can make the eyes of a fox
> or the eyes of keys that open locks.

For more information on using children's literature, check out the Math, Literature, and Nonfiction series from Math Solutions (mathsolutions.com). There you'll find a link to a chart of all of the children's books featured in these resources. Also, check out Scholastic's *Math Reads*, which I worked on with a team of Math Solutions colleagues (http://teacher.scholastic.com/products/math-concepts-skills/math-reads).

Ask students for their ideas about what they might make with one black dot, then two, three, and so on, up to ten black dots.

Pose the problem: *Make your own* black dots *book*. Plan for students to complete a page or two a day. Black adhesive dots, $\frac{3}{4}$- inch in diameter, are available at office supply stores and easy for students to use. Newsprint with an unlined top portion for illustrations and a lined bottom portion for their writing works well.

Pose another problem when students have completed and shared their books: *How many black dots did you use?* Ask the students to show their work and explain their reasoning. To help students begin their explanations, write on the board: *I used _____ dots. I got my answer by _____ .*

Additional Instructional Suggestions

The following instructional suggestions are for small groups of students. After students are familiar with the activities, some of the suggestions are suitable as independent investigations for individual or partner work, and for choice time explorations.

For more on using investigations with various instructional groups, see "Starting Point 20: Four Structures for Organizing and Managing Classroom Instruction" in Part 1 on page 111.

Build a Stack

You need: interlocking cubes, about 12 per student

This investigation is suitable for instruction with a small group of six to eight students. Give students directions that use the words more and less, such as the examples below and, for each, have students build stacks of interlocking cubes for each direction you give.

Build a stack that has one more than four.

Build a stack that has two more than six.

Build a stack that has one less than seven.

For an easier version: *Build a stack of four. Now build a stack that has one more than four. How many did you use?*

For more of a challenge: *What number do you think is one less than five? Let's build a stack and see.*

Teaching Tip
This investigation is useful for reinforcing or helping students understand the concepts of one more, one less, two more, and two less. I watch to see if, for example, when I ask them to build a stack that has one more than four, are they able to count one more cube? Or do they build a stack and have to count all of the cubes to check?

— MSB

Snap It

You need: interlocking cubes, 10 per student

This investigation is suitable for instruction with a small group of six to eight students. Ask students to each make a train using the same number of interlocking cubes. Then explain that on the signal "Snap," they break their train into two parts and hold the two parts behind their backs, one part in each hand. They take turns showing the cubes in one hand and then in the other while the other students say the combination.

Teaching Tip
Snap It is ideal as an independent partner activity. You can change the difficulty of the experience by increasing or decreasing the number you select for students to use for their trains.

— MSB

Grow and Shrink

You need: cubes, 6 per student
1–6 number cube
ten-frame recording sheet, **R** See Reproducible R.37
1 per student

This investigation is suitable for instruction with a small group of six to eight students. Students take turns rolling the 1–6 number cube. With the students (who are able) call out the number rolled. Then each student builds the number rolled on his or her ten-frame.

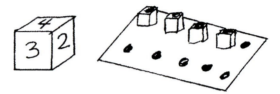

Yarn Shapes

You need: yarn, enough for each student to cut a piece the same length as his or her arm
tiles, about 100 per student

This investigation is suitable for instruction with a small group of six to eight students, or as a whole-class lesson. Model for students how to cut a piece of yarn as long as their arm and use it to outline a shape. Then fill in the shape with tiles and have the students count them with you. Repeat for several other shapes until you're sure they understand what to do. Ask students what they notice about shapes that hold more tiles and those that hold fewer tiles. (Long skinny shapes will hold fewer tiles than rounder or more square-like shapes.)

Trace and Compare

You need: tiles, about 50 per student

This investigation is suitable for instruction with a small group of six to eight students, or as a whole-class lesson. Students trace around one of their shoes. Ask them to predict if it will take more tiles to fill their foot shape or to place tiles on the outline like a fence. They then measure with the tiles to find out.

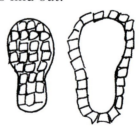

Students repeat the investigation by tracing other shapes—a book, their hand, a board eraser, and so on.

Grab-Bag Subtraction

You need: cubes or tiles, number to be decided by the teacher
5–10 number cube or spinner
small paper bag

Have students work in pairs. For each pair, select a number that is appropriate for them. One student fills the paper bag with the assigned number of cubes or tiles. The other student reaches in and takes out some, showing how many have been removed. Both students predict how many they think are in the bag. Then they check their predictions, and each student records the equation.

Assessing Understanding of Beginning Number Concepts

Observing students during classroom discussions and while they are working on independent investigations provides information about their understanding and skills. Also, one-on-one conversations with students reveal their individual understanding, misconceptions, and gaps, and provides valuable information that isn't always evident from classroom observations. The following suggestions can be used for both assessment approaches.

Observing Students

Students' verbal responses to questions and reactions to others' ideas reveal their levels of interest and understanding. Also, students' written work can be an indication of their thinking, especially when they've explained their reasoning processes.

It's important to look not only at whether students' answers to problems are right or wrong but also at how they arrive at their solutions. Important questions to ask yourself include:

- *Was the answer appropriate or reasonable?*

- *Did the student have a strategy for figuring out a solution or was the student guessing?*

- *What does the student's work reveal about the student's understanding of different-size numbers?*

To learn about students' numerical reasoning, probe by asking questions such as the following:

- *How did you figure that out?*

- *Can you explain why you're sure?*

- *What made you think of that?*

- *Can you think of another way to figure it out?*

When Observing
Seeing how students approach the problems from children's books such as One Gorilla (Morozumi 1996) on page 337 tells you about their comfort with numbers and their ability to calculate. Looking at their solutions to the number of macaroni needed in The Necklace Investigation on page 334 can tell you about their ability and comfort with larger numbers. Observing their strategies as they play Grow and Shrink on page 340 can reveal their understanding about relationships among numbers.

— MSB

Individual Assessments

The following assessment with cubes gives information about students' understanding of numerical relationships. Students' responses indicate their ability to decompose numbers and their confidence with number combinations.

TEACHER	STUDENT	INTERPRETATION
Say: *Count five cubes into my hand.*	Student is able to do so.	Student shows ability to count with one-to-one correspondence.
	Student is unable to do so.	Student doesn't show ability to count with one-to-one correspondence. Try with three cubes. If student is unsuccessful, don't continue.
Ask: *How many cubes do I have in my hand?*	Student says "five" without counting.	Student conserves for five. Ask next question.
	Student needs to recount.	Student doesn't conserve. Try with three cubes.
Hide some of the five cubes in one hand and show the others. Ask: *How many cubes am I hiding?*	Student answers instantly, correctly, and confidently.	Student indicates understanding of the quantity five. Check twice more by hiding different numbers of the five cubes to be sure student can decompose flexibly. Then assess with six cubes. As long as the student is successful, continue assessing up to ten cubes.
	Student doesn't answer, answers incorrectly, or has to count and doesn't know instantly with confidence.	Check twice more by hiding different numbers of the five cubes to be sure student can't decompose flexibly. If so, try again with three cubes, and then with four, to ascertain where students' understanding is weak.

Place Value

About Place Value

Our place-value system, which allows us to represent any number with just ten digits, is complex for students to understand. Students need to learn to make groups of ten items and then count those groups as if they were single items. They must learn that digits have different values, depending on their position in numbers. The difference between 36 and 63, for example, though obvious to adults, is not always easy for young students to understand.

When learning about place value, students benefit from grouping concrete materials into tens and hundreds to count them and linking the results to the standard numerical notation. Students also benefit from involvement with problem situations that call for estimating large numbers of things. This section suggests whole-class lessons and additional investigations in which students estimate and count large quantities of objects, look for patterns in the numbers on 0–99 and 1–100 charts, learn several games, and more.

Mathematical Practices

Developing understanding and skills with place value should support the mathematical practices described in the Common Core and other standards documents for students in all grades. The mathematical practices should be connected to the content standards by engaging students in solving problems, reasoning, making conjectures, applying math to everyday life, using appropriate tools, communicating precisely, looking for patterns and structure, and looking for regularity in mathematical methods. The investigations in this section provide ways to make connections between practice and content standards.

Mathematical Content

Instruction that focuses on place value begins in kindergarten and is part of the mathematics curriculum through grade 5. The standards that focus on building understanding are especially important for helping students engage with the mathematical practices. Below are content designations that align with the Common Core and other standards documents.

Kindergarten: Gain foundations for place value with numbers 11 to 19.

Grade 1: Understand place value and use place value to add and subtract within 100.

Grade 2: Understand place value and use place value to add and subtract within 1000.

Grade 3: Use place value to perform multidigit arithmetic, including adding and subtracting within 1000 and multiplying one-digit whole numbers by multiples of 10 up to 90.

Grade 4: Recognize in multidigit numbers that a digit represents ten times what it represents in the place to its right; round multidigit whole numbers to any place; use place value understanding to add, subtract, multiply, and divide whole numbers.

Grade 5: Recognize in multidigit numbers that a digit represents ten times what it represents in the place to its right and $\frac{1}{10}$ of what it represents in the place to its left; explain patterns in the number of zeroes when multiplying by powers of 10 and when decimals are multiplied or divided by a power of 10; compare decimals to thousandths.

Whole-Class Instruction

The following suggestions for whole-class instruction introduce students to important and basic ideas relating to place value. They are organized into four categories: counting large quantities, using money, a logic game, and looking for patterns.

A Problem-Solving Lesson: How Many Fingers?

Engage the students in a variety of problems in which they estimate and count large numbers of objects. Relating the problems to the students and their school environment helps them apply mathematics in contexts that are real to them. The following whole-class sample lesson engages students in figuring out how many fingers the students in the class have altogether.

Materials

interlocking cubes, at least as many as fingers in the room

Introducing

1. **Present or review concepts.** On the day you do this investigation, determine the number of people in the class—students who are present, you, and any other visitors. Write this number on the board.

2. **Pose a part of the problem or a similar but smaller problem.** Ask seven or eight students to come to the front of the room and hold up their hands. Ask the class for different ways to count how many fingers they have in all. Typically, students will suggest counting by twos, fives, tens, and, perhaps, ones. As each way is suggested, have the class count aloud with you. Also, suggest any of these ways to count that students didn't think of.

   Then ask, *How many students need to come up to the front of the room so there are 100 fingers altogether?* For some students, this will be obvious; others may be uncertain or have no idea at all. Whatever number students suggest, have that many come to the front. Have the students count along with you as you count their fingers. If no one suggests ten students, be sure to do so. For each suggestion, go through the process of counting by twos, fives, and tens, and even ones, if the students suggest it, to see how many fingers there are.

   Ask the students to estimate the total number of fingers in the room.

3. **Present the investigation.** Then present the problem for students to solve in pairs or small groups: *How many fingers are there altogether on all of our hands?*

4. **Discuss the task to make sure students understand what they are to do.** Remind the students of the number of people that you wrote on the board earlier.

For Younger Students
When smaller numbers are more appropriate, switch the investigation to How Many Thumbs? Have each student take two interlocking cubes to represent their two thumbs and then work together to snap them into trains with ten cubes in each, and then count them. Then break apart trains so that there are five of each and recount.
— MSB

Teaching Tip
Sometimes I've begun by asking only three students to come to the front of the room, which makes this introductory experience a little easier but a number large enough so that I can point out that counting by ones takes much longer and that it's always good to look for ways to solve math problems more efficiently.
— MSB

Teaching Tip
To guide students to think about a reasonable estimate (as well as assess students' understanding and reasoning) ask, Are there enough people in the class to have two hundred fingers altogether? How do you know? More than two hundred? More than three hundred?
— MSB

Exploring

Circulate and offer assistance as needed. Ask pairs or groups that finish more quickly than others to figure out how many thumbs are in the room altogether.

Summarizing

Ask student groups to report their solutions. Be sure to ask students to explain how they figured out their answers. To verify the correct answer, have each person in the room make a train of ten interlocking cubes, one for each finger. Then count the trains by tens. Also, record the final answer on the board in several different ways; for example, *two hundred and seventy, 27 tens, 100 + 100 + 70, 270.*

A Problem-Solving Lesson: How Many Pockets?

The following whole-class sample investigation builds students' number sense through engaging them in estimating how many pockets they have.

Materials

interlocking cubes such as Multilink, Snap, or Unifix cubes, at least 200

Introducing

1. **Present or review concepts.** Talk with the class about what an estimate is. Explain that estimating gives the opportunity to think about numbers, better understand what they mean, and make guesses about what answers might be. Also, tell the students that they'll be solving a problem that could have a large number as the answer. Ask them for ideas about what a large number might be.

2. **Pose a part of the problem or a similar but smaller problem.** Invite a student to come to the front of the room. Be sure to choose a student who is wearing clothing that has pockets. Ask the student to put one cube into each pocket. Then have the student remove the cubes, snap them together, and count them.

3. **Present the investigation.** Ask, *About how many pockets do you think there are altogether in our class?* Have students think first and then talk in pairs. Finally, have them report their estimates and explain why they think their estimates make sense.

   Tell them that they'll now each find out how many pockets they have. Explain that they'll put one cube in each of their pockets, as their classmate demonstrated. Then they'll remove the cubes from their pockets, snap them together, count them, and compare how many they have with their neighbors. Make cubes available in several locations so students have easy access to them.

4. **Discuss the task to make sure students understand what they are to do.** Ask several students to state the directions for what they are to do.

Exploring

Circulate and offer assistance if needed.

For more information about the "think, pair, share" routine, see "Starting Point 14: The Importance of Classroom Discussions" in Part 1 on page 67.

Summarizing

After students have had the opportunity to compare, bring them to attention for a classroom discussion. Begin by having students report the number of pockets they have. Ask, *Who has zero pockets? One? Two? Three?* Continue by asking, *Who has the most number of pockets?*

If you'd like, create a class graph by listing the numbers *0, 1, 2,* and so on, and having students each mark an *X* or a check next to the number of pockets they have. Then pose another problem: *How many pockets do you have altogether?* Ask students to combine their cubes, work with their neighbors to make trains with ten cubes in each, and bring each train of ten to the front of the room. Have the class count aloud with you by tens. Then have students bring up their extra cubes and use them to make additional trains of ten. Again, have them count aloud by tens. Count the extras. Record the number of tens and extras on the board as well as the final number (e.g., *6 tens and 8 ones = 68*).

Extension

How Many Pockets? Revisited. Tell the students they'll repeat the investigation for the next few days to see if the number of pockets changes. Continue the investigation for as many days as the students are interested.

Teaching Tip
After students put a cube in each pocket, I've found that it's good to collect the extra cubes so that they don't get mixed up with the cubes from students' pockets. (This tip comes from my experience where one boy got so involved snapping cubes together that he ignored the pocket connection and made a train that was seventeen cubes long.)

—MSB

FYI
It may seem that grouping by tens is the most efficient way to count the cubes, but left to their own choices, students may prefer to group objects in other ways, by twos or fives, for example. While grouping by tens relates to our place-value system, it takes time and many experiences for this to be compelling or even make sense to all the students.

—MSB

Additional Counting Investigations

How Many Fingers? and *How Many Pockets?* are examples of lessons that can be repeated during the year. Spacing out experiences like these provides the opportunity to assess changes that occur over time in how students think about large numbers. It's important to remember that teaching students the usefulness and logic of grouping objects into tens to make sense of large quantities is not a lesson objective, but a long-range goal that's best attached to repeated investigations. Students need many experiences over time to learn to connect the idea of counting by tens (which many can do by rote) to the structure of our place-value system.

While students are developing understanding of place value, it's important they feel that their own methods for counting large numbers of objects are also valid. The pedagogical challenge is to make the connection between grouping by tens and our number system. The goal is for students to have the chance to consider the connection, understand it, see its usefulness, and eventually use their experience to construct an understanding of place value for themselves. Additional counting investigations follow.

ADDITIONAL PROBLEMS FOR COUNTING LARGE QUANTITIES

- How many feet are there in class altogether? Thumbs?
- How many buttons are there on everyone's clothing?
- How many cubes would be in a box after each student puts in a handful?
- How many letters are there altogether in everyone's first names? Last names?
- How many books are in the class library?

When doing other explorations, such as figuring the number of buttons or books, vary the materials. For example, use beans to represent buttons and provide small cups for students to group them into tens. Use tally marks to record the number of feet in the room and, after counting by fives, draw circles around groups to count them by tens.

Classroom discussions are important because students have the opportunity to hear each other's ideas and you can get a glimpse into students' understanding. In classroom discussions, raise questions such as the following:

- *If you group the cubes (or other objects) by twos or fives or tens, will you get the same number when you count how many there are altogether? Always? Explain your thinking.*

- *Some people say it's easy to count by tens. Why do you think they say that?*

- *Which takes fewer numbers—to count to one hundred by fives or by tens? Why? How else can you count to one hundred?*

FYI
Though many young students can count by tens, when I've asked them to continue beyond one hundred, many continue incorrectly, next typically saying two hundred, three hundred, and so on, or 101, 102, and so on. I've found it useful to make time to listen to each student count by tens, hear how they extend the pattern past one hundred, and then provide experiences counting objects to develop their understanding.

—MSB

A Money Game: Race for $1.00

Money is a useful model for place value. The following game takes advantage of students' interest in and familiarity with money. Before introducing the game, however, review for the students the relationships of the denominations to each other.

Materials

pennies, 30 per pair of students
dimes, 20 per pair of students
pretend dollar bills, 2 per pair of students
1–6 dice, 2 per pair of students
small zip-top bag to hold the coins and dollar bills, 1 per pair of students

Teaching the Rules of the Game

Teach the rules of this two-player game by selecting two students to play while the rest of the class watches. The pair you chose should follow the directions as you read them.

RACE FOR $1.00: RULES OF THE GAME

You need: zip-top bag with pennies, dimes, and dollar bills
                    1–6 dice, 2 per pair of students

Play with a partner. Players take turns. Each turn has three steps.

1. Roll the two dice.

2. Add the numbers that come up and take that many pennies. If you have enough, exchange ten pennies for a dime. (You may only exchange when you have the dice.)

3. Pass the dice to the next person.

The first player to get a dollar is the winner.

Then choose two different students to play a new game. When you feel confident that the students understand how to play, distribute a zip-top bag of materials to each pair of students and have them play with partners. Circulate to be sure students are playing correctly. Notice if students take shortcuts; that is, when they roll a sum larger than 10, such as 12, some may take one dime and two pennies rather than count out twelve pennies. Others in the group may question this and ask if it's allowed. Respond that shortcuts are allowed only if everyone in the group understands what's being done and agrees.

Discuss the Game

After students have had a chance to play the game several times, lead a discussion about the game by asking the following questions:

What did you like about the game?

How would you explain how to exchange to someone who hadn't played the game yet?

Teaching Tip
Playing Race for $1.00 is a good option for students when they've finished assignments and have time available.
— MSB

A Logic Game: Digit Place

The game of *Digit Place* appears in the "Problem-Solving Investigations: Number and Operations" section of Part 2 on page 299. Students need to focus on the importance of the positions of the digits in numbers, while being challenged to think strategically. In the simpler version described that follows, the game is played with two digits instead of three, and the class plays against the teacher.

Teaching the Rules of the Game

To introduce the game, make sure all students can see what you'll write on the board. Draw a chart as shown and also write the numbers from 0 to 9.

Teach the rules of the game by playing a practice game. Tell the class that the goal of the game is to guess the two-digit number that you've chosen. To demonstrate how to play, you'll tell them that the number you've picked is seventeen. Show them how you would give clues for several pretend guesses. Write 74 for the first guess and explain that it has one correct digit, the 7, but neither is in the correct place. Record on the chart. Then repeat for a guess of 16, and then for 84. Tell them that each clue reveals how many of their digits are correct and how many of those are in the correct place. Show how to cross out numbers, here 8 and 4, when the clues reveal for sure that they aren't in the two-digit number they're trying to guess.

Next play a real game with the class, having students guess while you record the clues.

Play a game or two each day for several days to help the students learn the rules. Remember that each time you start a game, list the numbers from 0 to 9 and cross out numbers as they are eliminated for certain.

Discuss the Game

After you've played several games and the students understand how to play *Digit Place*, lead a discussion about the strategies they use when choosing numbers to guess.

```
0 1 2 3 4 5 6 7 8 9
Guess | Digit | Place
```

```
0 1 2 3 4̷ 5 6 7 8̷ 9
Guess | Digit | Place
  74  |   1   |   0
  16  |   1   |   1
  84  |   0   |   0
```

Patterns on the 0–99 Chart

Writing numbers on a 10-by-10 grid arranges them in an orderly way, making it possible for students to see patterns and relationships in our counting system. This investigation focuses students on patterns using the numbers from zero to ninety-nine.

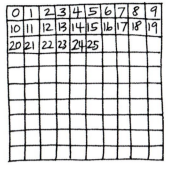

Teaching Directions

Post a blank 10-by-10 grid large enough to write numerals in each square that the class can see. Ask the students how many squares are on the grid. Have students think first and then talk in pairs. Finally, have them report their estimates and explain why they think their estimates make sense.

On the chart, write the numerals from *0* to *25* as shown.

Then ask questions like these and ask students to explain their reasoning:

What number would come next?

Where do you think forty will land? Fifty? Fifty-three? Sixty-three? [Have students come up and point to the squares.]

[Point to a square.] *What number do you think belongs here?*

Take several days asking questions like these and writing in numbers to completely fill in the chart. Don't rush the experience. The more time students have to examine the chart, the more support they have for noticing patterns.

Lead a Discussion

Lead a classroom discussion for students to share the patterns they noticed. Typically, students see patterns in the rows and columns. For example, the numbers in the first column on the 0–99 chart all end in 0; all the numbers in the bottom row start with 9. Students don't often look for diagonal patterns. You can prompt this by saying: "I see a pattern in the numbers that have both digits the same." Also, suggest that students look at patterns or characteristics of other numbers (see the box below). Ask students to locate the numbers on the 0–99 chart and describe the pattern they make. Repeat for other characteristics.

LOOKING FOR PATTERNS SUGGESTIONS

- odd numbers
- even numbers
- numbers with both digits the same
- numbers with a 6 in them
- numbers with digits that add to ten
- numbers with digits that add to nine (can repeat for digits that add to five, six, seven, and eight)

FYI
Teachers often ask if they should use 0-99 or 1-100 charts for an investigation like this one. My short answer is: I use them both and think that they both offer useful patterns for students to examine.
— MBB

For a more in-depth response, see "0–99 Chart versus 1–100 Chart" in Part 4 on page 464.

Teaching Tip
Using the "think, pair, share" routine is appropriate when asking students to make an estimate.
— MBB

For more information, see "Starting Point 14: The Importance of Classroom Discussions" in Part 1 on page 67.

Teaching Tip
If you have access to a pocket hundreds chart, it's wonderful for this investigation. Insert the number cards from 0 to 25. Put the rest of the cards in a basket and draw them out, one by one, for students to place. Sometimes I do this silently and have students come up and place numbers. Other times, I ask students to talk with a partner and then call on someone to explain where the number card goes and why.
— MBB

FYI
These suggestions can be used as part of a menu that students work on independently or with a partner.
— MBB

For more information on using a menu to structure independent work, see "Starting Point 20: Four Structures for Organizing and Managing Classroom Instruction" in Part 1 on page 111.

Teaching Tip
To provide extra structure for helping students with the tens structure of our place-value system, instead of drawing stars on blank paper, give students 10-by-10 grids. They'll easily be able to count by tens how many stars they drew.
— MBB

FYI
This investigation is similar to Fill the Cube (Version 2) in Part 3 on page 368. In Version 2, students figure the difference between the two counts.
— MBB

Teaching Tip
If you prefer, have students write the numbers from 1 to 100 instead of from 0 to 99.
— MBB

Additional Instructional Suggestions

The following instructional suggestions are for small groups of students. After students are familiar with the activities, some of the suggestions are suitable as independent investigations for individual or partner work, and for choice time explorations.

Stars in 1 Minute

You need: a timer (at least 1 minute)

1. Work with a partner. Predict how many stars you think you can draw in 1 minute.

2. Players take turns timing each other drawing stars. One partner draws and the other partner keeps time for 1 minute.

3. Count the stars in two ways, by circling them in fives and then in tens. On your paper, record how many stars you drew.

Fill the Cube (Version 1)

You need: Unifix cube
popcorn kernels, enough to fill the cube
lentils, enough to fill the cube

1. Predict how many kernels of popcorn you think will fill the cube. Record your prediction.

2. Fill the cube.

3. Count the kernels in two ways, by grouping them by twos or fives, and also by grouping them by tens.

4. Record the number of kernels.

5. Repeat with lentils. Use your popcorn count to make your estimate of lentils.

Number Puzzle

You need: 10-by-10 square of half-inch grid paper [R] See Reproducible R.3
envelope

1. Write the numbers from 0 to 99 on your grid.

2. Cutting only on the lines, cut the grid paper into seven interesting pieces. Write your name on the back of each piece.

3. Test your puzzle by fitting the pieces back together. Then put your puzzle pieces into an envelope. Write your name on the envelope and place it in the puzzle box for others to try.

4. Choose someone else's puzzle to put together. When you solve it, sign your name on the back of the envelope and return the puzzle to the puzzle box for others to try.

Five-Tower Game

You need: interlocking cubes, at least 200
1–6 dice, 2 per pair of students

1. Work with a partner and take turns.

2. Each player takes a turn rolling the dice. Add the numbers that come up and take that many cubes. Snap the cubes into a tower. Continue until both players each have five towers.

3. Each player figures out how many cubes he or she has.

4. Compare your counts. See if one of you has more than the other or if you both have the same number of cubes.

Pinch a 10

You need: small bag or bowl of kidney beans

1. Take a pinch of kidney beans and count. Did your pinch have fewer than ten, more than ten, or exactly ten? Make a chart as shown and record with a tally mark. Do this ten times.

(Tally like this: ⧠⧠⧠⧠⧠ ‖)

Fewer than 10	10	More than 10

2. Write a statement about your results. Repeat and see if you get better at pinching tens.

Make a Shape

You need: crayon or marker
tiles, 10 each of 4 colors

1. Work with a partner. On a plain sheet of paper, draw a shape that you and your partner think can be covered with thirty-two tiles.

2. Test your thinking with tiles. Use ten of one color, then use ten of another color, and so on, until your shape is covered. Record the number of tiles you used.

3. Try this investigation a second time, drawing a new shape that you think can also be covered with thirty-two tiles. Again, cover, count, and record.

Coloring 0–99 Patterns

You need: small 0–99 charts, 2 sheets   <u>R</u>   See Reproducible R.34
         crayon or marker

Work with a partner. Decide which numbers to color on one of the 0–99 charts. Each partner should color his or her own chart.

Write a description of the pattern of the numbers colored.

Repeat for the other directions, coloring on a separate 0–99 chart for each.

Directions:

1. Color all the numbers with both digits the same.

2. Color all the numbers with digits that add to 8.

3. Color all the numbers with first digits that are larger than the second digits.

4. Color all the numbers with a 4 in them.

5. Color all the even numbers.

6. Color all the numbers with digits that add to 10.

Assessing Understanding of Place Value

Observing students in classroom discussions and when they are working on independent investigations provides information about their understanding and skills. Having one-on-one conversations with students also provides information by revealing individual students' understanding, misconceptions, and gaps that aren't always evident from classroom observations. The following are suggestions for both assessment approaches.

Observing Students

When students are working on the independent tasks, circulate and observe them. Also, whole-class discussions can help reveal what students understand.

When students play *Race for $1.00*, notice how students organize their pennies and dimes. See if they exchange when possible and if they take shortcuts, such as taking one dime and two pennies when they roll a sum of 12. Interrupt them to ask who is winning and see how they compare their two quantities.

With *Stars in 1 Minute*, *Fill the Cube (Version 1)*, and *Five-Tower Game*, see which students group the objects into tens and which group by twos and fives or persist in counting by ones. Ask students how many groups they would have if they grouped by tens. Don't insist that students group by tens; there's no point in students doing something mechanically without understanding. Encourage them, talk about grouping by tens, but respect their need to do what makes sense to them.

For *Fill the Cube*, ask students how they could use the information from their popcorn count to predict how many lentils the cube will hold.

When students count the beans in *Pinch a 10*, notice how they count—by ones, twos, or some other way.

Notice how students fit together the pieces from each other's puzzles from *Number Puzzle*. Ask questions such as: *What clues do you look for? How will you know when the puzzle is together correctly? What's easy and what's hard about the puzzle?*

Individual Assessments

To assess students' understanding of place value, interview them using the following protocol.

TEACHER	STUDENT	INTERPRETATION
Put out a sheet of paper and ask the student to count ten cubes onto it.	Student is able to do so.	Student shows ability to count with one-to-one correspondence.
	Student is unable to do so.	Prompt: "Check that there are ten cubes." If student doesn't self-correct, don't continue.

(continued)

> FYI
> I interviewed Cena and Jonathan when they were second graders to assess their understanding of place value. I didn't use the simplified protocol discussed here, but talking with Cena and Jonathan helped me realize how valuable one-on-one interviews can be for assessing student understanding. Visit mathsolutions.com/teachers and choose Video Clip Library to view the videos.
>
> — MBB

(continued from page 357)

TEACHER	STUDENT	INTERPRETATION
Place a group of six cubes on the table next to the paper with ten cubes on it. Say: "You have ten cubes and I have six." Move your six cubes onto the paper and ask: "How many cubes altogether are on the paper?"	Student says "sixteen" without counting.	Knowing the sum of ten and a one-digit number is an indication of place-value understanding.
	Student has to count cubes to figure out how many.	Indicates lack of place-value understanding.
Ask: "If I take six cubes away, how many cubes will be left on the paper?"	Student says "ten" without hesitating or having to count.	Indicates place-value understanding.
	Student doesn't answer or has to remove cubes and count.	Indicates lack of place-value understanding.
To reestablish total number of cubes, ask: "How many cubes are there altogether on the paper?" Then ask: "If I take ten cubes away, how many cubes will be left on the paper?"	Student says "six" without hesitating or having to count.	Indicates place-value understanding.
	Student doesn't answer or has to remove cubes and count.	Indicates lack of place-value understanding.
On a corner of the paper, write the number 16. Ask: *What does the "six" mean?*	Student gives answer related to place value; for example, "It tells how many ones there are." Or indicates six of the cubes on the paper.	Indicates place-value understanding.
	Student doesn't answer.	Indicates lack of understanding of the place-value meaning of digits.
Ask: *What does the "one" mean?*	Student gives answer related to place value; for example, "It means one ten." Or indicates ten of the cubes on the paper.	Indicates place-value understanding.
	Student doesn't answer or indicates one tile on the paper.	Indicates lack of understanding of the place-value meaning of digits.
Add ten more tiles on the paper. Ask: "If I add ten more tiles to the sixteen, how many tiles will there will be?"	Student says "twenty-six" without counting.	Indicates place-value understanding.
	Student has to count cubes to figure out how many.	Indicates lack of understanding of the place-value meaning of digits.

Addition and Subtraction

About Addition and Subtraction

This section focuses on having students add, subtract, and compare whole numbers in the context of problem-solving investigations. The investigations draw on ideas from various topics in the math curriculum: number and operations, data, geometry, and measurement. In this way, while students are developing their understanding of number, they have opportunities to broaden their view of mathematics and see relationships among the different areas of the math curriculum. In all investigations, the emphasis is on having students use and explain their own strategies for adding and subtracting. As a regular part of their work, students are expected to justify their answers and explain why they make sense.

Mathematical Practices

Developing understanding and skills with addition and subtraction should support the mathematical practices described in the Common Core and other standards documents for students in all grades. The mathematical practices should be connected to the content standards by engaging students in solving problems, reasoning, making conjectures, applying math to everyday life, using appropriate tools, communicating precisely, looking for patterns and structure, and looking for regularity in mathematical methods. The investigations in this section provide ways to make connections between practice and content standards.

Mathematical Content

Addition and subtraction of whole numbers is a major emphasis in grades 1 and 2, with ongoing support and practice appropriate in grade 3. The standards that focus on building understanding are especially important for helping students engage with the mathematical practices. Below are content designations that align with the Common Core and other standards documents.

Grade 1: Understand place value and use place value to add and subtract within 100.

Grade 2: Understand place value and use place value to add and subtract within 1000.

Grade 3: Use place value to perform multidigit arithmetic, including adding and subtracting within 1000.

Whole-Class Instruction

The following suggestions for whole-class instruction introduce students to important and basic ideas relating to addition and subtraction. They are organized into three categories: a statistical investigation, measurement investigations, and number games.

A Statistical Investigation: Name Graphs

Statistical investigations offer rich opportunities for students to develop their number sense. In this lesson, the lengths of the students' names are organized into two class graphs. The students interpret the data and compare the number of letters in their first and last names.

Materials

3-by-3-inch sticky notes, 2 per student
interlocking cubes, about 300

Create a Class Graph

Tell the students that they're going to create a class graph to display information about their first names. Ask each student to write his or her first name on a 3-by-3-inch sticky note. List the numerals from 1 to 10 where everyone can see them and where there's room for students to post their sticky notes to make a graph. Have the students, one at a time, come up and post their name next to the numeral that indicates the number of letters it has.

Letters in Our First Names

Lead a classroom discussion about what the graph shows. Ask questions like these:

What's the least number of letters in a first name? Most?

Which length of our first names occurred the most?

What's the difference between the largest and smallest lengths in our names?

Pose a Problem

Then pose the problem of figuring out how many letters they think are in all of their first names together. First ask for estimates. Next talk about how they might determine the total from the information on the graph. Then have them work in pairs or small groups to figure out the total number of letters.

Teaching Tip
This is a good opportunity to introduce range and mode. On the graph shown, the range is 5, the difference between the largest and smallest numbers of letters. The mode is also five because there are more names with five letters than with any other number of letters.
— MSB

Teaching Tip
You might want to talk informally about the idea of average by asking the students how long they think a "typical" name is.
— MSB

FYI
Asking the students to estimate gives me the opportunity to reinforce for them the benefits of making estimates. I explain that estimating gives them the opportunity to think about numbers, better understand what they mean, and make guesses about what answers might be.
— MSB

Using the "think, pair, share" routine is appropriate when asking students to make an estimate. For more information, see "Starting Point 14: The Importance of Classroom Discussions" in Part 1 on page 67.

Teaching Tip
Creating class name graphs is ideal at the beginning of the year when students are getting to know one another. Other ideas for name graphs include: Do you have a middle name? Is your first name longer, shorter, or the same length as your last name? Do you have a nickname? How many syllables are in your first name? In your last name?

— MBB

For additional information about introducing graphs, see "Graphing in the Classroom" in Part 2 on page 174. To read about how to use name graphs for fraction instruction, see "Using Graphs to Build Understanding of Fractions" in Part 3 on page 427.

FYI
Choosing boxes for particular students is a way to differentiate the investigation. Larger boxes require students to combine larger numbers, and smaller boxes produce problems with smaller numbers.

— MBB

Using the "think, pair, share" routine is appropriate when asking students to make an estimate. For more information, see "Starting Point 14: The Importance of Classroom Discussions" in Part 1 on page 67.

Lead a Classroom Discussion

After students have shared the problem, ask them to share their answers and explain their strategies. Then, to confirm the total and also reinforce place value, ask students each to make a train of interlocking cubes with as many cubes as letters in their first name. Ask groups to organize their cubes into trains of ten and bring the tens to the front of the room. Then call for the extra cubes, making additional trains of ten. Count the tens and extras to arrive at the total.

Extension

Investigating Last Names. Give each student another sticky note. Have them write their last names, and organize these into another graph. Ask the students to look at both graphs and describe how the shapes of the data compare. Ask if they can tell from looking at the graphs if there are more letters in their first or last names altogether. Have students offer their opinions and explain their reasoning. Then have students figure how many letters are in their last names altogether and find the difference between the total numbers of letters in their first and last names.

A Problem-Solving Lesson: How Much Ribbon?

Measuring can provide numerical data to use for adding and subtracting. Students figure out how much ribbon or yarn they need to wrap a gift box. Although students work with different numbers, and therefore arrive at different answers, they'll be thinking about similar problem situations.

Materials

gift boxes, 1 per pair of students or small group (Collect a selection in different sizes, larger ones such as boxes for shoes, sweaters, blouses, kitchen pots or mixing bowls, and smaller ones, such as those for candy, ties, and other smaller gifts.)

yarn or ribbon, 1 yard cut for each pair of students or small group and additional available for students to cut

ruler, 1 per pair of students

scissors, 1 per pair of students or small group

Introducing

1. **Present or review concepts.** Review with the students what it means to make an estimate.

2. **Pose a part of the problem or a similar but smaller problem.** Show the students a box and ask them to estimate, in inches, how much yarn or ribbon they think they'd need just for making a bow. Then give each pair or group a yard-long length and have them tie a bow around a pencil, trim its ends, and measure the length they used. Tell them that it's up to them to decide on the size of the bow and the lengths of the ends. When all students have completed this step, have them show their bows and report their lengths. Record this information where everyone can see it.

3. **Present the investigation.** Then give each pair or group a gift box. Post the directions. Tell them that their job is to figure out how many inches of ribbon or yarn they would need to wrap their box, including the bow. (They can use their own measurement for the bow or any other one that is reasonable according to the class list of bow measurements.)

4. **Discuss the task to make sure students understand what they are to do.**

HOW MUCH RIBBON?

Directions

1. Talk about a plan to solve the problem.

2. Decide on the length of yarn you need.

3. Write about how you got your answer.

4. Measure and cut yarn to test your answer.

Teaching Tip
I've found it helpful to demonstrate with a box how they might wrap it, as in the picture shown. However, I leave it up to the students to decide how they will wrap the particular box they have.

— MSB

Exploring
Circulate and offer assistance as needed.

Summarizing
When all groups have completed the problem, have them present their results and procedures to the class. Presentations such as these help students learn about other ways to solve problems and work with numbers.

A Problem-Solving Lesson: How Big Is Your Hand?

This investigation involves the students with measuring area. On centimeter grid paper, students trace one of their hands with their fingers together and figure its area.

Materials
centimeter grid paper **R** See Reproducible R.2

Introducing

1. **Present or review concepts.** Show students a piece of centimeter grid paper and tell them that measuring how many squares fill a shape is a way of measuring area.

2. **Pose a part of the problem or a similar but smaller problem.** Demonstrate by tracing your hand and figuring its area. Show how to record by using sq cm and/or cm^2.

3. **Present the investigation.** Tell students that they will each trace a hand, fingers together, and then figure out about how much its area is.

4. **Discuss the task to make sure students understand what they are to do.**

Exploring

Circulate and offer assistance as needed. For students who finish more quickly, ask them how they think their hand area measurements would compare if they traced their hands with their fingers apart. Have them try this investigation.

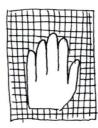 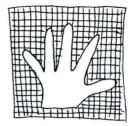

Summarizing

Have students report on how they dealt with the irregular squares to figure out their hand area.

Extension

Comparing Hand Areas. Have students figure the area of a kindergarten student's hand and an adult's hand and compare these areas with their own measurements.

A Number Game: Roll 15

Games are always appealing to students. The game of *Roll 15* gives practice adding within 20. After teaching the game to the whole class, students can play it independently.

Materials

0–5 number cubes, 2 per pair of students
5–10 number cubes, 2 per pair of students

Teaching the Rules of the Game

Explain that the object of the game is to get a score as close to 15 as possible. Teach the rules of the game by selecting two students to play while the rest of the class watches. Read each rule and have the pair you chose follow the directions.

ROLL 15: RULES OF THE GAME

You need: 0–5 number cubes, 2 per pair of students
5–10 number cubes, 2 per pair of students
Play with a partner. Take turns and follow these rules.

1. Choose any cube to roll, then roll a second cube, and add the two numbers rolled. Set the cubes aside. (If the two numbers rolled are 3 and 4, your sum is 7 so far.)

2. Either stop or roll a third cube (different from the other two) and add the number on to the previous sum. (If the third number rolled is a 9, your sum is now 16.)

3. After the third roll, if your sum is still less than 15, you may choose to roll the fourth cube.

The player with a sum closer to 15 is the winner.

Have the students play the game in pairs. Ask students to record each time they roll, keeping track of which cubes they roll, the numbers that come up, and the sums they have.

Discuss the Game

After students have played about five games, use the following questions for a classroom discussion:

How many times did you usually roll before stopping?

Which cube do you think is best to use first? Second?

How many times did you go over fifteen?

What might you roll to produce a result of exactly fifteen?

Have the students play five more rounds.

Teaching Tip
I love this game for its mix of chance and strategy. Be sure to remind students that on their turn, they may roll up to four times, but can roll each number cube only once.

—MSB

A Number Game: The Game of Pig

The *Game of Pig* gives students practice adding within 100.

Materials

1–6 dice, 2 per pair of students

Teaching the Rules of the Game

The object of the game is to be the first player to reach 100. Teach the rules of the game by selecting one student to play with you while the rest of the class watches. Read each rule and model the directions.

The Game of Pig also appears in Part 2 on page 200.

Teaching Tip

For the previous game, *Roll 15,* I suggested having two students model how to play. Here I suggest having a student play with you. I've found it easier to model the rules by playing myself than coaching students through them.

— MSB

THE GAME OF PIG: RULES OF THE GAME

You need: 1–6 dice, 2 per pair of students

Play with a partner. Take turns and follow these rules.

1. On your turn, roll the dice as many times as you like, mentally keeping a running total of the sum of the numbers that come up. Check that your partner agrees with your adding.

2. When you decide to stop rolling, record the total for that turn and add it to the total of previous turns.

Important: If a 1 comes up when you're rolling, your turn automatically ends and you score 0 for that round. If 1s come up on both dice, not only does your turn end, but the total you've accumulated so far resets to 0.

The first player to reach 100 is the winner.

Have the students play the game in pairs. Remind students to check each other's addition.

Discuss the Game

After all the students are familiar with the game and have had the opportunity to play it several times, lead a classroom discussion about their methods for adding mentally, their strategies for deciding when to roll and when to stop, and what they noticed about the sums that came up. Ask the following questions:

How did you decide when to keep rolling and when to stop and keep your score?

How often did a 1 come up?

How often did doubles come up?

If your total so far was fifteen and you rolled 9, what would your new total be? How did you figure that in your head?

If your total so far was nineteen and you rolled 11, what would your new total be? [Give all students who have strategies the chance to share them.]

What advice would you give to a new player?

Additional Instructional Suggestions

The following instructional suggestions are for small groups of students. After students are familiar with the activities, some of the suggestions are suitable as independent investigations for individual or partner work, and for choice time explorations.

These suggestions can be used as part of a menu that students work on independently or with a partner. For more information on using a menu to structure independent work, see "Starting Point 20: Four Structures for Organizing and Managing Classroom Instruction" in Part 1 on page 111.

How Old Is Ramona the Pest?

You need: *Ramona the Pest* (Cleary 1968)

In the book *Ramona the Pest*, Ramona is in kindergarten, which makes her about five years old. According to the copyright date, the book was written in 1968. How old is Ramona now?

Estimate and Measure

You need: interlocking cubes, about 50 per pair of students

Work with a partner. Using cubes, measure the length of at least five different things. For each, do the following:

1. Make an estimate and record.

2. Measure.

3. Count and record.

4. Figure out how far off your estimate was.

Record on a chart as shown.

Estimate and Measure			
Object	Est.	Meas.	How far off?

Teaching Tip
Before assigning this investigation, I either read this classic to the students or have them read it on their own.
— MSB

Management Suggestion
I like to post a copy of the chart and have students make their own. Organizing their work on paper is a valuable experience for them.
— MSB

In 1 Minute

You need: a way to time 1 minute

Work with a partner. While your partner times 1 minute, write the letters of the alphabet. (If you get to Z before time is up, start over with A.)

Repeat, this time writing numerals, starting with 1 and continuing until time is called.

Switch so your partner writes letters and numerals while you keep time.

Each of you counts the number of letters and numerals you wrote. See if you wrote more letters or more numerals, and figure out how many more.

Record your results and compare them with your partner's results.

Extension

In Half a Minute. Predict how many letters and numerals you think you would write in half a minute. Time each other to test your estimates. Compare your results with your 1-minute data. Write about what you notice.

FYI
I've used this investigation in various ways. Sometimes I assign it to individual students who need a challenge. Sometimes I ask students to work in pairs. I prepare baggies with the coins and put a card in each with 9 dimes and 50 pennies on it. Then I ask students to check when they're done that all of the coins are in the baggie.
— MBB

For a version of *Billy Goes Shopping* that gives students experience with addition and subtraction, see *Billy Wins a Shopping Spree* in Part 3 on page 381.

This investigation is similar to *Fill the Cube* (Version 1) in Part 3 on page 354. In this version, the students figure the difference between the two counts.

Billy Goes Shopping

You need: 9 dimes, per student
50 pennies, per student

Billy wants to buy some new school supplies. He has nine dimes to spend. He needs to save 25¢ for the bus. Look at the price list and choose some things for Billy to buy. (He can buy different things or more than one of the same thing.)

List the items you chose, along with the cost of each. Figure out the total. Use the dimes and pennies to figure out the change.

Figure out at least three ways Billy can spend his money. Remember, he needs 25¢ for the bus.

Price List

Erasers 10¢

Rulers 29¢

Pencils 25¢

Pens 39¢

Book covers 20¢

Covering Covers

You need: color tiles, about 100 per student
books, 6 per student

Choose two different books from the class or school library. Estimate which cover has the greater area. Measure each book cover with tiles and record. Figure out how many more tiles are needed for the larger cover and explain how you arrived at your answer.

Repeat for two other pairs of books.

Fill the Cube (Version 2)

You need: Unifix cube
popcorn kernels, enough to fill the cube
lentils, enough to fill the cube

Find out how many kernels of popcorn fill the cube. Record.

Predict how many lentils you think will fill the cube. Record your prediction and explain why you think it makes sense. Test your prediction.

Now figure out how many more lentils than popcorn kernels it took to fill the cube.

101 and Out

You need: 1–6 die or 0–9 spinner

This is a game for two or more players. Each player makes a recording sheet as shown.

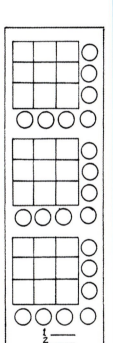

Follow these rules:
1. Take turns rolling the die or spinning the spinner.

2. On each turn, all players write the number in either the tens column or ones column of their recording sheet. Once a number is recorded, it cannot be changed.

3. After rolling or spinning six numbers, fill in any blank spaces in the ones column with 0s and add.

The player with a sum closest to 100 without going over is the winner.

Cross Out Singles

You need: 1–6 die or 0–9 spinner

This is a game for two or more players. Each player makes a recording sheet, as shown, for three rounds.

Follow these rules:
1. To begin, one player rolls or spins.

2. All players write the number in a square on their first chart. Once a number is recorded, it cannot be changed.

3. Take turns. Another player rolls or spins and everyone records in another square. Continue taking turns rolling or spinning until players have filled all nine squares.

4. Players add the numbers across, down, and on the diagonal, and record sums in the circle.

5. Players examine their sums. Any sum that appears in only one circle must be crossed out.

6. The total of the sums that are not crossed out is the player's score for that round. For example:

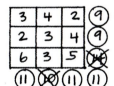

SCORE: 51

7. Play two more rounds. Then compare totals.

Extensions

Getting a Score of Zero. Find ways that produce a 0 score.

Getting the Highest Score. Using the numbers 1 to 9 once each, what's the highest score you can get?

Assessing Understanding of Addition and Subtraction

Observing students during classroom discussions and while they are working on independent investigations provides information about their understanding and skills. Also, one-on-one conversations with students reveal their individual understanding, misconceptions, and gaps, and provides valuable information that isn't always evident from classroom observations. The following suggestions can be used for both assessment approaches.

Observing Students

Classroom discussions can reveal how students think. For example, students' strategies for adding in *The Game of Pig* reveal information about their number sense and ability to add mentally. How they deal with the incomplete squares when figuring the area of their hands gives information about their understanding of fractional parts. How they decide whether there were more letters in their first or last names provides information about their number sense and ability to interpret statistical data. Although some of this information may not relate specifically to comparing quantities or the processes of addition and subtraction, it contributes to your understanding of students' mathematical thinking.

When students are working on the independent tasks, circulate, observe, and, at times, question students about their thinking and reasoning.

Individual Assessments

To find out about students' understanding of addition and subtraction and their abilities to compute, give them problems to solve that are similar to those they have been working on in class. Be sure to ask students to describe their thinking processes and explain why their answers make sense.

Such assessments are the same as learning tasks. However, looking at a class set of such papers gives you information about the abilities of the class in general and the progress of specific students. The following are some suggestions:

1. Give students problems to solve that use information from two or three of their results from *Estimate and Measure*. For example: *Lindsay and Laura measured Lindsay's height. Their estimate was 86 cubes. Their measurement was 69 cubes. What was the difference between their estimate and measurement?*

2. Give them the copyright date on one of their library books. Ask them to figure out how long ago the book was written. For easier problems, choose books written after 2000. Books written before 2000 give an extra challenge.

3. Ask them to write a paper titled "What Is Addition?" or "What Is Subtraction?"

4. Ask that they write an addition (or subtraction) word problem that follows two rules:
   a. It must end in a question.
   b. The question must be one that's possible to answer by adding (or subtracting).

Have them solve their word problem in as many ways as they can.

Introducing Multiplication

About Introducing Multiplication

Traditionally, instruction in multiplication has focused on two objectives: learning the multiplication facts and developing computational facility. After memorizing the times tables, students learn to multiply with paper and pencil, first practicing with one-digit multipliers and then progressing to two-digit and three-digit multipliers. Word problems are usually the vehicle for giving students practice with applying multiplication in problem situations.

The ideas in this section provide a shift toward a broader view of multiplication and a more active approach to learning. The investigations introduce multiplication from several perspectives: geometric, numerical, and through real-world contexts. To integrate multiplication with the rest of mathematics, the investigations include ideas from the topics of number and operations, geometry, statistics, and patterns and functions. The standard mathematical representation for multiplication is introduced in the context of the investigations, helping students connect the abstract representations to their own experiences.

Mathematical Practices

Developing understanding and skills with multiplication should support the mathematical practices described in the Common Core and other standards documents for students in all grades. The mathematical practices should be connected to the content standards by engaging students in solving problems, reasoning, making conjectures, applying math to everyday life, using appropriate tools, communicating precisely, looking for patterns and structure, and looking for regularity in mathematical methods. The investigations in this section provide ways to make connections between practice and content standards.

Mathematical Content

Multiplication of whole numbers is introduced in grade 2 and instruction continues in grades 3 through 5. The standards that focus on building understanding are especially important for helping students engage with the mathematical practices. Below are content designations that align with the Common Core and other standards documents.

Grade 2: Work with equal groups of objects to gain foundations for multiplication.

Grade 3: Represent and solve problems involving multiplication within 100; understand properties of multiplication; multiply one-digit number by multiples of 10 using strategies based on place value and properties of operations; by the end of grade 3, know from memory all products of two one-digit numbers.

Grade 4: Gain familiarity with factors and multiples; multiply to solve word problems; multiply a number up to four digits by a one-digit number and multiply two two-digit numbers using strategies based on place value and the properties of operations; use equations, rectangular arrays, and area models to explain calculations.

Grade 5: Fluently multiply multidigit whole numbers using the standard algorithm.

Whole-Class Instruction

The following suggestions for whole-class instruction introduce students to important and basic ideas related to multiplication. They are organized into four categories: multiplication in real-world contexts, multiplication as combining equal groups, a multiplication game, and a geometric model for multiplication.

A Problem-Solving Lesson: The Chopstick Problem

Having students investigate groups of objects in a real-world context helps them link the idea of multiplication to the world around them. This context also helps students avoid the pitfall of seeing mathematics as totally abstract and unrelated to themselves. Too often, math exists for students only on the pages of textbooks and worksheets. They need opportunities to see mathematics as integral to their daily experiences. Use this problem to introduce multiplication in a real-world context.

Materials
1 pair of chopsticks, more if you want students to try using them

Introducing

1. **Present or review concepts.** To begin, show students a pair of chopsticks and make sure students know that when people use chopsticks to eat, two chopsticks are required.

2. **Pose a part of the problem or a similar but smaller problem.** Ask, *How many chopsticks are needed for four people?* Hear from all students who want to respond, asking them to explain how they arrived at their answers.

3. **Present the investigation.** Ask, *How many chopsticks are needed for everyone in the class?* Write the number of people in the class on the board. Have the students solve this problem in pairs or small groups. Ask them to record their answer and describe their reasoning using words, numbers, and/or pictures.

4. **Discuss the task to make sure students understand what they are to do.**

Exploring
Circulate and offer assistance as needed.

Summarizing

1. **Have pairs or groups review their work and think about what to report in a classroom discussion.**

2. **Initiate a classroom discussion.** Ask groups to report how they worked together to come up with and agree on their response.

3. **Ask groups to report their results or solutions, explaining their reasoning or strategies.** When students report their answers, ask them to explain their reasoning. Keep the emphasis on students' different approaches for solving the problem. Record the methods students report, modeling for the students how to use

FYI
I like to talk with students about the history of chopsticks. According to the California Academy of Sciences, chopsticks were developed about 5000 years ago in China. The earliest versions were probably twigs used to retrieve food from cooking pots. Have students who are interested do research—there's lots of information online.
— MSB

mathematical notation to represent their ideas. For example, before students are introduced to multiplication, they typically add. To figure out how many chopsticks are needed for twenty-six people, some students may add (26 + 26 = 52); others may figure out the number chopsticks for twenty-five people first and then add on two (25 + 25 = 50, 50 + 2 = 52); others may figure out the number chopsticks for twenty people first and then for the other six people (20 + 20 = 40, 6 + 6 = 12, 40 + 12 = 52).

4. **Generalize from the solutions.** Use this opportunity to connect students' reasoning to multiplication as another way to represent their thinking. Explain, *You can think about 26 + 26 as two groups of 26 chopsticks, and we can write that as 2 × 26.*

A Problem-Solving Lesson: Things That Come in Groups

In this investigation, students look for real-world examples of different size equal groups.

Materials
12-by-18-inch newsprint, 1 sheet for each pair or small group
copy paper or 9-by-12-inch drawing paper for posting, 11 sheets titled *Things That Come in 2s, Things That Come in 3s, Things That Come in 4s,* and so on up to *Things That Come in 12s*

Introducing
1. **Present or review concepts.** Explain that "equal groups" means that each group contains the same amount of something.

2. **Pose a part of the problem or a similar but smaller problem.** Post the sheet of paper titled *Things That Come in 2s.* Ask the class to brainstorm things other than chopsticks that come in twos. List their suggestions on the sheet of paper. It's common for students to think of examples from their bodies (e.g., eyes, ears, hands, feet, thumbs, etc.).

3. **Present the investigation.** With students working in pairs or small groups, ask them to make lists of things for ten other numbers—threes, fours, fives, and so on—up to twelves. Give each group a sheet of 12-by-18-inch newsprint to organize their lists. Suggest that groups organize their paper into sections, one for each number.

4. **Discuss the task to make sure students understand what they are to do.**

Exploring
Circulate and offer assistance as needed.

Summarizing
Post the eleven sheets of 9-by-12-inch paper labeled for the numbers from 3 to 12. Have pairs groups take turns reading items from their charts. After a group reads an item, the other groups guess the list on which it belongs. Should uncertainty or a dispute arise about items, such as sides on a stop sign or wings on a butterfly, start a separate

---

Teaching Tip
When introducing multiplication, I find it helpful to read expressions like 2 × 26 as "two groups of 26" and "two times 26." Using both expressions reinforces the meaning of multiplication as equal groups.

—MBB

When introducing multiplication, I read aloud to the class *Amanda Bean's Amazing Dream* by Cindy Neuschwander (1998). You can tell from the book that Cindy has been teaching for many years. For more about how to use this book with students, see "Questions Teachers Ask" in Part 4 on page 457.

Teaching Tip
If students' ideas are limited to a particular category, such as their bodies, offer a few suggestions to broaden their thinking (e.g., wheels on a bicycle, wings on a bird, slices of bread in a sandwich, etc.)

—MBB

Teaching Tip
I model for groups how to fold their 12-by-18-inch newsprint into eight sections, folding in half twice to get four sections ("hamburger" folds), opening, and making a "hotdog" fold to get a total of eight sections. I number the sections on one side from 2 to 9, and then number three sections on the back for 10, 11, and 12.

—MBB

"research" list and resolve the questions at a later time. Continue until all students have reported all of their ideas. Keep the lists posted where all students can refer to them as a possible resource of ideas for multiplication problems to solve.

Also, encourage the students to continue thinking about other items to add to the lists. You may choose to give students the homework assignment of asking their parents to help think of additional items.

A Problem-Solving Lesson: Candy Boxes

Investigating rectangular arrays introduces students to a geometric model for multiplication. Students investigate rectangular arrays as they research how to package candy. The "candies" are 1-inch square tiles that are packed one layer deep in rectangular boxes. Students use the tiles to identify various dimensions of boxes for different numbers of candies.

Materials
tiles, 12 per student
half-inch grid paper   **R** See Reproducible R.3
scissors
tape and glue

Introducing

1. **Present or review concepts.** Distribute tiles so that each pair of students has twenty-four. Explain that the tiles are pretend candies that come in rectangular or square boxes and are always packed in just one layer.

2. **Pose a part of the problem or a similar but smaller problem.** Tell the students that a sampler box has four candies in it. Ask each student to take four tiles and see how the candies might be arranged to fit into a box. Draw them where everyone can see them. Write the dimensions 2 × 2 and 1 × 4 inside each rectangle you drew and read them aloud as "two rows of two" and "two by two" and "one row of four" and "one by four." Then, using half-inch grid paper, model how to cut out the two different arrays and record the dimensions on each.

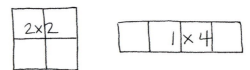

3. **Present the investigation.** Pose the problem: *Each pair of students is the design research team of the candy company. The president of the company has asked for a report about the different boxes possible for six, twelve, and twenty-four candies.* Give the following three directions:

   1. For each number of candies, use the tiles to find all possible rectangles.

> **Teaching Tip**
> Typically in a class, students produce two possible options. Draw them where everyone can see them. If students only find one option, draw the other on the board and have the students build it with the tiles. If students suggest an L-shaped arrangement, remind them that the boxes must be rectangular or square. This is a good opportunity to point out that squares are really special rectangles because each of their sides is the same length.
>
> — MSB

2. Cut out each rectangular shape as you find it, using half-inch grid paper.

3. Write a memo to the president explaining what you've learned about boxes for each quantity and your recommendation for the box shape. Include your cutout boxes with your memo.

4. Discuss the task to make sure students understand what they are to do.

Teaching Tip
I've found it helpful to post the directions for the problem where all students can see them.
— MSB

Exploring

Circulate and offer assistance as needed.

Summarizing

Have students report their findings and recommendations in a classroom discussion.

Extensions

Candy Box Research. Assign student pairs different numbers—from 1 to 36—and ask them to build all of the rectangular boxes possible for that number of candies. Then, ask pairs to cut out the shapes using half-inch grid paper and label their dimensions. Prepare a large horizontal chart with spaces marked for the numbers from 1 to 36 for students to post their rectangles. Also post the rectangles done in the whole-class investigation for four, six, twelve, and twenty-four candies.

Revisiting Candy Box Research. When the class has completed the chart for *Candy Box Research*, ask pairs to write answers to the following questions and then follow with a classroom discussion.

1. For which numbers are there rectangles that have sides with two squares on them? Write the numbers from smallest to largest.

2. For which numbers are there rectangles that have sides with three squares on them? Write the numbers from smallest to largest.

3. Do the same for numbers with rectangles that have four squares on a side.

4. Do the same for numbers with rectangles that have five squares on a side.

5. Which numbers have rectangles that are squares?

6. How many squares are in the next larger square you can make?

7. What is the smallest number with exactly two different rectangles? Three different rectangles? Four?

8. Which numbers have only one rectangle? List them from smallest to largest.

A Multiplication Game: Circles and Stars

This game introduces students to multiplication as combining equal groups, often referred to as *repeated addition*. Students interact with the idea of multiplication pictorially (by drawing circles and stars), symbolically (by writing the multiplication equations), and orally (by reading the equations).

Materials

1–6 dice, 1 die per pair of students

Teaching the Rules of the Game

Tell the students that you're going to teach them how to play a game called *Circles and Stars* and that they'll play in pairs. To model how to play, invite a student to be your partner and join you at the board.

Begin by rolling a die and reporting to the class the number that comes up. Draw that many circles on the board, pointing out to the class that you're drawing the circles large enough to be able to draw stars inside. Roll again, report the number to the class, and draw that many stars in each of your circles.

Ask your student partner to repeat the steps: roll the die, draw the appropriate number of circles, roll again, and draw stars in each circle. Ask the class to figure out how many stars each of you drew. Write the correct number of stars underneath each drawing.

Play another round to be sure the students understand, and then ask the volunteer to be seated. Demonstrate how to fold a piece of paper into eight sections. Ask students to write *Circle and Stars* and their names in the first section, and use the other sections to draw circles and stars as they play. Tell the class that a complete game takes seven rounds.

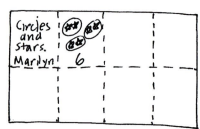

Tell the students that although they can see who wins each round by comparing how many stars each player drew, the winner of the game has more stars altogether. After seven rounds, students are to figure out the total and record it in the title section on their paper.

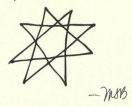

Have the students fold their paper and play the game. Those who finish more quickly can play again. Circulate and check that students consistently draw the same number of stars in each circle. (If they don't, this is an indication that they aren't clear about the rules for playing.) Also check that students recorded the correct number of stars for each round. If a number is incorrect, don't tell the student the correct answer but rather point out the error and ask the two students to figure it out together.

Introduce Recording Equations

Interrupt the class when all the students have completed at least one game to show them how to record a multiplication equation for each round. Draw on the board a sample page of three circles with two stars in each and underneath write: 3 × 2. Explain to the students that this is a way to write three groups of two with math symbols. Tell them that you can also read it as "three times two" and it means the same thing. Write = 6 and explain this completes the equation to tell how many stars there are in all for that round. Write on the board three ways to read 3 × 2 = 6:

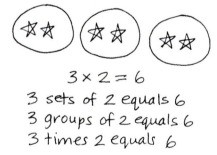

$$3 \times 2 = 6$$

3 sets of 2 equals 6
3 groups of 2 equals 6
3 times 2 equals 6

Ask students to work with their partners and agree on the math equation to write in each section of their paper. Tell them that as they write each math equation, they should read it aloud to each other in two different ways. Make time for students to play the game over a period of days.

Discuss the Game

After students have all played three or more games, lead a classroom discussion. Ask students to write their answers to these questions on their sheet:

> For the rounds you played, *which number of stars came up more often?*
>
> *Can you find two rounds with the same total but with different arrangements of circles and stars?* (For example, you can draw four stars with one circle and four stars in it, four circles with one star in each, or two circles with two stars in each.)
>
> *One is the smallest number of stars you can draw on a round. If you roll a 1 twice, draw one circle with one star in it. What do you think is the greatest number of stars possible in a round?*
>
> *Who drew twelve stars in one round? Describe how many circles you drew and how many stars you drew in each?* (Possibilities are 2×6, 3×4, 4×3, and 6×2.)

Extensions

Collect Data. List the numbers from 1 (the fewest number of stars possible in a round) to 36 (the most). Have students use their papers and make a tally mark for the number of stars from each round they played. Some numbers won't have any tally marks. (These include prime numbers greater than 5—7, 11, 13, 17, 19, and so on—and numbers with at least one factor greater than 6 so it won't be rolled—$21 = 7 \times 3$, $22 = 11 \times 2$, and so on.) While students typically won't make this generalization, seeing the data is a way to build their number sense about multiplication and factors.

A Homework Assignment. Have students teach someone at home how to play *Circles and Stars*. Either send students home with a die, or have them make a spinner with six sections and number them 1 to 6. For directions on making spinners, see "How to Make a Spinner That Really Spins" in Part 2 on page 171.

Additional Instructional Suggestions

The following instructional suggestions are for small groups of students. After students are familiar with the activities, some of the suggestions are suitable as independent investigations for individual or partner work, and for choice time explorations.

For more on using a menu to structure independent work, see "Starting Point 20: Four Structures for Organizing and Managing Classroom Instruction" in Part 1 on page 111.

Patterns in Multiples

You need: *Things That Come in Groups* charts ☒ See Reproducible R.32
 large 0–99 chart, 2 per pair of students

Choose an item from one of the *Things That Come in Groups* charts. List at least twelve multiples and write multiplication sentences. For example, if you choose "wheels on tricycles" from the *Things That Come in Threes* chart, you would list:

1 × 3 = 3

2 × 3 = 6

3 × 3 = 9

(and so on)

Color in the multiples on a 0–99 chart. Continue the pattern to the end of the chart.

Write about the patterns you see in the numbers on your list and on the 0–99 chart.

Repeat for an item from a different chart.

For information about these charts, see "A Problem-Solving Lesson: Things That Come in Groups" on page 375.

Billy Wins a Shopping Spree

Work with a partner. Billy won a $25.00 shopping spree at the Science Museum Store. He could choose items from the price list shown. Decide what Billy could buy. Make a receipt that shows how many items of each price Billy bought. Show the total he spent and the credit he has left, if any.

PRICE LIST

$3.00	$4.00	$5.00
1. origami paper	1. kaleidoscope	1. ball
2. crystal and gem magnets	2. large magnifying glass	2. glow-in-the-dark solar system stickers
3. furry stuffed seal pups	3. sunprint kit	3. inflatable world globe
4. prism	4. inflatable shark	4. wooden dinosaur model kit

Extension

Exactly $25.00. Find the combinations of different-priced objects that Billy could buy and spend $25.00 exactly. Note that buying five balls is the same price combination as buying three balls and two dinosaur model kits because in each case, Billy is buying five items at $5.00 each.

For a similar investigation that gives students experience with addition and subtraction, see *Billy Goes Shopping* on page 368.

Calculator Patterns

You need: calculator

Enter a number from 2 to 12. Press the + key. Press the = key. (You should see the same number you first entered.) Keep pressing the = key. Each time you press it, record the number displayed in a list. Continue until there are at least twelve numbers on your list. Write about the patterns you notice.

Multiplication Stories

Write a multiplication story that follows two rules:
1. It must end in a question.
2. The question must be one that can be answered using multiplication.

Solve your story problem in as many ways as you can.

Exchange papers with another student and solve each other's problems.

Times Table Plaids

You need: multiplication table **R** See Reproducible R.38

Choose a number from 2 to 12. List the multiples of the number up to 144. For example, if you chose the number 5, would list:

5

10

15

20

(and so on)

On a multiplication chart, color all the multiples on your list.

Compare your pattern with patterns others generated from the multiples of other numbers.

Write about the similarities and differences among the patterns.

FYI
The purpose of this investigation is for students to develop familiarity with multiples and look for patterns, not to memorize the multiplication facts. To avoid confusion with the products, it's helpful for students to use calculators and the method described in the Calculator Patterns investigation.

— MSB

Teaching Tip
Collect several different-sized candy boxes, each with seven cubes inside, from which students can choose.

— MSB

How Many Were Eaten?

You need: candy box with 7 cubes inside

There are seven candies left in the box. Figure out how many were eaten. Show your work and explain your reasoning.

How Long? How Many?

You need: Cuisenaire rods, 1 set per pair of students or student
1–6 die, 1 per pair of students or student
centimeter grid paper **R** See Reproducible R.2

Two versions of these two-player games are described here.

Version 1

Rules for Play

Each player cuts a centimeter square from centimeter grid paper. Players take turns and follow these rules.

1. Roll the die twice. The first roll tells *how long* a rod to use. The second roll tells *how many rods* to take.

2. Arrange the rods into a rectangle.

3. Trace the rectangle on your grid and write the appropriate multiplication equation inside.

The game is over when one of you can't place your rectangle because there's no room on the grid. Then figure out how many of your squares are covered and how many are uncovered. Check each other's answers.

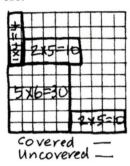
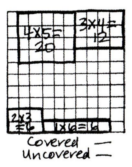

Version 2

Both players use the same full sheet of centimeter grid paper. The goal is to work together to cover as much of the paper as possible by tracing rectangles. As in the first version of this game, players take turns rolling the die and taking the appropriate rods. Together, decide how to form them into a rectangle and where to trace it on the paper. Continue until you can't place the rectangle for the numbers you rolled. Figure out how many of your squares are covered and how many are uncovered.

The Factor Game

You need: markers, 1 each of two different colors

sheet of paper with the numbers 1 to 30 written on it as shown, spaced so markers can cover numbers

```
The Factor Game
 1   2   3   4   5
 6   7   8   9  10
11  12  13  14  15
16  17  18  19  20
21  22  23  24  25
26  27  28  29  30
```

Play with a partner. Each player uses a different-colored marker. Follow these rules.

1. One player selects a number and circles it with his or her marker.

2. The other player finds all the proper factors of the number, circling each with his or her marker.

Switch roles and continue until no factors are left for the remaining numbers. Then each players adds the numbers he or she circled. The player with the larger score is the winner.

An Illegal Move Caution: Selecting a number with no factors left is an illegal move. If you make an illegal move, you add the number you chose to your score . . . but you lose your next turn to select a number.

Assessing Understanding of Multiplication

Observing students during classroom discussions and while they are working on independent investigations provides information about their understanding and skills. Also, one-on-one conversations with students reveal their individual understanding, misconceptions, and gaps, and provides valuable information that isn't always evident from classroom observations. The following suggestions can be used for both assessment approaches.

Observing Students

When students are working, circulate, observe, and, at times, question them about their thinking and reasoning. When students play *Circles and Stars*, for example, some students figure out how many stars there are on a page by counting each star. Others count by twos, or add, or know the multiplication fact. Asking students to explain how they figured the number of stars on one or more pages will provide insights into their thinking. For *Candy Box Research*, ask students how they know when they've found all the possible rectangles for a particular number. For *Billy Wins a Shopping Spree*, notice how students do the calculations when they decide what Billy can buy or how much he spent.

The students' stories for *Multiplication Stories* reveal whether students can relate contextual situations to the idea of multiplication. Their solutions from *How Many Were Eaten?* help you see if they can interpret multiplication geometrically.

Talk with students about the patterns they are noticing in *Candy Box Research*, *Patterns in Multiples*, *Calculator Patterns*, and *Times Table Plaids*. After they have the opportunity to play *How Long? How Many?* ask students to explain their strategies for filling as much as possible of the centimeter grid paper.

Individual Assessments

Give assessments that reveal students' thinking. The following are several suggestions.

1. Before beginning instruction, ask students to write what they know about multiplication. Have them do this again at the end of the instructional unit. Return both papers to the students and ask them to reflect on their learning.

2. Give the students a multiplication fact—6 × 5 or 7 × 6, for example. Ask them to explain how to figure out the answer. If students say they already know the answer, ask how they would tell a younger student how to figure it out.

3. Ask students to explain how they would figure out the answer to a multiplication problem using information from an easier but related problem. For example:

$6 \times 8 = 48$

$6 \times 9 = \underline{\quad}$

How would you use the answer to 6×8 to figure out the answer to 6×9?

4. Give students a word problem to solve and ask them to find the answer in as many ways as possible and explain why their solutions make sense.

Introducing Division

About Introducing Division

There are two different types of division. The first type is *sharing* or *partitioning*, which involves dividing a collection of objects into a given number of equal parts. Sharing twelve candies among three friends is a division situation of this type. The second type is *grouping*, which means dividing a collection of objects into groups of a known size. Figuring how many fifteen-cent pencils can be purchased with $1.00 is an example of division by grouping.

Students should become familiar with both types of division. Their formal instruction with division should begin with problem situations to solve that are then related to the standard symbolic representations. Also, students' understanding of division becomes more powerful when they begin to see the connections between division and multiplication, between sharing and grouping, and between division and the other operations.

When solving division problems, students often use a combination of operations. For example, consider the following problem:

> *A woman decided to knit socks for holiday presents for her family. She was able to knit one sock a week. One year, she began knitting on January 1 and knit steadily until December 15. Then she stopped so she could wrap each pair of socks. How many presents did she wrap?*

After students had time to think about how they might solve the problem, I had some report their methods. Some students solved the problem by counting to fifty by twos and kept track of how many twos they counted. I recorded this on the board by writing 2, 4, 6, 8, . . . , 50, and also by recording the multiplication and division notations that relate:

$$25 \times 2 = 50$$
$$50 \div 2 = 25 \qquad 2\overline{)50}^{\,25}$$

Other students solved the problem using a combination of multiplying, adding, and subtracting. One student explained, "For ten people, she would use twenty socks. For ten more, another twenty. That's forty socks altogether. So she has ten socks left. That's enough for five more people. So add ten plus ten plus five, and she has presents for twenty-five people." I asked her to repeat her explanation and, as she did so, I recorded equations to represent her thinking:

$$10 \times 2 = 20$$
$$20 + 20 = 40$$
$$50 - 40 = 10$$
$$10 \div 2 = 5$$
$$10 + 10 + 5 = 25$$

One boy used a different approach. He reported, "Each person needs two socks, and half of fifty is twenty-five. That means twenty-five people get presents." I recorded:

$$\tfrac{1}{2} \text{ of } 50 = 25$$

It's important that students understand that a situation such as this one presents a division problem. However, it's also valuable for students to know that there is more than one way to find the answer. Although students may use different operations when calculating, they are finding the answer to a division problem in a legitimate way.

Don't shy away from problems with large numbers or with remainders. The wider the variety of problems, the more support students have for developing number sense and the more mathematically flexible they will become. A note about calculators: Even if students use a calculator to find or verify an answer, have them explain why the answer makes sense. In problems with remainders, calculators are valuable for introducing students to decimals. Using a calculator to solve the problem of sharing seventeen cubes among four students, for example, presents the opportunity to talk about 4.25 as a number that is greater than 4 but less than 5.

Read more about a student who was frustrated on a standardized test by a division problem in "Starting Point 8: Word Problems: Developing Understanding of Arithmetic Operations" in Part 1 on page 36. For the problem, students weren't supposed to figure out a numerical answer, but rather indicate which operation they would use.

Mathematical Practices

Developing understanding and skills with division should support the mathematical practices described in the Common Core and other standards documents for students in all grades. The mathematical practices should be connected to the content standards by engaging students in solving problems, reasoning, making conjectures, applying math to everyday life, using appropriate tools, communicating precisely, looking for patterns and structure, and looking for regularity in mathematical methods. The investigations in this section provide ways to make connections between practice and content standards.

Mathematical Content

Division of whole numbers is introduced in grade 3 and instruction continues in grades 3 through 6. The standards that focus on building understanding are especially important for helping students engage with the mathematical practices. Below are content designations that align with the Common Core and other standards documents.

Grade 3: Interpret whole-number quotients; represent and solve problems involving division within 100; understand the relationship between multiplication and division.

Grade 4: Divide to solve word problems; find whole-number quotients and remainders with up to four-digit dividends and one-digit divisors using strategies based on place value, the properties of operations, and the relationship between multiplication and division.

Grade 5: Find whole-number quotients and remainders with up to four-digit dividends and two-digit divisors using strategies based on place value, the properties of operations, and the relationship between multiplication and division.

Grade 6: Fluently divide multidigit numbers using the standard algorithm.

Whole-Class Instruction

These suggestions for whole-class instruction introduce students to important and basic ideas relating to division. They are organized into four categories: division sharing problems, division grouping problems, using children's books with word problems, and division games.

A Problem-Solving Lesson: Division Sharing Problems

Presenting students with problem situations helps develop their familiarity with the language and process of division. Use the problem that follows about sharing money to introduce a sharing division problem in a real-world context.

Introducing

1. **Present or review concepts.** Review with students what "sharing equally" means.

2. **Present the investigation.** Tell students the following story:

   While walking to school one day, four students found a $5.00 bill. When they arrived at school, they told their teacher, and she asked them to tell the principal. The principal thanked the students and told them she would try to find out who lost the money. A week later, the principal called the students back to her office, and told them no one had claimed the money and that it was theirs to keep. However, they first had to figure how to share it equally among the four of them.

   Have the students work in pairs or small groups to figure out how the four students can share $5.00 equally among them. Write the following prompt on the board and ask students to use words, numbers, and/or pictures to record their answer and explain how they reasoned.

   Each person gets ____. We think this because ____.

3. **Discuss the task to make sure students understand what they are to do.**

Exploring

Circulate and offer assistance as needed. To give all students time to solve the problem, ask pairs or groups who finish first to solve a similar problem, but one that has a remainder: *If four students found 50¢ on the way to school, how much would each get if they had to share it equally?*

Summarizing

Have students report their answers and explain their reasoning. Keep the emphasis on the different approaches students use to solve the problem. Show students how to represent the problem and solutions mathematically:

$$50\cent \div 4 = 12\cent \ R\ 2\cent$$

$$4\overline{)50\cent}^{\,12\cent\,R2\cent}$$

Extensions

More Stories About the Four Students. In subsequent classes, continue with stories about the four students who find different things on the way to school. They can find a bag of marbles with fifty-four marbles, a train of seventeen interlocking cubes, a bag with twenty-two apples, and so on.

Problems with Other Divisors. Vary the contexts and the size of the divisors. Here are examples:

> *Suppose someone gives the class a gift of 100 pencils. If we divide them equally among all the students, how many pencils will each student get?*

> *If eight students were at a birthday party, and there were a box of cookies with three packets of ten cookies each to divide equally among them, how many cookies could each student get?*

A Problem-Solving Lesson: Division
Grouping Problems

Use the following problem about making omelets to introduce a grouping division problem in a real-world context. In contrast to sharing problems, here the division problem is to put eggs into equal groups with two eggs in each.

Introducing

1. **Present or review concepts.** Write the word *dozen* on the board and review that there are twelve objects in one dozen. Draw twelve eggs.

2. **Pose a part of the problem or a similar but smaller problem.** Ask, *If it takes three eggs to make an omelet, how many omelets can you make from a dozen eggs?* Discuss with the class.

3. **Present the investigation.** Introduce the problem:

> *There were two cartons in the refrigerator with a dozen eggs in each, plus three extra eggs in the holders in the refrigerator door. Mom liked to eat an omelet each day and used two eggs in each omelet. How many days could she make omelets before she had to buy more eggs?*

> Have the students solve this problem in pairs or small groups. Ask them to record their answer and use words, numbers, and/or pictures to explain how they figured it out.

4. **Discuss the task to make sure students understand what they are to do.**

Exploring

Circulate and offer assistance as needed.

Summarizing

Have students report their answers and describe how they reasoned. Ask students to report the different approaches they used to solve the problem. Reinforce for the students how to represent the problem and solutions mathematically:

$$27 \div 2 = 13 \, R \, 1$$

$$2 \overline{)27} \quad {}^{13 \, R \, 1}$$

Extensions

Making Sandwiches. Bring a loaf of sliced bread to class. Choose a loaf that is packaged in a clear wrap so students can count the slices. Present this problem: *How many sandwiches can be made from the loaf?*

Using Tiles. Tell the class that for a math investigation, each student needs eight tiles. One box can hold two hundred tiles. Present this problem: *Can everyone in the class participate in the investigation at one time?*

A Ream of Paper. Tell students that paper is packaged in reams, and that a ream contains five hundred sheets. Present this problem: *If each student needs 20 sheets of paper to make a recording book, how many books can be made from one ream of paper?*

Apple Giveaway. Present this problem: *A person with an apple tree had a giveaway celebration to get rid of fifty extra apples. She offered three apples to each person who asked. How many people could get free apples?*

A Problem-Solving Lesson: The Doorbell Rang

The classic children's book, *The Doorbell Rang* (Hutchins 1986), provides students the opportunity to model division sharing problems and reinforces standard division notation. The story begins with Victoria and Sam who are about to have a snack. Their mother had baked a dozen cookies. Just as they're about to divide the cookies, the doorbell rings and two friends enter. Then, just before the four children begin to eat cookies, the doorbell rings again and two more children enter. And once these six children are about to have their snack, the doorbell rings again and six more children arrive. Now there are twelve children and twelve cookies. The children freeze when the doorbell rings again, but this time it's Grandma with a plate of freshly baked cookies.

Materials

The Doorbell Rang by Pat Hutchins, 1 copy
tiles or interlocking cubes, 12 per pair of students

Introducing

1. **Present or review concepts.** Show students *The Doorbell Rang* and tell them that you're going to read them a story about sharing cookies. Be sure that students understand the idea of sharing equally.

2. **Pose a part of the problem or a similar but smaller problem.** Read the book aloud to the class so that the students can hear the story and see and enjoy the illustrations. Then read the story a second time, this time recording each of the sharing problems as it occurs showing two different mathematical representations.

$$12 \div 2 = 6$$
$$12 \div 4 = 3$$
$$12 \div 6 = 2$$
$$12 \div 12 = 1$$

$$2\overline{)12}^{\,6} \qquad 4\overline{)12}^{\,3}$$
$$6\overline{)12}^{\,2} \qquad 12\overline{)12}^{\,1}$$

3. **Present the investigation.** Distribute twelve color tiles or cubes to each pair of students. Explain that for each problem, one student reads the problem aloud and explains what happened in the story. The other student, using the twelve tiles or cubes to represent the cookies, shows how to share the cookies to get the answer. They switch roles for each problem.

4. **Discuss the task to make sure students understand what they are to do.**

Exploring

Circulate and offer assistance as needed.

Summarizing

1. **Focus on vocabulary.** Use this opportunity to introduce *dividend*, *divisor*, and *quotient*.

2. **Relate division to multiplication.** Point out the related multiplication equation for each problem. For example, if only Victoria and Sam shared all twelve cookies, they would each have six cookies, which can be represented with multiplication by $2 \times 6 = 12$. Read this as "two groups of twelve" and as "two times twelve." Repeat for the other problems.

Extensions

Sharing Grandma's Cookies. With Grandma's plate of cookies, there would be twenty-four cookies in all. Present this problem: *How many cookies would each of the twelve children get if they shared all twenty-four cookies equally?* Ask them to write the division problem in two ways.

Write a Story. Ask students to write and illustrate their own version of this story. Explain that they may change the number of cookies on the plate and also the number of children who arrive each time. Have students read their story to a partner.

FYI
Seeing the connection between division and multiplication helps deepen students' understanding of both operations. I think it's important to relate division to multiplication whenever the opportunity arises.
— MSB

A Division Game: Leftovers

The following game of chance gives students experience with sharing quantities into equal groups and relating the action to the appropriate mathematical representation.

Materials

1–6 die, 1 per pair of students
3-by-3 inch squares of construction paper, 6 per pair of students
tiles or other counters, 15 per pair of students
a cup to hold the tiles, 1 per pair of students

Teaching the Rules of the Game

Tell the students that you're going to teach them how to play a game called *Leftovers* that they'll play in pairs. To model how to play the game, invite a student to be your partner and join you at the board. Read each rule and follow the directions.

LEFTOVERS: RULES OF THE GAME

You need: 1–6 die, 1 per pair of students
  3-by-3 inch squares of construction paper, 6 per pair of students
  15 tiles per pair of students
  a cup to hold the tiles, 1 per pair of students

Play with a partner. Follow these rules.

1. One player rolls the die, puts out that number of 3-by-3-inch paper squares, and divides the tiles in the cup equally among the squares.

2. The other player records an equation to describe what occurred. For example: If a player rolled a four and divided the tiles onto four square, the equation would be: $15 \div 4 = 3 \text{ R } 3$.

3. The first player keeps the leftovers but puts the remaining tiles from the paper squares back into the cup.

4. Continue playing until there are no tiles left to divide.

When there are no tiles left, players count the leftover tiles they kept. The winner is the player who has the greater number of leftovers.

As you play the sample game, model how to record.

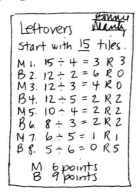

Teaching Tip
When you play a sample game, point out that after the first player's turn, there may be fewer than fifteen tiles in the cup if the first player had a remainder and therefore kept the leftover tiles. Also, when you record, use the players' initials to mark who had the leftovers.

— MSB

Exploring

Circulate and offer assistance as students play in pairs.

Summarizing

Lead a classroom discussion about what the students noticed while playing the game. Ask them which rolls were more favorable and why.

Extension

Remainders of Zero. On a class chart, they record their sentences with remainders of zero. (Ask students to record only those sentences that haven't already been recorded on the chart.)

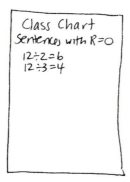

These suggestions can be used as part of a menu that students work on independently or with a partner. For more information on using a menu to structure independent work, see "Starting Point 20: Four Structures for Organizing and Managing Classroom Instruction" in Part 1 on page 111.

Additional Instructional Suggestions

The following instructional suggestions are for small groups of students. After students are familiar with the activities, some of the suggestions are suitable as independent investigations for individual or partner work, and for choice time explorations.

Leftovers with 20

You need: 1–6 die, 1 per pair of students
tiles, 20 per pair of students
3-by-3-inch squares of construction paper, 6 per pair
of students

This is an extension of *Leftovers*, the game the students learned in a whole-class lesson.

This is a two-player game. Play with a partner, following these rules:

1. One player rolls the die, puts out that number of 3-by-3-inch paper squares, and divides the tiles in the cup equally among the squares.

2. The other player records a mathematical equation to describe what occurred.

3. The first player keeps the leftovers but puts the tiles on the paper squares back in the cup.

4. Continue playing until there are no tiles left to divide. The winner is the player who has the greater number of leftovers.

Division Stories

Write a division story that follows two rules:

1. It must end in a question.

2. The question must be one that's possible to answer by dividing.

Solve your story problem in as many ways as you can.
Exchange papers and solve each other's problems.

The Kings-and-Elephants Problem

You need: *17 Kings and 42 Elephants* by Margaret Mahy, 1 book

This book tells the story of seventeen kings and forty-two elephants going on a journey through a jungle. Figure out how seventeen kings could divide up the work of taking care of forty-two elephants. Explain your reasoning.

Write other math problems that use the information in the story. For example: *How many elephant feet were there altogether?*

Chocolate Bars

Here is a picture of five chocolate bars. (Some chocolate bars are scored to make them easy to break apart and share.)

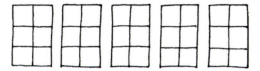

Figure out how to share the five chocolate bars equally among four people.

Explain how you solved the problem. Write: *Each person gets* _____. *I figured it out by* _____. Use words, numbers, and/or pictures.

Assessing Understanding of Division

Observing students during classroom discussions and while they are working on independent investigations provides information about their understanding and skills. Also, one-on-one conversations with students reveal their individual understanding, misconceptions, and gaps, and provides valuable information that isn't always evident from classroom observations. The following suggestions can be used for both assessment approaches.

Observing Students

When students are working on the independent tasks, circulate, observe, and, at times, question them about their thinking and reasoning. When students are playing *Leftovers with 20*, for example, ask them if they can predict whether there will be a remainder before they divide the tiles. The game gives students concrete experience with division problems that have a quotient of zero; make sure students understand when zero is an appropriate answer.

The students' stories for *Division Stories* reveal whether they can relate contextual situations to the idea of division. *More Candy Box Research* gives you information about students' comfort with numbers. If students are interested and able, discuss rules for divisibility with them.

Individual Assessments

The following written assignments offer ways to find out about students' understanding of division.

1. Before beginning instruction, ask students to write what they know about division. Have them do this again at the end of the instructional unit. Return both papers to the students and ask them to reflect on their learning.

2. Give the students a division problem, for example: *24 ÷ 3* or *65 ÷ 5*. Ask them to explain how to figure out the answer. If students say they already know the answer, ask how they would tell a younger student how to find out.

3. Ask the students to solve 21 ÷ 4 for the following four situations. For each situation, they are to report an answer, show how they arrived at it, and explain why the answer makes sense.

    1) Share 21 cookies among 4 students.
    2) Share 21 balloons among 4 students.
    3) Share $21.00 among 4 students.
    4) Do 21 ÷ 4 on a calculator.

4. Assign a problem, such as one of those suggested for whole-class lessons. Ask students to present a solution in writing and explain their reasoning.

Extending Multiplication and Division

About Extending Multiplication and Division

In the upper-elementary grades, students develop skills to estimate and calculate accurately when multiplying and dividing with large numbers. Students should be able to compute mentally as well as with paper and pencil and make estimates that allow them to judge the reasonableness of their answers. When confronted with problem situations, they should know when it's necessary to be accurate and when an estimate will suffice.

Traditionally, instruction related to multiplying and dividing large numbers has focused on computing accurate answers proficiently using paper-and-pencil algorithms. Unfortunately, the result of this focus has been that many students learn the algorithms for multiplication and long division without understanding why these algorithms make sense. Also, little emphasis has been given to calculating mentally.

Instruction should help students develop a repertoire of strategies for multiplying and dividing with large numbers both by figuring mentally and using paper and pencil. Learning different strategies requires that students understand several important ideas—how to multiply and divide by ten, powers of ten, and multiples of powers of ten; how to apply the distributive property to multiplication and division problems; and how multiplication and division relate to each other. When emphasis is placed on understanding and using these ideas, the role of paper and pencil expands beyond performing standard algorithms to keeping track of numerical reasoning and calculating in ways that relate to the specific numbers at hand. Standard algorithms are one way to perform computations, not the only or best way. Too often, for example, when faced with calculations like 463×100 and $360 \div 20$, students reach for pencil and paper to apply the algorithm rather than reason that for these problems, figuring mentally is more useful, appropriate, and efficient. Proficiency with multiplication and division shouldn't be judged by students' ability to perform one particular algorithm but by their ability to calculate answers to multiplication and division calculations accurately and efficiently using approaches that are appropriate to specific problems and the numbers at hand.

Mathematical Practices

Developing understanding and skills with multiplication and division should support the mathematical practices described in the Common Core and other standards documents for students in all grades. The mathematical practices should be connected to the content standards by engaging students in solving problems, reasoning, making conjectures, applying math to everyday life, using appropriate tools, communicating precisely, looking for patterns and structure, and looking for regularity in mathematical methods. The investigations in this section provide ways to make connections between practice and content standards.

Mathematical Content

Multiplication of whole numbers is introduced in grade 2 and instruction continues in grades 3–5; division instruction begins in grade 3 and continues in grades 4–6. The standards that focus on building understanding are especially important for helping students engage with the mathematical practices. Below are content designations that align with the Common Core and other standards documents.

Grade 2: Work with equal groups of objects to gain foundations for multiplication.

Grade 3: Interpret whole-number quotients; represent and solve problems involving multiplication and division within 100; understand properties of multiplication and the relationship between multiplication and division; multiply one-digit number by multiples of 10 using strategies based on place value and properties of operations; by the end of grade 3, know from memory all products of two one-digit numbers.

Grade 4: Gain familiarity with factors and multiples; multiply and divide to solve word problems; multiply a number up to four digits by a one-digit number, multiply two two-digit numbers, and find whole-number quotients and remainders with up to four-digit dividends and one-digit divisors using strategies based on place value and the properties of operations; use equations, rectangular arrays, and area models to explain calculations.

Grade 5: Fluently multiply multidigit whole numbers using the standard algorithm; find whole-number quotients and remainders with up to four-digit dividends and two-digit divisors using strategies based on place value, the properties of operations, and the relationship between multiplication and division.

Grade 6: Fluently divide multidigit numbers using the standard algorithm.

Whole-Class Instruction

The following suggestions for whole-class instruction introduce students to important and basic ideas relating to multiplication and division. They are organized into five categories: multiplying by ten and powers of ten, using the distributive property, connecting multiplication and division, multiplication and division through real-world problems, and multiplication and division games.

Multiplying by Ten and Powers of Ten

Because of the structure of our base ten place-value system, it's important for students to investigate the patterns of multiplying by ten and powers of ten.

Multiplying by Ten

Multiplying by ten is made simple, calling merely for adding a zero (for example, $6 \times 10 = 60$, $13 \times 10 = 130$, $247 \times 10 = 2470$, and so on). Learning this pattern allows students to multiply by ten in their heads easily. It's important, however, that even when students know the pattern of adding a zero they can also verify answers in other ways. For example, they might reason that 13×10 is 130 because ten 10s are 100, three more 10s is 30 more, and 100 plus 30 is 130. Or they can verify that 25×10 is 250 by thinking that 25×2 is 50, doubling that for 25×4 gives 100, doubling again for 25×8 gives 200, and adding two more 25s makes 250 altogether. Using these and other strategies not only helps students develop computational flexibility but also helps them verify that applying the shortcut makes sense.

Multiplying by Powers of Ten

The pattern of multiplying by ten extends to larger powers of ten. Multiplying by one hundred, for example, results in adding two zeros, so that 12×100 is 1200. (In this and similar problems, it seems to help students make sense of them if they read 1200 as "twelve hundred" rather than as "one thousand two hundred" or think of 3700 as thirty-seven hundred rather than three thousand seven hundred.) Again, although students know the pattern of adding two zeros, they should be expected to verify answers by reasoning (for example, 4×100 is the same as 4 groups of 100, which is $100 + 100 + 100 + 100$).

Using Different Approaches

It's a good idea to devote whole-class discussions to solving a few multiplication and division problems with ten and powers of ten. Encourage students to think of multiple approaches and record their ideas on the board as they present them. Recording their reasoning models for students how to represent their thinking symbolically. For example, here are three different ways to think about solving the problem 25×10.

$25 \times 2 = 50$	$10 \times 10 = 100$	5 tens $= 50$
$50 + 50 = 100$ (25×4)	$10 \times 10 = 100$	Count by 50 five times
$100 + 100 = 200$ (25×8)	$5 \times 10 = 50$	50, 100, 150, 200, 250
$200 + 50 = 250$ (25×10)	$100 + 100 + 50 = 250$	

Focus on how students reason as well as on how to verify correct answers. Start a class list of strategies. Talk about which strategies are better suited for specific problems so that students think about the efficiency of certain methods. Keep in mind that the goal of this instruction is to develop students' ability to reason mentally both accurately and efficiently. Follow your classroom discussions with partner or small-group work and individual assignments, asking students to solve a few problems in several different ways. Share the student work samples during subsequent classroom discussions so that students can explain how they used paper and pencil to keep track of and explain their numerical reasoning, making a bridge between reasoning mentally and using paper and pencil. Also, having students share work encourages others to think about how their classmates' reason.

Using the Distributive Property

It's helpful to have frequent whole-class discussions about strategies for mentally multiplying and dividing, presenting problems that traditionally have been relegated to paper-and-pencil solutions. It's helpful to use the same structure:

1. Present the class with a problem.

2. Ask the students to take a few minutes and think about the problem.

3. Have students then share their ideas with a partner.

4. Lead a classroom discussion during which students share their ideas.

Using the "think, pair, share" routine is appropriate when asking students to make an estimate. For more information, see "Starting Point 14: The Importance of Classroom Discussions" in Part 1 on page 67.

An Example: 13 × 5

When asked to calculate mentally the answer to 13×5, for example, one student may report that 10×5 is 50, 3 more 5s is 15, and $50 + 15$ is 65. Another student may reason that 6×5 is 30 and another 6×5 makes 60 altogether; this takes care of twelve 5s, and 1 more 5 makes 65. Or a student may think that 13×2 is 26, so 13×4 is twice that, or 52, and 1 more 13 makes 65. As described in the previous section about multiplying by ten and powers of ten, record as each student reports.

$$13 \times 5$$

$10 \times 5 = 50$	$6 \times 5 = 30$	$13 \times 2 = 26$
$3 \times 5 = 15$	$6 \times 5 = 30$	$13 \times 4 = 52$
$50 + 15 = 65$	$30 + 30 = 60$	$52 + 13 = 65$
	$60 + 5 = 65$	

Be sure to talk with the class about how recording is a useful tool for keeping track of and describing how you reason, not only for following a formerly learned procedure. In each of the previous strategies, students do simpler multiplications, figure out partial products, and then combine the results for a final answer. Students will usually do this when multiplying by ten and powers of ten, but other numbers provide new challenges. At first, if students don't offer strategies like these in classroom discussions, jump-start their thinking by encouraging them to begin with what they know. Or give them a suggestion about a place to start, such as multiplying 10×5, and have them talk in pairs or small groups about how that might help. You can also model one way as an example and then ask students to think of other approaches. Thinking about multiplying or dividing in this way is new for some students, and they need time to expand their computational repertoire to include ways other than using the procedures they may have learned and practiced.

Connecting the Distributive Property to Rectangular Arrays

Relating multiplication to rectangular arrays is a way to show why a particular way to reason numerically makes sense and offers a geometric interpretation of multiplication that can help students see how the areas of number and geometry can relate to each other. For example, a 5-by-13 array can be split into a 5-by-10 array and a 5-by-3 array, as shown here:

For more information about relating multiplication to rectangular arrays, see *Candy Boxes* on page 376.

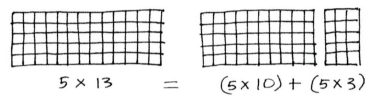

$$5 \times 13 \quad = \quad (5 \times 10) + (5 \times 3)$$

All of the strategies described for multiplying 13×5 make use of the distributive property of multiplication over addition. This means that instead of thinking of 13×5 as one multiplication problem, we split the problem into two or more problems. For example, by thinking of 13 as $10 + 3$, we can distribute multiplying by 5 over the two addends by doing 10×5 and 3×5.

Similarly, for division, students can figure the answer to $150 \div 6$ by using the distributive property, this time distributing the division over addition. One way to do this is to think about 150 as $60 + 60 + 30$. Divide 60 by 6 to get 10 and then divide 60 by 6 for 10 more. This accounts for 120 of the 150, leaving $30 \div 6$ for 5 more. Adding two 10s and 5 gives 25, the answer to $150 \div 6$.

Making use of the distributive property helps students develop strategies for computing. Also, because applying the distributive property depends on the specific numbers involved, it helps develop students' number sense as well. For example, when thinking about dividing 150 by 6, as explained previously, choosing to think of 150 as $60 + 60 + 30$ helps make the problem more manageable. If the problem called for dividing 150 by 7, however, it might make more sense to think of 150 as $70 + 70 + 10$ or $140 + 10$. Making decisions like these focuses students on the particular characteristics of numbers and helps refine their number sense.

The distributive property is also the basis of why standard algorithms work, producing partial products for multiplication and the individual digits in quotients of long-division problems. However, the focus of lessons should be on finding ways to make complicated computations simpler and more manageable, not on learning what the distributive property is. (I remember learning about the distributive property by being shown that $a(b + c) = ab + ac$, but never understanding why it was important or how it might be useful.) Keep the emphasis on making numerical calculations. It's fine to identify that what your students are doing is applying the distributive property, but don't make the distributive property the goal of instruction.

A Problem-Solving Lesson: Beans and Scoops

Jars, scoops, and various sizes of dry beans are easily accessible materials that are effective for engaging students with multiplication, division, and the relationship between them. The emphasis of lessons using these materials should be on having students solve problems for which they use multiplication and explain how they reasoned. Lessons like these can be done from time to time during the year, varying the problems as well as the sizes of the jars, scoops, and beans. The following are directions for an initial lesson, followed by extensions for subsequent experiences.

Materials
jar
beans
1-ounce scoop (a 1-ounce coffee scoop works well)

To prepare for the lesson, fill a jar with scoops of beans, counting the number of scoops it takes. Also count the number of beans in the jar.

Introducing
1. **Pose an introductory problem.** Show the class the coffee scoop and the jar filled with beans. Ask, *How many scoops do you think it took to fill the jar?*

2. **Present the investigation.** Reveal the number of scoops the jar holds and also how many beans are in the jar. Write these numbers on the board and pose a problem: *Figure out about how many beans fill the scoop.* Have students work individually or in pairs, and write about how they solved the problem.

3. **Discuss the task to make sure students understand what they are to do.**

Exploring
Observe the interaction, listening to how groups organize working together, the ideas they discuss, and the strategies they use. Offer assistance when needed.

Summarizing
1. **Have students report their answers and explain how they reasoned.**

2. **Verify their answers.** To do this, go around the room and give each pair of students a scoop of beans to count. Of course, the number of beans in different scoops will vary as measurement is never exact. This gives students the chance to talk about the problem as one for which an accurate answer doesn't make the most sense but for which an estimate will suffice or be even more appropriate.

Teaching Tip
After trying different jars, I decided on a jar that's a little more than 10 ounces and holds a dozen or so scoops of beans. I've used different size beans—kidney or pinto with older students and lima beans for an easier investigation with younger students.
— MSB

FYI
Asking students to estimate isn't crucial to the investigation, but it engages students' interest and helps them think about the context of the problem. Also, I never pass up an opportunity to ask students to make an estimate.
— MSB

Extensions

How Many Scoops Fill the Jar? As a variation on this lesson, tell students only how many beans are in the jar. Then give them a scoop of beans to count and use that information to figure out about how many scoops filled the jar. After discussing their solutions and methods, empty the jar and then refill it with scoops as the students count.

How Many Beans Fill the Jar? For another variation on this lesson, have students figure out how many beans fill a jar. Using a larger jar, like quart size, gives students experience with greater numbers. Show the class an empty jar, a scoop, and a bag of beans. Ask the students to estimate about how many beans they think the jar will hold. After listening to their estimates, pour a scoop of beans on one student's desk to count. Ask, *What other information do we need to figure out the total number of beans that fill the jar?* After the students determine that multiplying the number of beans in one scoop by the number of scoops in the jar will produce a reasonable estimate, begin filling the jar with scoops of beans. Stop after several scoops and ask, *How many beans are in the jar so far?* Have the students calculate mentally the number of beans and discuss their methods. Continue adding scoops and having students calculate the number of beans until the jar is full. Repeat on other days with different-size beans and jars.

Multiplication and Division Through Real-World Problems

Using situations that call for multiplying and dividing with large numbers as the basis for whole-class discussions provides opportunities for students to explain their strategies and listen to strategies other students have used. As much as possible, choose contexts that relate to students' lives or are familiar to them. Also, ask students to make up their own multiplication and division problems to solve. The following examples can get you started.

Replacing Floor Tiles

Figure out the number of floor tiles needed to tile the floor of the classroom. Then calculate the number of floor tiles needed for our wing and for all the classrooms in the school.

Stacking Chairs

If we stacked all of our chairs on top of one another, how high would the stack reach?

Head to Heels

If four students in the class were to lie in a straight line head to heel, how long would the line be? Then use that information to approximate the length of all the students in our class lying head to heel.

School Days

About how many days are students expected to come to school each month? How many school days are there in a year?

The first three examples come from *50 Problem-Solving Lessons* (Burns 1996) in which I report how David Ott created problems for his sixth graders to solve that involved data collection and measurement as well as multiplication and division.

What's in a Name?

What's the average length of the first names of students in our school? What's the average length of last names?

Milk Money

How much do students in our class spend on milk for lunch weekly? In the entire school year? How much do all students in school spend on milk weekly? In the entire school year?

Soccer Statistics

If our town has eight teams in the soccer league, how many players are needed altogether?

A Multiplication Game: Hit the Target (Version 1)

Games are useful for instruction because they motivate students, offer a change of pace, and stimulate both thinking and practice. This two-person game engages students with multiplication. Students can play it either by figuring mentally or with paper and pencil. The purpose of using this and other games should be to help students learn new strategies for computing and to refine and reinforce the strategies they already know.

> In *Developing Number Sense, Grades 3–6* (Bresser and Holtzman 1999), the authors present a full classroom vignette of this game, along with samples of student work and extensions.

Teaching the Rules of the Game

Explain that the goal of the game is to use multiplication to hit a target range in as few tries as possible. To introduce the game, write on the board, *Target Range: 800–850*. Choose a student to play with you. Read the rules and follow the directions. Let the student be the first player. That way, as the second player, you can ask for suggestions from the rest of the class about what you might do next. For example, if the student chooses 12 as the initial number, ask the class to suggest a number you can multiply by 12 to get a product between 800 and 850. Asking students to explain how they would do the multiplication keeps the emphasis of the game on strategies for mental multiplication.

HIT THE TARGET (VERSION 1): RULES OF THE GAME

Play with a partner. Follow these rules.

1. The first player picks a number between one and one hundred.

2. The second player then chooses a number to multiply this initial number by, with the goal of reaching the target range.

3. Player 2 does the multiplication mentally and then Player 1 checks and records it. If the product isn't in the target range, Player 2 chooses another number to multiply the original number by.

4. Continue until the product hits the target range.

Play again, switching roles.

Discuss the Game

After students have had experience playing the game, lead a classroom discussion about which initial numbers were easy and which were difficult and why. Also ask students to describe the strategies they used for calculating mentally.

Play the game again with the class from time to time, changing the target range and/or the possible range for the initial number.

A Division Game: Leftovers from 100

For another version of the game *Leftovers* that involves smaller numbers, see page 394.

This two-person game engages students with division. Students can play it either by figuring mentally or with paper and pencil. The purpose of using this and other games should be to help students learn new strategies for computing and to refine and reinforce the strategies they already know.

Teaching the Rules of the Game

Tell the students that this is a game they'll play in pairs and have one recording sheet for the two of them. The goal of the game is to get the highest score possible.

LEFTOVERS FROM 100: RULES OF THE GAME

You need: recording sheet with the numbers 1 to 20 at the top

Play with a partner. Follow these rules.

1. One player chooses a number from one through twenty, divides one hundred by that number, and keeps the remainder as his or her score.

2. The other player crosses out the number chosen, records the division sentence, and marks the sentence with the first player's initial. (See the sample.)

3. Both players then subtract the remainder from one hundred to determine the next starting number. (Having both players do this is a way to check the subtraction.)

4. Change roles and repeat Steps 1, 2, and 3.

5. Continue alternating roles and playing until the starting number becomes zero or it's no longer possible for either player to score.

6. Figure out the total remainders for each player. The player with the greater total is the winner.

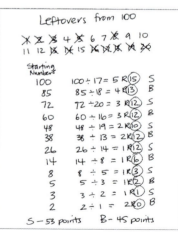

Discuss the Game

After students have played the game enough times to feel comfortable with how to play, lead a classroom discussion about what the students noticed while playing the game. Ask the following questions:

1. *What's the best number to use for a first move? Why?*

2. *What strategies did you use to decide which number was the best to choose?*

3. *How would your strategies change if the starting number was ninety-nine?*

4. *When a game is finished, the total of both players' scores, plus the last starting number that remains (if it's greater than zero), should add up to the original starting number of one hundred. Why is this so?*

5. *How do you think the game would change if the divisors were limited to one through fifteen or included one through twenty-five? Try these versions to see which would be the best game.*

Extension

Changing the Starting Number. For other versions of the game, change the original number. For example, playing *Leftovers from 200, Leftovers from 240,* or *Leftovers from 400* engages students with greater numbers. Playing *Leftovers from 60* may make the game more accessible for some students.

Using Calculators. Suggest that students use calculators to see whether this makes the game easier to play and, if so, how. For example, dividing 100 by 8, 12, and 16 all produce a whole number remainder of 4; on a calculator, however, $100 \div 8 = 12.5$, $100 \div 12 = 8.333$ [. . .], and $100 \div 16 = 6.25$.

Teaching Tip
Changing the starting numbers in *Leftovers* from 100 is a way to differentiate the game to meet students' varying needs.
—MSB

FYI
Having students use calculators to play the game gives them the chance to think about the relationship between the whole number remainders used in this game and decimal remainders represented on calculators.
—MSB

These suggestions can be used as part of a menu that students work on independently or with a partner. For more information on using a menu to structure independent work, see "Starting Point 20: Four Structures for Organizing and Managing Classroom Instruction" in Part 1 on page 111.

Additional Instructional Suggestions

The following instructional suggestions are for small groups of students. After students are familiar with the activities, some of the suggestions are suitable as independent investigations for individual or partner work, and for choice time explorations.

The Greatest Product

You need: 1–6 die, 1 per student

Roll the die four times, recording the number that comes up each time. Use the four numbers to make a multiplication problem that produces the greatest possible product. For example, if you roll 2, 5, 6, and 1, some problems you could make are 52×61, 51×62, and 612×5. Repeat for at least five sets of numbers. Then investigate the following:

1. If you rolled the same number four times, for example four 2s, your choices are 22×22 or 222×2. Which problem gives the greater product? Does the same configuration of any number rolled four times give the greater product?

2. Repeat the investigation, trying to make the smallest product each time.

3. Repeat the investigation rolling five times.

4. Do the investigation with a 0–9 die or spinner so that you have more numbers to use.

Leftovers Revisited

You need: 1–6 dice, 2 per pair of students

Work with a partner. This two-player game is an extension of the whole-class lesson *Leftovers from 100*. As with the previous game, the goal is to get the highest score possible. Play the game using the following rules.

1. Agree on a starting number between 200 and 500.

2. One player rolls the two dice and uses the numbers to make a two-digit divisor. For example, if the player rolls a 3 and a 5, the player can use 35 or 53 as the divisor. The player divides the starting number by the divisor and keeps the remainder as his or her score.

3. The other player records the division sentence, marking the sentence with the first player's initial.

4. Both players subtract the remainder from the starting number to determine the next starting number.

5. Students then change roles and repeat Steps 2, 3, and 4.

6. Continue alternating roles and playing until the starting number becomes zero or it's no longer possible for either player to score.

7. Figure out the total remainders for each player. The player with the greater total is the winner.

Remainders of Zero

You need: 1–6 die, 1 per student

Roll the die four times, recording the number that comes up each time. Use the four numbers to make division problems that have a remainder of zero. For example, if you roll 2, 5, 6, and 1, one problem that you could make is 156 ÷ 2. See how many different problems you can find for the four numbers. If you are convinced that it isn't possible to make any problem with a remainder of zero, explain why you think this is so.

Then do the following:

1. Repeat the investigation, trying to make problems with the largest remainder possible.

2. Repeat the investigation, rolling five times.

3. Do the investigation with a 0–9 die or spinner so that you have more numbers to use.

Factor Fiddling

When multiplying two factors, suppose you double one. For example, change 5 × 3 to 5 × 6 (doubling the 3) or to 10 × 3 (doubling the 5 instead). What happens to the product? Try this for many other problems as well.

Then investigate what happens to the product of two factors when you fiddle with one or both of the factors in other ways:

1. Triple one factor.

2. Halve one factor.

3. Double one factor and halve the other factor.

4. Think of other ways to fiddle with factors and see what you discover.

Hit the Target (Version 2)

You need: 1–6 die, 1 per pair of students

Play with a partner. The goal of the game is to hit the target range in as few steps as possible. Play the game using the same rules as for *Hit the Target (Version 1)*, except use a die to determine the target range, as explained in Step 1.

1. To choose a target range, roll the die three times (or four times to use greater numbers). Arrange the three or four numbers into the greatest possible number; this is the lower end of your target range. (For example, if you roll 2, 6, and 3, then the number you make is 632.) Add 50 to your original number to determine the upper end of your range. (In the case of the example, the target range is 632–682.)

2. Player 1 chooses a number between one and one hundred (fourteen, for example).

3. Player 2 chooses another number to multiply the first number by, and Player 1 verifies and records the result (for example, $14 \times 50 = 700$).

4. If the product doesn't hit the target range, Player 2 goes back to the original number and multiplies it by any another number. Player 1 verifies and records the result.

5. Players repeat Step 4 until the product falls within the target range.

6. Players repeat the game, alternating roles.

Sample Game Scenario

The following is an example of how a game might progress.

Target Range: 632–682

Starting Number: 14
$14 \times 50 = 700$	The number is too high.
$14 \times 40 = 560$	The number is too low.
$14 \times 45 = 630$	The number is closer but still too low.
$14 \times 46 = 644$	The number is within the target range.

Assessing Understanding of Multiplication and Division with Large Numbers

Observing students during classroom discussions and while they are working on independent investigations provides information about their understanding and skills. Also, one-on-one conversations with students reveal their individual understanding, misconceptions, and gaps, and provides valuable information that isn't always evident from classroom observations. The following suggestions can be used for both assessment approaches.

Observing Students

During classroom discussions and when students are involved with independent investigations, circulate among them, observe what they are doing, and talk with them about their numerical reasoning. When students are engaged in small-group or individual written assignments, ask them to explain how they reasoned.

Individual Assessments

1. Assign a multiplication or division problem and ask students to show at least three different ways to figure the answer and explain their reasoning.

2. Give students real-world problems along the lines of the examples suggested for the whole-class lessons. Ask students to present their solutions in writing and to explain their reasoning.

Fractions

About Fractions

Students' introduction to fractions initially occurs outside of school. They hear adults use fractions in different ways and in a variety of circumstances:

- I'll be back in three-quarters of an hour.
- I need two sheets of quarter-inch plywood.
- The recipe says to add two-thirds of a cup of water.
- The trim calls for two and a half yards of ribbon.
- There's a quarter moon tonight.
- The dishwasher is less than half full.

Also, students have learned to use the language of fractions to describe events in their own lives:

- You can have half of my cookie.
- Here, use half of my blocks.
- It's a quarter past one.
- I need half a dollar.

From their experiences, a number of ideas about fractions take shape informally in students' thinking. However, students' understanding of fractions typically is incomplete and confused. For example, they often think of half as any part of a whole, rather than one of two equal parts. Also, they often refer to one-half as being larger than another. (It's common to hear students say, "My half is bigger than your half.") They may be familiar with $\frac{1}{2}$, $\frac{1}{3}$, and $\frac{1}{4}$ of a unit, but not with $\frac{2}{3}$ or $\frac{3}{4}$. They may not have noticed relationships between fractions, for example, that $\frac{2}{4}$ of an orange is the same as $\frac{1}{2}$ of an orange, or that $\frac{3}{4}$ of an inch is $\frac{1}{4}$ less than 1 inch. Also, students' informal learning has most likely not been connected to the standard symbols of fractional notation.

Classroom instruction should build on students' previous experiences and help students clarify the ideas they're forming. It should provide many opportunities throughout the year for students to make sense of fractions, use fractional language, and learn to represent fractions with the standard symbols. Students should deal with fractions concretely and in the context of real-world situations before they focus on symbolic representations.

Some of the investigations suggested in this section present fractions as parts of a whole and others present fractions as parts of sets of objects. Various concrete materials are used so that the students do not link the concepts to the attributes of any particular material. (It may seem ludicrous to think students might generalize that fractions are round, but if their experiences with fractions deal only with fraction "pies," that misconception is not so improbable.)

The essential topics for instruction in fractions include naming fractions, comparing fractions, studying equivalence of fractions, and performing operations with fractions. In my experience, it's fairly easy to help students develop understanding fractions with a numerator of 1 (called *unit fractions*). Yet when fractions such as $\frac{2}{5}$ and $\frac{3}{4}$ enter the picture, so does confusion. Also, students have difficulty deciding which of two fractions is greater, $\frac{2}{3}$ and $\frac{4}{5}$, for example, or even $\frac{1}{8}$ and $\frac{1}{16}$, and why fractions such as $\frac{3}{6}$ and $\frac{4}{8}$ describe the same part of a unit. These types of difficulties indicate the need for further concept development with concrete materials and real-world situations.

When teaching older students who lack basic understanding of fractions, it's not uncommon for teachers to feel the pressures of time and the demands of the curriculum. In that situation, it's often tempting to speed up instruction and teach the rules for operating with fractions. Some teachers resort to telling students, for example, that multiplying the numerator and denominator by the same number gives an equivalent fraction, or that in order to divide you invert the fraction on the right and multiply across the tops and across the bottoms.

Giving students rules to help them develop facility with fractions doesn't help them develop understanding of the concepts. The risk is that when students forget a rule, they'll have no way to reason through a process. Try this test with your students: Give students a fraction problem they're "supposed" to understand, $\frac{1}{2} + \frac{1}{3}$, for example. Ask them to show you what the problem means with any concrete material, or a drawing, or by relating it to some real-world situation. Watch the students' responses and let their responses guide you when making instructional choices.

It's important to provide a variety of ways students can learn about fractions—with concrete materials, from a geometric perspective, with a numerical focus, and related to real-world situations. Let the students know that different people learn in different ways, and that they should pay attention to the kinds of investigations that help them develop understanding. Encourage them on investigations with which they are less comfortable. Don't expect immediate results from any one investigation. Students need time to absorb new ideas and integrate them with the understanding they already have.

The ideas in this section don't provide a comprehensive guide for teaching fractions. Rather, they offer models of ways to introduce ideas about fractions, suggest problem situations that engage students, and give alternative methods for assessing what students understand. Not included are suggestions to help develop understanding and skill with fraction operations.

Mathematical Practices

Developing understanding and skills with fractions should support the mathematical practices described in the Common Core and other standards documents for students in all grades. The mathematical practices should be connected to the content standards by engaging students in solving problems, reasoning, making conjectures, applying math to everyday life, using appropriate tools, communicating precisely, looking for patterns and structure, and looking for regularity in mathematical methods. The investigations in this section provide ways to make connections between practice and content standards.

For comprehensive help with teaching how to add, subtract, multiply, and divide fractions, you might be interested in two Teaching Arithmetic resources that I wrote: *Lessons for Extending Fractions* and *Lessons for Multiplying and Dividing Fractions* (2003).

Mathematical Content

Fractions are introduced informally in grade 2, typically as part of instruction in geometry with students dividing circles and rectangles into equal shares. Formal instruction continues from grade 3 on. The standards that focus on building understanding are especially important for helping students engage with the mathematical practices. Below are content designations that align with the Common Core and other standards documents.

Grade 2: Partition circles and rectangles into two, three, or four equal shares and name them as halves, thirds, and fourths.

Grade 3: Develop understanding of fractions as numbers beginning with unit fractions ($\frac{1}{2}$, $\frac{1}{3}$, $\frac{1}{4}$, and so on); use fractions to represent parts of a whole; use fractions to represent numbers equal to, less than, and greater than one; explain equivalence of fractions; compare fractions by using visual fraction models and strategies based on noticing equal numerators or denominators.

Grade 4: Extend understanding of fraction equivalence; compare and order fractions; build fractions from unit fractions (e.g., $\frac{2}{3} = \frac{1}{3} + \frac{1}{3}$); develop understanding of adding and subtracting fractions with like denominators; use the meaning of fractions and of multiplication to multiply a fraction by a whole number; solve word problems.

Grade 5: Use equivalent fractions as a strategy to add and subtract fractions; interpret a fraction as division of the numerator by the denominator; use the meaning of fractions, of multiplication and division, and the relationship between multiplication and division to understand and explain why the procedures for multiplying and dividing fractions makes sense (limited in division to dividing unit fractions by whole numbers and whole number by unit fractions); solve word problems.

Grade 6: Use the meaning of fractions, of multiplication and division, and the relationship between multiplication and division to understand and explain why the procedures for dividing fractions make sense; solve word problems involving multiplication and division of fractions.

Grade 7: Recognize fractions, decimals, and percents as different representations of rational numbers.

Whole-Class Instruction

These suggestions for whole-class instruction introduce students to basic fraction concepts and fractional notation and include the following: introducing fractions in real-world contexts, fractions with two-color counters, the fraction kit, using graphs to build understanding of fractions, exploring fractions through sharing problems, comparing and ordering fractions, and mental calculation with fractions.

Introducing Fractions in Real-World Contexts

Students need many opportunities to talk about fractional parts, see examples, work with concrete materials, and relate their experiences to the standard mathematical notation. Such experiences are best done over time so that students can develop familiarity and understanding. The following suggestions are for introducing fractions as parts of sets and the structure of fractional notation. All of them use real-world objects: a six-pack of soft drinks, bananas, a package of chewing gum, crackers, birthday candles, apples, pencils, and more. Using a six-pack of soft drinks illustrates a structure for these experiences that can then be used with the other objects.

Materials

six-pack of soft drinks
various size sets of objects, such as a bunch of seven bananas, a package of five sticks of gum, a box of crackers with three separately wrapped packages, a box of colored birthday candles, a bag of red and green apples, pencils with and without erasers, some sharpened and some new (for extensions)

Fractions with a Six-Pack

For a first experience, show the students a six-pack of soft drinks and remove one can from the package. Tell the students, "If I drink this soft drink, I can write a fraction that describes what part of the six-pack I drank." On the board, write $\frac{1}{6}$. Tell the students that this means one of six parts and we read it as "one-sixth." Also write *one-sixth* on the board. Then pose the following questions. For each, have students explain their thinking. Correct any erroneous notions. If this is the first time students have been introduced to this notation, remember they'll need time to understand and become comfortable with it.

> *What do you think the bottom number in the fraction refers to?* [The number of cans in a full six-pack.]
>
> *What do you think the top number in the fraction refers to?* [The number of cans I removed from the six-pack.]
>
> *Why does this mathematical notation make sense?* [You can tell how many are in the whole group and also how many you removed.]
>
> *What fraction can I write to describe the rest of the six-pack, the part I didn't drink?* [$\frac{5}{6}$]
>
> *What do the numbers in this fraction mean?* [The 6 tells the number of cans in a full six-pack and the 5 tells the number of cans left after one is removed.]

When posing questions to the class for discussion, I find it useful to use the "think, pair, share" routine. I ask students to think by themselves first, then turn and talk with a neighbor, and finally participate in a classroom discussion. For more on this routine, see "Starting Point 14: The Importance of Classroom Discussions" in Part 1 on page 67.

Remove another can and say, "Suppose I drink this can as well." Write $\frac{2}{6}$ and *two-sixths* on the board and ask the same questions. Continue introducing three-sixths, four-sixths, five-sixths, and six-sixths. Be sure to point out that six-sixths equals one whole six-pack.

$\frac{1}{6}$ one-sixth

$\frac{2}{6}$ two-sixths

$\frac{3}{6}$ three-sixths

$\frac{4}{6}$ four-sixths

$\frac{5}{6}$ five-sixths

$\frac{6}{6} = 1$ six-sixths

Teaching Tip
This is when I also introduce the terminology of numerator and denominator. I write them on the board and, as I continue with the lesson, I use them interchangeably with *top number* and *bottom number*.
— MSB

Fractions with Other Objects

Follow the same procedure for other sets of objects—a bunch of seven bananas; a pack of five sticks of gum; a box of crackers with three separately wrapped packages; a group of students in the class; a box of colored birthday candles; a bag of apples, some red and some green; a collection of pencils, with and without erasers, some sharpened and some new; a set of textbooks; shoes; and tiles.

- Show a bunch of seven bananas: *What fractional part is one banana? Two? Etc.*

- Show a pack of five sticks of gum: *What fractional part is one stick? Two? Etc.*

- Open a box of crackers and show the three identical packages inside: *What fractional part is one package. Two? Also, what fractional part of a package is one cracker? Two? Etc.*

- Ask a group of eight students to come to the front of the room: *What fraction of the group are boys? Girls? What fraction are wearing blue? Are wearing long sleeves?*

- Show a box of colored birthday candles: *What fraction of the candles in the box are pink? Blue? Green?*

- Bring to class a bag of apples, some red and some green: *What fraction of the apples are red? Green?*

- Show a set of pencils, some sharpened and some new: *What fraction of the set are sharpened? New? Have good points? Have erasers?*

- Stack about a dozen textbooks on a table: *What fraction of the set are math books? Science books? Social studies books?*

- Have nine students each take off one shoe. Set the shoes on a table at the front of the room, or have students gather so all can see them. Ask: *What fraction of the set are tennis shoes? Have laces? Don't have laces? Have bumpy soles?*

- Take a handful of tiles, with some each of red, yellow, blue, and green: *What fraction of the set are red? Yellow? Blue? Green?*

Teaching Tip
At times I've used all of these suggestions in a one-day lesson and other times I've spread out the experiences over several days. Both seem equally effective.
— MSB

For more information about using the "think, pair, share" routine, see "Starting Point 14: The Importance of Classroom Discussions" in Part 1 on page 67.

Fractions with Two-Color Counters

As with the previous idea about introducing fractions in contexts, this suggestion also introduces fractions as parts of sets, here using the concrete material of two-color counters.

Materials

two-color counters, 12 per student

Distribute twelve two-color counters to each student. Use the same format for all of the experiences in this lesson.

1. First give students a direction about how to arrange their twelve counters.

2. Ask questions to connect the experience to fractional ideas.

3. Record using fractions (optional).

For each question, first have students think on their own, then discuss with a partner, and finally have students share their thinking with the class.

Twelve Counters in Three Equal Groups

Direction 1: *Divide the set of twelve counters into three equal groups with all yellow sides showing.*

Questions: *What fractional part of the whole set is represented by each group?* [$\frac{1}{3}$]

How many counters are in $\frac{1}{3}$ of the set? [4]

Record: $\frac{1}{3}$ of 12 = 4

Direction 2: *Flip the counters in one of the three groups.*

Questions: *What fractional part of the whole set is red?* [$\frac{1}{3}$] *Yellow?* [$\frac{2}{3}$]

How many are in $\frac{1}{3}$ of the set? [4]
In $\frac{2}{3}$ of the set? [8]

Record: $\frac{2}{3}$ of 12 = 8

Direction 3: *Flip the counters in another of the three groups.*

Questions: *What fractional part of the whole set is red?* [$\frac{2}{3}$] *Yellow?* [$\frac{1}{3}$]

How many are in $\frac{1}{3}$ of the set? [4] *In $\frac{2}{3}$ of the set?* [8]

Record: [Point to connect to what you've already recorded.]

Twelve Counters in Four Equal Groups

Direction 1: *Rearrange the counters into four equal groups with all yellow sides up. Flip the counters in one group.*

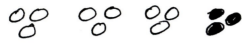

Questions: *What fractional part of the whole set is red?* [$\frac{1}{4}$]
Yellow? [$\frac{3}{4}$]

How many are in $\frac{1}{4}$ of the set? [3]
In $\frac{3}{4}$ of the set? [9]

Record: $\frac{1}{4}$ of 12 = 3

$\frac{3}{4}$ of 12 = 9

Direction 2: *Flip the counters in another group.*

Questions: *What fractional part of the whole set is red?* [$\frac{2}{4}$]
Yellow? [$\frac{2}{4}$]

How many are in $\frac{2}{4}$ of the set? [6]

Record: $\frac{2}{4}$ of 12 = 6

Twelve Counters in Six Equal Groups

Direction 1: *Rearrange the counters into six equal groups with all yellow sides up. Flip the counters in one group.*

Questions: *What fractional part of the whole set is red?* [$\frac{1}{6}$]
Yellow? [$\frac{5}{6}$]

How many are in $\frac{1}{6}$ of the set? [2]
In $\frac{5}{6}$ of the set? [10]

Record: $\frac{1}{6}$ of 12 = 2

$\frac{5}{6}$ of 12 = 10

Direction 2: *Flip the counters in another group.*

Questions: *What fractional part of the whole set is red?* [$\frac{2}{6}$]
Yellow? [$\frac{4}{6}$]

How many are in $\frac{2}{6}$ of the set? [4]
In $\frac{4}{6}$ of the set? [8]

Record: $\frac{2}{6}$ of 12 = 4

$\frac{4}{6}$ of 12 = 8

Direction 3: *Flip the counters in another group.*

Questions: *What fractional part of the whole set is red?* [$\frac{3}{6}$]
Yellow? [$\frac{3}{6}$]

How many are in $\frac{3}{6}$ *of the set?* [6]

Record: $\frac{3}{6}$ *of 12 = 6*

Riddles with Two-Color Counters

For each of these riddles, students answer by showing an arrangement of twelve, two-sided counters.

Riddle 1: Arrange the set of twelve counters so that $\frac{1}{4}$ has red sides showing.

Riddle 2: Show another set with fewer than twelve counters that also has $\frac{1}{4}$ of the set with red sides showing.

Riddle 3: For what other size sets can you show $\frac{1}{4}$ of the set with red sides showing?

Repeat the riddles for $\frac{1}{3}$ and $\frac{1}{6}$.

The Fraction Kit

The fraction kit introduces students to fractions as parts of a whole and has been the mainstay of how I've taught fractions for many years. Here I describe how students each cut their own fraction strips to make their kit, and then what they do with the kits to build their understanding and skills.

Materials

five 3-by-18-inch strips of construction paper in five different colors, 1 set per student
number 10 envelopes, 1 per student
scissors

Cutting the Fraction Kits

Give each student a set of five strips and have them follow your directions to cut and label them. They'll leave one strip whole and cut the others into halves, fourths, eighths, and sixteenths. Decide ahead of time which color strip they'll leave whole and which they'll cut into each fraction. This way, their fraction kits will all be the same. Give directions for cutting.

> **Teaching Tip**
> For a challenge for students who are ready and interested, I repeat the riddles for other fractions: $\frac{2}{8}$, $\frac{5}{6}$, and $\frac{3}{5}$.
> — MBB

> Either cut strips from 12-by-18-inch sheets of construction paper, or purchase fraction kit materials that come with precut strips, a magnetic set for the board, and the number cubes. Visit mathsolutions.com for more information about fraction kits.

DIRECTIONS FOR CUTTING A FRACTION KIT

1. Choose a color and model for the students how to fold it in half, open and label each section $\frac{1}{2}$, cut on the folds so they have two pieces, and write their initials on the back of each piece. Review the rationale for the notation $\frac{1}{2}$ by explaining that they divided the whole into two sections the same size, that each piece is one of the two sections, and that $\frac{1}{2}$ means one of two equal pieces.

2. Choose a color for the second strip and model for the students how to fold it in half and then half again, open and label each section $\frac{1}{4}$, cut on the folds so they have four pieces, and write their initials on the back of each piece. Talk about each piece being one of four, or one-fourth.

3. Choose a color for them to fold into eight sections. Have them label each section $\frac{1}{8}$, cut, and initial.

4. Next they fold a fourth strip into sixteen sections. Have them label each section $\frac{1}{16}$, cut, and initial.

5. Students leave the fifth strip whole, and label it three ways: *1 whole*, *1*, and $\frac{1}{1}$.

Each student now has a fraction kit to use. Having students cut and label the pieces helps them relate the fractional notation to the concrete pieces and compare the sizes of fractional parts. They can see that one-fourth, for example, is larger than one-sixteenth, and they can measure to prove that two of the one-eighth pieces are equivalent to one-fourth. Give them envelopes to keep their kits.

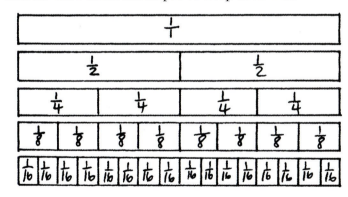

A Fraction Game: Cover Up

After students have cut their fraction kits, introduce this game.

Materials

fraction kit, 1 per student

fraction cube with the faces labeled $\frac{1}{2}, \frac{1}{4}, \frac{1}{8}, \frac{1}{8}, \frac{1}{16}, \frac{1}{16}$, 1 per pair or group

Teaching the Rules of the Game

Explain that this is a game for two or more players. Each player starts with a whole strip. The goal is to be the first to cover up the whole strip completely with other pieces of the fraction kit. No overlapping pieces are allowed.

COVER UP: RULES OF THE GAME

You need: fraction kit

fraction cube with the faces labeled $\frac{1}{2}, \frac{1}{4}, \frac{1}{8}, \frac{1}{8}, \frac{1}{16}, \frac{1}{16}$

Play with a partner. Follow these rules.

1. Both players start with a blue whole strip to cover up.

2. One player rolls the fraction cube. The fraction face up on the cube tells what size piece to place on the whole strip.

3. The player passes the number cube to the other player. Now he or she rolls and repeats the process.

4. Continue until someone has covered the whole strip completely, with no overlaps.

Note: When only a small piece is needed to cover the whole exactly, such as $\frac{1}{8}$ or $\frac{1}{16}$, rolling $\frac{1}{2}$ or $\frac{1}{4}$ won't work. You have to roll exactly what's needed. If you roll a fraction that's too big, don't play and give the fraction cube to the other player.

A Fraction Game: Uncover

Once students are comfortable playing *Cover Up*, I introduce this game.

Materials

fraction kit, 1 per student

fraction cube with the faces labeled $\frac{1}{2}, \frac{1}{4}, \frac{1}{8}, \frac{1}{8}, \frac{1}{16}, \frac{1}{16}$, 1 per pair or group

Teaching the Rules of the Game

This game gives students experience with equivalent fractions. Each student starts with the whole strip covered with the two $\frac{1}{2}$ pieces. The goal is to be the first to uncover the whole strip completely.

UNCOVER: RULES OF THE GAME

You need: fraction kit

fraction cube with the faces labeled $\frac{1}{2}, \frac{1}{4}, \frac{1}{8}, \frac{1}{8}, \frac{1}{16}, \frac{1}{16}$

Play with a partner. Follow these rules.

1. Both players start with a blue whole strip to cover up.

2. One player rolls the fraction cube. The fraction face up on the cube tells what size piece to remove from the whole strip. There are three options: remove a piece (only if there's a piece the size indicated by the fraction face up on the cube), exchange any of the pieces left for equivalent pieces, or do nothing and pass the fraction cube to the next player. (A player may not remove a piece and trade on the same turn, but can do only one or the other.) It's important for students to check that each other exchanges correctly.

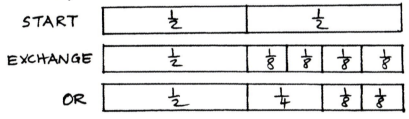

3. The player passes the number cube to the other player.

4. Continue until someone has uncovered the whole strip completely, with no overlaps.

Recording Cover Ups

When playing *Cover Up* and *Uncover*, the only fractions used are the unit fractions $\frac{1}{2}, \frac{1}{4}, \frac{1}{8}$, and $\frac{1}{16}$. When playing, however, students often use the language of those fractions: *I've got just three more sixteenths to take off. I can exchange this one-half piece for two fourths.* After students are familiar with both games, they can be introduced to writing fractions with numerators other than 1 so that the symbolism for these fractions is connected to their concrete experiences. To do this, follow these directions.

1. Ask the students to cover their whole strip with whatever smaller pieces they choose.

2. On the board, record equations for several of their examples. For example, if a student used three $\frac{1}{4}$ pieces and two $\frac{1}{8}$ pieces, record: $\frac{1}{4} + \frac{1}{4} + \frac{1}{4} + \frac{1}{8} + \frac{1}{8} = 1$.

3. Explain how to shorten the equation by counting the fourths and writing $\frac{3}{4}$ and counting the eighths and writing $\frac{2}{8}$: $\frac{3}{4} + \frac{2}{8} = 1$. Have students help you shorten several other of the recordings.

4. Then have them each cover their whole strip with at least five different combinations of pieces, record an equation, and then record it again combining fractions when possible. Have students exchange and check each other's papers.

Extension

Extend the Fraction Kit. Use different-color construction paper strips to have students extend the fraction kit to include thirds, sixths, and twelfths. Have them use a fraction cube with the faces labeled $\frac{1}{2}, \frac{1}{3}, \frac{1}{4}, \frac{1}{6}, \frac{1}{6}, \frac{1}{12}$, to play *Cover Up* and *Uncover*, and to record equations.

Completing Fraction Equations

Give students incomplete fraction equations and have them use their fraction kits to decide how to complete them. This is fairly standard fraction practice, but in this case the practice relates to students' concrete experience with the fraction kits. In all cases, have students explain, orally and in writing, why their answers make sense. These problems can have several forms:

- Give pairs of fractions and have students insert >, <, or = to make a true sentence; for example, $\frac{3}{4} \;\square\; \frac{7}{16}$

- Ask students to supply the missing number to make the fractions equivalent; for example, $\frac{\square}{4} = \frac{6}{8}$.

- Have students write other fractions that are equivalent to the one you give; for example, $\frac{1}{2} = \frac{\square}{\square}$.

- Have students figure out how to write one fraction to replace an addition expression. They make a train of the pieces and then use their fraction kits to cover the pieces with pieces of the same size so that they can write one fraction.

Using Graphs to Build Understanding of Fractions

Use data from class graphs for classroom discussions about fractions. Over time, such discussions help students develop and secure their understanding of fractional concepts. The graphing ideas that follow present variations on graphs about names.

Check the list of graphs in Part 2 on page 176 for other graphing ideas that you may find useful.

Is your last name longer, shorter, or the same length as your first name? (Ask, *What fraction of the class has last names that are longer? Shorter? The same length?*)

How many letters in your last name? (Ask, *What fraction of the class has last names with more than five letters? More than seven? Fewer than six?*)

How many syllables in your first name? (Ask, *What fraction of the class has one syllable in their first names? Two? Three? More? What fraction of the class has fewer than three syllables in their first names?*)

Do you have a middle name? (Ask, *What fraction of the class has a middle name? What fraction doesn't?*)

Were you named after someone special? (Ask, *What fraction of the class was named after someone special? What fraction wasn't?*)

A Problem-Solving Lesson: Sharing Cookies

Students benefit from a variety of sharing problems that call for fractional solutions. They can use circles to share cookies, squares to share brownies, and rectangles to share apple crisp bars. Although the problems presented for each of the shapes can be the same, for some students changing the shapes seems to change the problem and present a new challenge. In the following investigation, students share different numbers of "cookies" among members of a group.

Materials

Fractions with Cookies R See Reproducible R.39
scissors
glue

Introducing

1. **Present or review concepts.** Remind students that when sharing fairly, each person should get the same amount.

2. **Pose a part of the problem or a similar but smaller problem.** Ask, *If I give each group of four students four cookies to share, how many cookies would each person get?* This will most likely be obvious to them, but it will give you the chance to reinforce what is meant by "sharing equally."

3. **Present the investigation.** Then explain that they are to solve the problems of sharing one, two, three, five, and six cookies among four people. Either duplicate the reproducible as shown or post a model for students to replicate. Provide paper circles to represent cookies. Ask them to cut the circles, paste each person's share on a sheet of paper, and record how much each person gets.

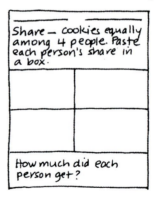

4. **Discuss the task to make sure students understand what they are to do.**

Exploring

Circulate and offer assistance as needed.

Summarizing

Have groups present and explain their solutions.

Extensions

More Sharing Cookies Problems. Extend the investigation by changing the number of cookies students are sharing, by changing the size of the group to six or eight people, or by substituting rectangular "bars"

[R] See Reproducible R.39 for the cookies.

Who Ate More Pizza? Problems. Build on the experience students have gained through thinking about fractional parts of circles in *Sharing Cookies* by having them compare shares of pizza. Vary the problems by changing the number of pieces cut and eaten. Either present the problems to the whole class, or first ask pairs or small groups to consider them before leading a classroom discussion.

> *Joey and Roberta each had individual pizzas that were the same size. Joey cut his into four pieces and ate three of them. Roberta cut hers into six pieces and ate four of them. Who ate more pizza?*
>
> *Mario cut his pizza into eight pieces and ate two of them. Kim cut hers into four pieces and ate one of them. Who ate more pizza?*
>
> *William cut his pizza into eight pieces and ate five of them. Elissa cut hers into six pieces and ate four of them. Who ate more pizza?*
>
> *Sara cut her pizza into three pieces and ate one of them. Tomas cut his into eight pieces and ate two of them. Who ate more pizza?*

To extend this experience into decimals, see "Using Sharing Cookie Problems to Introduce Decimals" on page 441.

A Problem-Solving Lesson: Sharing Brownies

Using the context of brownies, students figure out different ways to divide the grids into halves, fourths, and eighths. Although these are the same fractional parts the students investigated when they constructed fraction kits, using grids gives them another way to build their understanding.

Materials

Fractions on Grids (4-by-4 squares), 1 per student

[R] See Reproducible R.41

Fractions on Grids (6-by-4 rectangles), 1 per student

[R] See Reproducible R.42

Introducing

1. **Present or review concepts.** Remind students that when sharing fairly, each person should get the same amount.

2. **Pose a part of the problem or a similar but smaller problem.** Begin with halves. On the board, draw several 4-by-4 grids. Ask students how to divide the grids in half so that two people would each get the same amount of brownie to eat. Students typically suggest the following three ways.

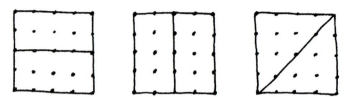

If students don't offer other ways, suggest that they think of ways that don't use one straight cut but that still produce two pieces the same size. Show one of these examples.

3. **Present the investigation.** Have students work in pairs or small groups to find as many other ways as they can to divide the brownies into halves. Distribute worksheets of 4-by-4 grids on which they can record their work.

4. **Discuss the task to make sure students understand what they are to do.**

Exploring
Circulate and offer assistance as needed.

Summarizing
Lead a classroom discussion during which students show their favorite solutions and explain how they know the two parts really are halves.

Extensions
Change the Fractions. Repeat for fourths and again for eighths.

Change the Grids. Repeat with 6-by-4 grids [R] See Reproducible R.42 and ask students to share these rectangular brownies among 2, 3, 4, 6, and 8 people. This provides experience with halves, thirds, fourths, sixths, and eighths.

A Fraction Investigation: Put in Order
Learning to compare and order fractions is important to developing an understanding of fractions. Students must recognize that the size of the denominator affects the size of fractional parts of the same whole—the larger the denominator, the smaller the pieces. Students must also be able to determine when fractions are equivalent—that two-fourths, for example, represents the same part of a whole as does three-sixths, four-eighths, and so on. In this investigation students place fractions in order from smallest to largest. *Put in Order* is an appropriate follow-up to the fraction kit investigations after students have made kits and have played *Cover Up* and *Uncover*. When first experiencing *Put in Order*, it's helpful for students to use their fraction kits to help them reason.

Materials
4-by-6-inch index cards, 12 for the initial investigation and more for extensions
fraction kit, 1 per student

Teaching the Lesson
Write twelve fractions (see below) on 4-by-6-inch index cards, one fraction per card, large enough for everyone to see. Prop one card up where everyone can see it. Tell the students that their task is to place the rest of the fractions in order from smallest to largest. Show the cards one at a time, each time asking a student to place it and explain their reasoning.

The following set of fractions works well for a first lesson with this investigation. Begin by propping up the card with $\frac{1}{2}$ on it to provide a familiar landmark fraction to use.

$$\frac{1}{16}, \ \frac{1}{8}, \ \frac{3}{16}, \ \frac{1}{4}, \ \frac{3}{8}, \ \frac{1}{2}, \ \frac{5}{8}, \ \frac{3}{4}, \ \frac{15}{16}, \ \frac{1}{1}, \ \frac{9}{8}, \ \frac{3}{2}$$

Repeat with different sets of fractions or using previous sets but presenting the fractions in a different order. When making sets of cards, avoid including equivalent fractions so students don't try to order two fractions that have the same value.

$$\frac{1}{8}, \ \frac{1}{6}, \ \frac{1}{4}, \ \frac{1}{3}, \ \frac{1}{2}, \ \frac{2}{3}, \ \frac{3}{4}, \ \frac{15}{16}, \ \frac{8}{8}, \ \frac{17}{16}, \ \frac{7}{6}, \ \frac{4}{3}$$

$$\frac{1}{16}, \ \frac{1}{12}, \ \frac{2}{8}, \ \frac{3}{8}, \ \frac{3}{6}, \ \frac{3}{4}, \ \frac{7}{8}, \ \frac{11}{12}, \ \frac{3}{3}, \ \frac{17}{16}, \ \frac{9}{8}, \ \frac{5}{4}$$

Extensions
Students Create Put-in-Order Cards. After the class is familiar with the investigation, have students work in pairs or small groups and create sets of fractions to present to the class. Have them first justify in writing the order of their fractions; after you check their reasoning, have them lead the investigation for the rest of the class.

Fractions on a Number Line. In the *Put in Order* investigation, students don't pay attention to positioning the fractions according to their sizes. Use the same cards to shift the students' thinking to positioning the fractions as they would appear on a number line. On the board, draw a line equal in length to two fraction kit whole strips. Mark and label points for *0, 1,* and *2.*

Then use the fraction cards from *Put in Order* and have students use fraction kit pieces to locate the fractions. For each, have a student come and eyeball where the fraction might go; then check with the fraction pieces.

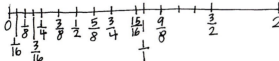

For seatwork, have students reproduce the number line on a smaller number line that fits on a piece of paper.

Mental Calculation with Fractions

A great deal of emphasis traditionally has been put on paper-and-pencil algorithms for addition, subtraction, multiplication, and division of fractions. The following suggestions offer ways to have students calculate mentally with fractions. The emphasis shifts from paper-and-pencil computation with the goal of arriving at exact answers to mental calculation with the goal of arriving at estimates and being able to explain why they're reasonable.

Closest to 0, $\frac{1}{2}$, or 1?

Give students fractions that are less than 1—$\frac{3}{8}$, $\frac{1}{6}$, or $\frac{5}{7}$, for example—and have them decide if the fraction is closest to 0, $\frac{1}{2}$, or 1. Have students discuss in pairs or groups and then report back to the class, explaining their reasoning.

For an individual assignment, give students a collection of a dozen or so fractions to sort into three groups: closest to 0, closest to $\frac{1}{2}$, and closest to 1. Students should record their answers and write about the methods they used to sort their fractions.

Fractions in Contexts

Give students problems for which they are to find estimates mentally. Have students work in pairs or groups so they can talk about their ideas. As with all investigations, have students defend their answers by explaining their methods.

Finding Fractional Parts

In order to do these problems, students should be able to figure mentally fractional parts such as $\frac{1}{3}$ of 30, $\frac{1}{2}$ of 24, and $\frac{1}{4}$ of 32.

A full tank of gas holds 14 gallons. The fuel gauge reads $\frac{1}{4}$ full. About how many gallons are left? (If you get 20 miles per gallon, how much farther can you drive?)

Jill's mother and aunt together have agreed to split equally $\frac{1}{2}$ of the cost of a baseball glove with Jill. The glove costs $25.99. About how much does Jill need to contribute?

A $7.98 shirt is on sale at $\frac{1}{3}$ off. About how much will Tony save if he buys it?

Have students make up situations such as these for their classmates to solve.

Fraction Word Problems

Have students try the following problems. Be sure to keep the emphasis on reasonable answers and on the different methods they used.

A bookshelf measures $2\frac{1}{2}$ feet. How many could you fit against a wall that measures $14\frac{1}{2}$ feet?

If it takes $1\frac{1}{4}$ yards of fabric to make a cape and each of the six people on the cheering squad needs a cape, how much fabric should you buy?

Then have them try some of their textbook word problems, not to calculate exact answers, but to arrive at acceptable estimates and to be able to explain their reasoning.

Strategies for Operations

Encourage students to invent their own strategies for mentally estimating sums and differences. You may want to present a sample strategy to the class. For example, estimating whether fractions are close to 0, $\frac{1}{2}$, or 1 can help in estimating sums. To estimate $\frac{12}{13} + \frac{4}{9}$, you could think: *$\frac{12}{13}$ is close to 1 and $\frac{4}{9}$ is close to $\frac{1}{2}$, so the sum is about 1$\frac{1}{2}$. But it's a little less, since the actual numbers were less than 1 and $\frac{1}{2}$.* Try some exercises with the whole class and then give small groups problems to discuss and estimate together.

In the same way, model techniques for estimating products and quotients. For example, to estimate the answer to $2\frac{7}{8} \times 15\frac{3}{4}$, you can think: *$2\frac{7}{8}$ is close to 3 and $15\frac{3}{4}$ is close to 16, and 3 × 16 is 48. So the answer is close to but less than 48.*

Additional Instructional Suggestions

The following instructional suggestions are for small groups of students. After students are familiar with the activities, some of the suggestions are suitable as independent investigations for individual or partner work, and for choice time explorations.

Fractions Close to $\frac{1}{2}$

For each situation, decide whether the best estimate is more or less than $\frac{1}{2}$. Record your conclusions and reasoning.

1. When pitching, Joe struck out 7 of 17 batters.
2. Sally made 8 baskets out of 11 free throws.
3. Bill made 5 field goals out of 9 attempts.
4. Maria couldn't collect at 4 of the 35 homes on her paper route.
5. Diane made 8 hits in 15 times at bat.

Make up three situations and exchange papers with a classmate.

Building Rectangles

You need: tiles, about 10 of each color
      half-inch grid paper, several sheets   **R** See Reproducible R.3
      markers or crayons, 1 each of red, yellow, green, and blue

Use tiles to build a rectangle that is $\frac{1}{2}$ red, $\frac{1}{4}$ yellow, and $\frac{1}{4}$ green. Record and label it on grid paper.

Find at least one other rectangle that also works. Build and record.

Now use the tiles to build each of the rectangles below. Build and record each in at least two ways.

$\frac{1}{3}$ green, $\frac{2}{3}$ blue

$\frac{1}{6}$ red, $\frac{1}{6}$ green, $\frac{1}{3}$ blue, $\frac{1}{3}$ yellow

$\frac{1}{2}$ red, $\frac{1}{4}$ green, $\frac{1}{8}$ yellow, $\frac{1}{8}$ blue

$\frac{1}{5}$ red, $\frac{4}{5}$ yellow

$\frac{1}{8}$ red, $\frac{3}{8}$ yellow, $\frac{1}{2}$ blue

 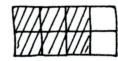

These rectangles show two solutions for $\frac{3}{4}$ red, $\frac{1}{4}$ yellow.

Fraction Riddles

You need: tiles, about 10 of each color
half-inch grid paper, several sheets **R** See Reproducible R.3
markers or crayons, 1 each of red, green, blue, and yellow

Solve each of the following riddles.

Riddle 1: A rectangle is $\frac{1}{2}$ red, $\frac{1}{5}$ green, $\frac{1}{10}$ blue, and the rest yellow. How much of the rectangle is yellow? Draw the rectangle on grid paper and record the fraction that tells which part is yellow.

Riddle 2: A rectangle is $\frac{3}{5}$ red. The rest is blue and yellow but not in equal amounts. What could the rectangle look like? Record.

Riddle 3: A rectangle is $\frac{1}{2}$ red and $\frac{1}{3}$ blue. Also, it has one green tile and one yellow tile. What could the rectangle look like? What fractional part is green? Yellow? Record.

Make up three riddles like these for others to solve.

Teaching Tip
This investigation is suitable for students after they have tried the Building Rectangles investigation.
—MSB

Rod Relationships

You need: Cuisenaire rods, 1 set

The yellow rod is half as long as the orange rod. (Prove this to yourself with the rods.) This relationship can be written:

$$\frac{1}{2}o = y$$

Find all the other pairs of halves you can with the rods and build them. Record each.

Then do the same with thirds. For example, it takes three light green rods to make a train as long as the blue rod, so light green is one-third of blue. (Prove it with the rods.) Record like this:

$$\frac{1}{3}e = g$$

Find all the fractional relationships you can for halves, thirds, fourths, fifths, and so on, up to tenths. Explain why you think you've found them all.

Build the Yellow Hexagon

You need: pattern blocks, 1 set

Find all the different ways you can build the yellow hexagon from different assortments of blocks. Count only different combinations of blocks. For example, if you use two blues and two greens, that combination counts as only one way even if the arrangements look different.

These count as one way.

Use fractions to record the different ways you found. For example, the green triangle is $\frac{1}{6}$ of the hexagon and the red trapezoid is $\frac{1}{2}$ of the hexagon. Therefore, if you build the hexagon using one red and three greens, you can record as follows: $\frac{1}{2} + \frac{1}{6} + \frac{1}{6} + \frac{1}{6} = 1$. Also, you can shorten that by combining the three greens into one fraction: $\frac{1}{2} + \frac{3}{6} = 1$. Record each of the ways you built the yellow hexagon, recording each in different ways.

Wipeout

You need: pattern blocks, 1 set
fraction cube with the faces labeled $\frac{1}{2}$, $\frac{1}{3}$, $\frac{1}{3}$, $\frac{1}{6}$, $\frac{1}{6}$, $\frac{1}{6}$

This is a two-person game. The goal is to be the first to discard your blocks. You each should start with the same number of hexagons, either one, two, or three. Follow these rules:

1. Take turns rolling the cube.

2. You have three options on each turn: remove a block (only if it's the fractional part of the hexagon indicated by the fraction face up on the cube), exchange any of your remaining blocks for equivalent blocks, or do nothing and pass the cube to your partner. You may not remove a block and trade on the same turn—you can do only one or the other.

Be sure to pay attention to each other's trades to make sure they are done correctly.

Assessing Understanding of Fractions

Observing students during classroom discussions and while they are working on independent investigations provides information about their understanding and skills. Also, one-on-one conversations with students reveal their individual understanding, misconceptions, and gaps, and provides valuable information that isn't always evident from classroom observations. The following suggestions can be used for both assessment approaches.

Observing Students

During classroom discussions and when students are working on the independent tasks, circulate, observe, and question them about their thinking and reasoning.

Individual Assessments

The following written assignments offer ways to find out about students' understanding of fractions.

1. Before beginning instruction, ask students to write what they know about fractions. Have them do this again at the end of the instructional unit or even midway through. Return papers to the students and ask them to reflect on their learning.

2. Assign problems such as those suggested for whole-class lessons. Ask students to present solutions in writing and explain their reasoning.

3. Ask the students to draw pictures to show the following fractional parts:

   a. $\frac{2}{5}$ of a set of circles are shaded

   b. $\frac{4}{5}$ of the squares are red

   c. $\frac{3}{4}$ of the triangles are blue

   d. $\frac{1}{3}$ of the balls are footballs

   e. $\frac{4}{9}$ of the fruit are apples

4. Show students a pattern block design made with three green triangles, six blue parallelograms, three red trapezoids, and one yellow hexagon. Ask students to respond in writing to the problem: *What fraction of the design is blue?* (Caldwell 1995).

   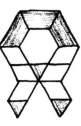

5. Ask students to choose the best estimate for the answer to $\frac{12}{13} + \frac{7}{8}$.

   a. 1

   b. 2

   c. 19

   d. 21

Decimals

About Decimals

Decimals make it possible to use our place-value system of notation to represent fractions with denominators of ten, hundred, thousand, and so on. The investigations in this section assume that students have learned about fractions and have a base of understanding that can be expanded to incorporate the symbolism of decimals. They suggest ways to connect students' former experiences to the new notation.

When students are learning about decimals, it's helpful to distinguish between the way decimals are commonly read and what they mean. It's natural to read decimals such as 2.7 and 0.34, for example, as "two point seven" and "point thirty-four." However, students should know that these decimals can also be read as "two and seven-tenths" and "thirty-four hundredths," and they should be able to relate decimal fractions to common fractions. Paying attention to this difference reinforces the fact that decimals are fractions written in different symbolic notation.

The lessons in this section suggest several ways to introduce students to decimals and to help them discover how decimals relate to our number system. The emphasis is on helping students make sense of decimals in several different ways and building a foundation of understanding from which students can later learn about repeating decimals, scientific notation, and other related topics.

The ideas in this section don't provide a comprehensive guide for teaching decimals. Rather, they offer models of ways to introduce ideas about decimals, suggest problem situations that engage students, and give alternative methods for assessing what students understand. Not included are suggestions to help develop understanding and skill with decimal operations.

Mathematical Practices

Developing understanding and skills with decimals should support the mathematical practices described in the Common Core and other standards documents for students in all grades. The mathematical practices should be connected to the content standards by engaging students in solving problems, reasoning, making conjectures, applying math to everyday life, using appropriate tools, communicating precisely, looking for patterns and structure, and looking for regularity in mathematical methods. The investigations in this section provide ways to make connections between practice and content standards.

Mathematical Content

Instruction with decimals begins in grade 4. The standards that focus on building understanding are especially important for helping students engage with the mathematical practices. Below are content designations that align with the Common Core and other standards documents.

Grade 4: Understand decimal notation for fractions with denominators of 10 and 100; compare decimals to hundredths.

For comprehensive help with teaching decimals, you might be interested in a Teaching Arithmetic resource that I wrote with Carrie De Francisco: *Lessons for Decimals and Percents* (2002). Visit mathsolutions.com for more information.

Grade 5: Read, write, and compare decimals to thousandths; perform operations with decimals to hundredths.

Grade 6: Fluently add, subtract, multiply, and divide multidigit numbers; apply and extend previous understandings of numbers to the system of rational numbers; understand ordering of decimals.

Grade 7: Develop a unified understanding of number, recognizing fractions, decimals (that have a finite or a repeating decimal representation), and percents as different representations of rational numbers; know that the decimal form of fractions terminates in zeros or eventually repeats.

Whole-Class Instruction

These suggestions for whole-class instruction introduce students to important and basic ideas relating to decimals. They are organized into three categories: using sharing cookie problems to introduce decimals, a geometric perspective on decimals: decimals on grids, and mental calculation with decimals.

A Problem-Solving Lesson: Sharing Cookie Problems to Introduce Decimals

Students solve division word problems of sharing cookies for which they can use fractions to express the remainders. They compare the answers to the decimal answers a calculator would give. These problems provide a preliminary decimal experience. The goal isn't for students to understand decimal and fractional equivalents, but rather to begin to build their intuition about how fractions and decimals relate.

Materials

    calculators, 1 per student or pair
    Fractions with Cookies, optional **R** See Reproducible R.39

Introducing

1. **Present or review concepts.** Tell students that they'll solve some division problems in two ways, first without a calculator and then with a calculator. Be sure they know how to use a calculator to solve division problems.

2. **Pose a part of the problem or a similar but smaller problem.** Give students a problem to solve in pairs or small groups: *Two children share seven cookies equally. How much does each child get?* Have students solve this and report their solutions and strategies. If it would be helpful, have students actually cut out circles (to represent the cookies) and share them, cutting cookies as needed. Some may report the answer with a remainder (3 R1). Talk about how to share the remaining cookie to establish the answer that each child gets $3\frac{1}{2}$ cookies.

    Then ask what answer they think they'd get if they divided on a calculator. Have them use calculators for $7 \div 2$ and discuss the answer of 3.5. Tell them that this number is called a decimal and is how the calculator represents a number that's greater than 3 but less than 4, and that 3.5 means the same as $3\frac{1}{2}$.

3. **Present the investigation.** Tell students that they are to solve five sharing cookie problems in two ways—figuring out the answers on their own and then using a calculator—and compare the answers.

    Share seven cookies among three students. How much does each student get?

    Share nine cookies between two people. How much does each person get?

For this sample lesson, I used the Introducing/Exploring/ Summarizing model for problem-solving lessons, described in Part 2 on page 135.

This investigation is an appropriate extension for "A Problem-Solving Lesson: Sharing Cookies" in Part 3 on page 428.

Share five cookies among four students. How much does each student get?

Share seven cookies among four students. How much does each student get?

Divide one large cookie among ten people. How much does each person get?

4. Discuss the task to make sure students understand what they are to do.

Exploring
Circulate and offer assistance as needed. If students need help or want to verify their solutions, provide them the circles and scissors to cut "cookies."

Summarizing
Lead a classroom discussion about what students notice about the decimal answers. Ask for conjectures about how the fractions in their answers compare with the decimals in the calculator answers.

A Problem-Solving Lesson: Decimals on Grids
Some students benefit from being able to visualize decimals. A 10-by-10 grid is useful for introducing tenths and hundredths, helping students see the relationship between decimals and common fractions, and giving them initial experiences operating with decimals.

Materials
10-by-10 grids, 1 per student and more as needed **R** See Reproducible R.43
markers or crayons

Introducing
1. **Present or review concepts.** Post or draw three 10-by-10 grids so everyone can see them. Talk with the students about the grids—the number of rows, columns, and small squares in each.

2. **Pose a part of the problem or a similar but smaller problem.** On one grid, shade the first three columns of squares, as shown. Ask: *What fractional part of the grid have I shaded?*

Students may respond with three-tenths or thirty-hundredths. Record the fractions and have the students explain why those fractions make sense. If students suggest only one possibility, then record the other and have them discuss why this also makes sense. Then show the class how to represent these fractions as decimals: 0.3 and 0.30. Talk about the differences between these two numerals.

Repeat with two other examples. For one, shade three small squares and again ask, *What fractional part of the grid have I*

For this sample lesson, I used the Introducing/Exploring/Summarizing model for problem-solving lessons, described in Part 2 on page 135.

FYI
I've often been surprised by students' lack of experience with 10-by-10 grids. It seems obvious to me that ten rows and ten columns produce one hundred small squares, but this isn't always obvious to students.
— MSB

FYI
Teachers have often asked me which is correct when writing decimals—.03 or 0.03. Both are mathematically correct. The benefit of using 0.03 is that it reinforces the whole number part of the decimal that, in this case, is zero.
— MSB

shaded? As before, record the common fraction, $\frac{3}{100}$, and the decimal fraction, 0.03. Choosing this example gives you the opportunity to discuss the importance of the placement of the digits.

Next shade two columns of ten squares and seven additional squares on the next column. Have students explain why $\frac{27}{100}$ makes sense and show them how to write it as a decimal. Also point out that this could be written as $\frac{2}{10} + \frac{7}{100}$. Have students discuss why this makes sense. Write both representations as decimals: 0.27 and 0.2 + 0.07.

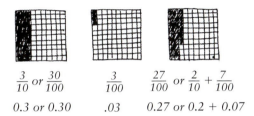

$\frac{3}{10}$ or $\frac{30}{100}$ $\quad$ $\frac{3}{100}$ $\quad$ $\frac{27}{100}$ or $\frac{2}{10} + \frac{7}{100}$

0.3 or 0.30 $\quad$ .03 $\quad$ 0.27 or 0.2 + 0.07

3. **Present the investigation.** Distribute to each student the reproducible that has nine 10-by-10 grids on it. Direct them to color in some rows and/or squares on each, as you did, and record how much they colored using fractions and decimals. Encourage students to record the different ways possible to represent the portion of the grid they shade.

Exploring

Circulate and offer assistance as needed. Check that students are representing how much they shade in more than one way.

Summarizing

Have students report their findings and recommendations in a classroom discussion. One way to do this is to have a student come up and shade in a 10-by-10 grid from his or her paper and have the others name the matching fractions and decimals.

Extensions

Relating Decimals to Money. It's useful to relate the decimal notation you've presented to our system for recording money. Ask students to think of the 10-by-10 grid as $1.00. Discuss why pennies can be thought of as hundredths and dimes as tenths. Compare notations to see how they are alike and different. For example, on a grid, 0.14 can be described as one column and four extra squares or as fourteen squares; similarly with money, $0.14 can be one dime and four pennies or fourteen pennies. However, while three columns on a grid can be represented as 0.3, three dimes isn't written as $0.3, but as $0.30. These are social conventions that students must learn.

Relating Decimals to Mixed Numbers. Introduce how to use grids to represent numerals. Show how to shade on three grids to show $2\frac{3}{10}$, or 2.3.

2.3 or $2\frac{3}{10}$

Teaching Tip
Sometimes students ask if they have to color in rows or parts of rows as I did, but instead if they can color squares in a design or more randomly. I ask them to color in as I did so that I could have a sense just by looking of about how many squares were colored in before counting them. The goal is to build some intuitive connection between part of a grid and its decimal representation, and this isn't effectively done by coloring in scattered squares.
— MSB

Comparing and Ordering Decimals. Students can use the grids to compare decimals. When they focus on the visual representations of decimals, they are less apt to mistakenly interpret that 0.52, for example, is greater than 0.6. Also, coloring on grids helps reinforce that decimals such as 0.4 and 0.40 are equivalent. Give students pairs of decimals to compare, or assign a page from their textbook and have them use the grids to decide for each. Also, give students several sets of decimals to put in order, such as 0.15, 0.2, 0.46, and 0.3.

Writing Decimals for Fractions with Denominators Other Than 10 or 100. Talk with students about how to use decimals to represent common fractions that are not expressed as tenths or hundredths. Begin with one-fourth, one-half, and three-fourths so that students can relate these fractions to money.

Multiplying Tenths by Tenths. Introduce students to using rectangular arrays to multiply tenths by tenths. It may be necessary to review how arrays model multiplication of whole numbers.

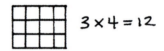

The following two examples show how to use grids to multiply decimals. Examples such as these may help students see why multiplying tenths by tenths produces hundredths.

Mental Calculation with Decimals

A great deal of emphasis traditionally has been put on paper-and-pencil algorithms for addition, subtraction, multiplication, and division of decimals. The focus is often put on how to do the problem rather than on what makes sense. The following suggestions offer ways to have students calculate mentally with decimals. The emphasis shifts from paper-and-pencil computation with the goal of exact answers to mental calculation with the goal of arriving at estimates and being able to explain why they're reasonable.

Closest to 0, 0.5, or 1?

Give students decimals that are less than 1—0.4, 0.15, or 0.7, for example—and have them decide if they are closest to 0, 0.5, or 1. Have students discuss in groups and then report back to the class, explaining their reasoning. Include decimals with tenths, hundredths, and, if the students are able, thousandths.

Decimals in Contexts

Give students problems for which they are to make estimates mentally. Have students work in pairs or groups so they can talk about their ideas. As with all investigations, have students defend their answers by explaining their methods.

Jenny started jogging. Her dad clocked her distances by car. On Monday, she ran 1.4 miles; on Tuesday, she ran 2.2 miles; and on Wednesday, she ran 1.9 miles. About how many miles did she run in the three days?

Raul bought three small bags of potato chips that cost $0.69 each. About how much did they cost altogether?

Maria had $4.65 in nickels. About how many nickels did she have?

Then have students try some of their textbook word problems, not to calculate exact answers, but to arrive at acceptable estimates and be able to explain their reasoning.

Strategies for Operations

Encourage students to invent their own strategies for calculating mentally. You may want to present a sample strategy to the class for estimating products and quotients. For example, to estimate the answer to 3.24×4.9, you can say that 3.24 is close to 3 and 4.9 is close to 5, and 3×5 is 15. Then you can decide if the answer will be greater than or less than 15. Do some exercises with the whole class and then give pairs or groups some problems to discuss and estimate together. After students make estimates, have them use a calculator check to check how close they were.

Teaching Tip
Some students figure out the exact answers to problems like these, either because they're unaccustomed to giving estimates for answers or because they were able to figure out the exact answer mentally. Accept all answers and talk about which are exact and which estimates are reasonable.

— MSB

For more on using a menu to structure independent work, see "Starting Point 20: Four Structures for Organizing and Managing Classroom Instruction" in Part 1 on page 111.

Additional Instructional Suggestions

The following instructional suggestions are for small groups of students. After students are familiar with the activities, some of the suggestions are suitable as independent investigations for individual or partner work, and for choice time explorations.

Decimals in the Newspaper

You need: a newspaper

Look for articles in which decimals are used. Choose one to present to the class. In your presentation, explain the meaning of the decimals.

Multiplication Puzzlers

You need: a calculator

For each problem shown here, find the missing number by using your calculator and the problem-solving strategy of guessing and checking. Don't solve the problems by dividing, but instead see how many guesses each problem takes you. Record all of your guesses.

For example, to solve $4 \times \underline{\hspace{1cm}} = 87$, you might start with 23 and then adjust.

Solve:

$5 \times \underline{\hspace{1cm}} = 96$

$6 \times \underline{\hspace{1cm}} = 106$

$4 \times \underline{\hspace{1cm}} = 63$

$8 \times \underline{\hspace{1cm}} = 98$

$4 \times \underline{\hspace{0.5cm}} = 87$

$4 \times 23 = 92$
$4 \times 22 = 88$
$4 \times 21 = 84$
$4 \times 21.5 = 86$
$4 \times 21.6 = 86.4$
$4 \times 21.7 = 86.8$
$4 \times 21.8 = 87.2$
$4 \times 21.74 = 86.96$
$4 \times 21.75 = 87$ ★
It took 9 guesses

Adding to 1

You need: calculator

Try this first: Enter the number 3 into the calculator. Press the + key and then press the = key. (You should still see the number 3 displayed.) Continue to press the = key and notice that each time the calculator will add 3 over and over and you'll see 3, 6, 9, 12, 15, and so on. Try this with other numbers as well.

The challenge is to find numbers to enter on a calculator so that by following the procedure of pressing the + key and then pressing the = key over and over, the display will eventually show 1 on the display. For example, enter .5 and then press the + key, followed by pressing the = key twice. The total is 1. You can record this: .5 + .5 = 1.

Find as many different ways as you can to repeat the same addends and get a total of 1. Record each.

The Place-Value Game

You need: 1–6 die or 0–9 spinner

Play with a partner or small group. The goal of this game is to make the largest number possible. Each player should draw a game board as shown:

— — — — . — —

Players take turns rolling the die or spinning the spinner. Each time a number comes up, every player writes it in one space on his or her game board. Once written, the number cannot be moved. After you've all filled in six blanks, each player reads aloud his or her number. The player with the greatest number is the winner.

For an online interview protocol for assessing students about decimals, visit Math Reasoning Inventory (mathreasoninginventory.com). This is a free online tool that I developed with a team of colleagues. At the site, you can also view video clips of students responding to the questions.

Assessing Understanding of Decimals

Observing students during classroom discussions and while they are working on independent investigations provides information about their understanding and skills. Also, one-on-one conversations with students reveal their individual understanding, misconceptions, and gaps, and provides valuable information that isn't always evident from classroom observations. The following suggestions can be used for both assessment approaches.

Observing Students

During classroom discussions and when students are working on the independent tasks, circulate, observe, and, at times, question them about their thinking and reasoning. Look and listen for evidence of students' understanding of decimals and their relation to fractions.

Individual Assessments

Give assessments that reveal students' thinking and understanding of decimals. The following are several suggestions.

1. Before beginning instruction, ask students to write what they know about decimals. Have them do this again at the end of the instructional unit or even midway through. Return papers to the students and ask them to reflect on their learning.

2. Ask students to write about the ways our systems for decimals and money are alike and different. Ask them to include examples.

3. Assign problems such as those suggested for whole-class lessons. Ask students to present solutions in writing and to explain their reasoning.

Percents

About Percents

Students have many experiences with percents before they study them formally in school. They know that a 50 percent sale means that prices are cut in half and that a 10 percent sale doesn't give as much savings. They understand what it means to earn a 90 percent grade on a test. They hear on TV that some tires get 40 percent more wear, that a tennis player gets 64 percent of her first serves in, that there's a 70 percent chance of rain tomorrow. Common to these sorts of experiences is that percents are presented in the context of situations that occur in students' daily lives.

The goal for instruction in percents should be to help students learn to use percents appropriately and effectively in problem situations. This means that when given a situation that involves percents, students should be able to reason mathematically to arrive at an answer, to explain why that answer is reasonable, and to make a decision about the situation based on the answer.

The investigations presented in this section are designed to build on what students already know and to help them extend their understanding of how to reason with percents. The ideas don't provide a comprehensive guide for teaching percents. Rather, they offer models of ways to introduce ideas about percents, suggest problem situations that engage students, and give alternative methods for assessing what students understand.

For comprehensive help with teaching percents, you might be interested in a Teaching Arithmetic resource that I wrote with Carrie De Francisco, *Lessons for Decimals and Percents* (2002).

Mathematical Practices

Developing understanding and skills with percents should support the mathematical practices described in the Common Core and other standards documents for students in all grades. The mathematical practices should be connected to the content standards by engaging students in solving problems, reasoning, making conjectures, applying math to everyday life, using appropriate tools, communicating precisely, looking for patterns and structure, and looking for regularity in mathematical methods. The investigations in this section provide ways to make connections between practice and content standards.

Mathematical Content

Formal instruction with percents typically appears in grades 6 and 7. The standards that focus on building understanding are especially important for helping students engage with the mathematical practices. Below are content designations that align with the Common Core and other standards documents.

Grade 6: Find a percent of a quantity as a rate per 100 (e.g., 30% of a quantity means $\frac{30}{100}$ times the quantity); solve problems involving finding the whole, given a part and the percent.

Grade 7: Use proportional relationships to solve real-world percent problems.

Whole-Class Instruction

These suggestions for whole-class instruction introduce students to important and basic ideas relating to percents. They are organized into four categories: introducing percents in contexts, a geometric perspective on percents, using graphs to build understanding of percents, and mental calculation with percents.

A Problem-Solving Lesson: Sense or Nonsense?

It makes sense for formal instruction on percents to build on what students already know. Investigations should expand students' knowledge from their daily life experiences into more general understanding. In this lesson, students decide whether statements that include percents are reasonable and explain their reasoning.

Materials

Sense or Nonsense statements, either posted or duplicated, 1 per pair or group   **R**   See Reproducible R.44

Introducing

1. **Present or review concepts.** Using contexts that are familiar to the students, discuss examples of 100 percent, 50 percent, and 0 percent. (For example, I ate 100 percent of the apple; I ate 50 percent of the apple; I ate 0 percent of the apple.)

2. **Pose a part of the problem or a similar but smaller problem.** Read the first *Sense or Nonsense* statement to the class: *Mr. Bragg says he is right 100% of the time. Do you think Mr. Bragg is bragging? Why?* Ask students to talk with their partner or group and then lead a classroom discussion. Have several students report their reasons for deciding that Mr. Bragg is bragging.

3. **Present the investigation.** First students record a statement about why Mr. Bragg was bragging. Then they discuss the rest in pairs or groups and record their conclusions.

4. **Discuss the task to make sure students understand what they are to do.** It's helpful to have one or two students restate the directions.

FYI
For this initial statement, students' typically agree but express their ideas differently. There are two benefits from having several students report—it reinforces that there are different "right" explanations, and students hear options that can be helpful to them as they craft their own reasons.

— MSB

SENSE OR NONSENSE

1. Mr. Bragg says he is right 100% of the time. Do you think Mr. Bragg is bragging? Why?

2. The Todd family ate out last Saturday. The bill was $36.00. Would a 50% tip be too much to leave? Why?

3. Joe loaned Jeff a dollar. He said the interest would be 75% a day. Is this a pretty good deal for Joe? Why?

4. Cindy spends 100% of her allowance on candy. Do you think this is sensible? Why?

5. The Never Miss basketball team members made 10% of the baskets they tried. Do you think they should change their name? Why?

6. Sarah missed 10 problems on the science test. Do you think her percent is high enough for her to earn an A? Why?

7. Rosa signs up customers for her sister's lawn mowing business. She gets to keep 25% of whatever her sister earns. Do you think this is a good deal? Why?

8. The weather reporter said, "There's a one hundred percent chance of rain for tomorrow." Is this a reasonable prediction for this month? Why?

9. Ms. Green was complaining, "Prices have gone up at least two hundred percent this past year." Do you think she is exaggerating? Why?

10. A store advertised, "Best sale ever, 10% discount on all items." Is this a good sale? Why?

Exploring

1. **Offer assistance as needed.** Observe the interaction and listen to how groups organize working together, the ideas they discuss, and the strategies they use. Listen for different explanations that could be useful for a later classroom discussion. Sometimes students in pairs or groups have different ideas. I tell them that it's OK for them to record their own ideas.

2. **Provide an extension to groups that finish more quickly than others.** Ask them to think of two more statements that you could add to the ones on the list.

Summarizing

1. **Have pairs or groups review their work and think about what to report in a classroom discussion.**

2. **Initiate a classroom discussion.** Have groups report how they organized working together. Ask if they ever had different opinions and how they resolved them.

3. **Ask groups to report their results or solutions, explaining their reasoning or strategies.** For each statement, first discuss whether the students agree or disagree with the statement, and then have several students present their ideas.

A Problem-Solving Lesson: What Percent Is Shaded?

This investigation presents students with a spatial model for thinking about percents. It is valuable for introducing or reinforcing the idea that percents are parts of one hundred and gives students the opportunity to estimate areas and express their estimates as percents.

Materials

transparencies of the sheet of 10-by-10 grids, enough so you can cut the grids apart and give each student one grid **R** See Reproducible R.43
sheet of squares the size of the 10-by-10 transparencies, each with a region shaded, 1 per student
How Much Is Shaded? **R** See Reproducible R.45

Introducing

1. **Present or review concepts.** Draw three squares on the board and label them *100%*, *50%*, and *0%*. Discuss how you could shade in part of each square to represent the percent. Demonstrate or have students come up and demonstrate.

2. **Pose a part of the problem or a similar but smaller problem.** Refer students to the first square on the *How Much Is Shaded?* sheet. Ask them to estimate the percent of the square that's shaded. Have them discuss in pairs or small groups and then report their estimates.

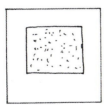

Next show students a transparent 10-by-10 grid. Ask them to discuss among themselves how to use the grid to figure out the shaded portion of the first square. It's important to reinforce for students that *percent* means "part of one hundred." Since there are one hundred small squares on the grid, the number of small squares that are shaded tells what percent of the grid has been shaded.

Repeat with the second shape on the worksheet. Again, have students estimate and then use their transparent grids to figure.

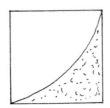

Management Tip
Working in pairs supports students, but each student should have a copy of the shapes so they can also figure individually.

— MSB

3. **Present the investigation.** Direct students to figure out exactly or make an estimate of the area of each shaded shape. They should write the percentage shaded below each square.

4. **Discuss the task to make sure students understand what they are to do.**

Exploring
Offer assistance as needed. For students who finish more quickly, suggest that they trace a square on another sheet of paper, shade a portion, and estimate what percent they shaded.

Summarizing
1. **Have pairs review their work.** Ask them to decide which were which were the three most difficult shapes to figure out.

2. **Review and have students report.** Review the percentages. Be sure to talk about the shapes that gave students difficulty.

Extension
Students Draw Shapes. Have students create shapes for others to try. Have them draw their shapes on index cards, first drawing a 2-inch square so it's the same size as the squares on their sheet.

Using Graphs to Build Understanding of Percents

Creating class graphs can provide an abundance of information for engaging students with percents. See the following graphing ideas and statistics about each topic. For each graph, students compare the statistical result of their class samples with the percentages reported for the population at large. Have students answer the following questions for each graph. (For each graph, insert the relevant piece of information in the blank.)

For more information about making class graphs, see "Graphing in the Classroom" in Part 2 on page 174.

- How many students indicated _____?

- Is this more or less than 50 percent? Explain how you know.

- About what percent of our class reported _____?

- Explain how you figured out that percent?

- The national statistic is _____. How does our class sample compare with this national statistic?

GRAPHING IDEAS FOR INVESTIGATING PERCENTS

1. Do you bite your fingernails? (About 44 percent of adolescents bite their fingernails.)

2. How many hours a day do you sleep? (About 60 percent of Americans sleep between seven and eight hours a day.)

3. Do you do chores in order to earn an allowance? (Eighty percent of eighth graders have to do chores for their allowance.)

4. Do you view smoking as a sign of weakness? (Seventy-five percent of Americans do.)

5. Which do you generally take, a shower or a bath? (Fifty-nine percent of teenage girls and seventy-eight percent of teenage boys take showers rather than baths.)

6. What is your favorite animal? (Nine percent of students report that the horse is their favorite animal.)

7. Does a dog live in your home? (Dogs live in 39 percent of U.S. households.)

8. Does a cat live in your home? (Cats live in 33 percent of U.S. households. More than one cat lives in 51 percent of those households.)

9. Does a bird live in your household? (Just 3 percent of households have a bird.)

10. Are you right- or left-handed? (About 10 percent of Americans are left-handed.)

> **FYI**
> I gathered this information from searching a variety of internet resources. It took a good deal of time, but was an interesting search.
> —MSB

Mental Calculation with Percents

It's useful for students to learn to calculate mentally with percents and have practice using strategies that make sense to them.

Percents of $100

Ask, *What is 50 percent of one hundred dollars?* Have students explain how they knew that $50 is the correct answer.

Then ask, *What is 25 percent of one hundred dollars?* Again, have students present answers and explain their reasoning. Typically, fewer students are sure about this problem. If no one can explain, offer several ways for them to think about the problem:

- 25 percent is half of 50 percent, so the answer is half of $50.00;

- there are four $0.25 in $1.00 and similarly there are four $25.00 in $100.00; and

- 25 percent is one-fourth of 100 percent and one-fourth of $100.00 is $25.00.

Continue the same sort of discussion for 10 percent, 5 percent, and 1 percent of $100.

> **Teaching Tip**
> It's important for students to know that you value their thinking, not just their right answers. Don't stop after just one student's explanation, but have others also explain their reasoning.
> —MSB

Percents of $200

Write the following on the board:

100% of $200 is _____.   10% of $200 is _____.

50% of $200 is _____.   5% of $200 is _____.

25% of $200 is _____.   1% of $200 is _____.

Have students work in pairs or small groups to figure out the answers. Then lead a classroom discussion in which students present their answers and reasoning.

Extend this by changing the $200 to another number, for example $500, $300, or $75.

More Percent Problems

Have students solve problems like the following:

If financing a loan costs approximately 5% a year, about what is a year's interest charge for a $400 loan?

A poll reported that 97.6% of a town's voters support the mayor. The voter population of the town is 12,500. About how many voters support the mayor?

If dinner in a restaurant costs $37.90, how much is a 20% tip?

Additional Instructional Suggestions

The following instructional suggestions are for small groups of students. After students are familiar with the activities, some of the suggestions are suitable as independent investigations for individual or partner work, and for choice time explorations.

These investigations can be used as part of a menu that students work on independently or with a partner. The independent investigations provide students with a variety of experiences for exploring percents.

Have students work on independent investigations in pairs or small groups. Then lead classroom discussions in which students present their findings, the different methods they used, and the difficulties they encountered.

For more information about using a menu, see "Starting Point 20: Four Structures for Organizing and Managing Classroom Instruction" in Part 1 on page 111.

Percents in the Newspaper

You need: newspaper

Look for articles (not advertisements) in which percents are used. Choose one to present to the class. In your presentation, explain the meaning of the percents.

Figuring Tips in Restaurants

Read the following story.

Four people went to a restaurant for pizza. They ordered two medium pizzas: one pepperoni and one plain. They each ordered a soft drink. The waitress brought their drinks right away, which was good since they were all thirsty. The pizzas were ready soon afterward, and she brought them right over, with a stack of extra napkins for them to use. The bill was $18.90 without tax.

Answer two questions:

1. What percent tip would you give?

2. How much money would you leave?

Explain your reasoning for each.
Write a restaurant story for others to solve.

Comparing Advertisements

You need: assortment of magazines or newspaper supplements that contain advertisements

Cut out four advertisements that offer discounts for items and paste them on a sheet of paper. Include one that indicates the percent the customer will save, one that gives the sale price, and two of your choice.

Decide which of the advertisements gives the customer the best deal. Record your decision on the back, including an explanation of your reasoning.

Trade with other groups and decide on the best deal for the advertisements they clipped. Compare your decisions.

The Photocopy Problem

You need: copies of a cartoon or drawing, including 1 full-size copy, 3 reductions, and 2 enlargements

Figure out what percent was used for each reduction and enlargement.
Record your solutions and explain the procedures you used.

Block Letters

You need: 10-by-10 grids, 1 sheet [R] See Reproducible R.43

Make block letters on 10-by-10 grids, trying to make each one so it covers as close to 50 percent of the grid as possible.

The Discount Coupon

You need: discount hamburger coupon

About what percent discount do you get with this coupon? Show your work and explain why your method and answer make sense.

Find one or two other coupons or advertisements that could be used for the same sort of investigation. Figure out the percent discount for each of them.

Try the investigation for coupons other students have found.

The Warehouse Problem

For the following problem, explain your thinking and show all the work that helps make your explanation clear.

A warehouse gives a 20% discount on all items, but you also must pay 6% in sales tax. Which would you prefer to have calculated first—the discount or the tax? Does it matter? Explain.

Percent Stories

Write a percent story problem that follows two rules:

1. It must end in a question.

2. The question must require that percents be used to answer it.

On a separate paper, solve your problem. Show your work and include an explanation of why your method makes sense.

Exchange papers and solve each other's problems.

Assessing Understanding of Percents

Observing students during classroom discussions and while they are working on independent investigations provides information about their understanding and skills. Also, one-on-one conversations with students reveal their individual understanding, misconceptions, and gaps, and provides valuable information that isn't always evident from classroom observations. The following suggestions can be used for both assessment approaches.

Observing Students

During classroom discussions and when students are working on the independent tasks, circulate, observe, and, at times, question them about their thinking and reasoning. Look and listen for evidence of students' ability to calculate with percents and relate percents to contextual situations.

Individual Assessments

The following written assignments offer ways to find out about students' understanding of percents.

1. Before beginning instruction, ask students to write what they know about percents. Have them do this again at the end of the instructional unit or even midway through. Return papers to the students and ask them to reflect on their learning.

2. Assign problems such as those suggested for whole-class lessons. Ask students to present solutions in writing and to explain their reasoning.

Questions
Teachers Ask

(continued from page 461)

Overview

Over the years, I've responded to many questions sent to me by teachers and parents. For this section, I rummaged through my file (now quite large), picked out the questions that I thought had the most general appeal, and included them here along with my responses.

Different from the math questions I received that led to the mathematical discussions for some of the investigations in Part 2, the questions in this section are pedagogical and focus on classroom management and instructional issues. My answers are meant to offer one way to think about the question raised—a way to spark ideas so teachers can use my responses in their own ways with the special needs of their own students at the forefront. I offer them in the spirit of sharing rather than providing definitive answers.

I suggest that you scan the title I provided for each question for a hint about its content. Each question also includes the grade level of the teacher who asked it, though most questions can apply to other grade levels as well. Also, I've included one question I received from a parent. I included this for two reasons. One is because the issue—memorizing multiplication and division facts—is one that teachers have raised as well. The other reason is because it models a way to communicate with parents about an issue that often concerns them.

I've enjoyed responding to teachers' queries. Writing answers sometimes gives me the opportunity to share my experiences, and at other times it helps me clarify my thinking, expand on my ideas, or reflect on new issues. Also, teachers' questions have helped me stay in touch with what's on their minds as they make changes in their classroom mathematics instruction.

0–99 Chart versus 1–100 Chart

Q. I notice that sometimes you use a 0–99 chart for an investigation, sometimes you use a 1–100 chart, and sometimes you suggest that either will do. How do you decide? —Grade 2

A. For many years, I used only the 0–99 chart and had several reasons for doing so. I wanted to be sure that students learned that zero is a number, not merely a placeholder, and also that it is an even number. Having zero on the chart gives zero status as a number that, as other numbers, tells how many. (Zero is the answer to the question, "How many elephants are in the room?" I like to ask this question and then ask students to think of other questions for which the answer is zero.) And including zero presents the opportunity, when talking about whether numbers are even or odd, to establish zero correctly as an even number by helping students see that it fits the same pattern as all of the other even numbers on the chart.

Also, I'm always fascinated to hear second graders' responses when I ask, "How many numbers are on the zero to ninety-nine chart?" Some insist that there are ninety-nine "because the last number is ninety-nine." Others reason that it's one hundred, most often "because there are ninety-nine but you have to count the zero, too," and sometimes "because you can count by tens since there are ten numbers in each row." A wonderful discussion typically results.

However, since then I've thought about several features that I especially like about the 1–100 chart, which I typically refer to as "the hundreds chart," and I've shifted to using it as well. The 1–100 chart begins with the first counting number. (Zero isn't considered a counting number.) Also, it includes the number one hundred, which is an important landmark number; continues the counting pattern into the first three-digit number; and allows for a natural extension to a 200 chart, a 300 chart, and so on.

So I now use the 0–99 and 1–100 charts interchangeably and have even posted one of each and asked students to talk about the similarities and differences between them.

For investigations that use these charts, see *Arrow Arithmetic* in Part 2 on page 286 and *The 0–99 Chart* on page 295.

Addition

Q. I teach second grade and am looking for a way to teach addition that helps students really understand why they are regrouping. —Grade 2

A. Building students' number sense is the key. Make sure to give your students ample experience taking numbers apart in various ways. For example, they should know that 10 can be broken into 6 + 4 or 9 + 1 and that it's also possible to break 10 into more than two parts, such as 2 + 3 + 5. Students need to be comfortable breaking apart all numbers up to 10, but breaking apart 10 is especially important as preparation for dealing with greater numbers.

It's also important that students can easily find the answers to problems like 10 + 7 and 10 + 3, where they are adding a number to 10. The pattern seems obvious to us as adults, but it often takes time for students to see and trust it. Try working with a 1–100 chart so students can see that going down to the number underneath is the same as adding 10.

As students begin to think about larger numbers, they need to see how tens fit into larger numbers. They should see that 15, for example, is $10 + 5$ and that 26 is $20 + 6$.

Finally, students should be asked to figure out their own ways for adding greater numbers. In my experience, most begin by adding the tens first. For example, to add 15 to 26, they typically add the tens to get 30, then add the ones to get 11, and finally combine 30 and 11 to get 41. While this isn't the standard procedure that we teach, it's efficient and shows good number sense.

Give students a good deal of practice adding problems in their own ways and sharing their methods. Introducing the standard procedure before they have a base of understanding runs the risk of having them think about *what to do* instead of *how to make sense*.

Algorithms and Basic Facts

Q. Should I ever teach the standard algorithms? —Grade 3

A. Yes. Along with students inventing their own strategies for calculating, teachers should also introduce the standard algorithms, explain why they make sense, and offer them as another way to calculate. It's important, however, that standard algorithms be presented not as better ways or the real ways, but as reliable procedures that are based in logic. Teaching algorithms should enhance—not replace—students finding ways that are appropriate and make sense to them.

Also, know that your explanations of standard algorithms may not make sense to all students. Similarly, when students present their methods for calculating, it's unlikely that all the others in the class will understand them. It's difficult to follow how other people reason. Encourage students to seek the meaning in each other's ideas, continue to have students explain why their ideas make sense, and keep true to the principle that students are to do only what makes sense to them and to persist until it does.

The instructional approach of having students invent their own algorithms does not eliminate the need for students to learn the basic facts. Being able to compute by any method, whether figuring an accurate answer, estimating, or justifying the reasonableness of a calculator answer, requires facility with addition and multiplication facts. Ideally, students would learn these facts from repeated use in problem-solving situations. However, additional practice is typically needed for students to commit basic facts to memory.

Several guidelines are important, however. It's not wise to focus on learning basic facts when students are initially studying an operation. A premature focus gives weight to rote memorization, instead of keeping the emphasis on developing understanding of a new idea. The danger to avoid is having students believe that giving quick, right answers is really what is most important when learning arithmetic.

Also, when learning facts, students should build on what they already know and focus on strategies for computing. For example, the doubles in addition, such as $5 + 5$ and $8 + 8$, are easier for students to remember. It's helpful for students to see how other combinations, such as $5 + 6$ and $7 + 8$, relate to the doubles.

Changing Instruction

Q. I am trying to implement changes into my math teaching so that I do less telling my students what needs to be done and more fostering their thinking. But I worry that they won't learn all that they need. I would appreciate any ideas that would bring my math class alive. —Grade 6

A. I remember clearly how hard it was for me to shift away from teaching by telling. We tend to teach the way we were taught, and I was certainly schooled under a teaching-by-telling regime. And I also know how hard it is to change well-entrenched habits. (Why do people have to start diets or give up smoking over and over again?)

That said, I'd like to offer some general thoughts about making changes.

It's hard to make changes by yourself.

It's very, very difficult to make changes in the classroom when you're working by yourself. It's hard enough to take the plunge and risk trying something new, and it's especially hard to do so alone. Most of my own thinking about what makes sense in the classroom has developed from collaborating with others and getting support from colleagues. I urge you to find another teacher with whom you can talk about planning lessons, analyze about how they went, look at student work, discuss management issues, or talk about whatever else you'd like to examine.

Focus on one teaching change at a time.

As a beginning middle school teacher (actually, it was junior high school then), I taught five classes each day and spent a good deal of time preparing and honing my lessons. At the time, my goal was getting better at explaining what it was that students needed to learn. Then I shifted my goal to seeing the benefit of not doing all of the explaining myself, but asking questions and eliciting responses from students. My classes came alive in a new way.

After making this one change, I learned about *wait time* in a conference workshop and decided that I wasn't allowing students enough time to think after I asked a question. I was so eager to hear a response and move on to the next question I had ready that I tended to call on the same few students who raised their hands quickly and waved them enthusiastically. So I decided to try what I had learned at the workshop. After I'd ask a question, I'd say to the class, "Raise your hand when you're ready to answer." Then I'd stand silently and slowly count to ten as I looked around the room. Sometimes I'd wait longer before calling on anyone, until at least more than half of the students had a hand raised. The change was amazing. Students realized that I was expecting them all to think, that they couldn't rely on those few who were always eager to reply. It took time and discipline for me to change my former habit, but I did it.

Sometime in the next few years, I put students into groups of four for the first time to facilitate even more of them contributing in class. (This was an idea I learned in another workshop.) When the students were in groups, not only did more students have a chance to talk but I was able to hear more of their thinking as I circulated in the room. It was hard at first to enforce the procedure of not responding to a student until everyone in the group had the same question, but with practice that, too, became a regular part of my teaching. Later I moved to having students work in pairs, and I found that easy to manage and in some cases more productive for the students.

I became a better teacher for these changes, but it took a year or so to make each of them staples in my instructional repertoire. Since then, each year I've found at least one way to improve my classroom teaching.

Look at the questions you ask.

Once I incorporated questioning, wait time, and small-group work into my instructional practice, I began what I think was the most significant shift in my classroom teaching—I broadened my attention from what I was teaching to figuring out what the students were really learning. I began this shift by rethinking the questions I posed to students. I did this in stages. First, I made a concerted effort to avoid asking questions students could answer merely with *yes* or *no* and, instead, began formulating questions that required students to explain their thinking. (And when I reverted to a yes-or-no question, I followed it with "Can you explain why you think that?") Then I moved to questions that didn't have a right answer but aimed to find out how a student was thinking. Finally, in my most profound change, I began to focus more intently on what students were saying, shifting my emphasis from listening for what I hoped to hear to listening to how the students were thinking and what they were understanding. It took several years of work to get my teaching skills in this area to where they are now.

I applaud your determination to change your teaching. Keep in mind that making substantive changes typically takes time. Good luck.

Decimals

Q. My third graders have trouble understanding the concept of decimals. They do not understand tenths, hundredths, and numbers smaller than one. They also have trouble transferring this knowledge to money; they'll write $3.5 for three dollars and five cents.
—Grade 3

A. Over the years, I've learned that the most effective way to introduce math concepts or skills that are new for students is a two-pronged approach: build on their prior knowledge and give them concrete experiences with the new ideas. Once students have a base of understanding, I help make the connections to the mathematical symbolism and vocabulary.

In order to introduce decimals, for example, I find it useful to rely on students' prior knowledge about money—specifically pennies, dimes, and dollars—and also to provide them the concrete tools of pennies and dimes (real or play) and replicas of $1 bills. First, I check to be sure that the students understand the relationships among pennies, dimes, and dollars—for example, 10 pennies are equivalent to 1 dime, and 100 pennies are equivalent to 1 dollar, and 10 dimes are also equivalent to 1 dollar. I also check that students can represent these amounts symbolically. I typically find that while students use the dollar sign to show 1 dollar ($1), they rely on the cents sign to show amounts less than 1 dollar (e.g., 10¢, 23¢).

Then I teach a game using the money that builds their number sense and lays the foundation for introducing decimal notation. *Close to $1.00* works well. Students play in pairs. Each pair needs a 1–6 die, a supply of about twenty dimes and twenty pennies, and two play dollar bills. Also, draw a recording sheet on the board and have each player make one to use (see below, left).

Players take turns rolling the die. Each player chooses to take the number rolled in pennies or dimes and writes his or her choice on the recording sheet. After six rolls, players figure out how much money they have and record their total. They check each other's figuring and see who got closer to $1. (It's OK to go over $1.) For an extra bit of mathematical oomph, they also calculate and record how far each total is from $1.

When first teaching the game, don't focus the students on the notation, but rather have them learn the rules and become comfortable with the game. Then use their familiarity with the game to introduce the decimal notation for money. Here's where you establish that the number of each of the coins has its own place in the number. Have them practice reading different amounts—$0.35, $0.71, $0.05, and so on. Have them write amounts that you give them. Then have them play again, this time using a recording sheet that has them record with the notation (see below, right).

Close to $1.00			Close to $1.00	
	Dimes	Pennies	Roll 1	$0._____
Roll 1			Roll 2	$0._____
Roll 2			Roll 3	$0._____
Roll 3			Roll 4	$0._____
Roll 4			Roll 5	$0._____
Roll 5			Roll 6	$0._____
Roll 6				
Total			Total	$_____

To change the game, have them play *Close to $2.00*. The rules are the same but the new goal of $2 requires them to change their numerical strategy.

As students become more comfortable, add in information about the values of the places and the relationship of these decimal numbers to the whole numbers they're already familiar with. All of their learning is based on place value, one of the most important big ideas of students' mathematics learning and an idea with which third graders need many experiences to help them cement and extend their understanding. We've traditionally asked students to demonstrate their place-value knowledge by identifying the place a digit in a particular number holds. For example, we might ask students, *How many hundreds are there in 3,412?* or *What place does the 4 hold in 3,412?* A correct response to either of these types of questions would indicate that the student knows where the hundreds place is. But a correct response does not necessarily mean that the student understands the meaning of the 4, that it represents four groups of one hundred. This sort of understanding develops from students exploring how to group different numbers of objects, seeing that when they have 132 objects, they can make one group of 100, three groups of 10, and have 2 extras.

Money can also be helpful for giving third graders experience with adding and subtracting decimals. For example, present a problem: *If you want to buy an apple for $0.39 and raisins for $0.25, how much money do you need?* First, ask the students to estimate if they need more or less than $1.00. (Playing the games should have helped them think about making an estimate.) Then have them figure, using the coins if needed. Finally, connect their reasoning to the correct terminology and record both horizontally and vertically:

$$\$0.39 + \$0.25 = \$0.64 \qquad \begin{array}{r} \$0.39 \\ + \ 0.25 \\ \hline \$0.64 \end{array}$$

Connecting Decimals and Fractions

Q. I know that decimals and fractions connect and I'm struggling for ways to help my students see the connection. Any suggestions? —Grade 6

A. Helping students make connections among all of the mathematical ideas they are learning is important, and the best way to learn something new is to connect it to something you already know. In this light, what students already know about common fractions is a useful springboard for introducing decimals. Like fractions, decimals represent numbers less than one or numbers that are in between two whole numbers. Students' initial learning about decimals can build on what they already know about fractions and introduce them to another convention for representing these numbers.

Here's something I've done with students. I draw a pizza on the board, "cut" it into four equal-size pieces, and write in one of the pieces. Then I ask students to think about why mathematicians decided to use this symbolism to represent each part of the cut-up pizza—what the 4 means and what the 1 means. We discuss their ideas and I reinforce what the two numbers represent. Then I draw another pizza, divide it into just two equal-size wedges, and ask the students how to label one piece. I repeat for a pizza cut into ten pieces.

Now to make the connection to decimals: I focus the students on the pizza divided into ten slices and introduce the students to the decimal representation for $\frac{1}{10}$. I write on the board *0.1* and explain that this is another way to write the fraction $\frac{1}{10}$. When I introduce this notation, I am consistent in reading both $\frac{1}{10}$ and 0.1 as "one-tenth." (Later I'll introduce "point one" as another way to *say* 0.1, but I always emphasize that it *means* one-tenth.) We talk about how $\frac{2}{10}$ can be written as 0.2, $\frac{3}{10}$ can be written as 0.3, and so on. I list on the board:

$$\frac{1}{10} = 0.1$$
$$\frac{2}{10} = 0.2$$
$$\frac{3}{10} = 0.3$$
$$\frac{4}{10} = 0.4$$
$$\frac{5}{10} = 0.5$$
$$\frac{6}{10} = 0.6$$
$$\frac{7}{10} = 0.7$$
$$\frac{8}{10} = 0.8$$
$$\frac{9}{10} = 0.9$$
$$\frac{10}{10} = 1.0 = 1$$

I explain that the decimal point is a mathematical convention that indicates an important shift in a number. With money, it separates the dollars from the cents. With measurements, it separates whole units from the parts of units. With numbers, it allows us to describe numerical quantities that are less than one or that are in between whole numbers.

Then I return to the pizza on the board that is divided into two pieces. We talk about $\frac{1}{2}$ being equivalent to $\frac{5}{10}$ so another way to write $\frac{1}{2}$ is 0.5. Depending on the class, I may continue on to hundredths and then talk about how to represent $\frac{1}{4}$ as a decimal, or I may wait to do that another day. Relating to money is a good way to talk about why 0.25 makes sense.

While the decimal point is a mathematical convention, it also has a logical underpinning that's important for students to understand. For example, the meanings of the 0 and the 4 in 3.04 are based on the logical structure of our place-value system, extending the pattern that each place is a successive power of ten. Decimals may be difficult to grasp for students who do not yet fully understand the structure of our place-value system with respect to whole numbers but have only learned the pattern of writing numbers.

Long Division

Q. Is there a way to teach long division so that students understand what is happening? My students have difficulty understanding the steps involved. —Grade 5

A. Long division is hard. First of all, after students go through many years of learning to compute by starting at the right, with the numbers in the ones place, the standard long-division procedure asks them to start at the left. Also, even though the procedure is for division, students learn that, after they divide, they have to multiply, then subtract, and finally bring down a number to start the process all over again. Students wonder why division also involves multiplying and subtracting, and what "bringing down" really means. It's no wonder that few people can explain why the long-division method works, even when they can do it correctly.

The key to all of students' mathematical learning is that they do what makes sense to them, look for the sense in all situations, and persist in their thinking until something does make sense. And this is also true for long division. Let's try it. Think about this problem:

$$6\overline{)875}$$

The standard long-division algorithm calls for beginning by asking: How many 6s are there in 8? Asking this question calls for looking just at one digit in 875 and doesn't focus on the meaning of 875. Another way to think about this problem is to begin by asking, About how many 6s can fit into 875? The word *about* is important here. We're looking for an estimate that's a number that's friendly and easy to think about. Then we can refine. I know, for example, that there are more than 100 6s in 875 because 100 6s is only 600, and that's less than 875. But it's a place to start, so I write 100 to keep track of part of the answer. Now I've "used up" 600, with 275 still left. (That's where the subtraction comes in, to find out how much is still left to deal with.) Next I think, About how many 6s are in 275? I know that there are at least 10, so I write *10* as another part of the answer. That takes care of 60, which leaves 215 more. Ten more 6s work, so I write another *10* and subtract 60 to find out that now 155 is left. Now I can take out 120, which is 20 6s, so I write *20*. Now with only 35 left, I can figure that there are 5 more 6s, or 30, so I write 5 in the answer. There's less than 6 left, so there's a remainder of 5. What's the answer? Add up all the parts: 100 + 10 + 10 + 20 + 5. The answer is 145 R5. Here are two ways to record:

For more instructional strategies for teaching division, see *Teaching Arithmetic: Lessons for Extending Division, Grades 4–5*, a book I coauthored with Maryann Wickett (2003).

Will this be easy for students to learn? Not for all students—the reality is that math is hard and that some students learn more easily than others. But at least this method is one that I can make sense of for myself and, therefore, help students understand, something that I've found difficult to do with the divide-multiply-subtract-bring-down procedure for long division.

Using Fingers for Computing

Q. I teach first grade and I encourage students to use their fingers when adding or subtracting. My daughter's teacher has a "strict rule" against using fingers when adding. Can you clear this up for me? —Grade 1

A. I think that we need to consider counting on fingers in the context of our larger goals for students' arithmetic competence. Our goals for students include that they learn to add, subtract, multiply, and divide accurately and efficiently and also learn to reason flexibly and confidently with numbers. Skills for computing are best built on a solid base of understanding and rely on repeated experiences over time.

That said, I don't think it's harmful for students to use their fingers when first learning to compute. Their fingers are their way of making numbers concrete and being sure of their answers. As their confidence develops, students' reliance on their fingers diminishes and, finally, ends completely. Rather than ban using fingers, I prefer to find ways to develop students' understanding, confidence, and skill with computing. For example, it's important for first graders to develop strategies for adding. Counting on is a beginning strategy that young students learn to use; for example, a student might find the answer to a problem like 9 + 3 by saying, "Nine, . . . ten, eleven, twelve," thus counting on three more from the nine. Making a ten is another strategy; for 9 + 3, a child may think, "Nine and one more from the three makes ten, and then I have to add two more to get twelve." Students often learn the doubles first, such as 3 + 3 and 4 + 4. While using doubles isn't particularly useful for 9 + 3, it helps with a problem like 6 + 7, when a child might think, "Six and six is twelve and one more is thirteen." Emphasizing strategies like these helps build students' understanding, number sense, and confidence.

From my more than fifty years of teaching experience, I've learned that students learn at different rates and on their own time schedules. The support we offer students should always aim at building their understanding and nurturing their interest in learning. I worry that banning fingers is asking your child to give up what makes sense to her at this time. I don't see any problem with letting students use their fingers in first grade.

Formative Assessment in the Classroom

Q. Other than the district tests we have to give, how do you recommend that I assess my students? —Grade 4

A. Assessing what students are learning is essential for knowing whether the instruction we're providing is accessible and effective for all students. Different from once-a-year district-level tests, the assessments I'm referring to are ongoing, are an integral part of instruction, and inform me about what and how students are learning from the instruction I'm providing.

I assess students in various ways—by listening to them during whole-class discussions, observing and listening to them as they work in pairs or small groups, and reviewing assignments that students complete individually. And while all of these are useful, I find that individual assignments provide me with specific evidence about each student's learning. Over the years, I've learned more about the sorts of assignments that are effective for giving me insights into what students understand, what they don't yet know, and how they are thinking.

The individual assignments I gave when I first taught mostly asked students to figure out answers. Now, I ask students to write, explain, include diagrams or sketches when appropriate, communicate about their confusion as well as their knowledge, and provide as much information as possible so that I have a view into their thinking.

I pore over papers to understand students' thinking, revisit papers from time to time, draw from them when planning follow-up instruction, use them for parent conferences, and keep them as a way to track each student's yearlong progress. I'm lost without student work. Not only does students' work serve to help me assess individual students' progress but it also helps me assess my own instruction in ways that I never was able to do in my earlier years.

For more on assessment, see "Starting Point 13: Making Formative Assessment Integral to Instruction" in Part 1 on page 62.

Homework

Q. I am a middle school math teacher. I grade nearly every homework assignment that I assign. I know math teachers who have their students grade work in class prior to collecting it. I have done this in the past but felt that students were not accurate in their grading or, at times, were even dishonest. I feel that by grading most assignments, I have a strong feel for where each and every student is comprehension-wise. But I also feel that my job is taking over my life. I would like some insights into the best ideas to approaching homework assessment/assigning a homework grade. —Middle School

A. My suggestions for dealing with homework come from my experience in working with middle school students (I taught eighth-grade math for six years). Although these suggestions don't deal extensively with the grading issue, they do deal with how to process homework more efficiently and in ways that will both inform you and provide opportunities for students to learn from each other. I hope you find something to try that is consistent with your interest in supporting student learning and making your life a bit easier.

Get students involved in talking about their homework. Here are some of the ways we processed homework:

- In pairs and sometimes groups of four, students talked about their homework problems and worked on coming to consensus on their answers or solutions. I walked around, listening to

FYI

Math Homework That Counts, Grades 4-6, written by Annette Raphel (2000), is a book that has been helpful to me in thinking about homework. It asks and explores such questions as "What constitutes good and meaningful math homework?" "What are the purposes of math homework?" "What makes a 'good' worksheet?" and "What does research say about homework?" Although the examples given are for grades 4-6, other grades will find the resource thought provoking.

— MSB

conversations and, at that time, noting who had not done the homework assignment. This process allowed students access to other students' ideas and a chance to correct their own mistakes. Also, those who didn't do the assignment had the opportunity to learn.

- Often I had the pairs or groups record problems they were uncertain about on the board so that we could talk about them as part of a class discussion. We could skip or deal quickly with those that didn't appear on the list, giving us time to dig into those that were difficult for students.

- Sometimes I had students come to consensus on their homework papers and I took one paper from the group to represent the thinking of the group.

One final thought: I gave only a few problems for homework so that there would be time to process them in some way the next day and then get on to that day's lesson.

The Language of Math

Q. Do you have any ideas for reinforcing the "language" of math for students? —Grade 2

A. This question is appropriate for all grade levels. Acquiring new language in any subject, not just in mathematics, calls for hearing words and phrases used in contexts that help bring meaning to them. I remember when a friend came to visit with her young daughter, Maria. As we settled in to chat, my friend said to Maria, "Please sit on the sofa." Maria looked around, not yet familiar with the word *sofa*, and noticed several things to sit on. Not sure what to do, she perched on an ottoman. "No, honey," Maria's mother said, "you can sit over there, on the sofa." She pointed to the sofa. This one experience with the word *sofa* wasn't enough. Maria would need to hear the word *sofa* more times before she would be comfortable knowing what it meant, and even more times before she would be comfortable using it herself.

It's no different with mathematical language. It's important, as often as possible, for teachers to use the standard terminology of mathematics and to encourage students to do so as well. When students are introduced to pattern blocks, for example, they often describe the blue block as a diamond. I point out to them that this blue block has other names, too; I introduce the terminology of *parallelogram* and *rhombus* and encourage students to use these labels.

In a geometry lesson with fourth graders, Todd asserted that he thought that all squares were the same but that rectangles could be different. I wrote his idea on the board so that everyone could think about it: *All squares are the same, but rectangles can be different.* Then I pressed Todd to explain his idea further. He said, "All squares look the same, but rectangles can be fat or skinny."

Ella said that she disagreed with part of what Todd said. "Some squares are bigger than others, so they're not really the same."

Alma, however, defended Todd's idea. "But you can still tell that they're squares because their sides are the same."

The discussion continued with others weighing in with their ideas. Finally, we agreed that while all squares have the same shape, no matter if they are large or small, all rectangles don't have the same shape. In the context of this discussion, I introduced the mathematical terminology of *similar*. "When shapes look the same, even if they are different sizes, they're called *similar*," I explained. I wrote *similar* on our "Math Words" chart and drew two squares of different sizes next to the word as a reminder. I asked the students to say the word aloud. I asked them to think of other shapes that would be mathematically similar. They thought of circles, some triangles, regular hexagons, and others.

One of the challenges of mathematical vocabulary is that often the words have other meanings in common usage, as does similar and words such as *even*, *odd*, *multiply*, *factor*, *prime*, and *power*. It's important to talk about the difference in meanings when common words have special mathematical meanings.

Also, after introducing new vocabulary, it's important to use the words often and in the context of experiences. I had the students explore similarity further. (Pattern blocks are good for this since the students can build larger and mathematically similar versions of all of the blocks with the exception of the yellow hexagon.) Sometimes I ask students to write the definition of a math term in their own words, but I do so only after they've had many experiences with the terminology.

For more on mathematical vocabulary, see "Starting Point 22: Teaching Math Vocabulary" in Part 1 on page 122.

Finally, keep in mind that language acquisition takes time and occurs from connecting words to experiences.

Math Centers

Q. I am a first-grade teacher with twenty very lively students in my classroom. How can I incorporate math center investigations into my daily schedule? —Grade 1

A. Spend the time it takes to establish routines so that students know how to operate during math time. One way to begin is to introduce just one math center investigation. For example, students can measure several objects with interlocking cubes and count to see how many cubes they used. Place the materials the students need—cubes, objects to measure (lengths of different-colored yarn, books, a paintbrush, and so on), and a supply of recording sheets—in a box or container. Gather the students and demonstrate what they are to do. Show them where the materials will be placed and tell them how many students may be at the center at one time. Talk about how to put the materials back when they are done and what to do with their paper. Then, choose students to try the investigation while you work with the rest of the class. Have them do so for ten or fifteen minutes. Then gather the class again and have the students who worked at the center report on their experiences. Allow time for others to ask questions. Over the next several days, give all of the students a chance to go to the center.

Next introduce two other investigations to the whole class. Again, demonstrate and set the parameters—how many students can work at one time, where they are to work, how they are to record, and so on. This time, have two groups try the centers while you work with the rest of the class.

If you work in this way, you'll soon be able to have enough math center investigations set up so that all of the students can work at a center at the same time.

Math Portfolios

Q. I'd love advice on how to set up well-rounded math portfolios. How can I start this process at the beginning of the year so that I can have a good picture of a child's abilities for assessment and conferences? —Grade 4

A. I've tried many different systems over the years for saving and organizing students' math work. I always look for a system that gives me access to a chronological view of each student's progress through the year and provides a sampling of student work that's useful for parent conferences. Also, because I believe that it's appropriate and beneficial for students in the intermediate grades to reflect on their own learning, I want a system that allows students to review their own progress from time to time. Finally, I know that a system must be easy to manage in order for it to have staying power in the classroom.

One system that I've found to work well is to set up a file box with a folder for each student. The logistics first: To make managing the folders really easy, arrange them in alphabetical order according to the students' first names, and then number them. As a regular routine for headings on papers, ask students to write their number after their name. This makes for easy filing later and for easy locating of their folders. Keeping the box on a counter makes the folders easily accessible both to you and to the students.

Next, explain to the students how you plan to use these folders. I tell students, "It's important that I know as much as possible about what you are learning during the year, so I'm going to ask you to put into this math folder some of the math assignments you do. You won't file all of the work you do, but I'll pick assignments that are especially useful for showing what you are thinking, how you are reasoning, what you're learning, and what additional help I might give."

I also tell students, "Later in the year, we'll have a chance to look over your work and talk about your progress. Also, we'll be able to share your work with your parents so they also can see how you're doing in math."

There are times when students work in pairs on an assignment that I'd like them to include in their folders. Sometimes I'd like students also to take their papers home to share with their families. And sometimes students would like to take a particular paper home to share. In these instances, I make copies of the papers so that they can serve each of these purposes.

To get the folders started, try a beginning assignment that gives you information about how the students feel about math and their own math learning. You might ask them to write a math autobiography about their math experiences in school so far. Or you might ask them to record something they especially like about math or think is easy and something they don't like about math or think is hard. Or begin by assigning a problem that's useful for assessing students' mathematics understanding and also how they can organize themselves on paper. For example, asking them how they might make change for one dollar using quarters, dimes, and nickels will inform you about their understanding of money and their number sense. (Ask older students to find all the possible ways, but don't expect third graders to do so.) For an assignment that focuses on place value, ask the students to write down as many numbers as they can think of between 500 and 800 that have one 0 in them. (Again, ask older students to find all the possible numbers, but not third graders.) To focus on addition and learn about students' numerical comfort, ask them to find five numbers that add up to an odd number. (Also ask older students what they know about the five numbers and see if any come to the conclusion that one, three, or all five of the numbers have to be odd.)

Typically, I review a class set of papers in order to decide whether to file them. When I find a set that is useful for revealing students' strengths and weaknesses, I bring them back to class and ask a student to file them. Doing this throughout the year provides a chronological record of each student's math progress for each reporting period and for the entire year. Different from using a portfolio as a sampling of best work, this is a system that can show progress over time. Also, looking at the portfolios together gives me a sense of different students' experiences with the instruction I offered. I don't have a rule about how many papers to keep, but I think that about one a week is a general average so I have about thirty-five or so per student by the end of the year.

If you're not sure about what sort of work to save, you might start by saving all of the students' papers for several weeks. Then, after a month or so, look through the files and see which papers give you insights into how students reason, what their strengths are, and where they are having difficulty. Save these and use them as a guide for selecting future assignments that are useful for assessing your students' progress.

Be sure that the students know that the work that isn't filed is also important. Explain that all of their work has value, but you're looking particularly for examples that show you how they are thinking. Also, if a student has a piece of work that he or she wants to file, that's fine. The more involvement students have with collecting samples of their work, the more attention they give to their own learning.

Meeting the Needs of All Students

Q. How can I challenge my students who are above grade level, but still teach to the whole class? —Grade 5

A. We all have students who learn quickly and can handle additional challenges, while others require more time to learn and often need additional attention on the basics. Here are three ideas for dealing with this in the classroom.

1. Make math choices available.
Provide options that can keep students mathematically engaged in ways that support your learning focus. Post a large sheet of drawing or chart paper, title it *Math Choices*, and explain to the students that

you'll list investigations that are available to them when they finish assignments and have extra time. That way, you'll have time to work with students who need additional help. To begin, list just one or two investigations, and change the list to keep up students' interest. Also, avoid one-shot investigations and instead include investigations that students can do multiple times. For example, to help build second graders' familiarity with the number 10 and also think about combining three addends, introduce the whole class to *All About 10*. Give each child ten interlocking cubes or other counters and have students organize them into three groups. Ask a child to report, and record his arrangement as an addition equation, for example,

$$10 = 3 + 3 + 4$$

Repeat for several other students' arrangements. Then have students work on their own to record as many different equations as they can. Once the students are familiar with the investigation, list variations as math choices—*All About 12* and/or *All About 20*—choosing numbers that are appropriate for your students. Also, as an extension, have them write equations with four or more addends.

I'm careful, however, to avoid making math choices available only to the more capable students; I want all students to have opportunities to make choices. To accomplish this, I sometimes give choice time to the entire class. Not only is it useful for me to observe which investigations students choose but it also gives me the chance to observe how students work independently and give help as needed.

2. Teach games.

Games are also useful, especially when they offer variations that provide for additional options. For practice with multiplication facts combined with the chance to spark thinking about probability, teach your students how to play *Multiplication Bingo*. Give each student a blank 5-by-5 grid with the center marked FREE, as in regular bingo, and tell students that they are to fill in their own numbers on the other twenty-four squares. Explain the rules: Once they have their cards filled in, you'll roll two dice and they will multiply the numbers that come up. If the product is on their grid, then they cross it out. The winner is the first to get a bingo, as in the regular game. (Keep track of the numbers rolled so you can check the products the students crossed out.) While all students can easily play the game and get practice with basic multiplication facts, some students will be challenged to figure out the best numbers to write on their cards.

To vary the game, instead of using standard 1–6 dice, use 1–10 dice, or one 1–6 die and one 5–10 die. Students can also play *Baby Bingo Blackout* using 3-by-3 grids with no free space. Again, they first fill in their own grids. For this game, the winner is the first player to cross out all nine numbers.

After introducing the games to the whole class, you can add them to the list of math choices for students to play independently in pairs or small groups.

3. Give assignments that allow students to set the parameters.

It's helpful if assignments are appropriate for different students' levels of proficiency and also provide information about their mathematical skill and comfort. For example, for an assignment for fifth graders on comparing fractions, I listed on the board six pairs of fractions:

$$\frac{1}{2} \text{ and } \frac{1}{3} \quad \frac{2}{3} \text{ and } \frac{3}{4} \quad \frac{3}{8} \text{ and } \frac{1}{4}$$

$$\frac{3}{8} \text{ and } \frac{1}{3} \quad \frac{5}{6} \text{ and } \frac{7}{8} \quad \frac{6}{8} \text{ and } \frac{4}{5}$$

I explained the directions: "Choose one pair of fractions to compare, copy it on your paper, circle the fraction that's larger, and explain how you know in two ways using numbers, pictures, and/or words." This kind of assignment works for any set of problems with varying difficulty. As a variation, ask students to choose any two or three of the problems to solve instead of just one.

For another example, to provide practice for third graders learning about multiplication, write on the board:

Which Has More Wheels?

7 bicycles

5 tricycles

Ask students to figure in their heads which has more wheels and check their answer with a partner. (For older students, use larger numbers—seventeen bicycles and twelve tricycles, or forty bicycles and twenty-five tricycles.) Have a student explain his or her reasoning. Then have students make up three more *Which Has More Wheels?* problems, choosing their own numbers and solving them. Having students exchange papers to check one another's work provides additional practice.

Money

Q. Many of my students are confused about the value of coins and the counting of money. Do you have any investigation ideas to help? —Grade 1

A. Instruction about money not only helps students learn about our monetary system but it also can promote and develop students' number sense. It's a win-win effort. I think that beginning instruction about money should focus students' learning in three areas: the names of coins, the values of coins, and how to represent amounts of money symbolically.

For a whole-class investigation, I like to give students each a penny, a nickel, and a dime. I ask them to examine each coin to see what's the same and different about them. (If you have magnifying lenses, this is a good time to have the students use them.) We discuss our discoveries and then I pose coin riddles:

Which coins have a building on the back?

There's a picture of a U.S. president on the front of each coin.

On which two coins do the presidents face the same way?

Which coin says ONE CENT on the back? [I write ONE CENT on the board.]

Which coin says FIVE CENTS on the back? [I write *FIVE CENTS* on the board.]

Which coin is a penny? A nickel? A dime?

Games with Money

I find games to be useful for teaching money concepts. For a two-player game, each pair needs a small paper bag with nine coins in it—three pennies, three nickels, and three dimes. One player names a coin—penny, nickel, or dime. The other player reaches into the bag and without peeking tries to remove the specified coin. They take turns.

For a harder version of the game that also focuses on the values of coins, I prepare a set of cards for various money values that can be made from three of the coins in their bag—1¢, 5¢, 10¢, 3¢, 6¢, 12¢, 21¢, 25¢, and so on. I choose amounts that I think are appropriate for them and sometimes vary the way I write the amounts, including some written as $0.01, $0.05, $0.10, and so on. One player chooses a card, the other reaches into the bag to remove the coins without peeking, and together they count up how much money they have to see if they match. If this game is too hard, I have the students put the coins in a container, choose a card, and work together to pick out the coins. For either game, players can record their answers by writing the values, using money stamps, or drawing coins to represent the coins they chose.

When students are ready, I like to teach the game *Race for $1.00*, a two-player game that helps them learn about place value as well as money (see page 351). Players need two dice and a zip-top bag with thirty pennies, twenty dimes, and two play dollars. They follow these rules:

1. On your turn, roll the dice, add the numbers, and take that number of pennies. If you have enough pennies, exchange ten pennies for a dime.

2. Give the dice to your partner.

3. Play until one player can exchange ten dimes for a dollar.

I model the game for the class by playing with a child, being especially careful to emphasize that they are to watch each other's moves and to exchange coins only when they have the dice.

To involve parents in supporting students' learning about money, it's useful to send home a note asking parents to empty the change from their pockets or purse each night and, with their students, count the coins.

Experiences with money should be ongoing during the year. I think that it's ideal for students to use actual coins for investigations and worth the time to help students develop the responsibility necessary for dealing with money in the classroom. For the investigation with magnifying lenses, real coins are essential, but play money will work for the other investigations.

For more money investigations, see *Why Can't I Have Everything? Teaching Today's Children to Be Financially and Mathematically Savvy*, a pre-K–2 resource written by Jane Crawford (2011).

Learning Multiplication and Division Facts

Q. My fourth-grade daughter is struggling to learn her multiplication and division tables. She takes timed tests at school and doesn't do very well. How can I help her? —Grade 4

A. Your daughter's problem isn't uncommon, and I've found that getting assistance at home is a wonderful way to help students shift from being discouraged to developing confidence and experiencing success. Following are some ideas I hope will be useful.

First, it's important your daughter sees the usefulness of memorizing the multiplication and division tables. Without having these committed to memory, all calculations, whether done mentally or with paper and pencil, will be difficult and laborious. If you think that your daughter would benefit from some encouragement to think about reasons for learning the tables, consider the books described below.

- *Amanda Bean's Amazing Dream* by Cindy Neuschwander (1998) was written by a third-grade teacher who wanted to motivate her students to think about multiplication. At the end of the book are investigations I wrote for parents to do with their students. While the book and investigations focus on multiplication, they also provide a good foundation for thinking about division.

- *One Hundred Hungry Ants* (1999) and *A Remainder of One* (1995), both by Elinor J. Pinczes, are quite helpful. The ideas in these books can spark discussions between parents and their children about both multiplication and division.

I like using students' books to support students' math learning. They help make abstract math ideas real and help stimulate students' imaginations. I know that they won't solve your daughter's problem, but they're a good starting place.

When helping your daughter, it's important to keep in mind that not only should students understand why memorizing basics is important but a focus on memorization should follow understanding the concepts of multiplication and division. Students should first learn how multiplication relates to repeated addition, how to interpret division, and how multiplication and division relate to each other. When I work with students, I check first that a child can figure out the answers to single-digit problems, such as 7×8 or $24 \div 3$, before they focus on memorizing answers. I want to be sure that a child knows that 7×8 can be interpreted as seven eights, or $8 + 8 + 8 + 8 + 8 + 8 + 8$, and that thinking about the problem as adding eight sevens, or $7 + 7 + 7 + 7 + 7 + 7 + 7 + 7$ will produce the same answer. For division problems like $24 \div 3$, a child should understand that the answer can be found by putting twenty-four into groups of three, by sharing twenty-four into three groups, or by relating the problem to multiplication and thinking, "Three times what number gives twenty-four?" The goal for your daughter is clear—quick and effortless recall of products and quotients with factors from one to twelve. But the memorization should follow learning the concepts.

After checking that your daughter has developed understanding of the concepts, you might look together at the multiplication table. Look for patterns in the rows and columns of numbers. Notice which products appear only once, exactly twice, or more than twice. Find the product that appears most often and talk about why this is so. Think about numbers that aren't products—like 17 and 31, for example—and talk about why these don't appear. Find out if there are more even or odd products and, again, discuss why.

Use a calculator to help familiarize your child with multiples. Most calculators have the capability to do repeated additions. Try it with a calculator you have at home. Press 8, then +, then =, and the display should show 8. Press the = key again, and you should see 16 on the display. Keep pressing the = key and the display will continue to show multiples of 8—24, 32, 40, 48, and so on. Have your daughter predict what number will show next before she presses the 5 key each time. Doing this will familiarize your daughter with the multiples of 8. Start with other numbers to practice other multiples.

Brainstorm with your daughter all of the possible ways she might memorize the table. Have her choose one way to try with just one set of numbers, say the eights. When she's ready, quiz her. Together decide if the method she used to study helped or if she'd like to switch to a different method for another number.

Good luck—to you *and* your daughter!

Interpreting Multiplication

Q. While I was at a math conference, the speaker of a session I attended emphasized that in "real" life, 12 × 2 is not the same as 2 × 12. He used the example of sending a kid to the store for twelve packages of two eggs or two packages of twelve eggs. I know this is getting picky, but in order for students to do well in upper grades, I believe the foundation has to be solid in every way. Should I address this with my students? —Grade 3

A. I agree with the speaker, that in real-world situations, 12 × 2 is not the same as 2 × 12, and I don't think this is a picky distinction. I think it's important. One way to interpret 12 × 2 is as twelve groups of two or twelve twos; another way to interpret it is as twelve two times. Using addition, the first interpretation can be represented as 2 + 2 + 2 + 2 + 2 + 2 + 2 + 2 + 2 + 2 + 2 + 2 and the second as 12 + 12. Since both interpretations produce the same correct answer, and multiplication is commutative, it's just an issue of mathematical semantics. When you think about 12 × 2 abstractly, out of any context, the interpretation is arbitrary.

Most elementary instructional programs use the first interpretation, referring to the times sign (×) as "groups of." If I were asking students to think about the number of eggs in two dozen, I would use 2 × 12 to represent the total number of twenty-four eggs—two groups of twelve or two twelves. When students think about multiplication in a context, it's important for them to be able to explain how the symbolism relates to the situation.

Multidigit Multiplication

Q. What do students need to understand to be successful with multidigit multiplication? How can I help my students? —Grade 4

A. There are three instructional ideas of fundamental importance that I introduce to students to build a foundation of understanding for multidigit multiplication. I introduce these ideas by having students practice figuring out the answers to carefully chosen multidigit multiplication problems. I have them figure mentally, rely on their number sense, and use paper-and-pencil recording to keep a record of their reasoning. I keep their focus on making sense of the computations. These three ideas follow.

1. Multiplying any number by ten results in adding a zero.

To teach this pattern, I assign each pair of students a "times ten" multiplication problem to solve. I don't tell them the pattern—merely memorizing the trick isn't sufficient. Rather, I have them figure out the answer by counting by tens or in some other way that makes sense to them. As each pair reports the answer and explains how they figured, I record a multiplication equation:

$6 \times 10 = 60$

$2 \times 10 = 20$

$13 \times 10 = 130$

And so on.

Then we talk about the pattern being a useful shortcut to figuring. It's also important for students to extend this pattern to multiplying numbers by one hundred, one thousand, or any power of ten. I repeat this process for "times one hundred" multiplication problems—$6 \times 100 = 600$, $13 \times 100 = 1300$, and so on. And then I repeat it once again for "times one thousand" multiplication problems.

2. When multiplying, split numbers into smaller parts, multiply each part, and then combine the partial products.

Solving a problem such as 14×6, for example, is possible to do mentally if you think of 14 as $10 + 4$, multiply each part by 6 to get $60 + 24$, and then add the partial products to get 84:

$10 \times 6 = 60$

$4 \times 6 = 24$

$60 + 24 = 84$

Or you could solve 14×6 by splitting 14 into 7×7, then multiplying 7×6 twice, and adding $42 + 42$, which also results in 84:

$7 \times 6 = 42$

$7 \times 6 = 42$

$42 + 42 = 84$

I give students practice with this strategy, first recording their thinking with equations as shown and then having them record. I emphasize that I use paper and pencil to keep track of how I (or they) reason. I've found that splitting numbers and distributing the multiplication over smaller numbers is accessible to students, and I choose the problems carefully to give them access to this strategy. Good beginning problems involve multiplying a number in the teens (12, 13, 14, or 15) by a single-digit number (3, 4, 5). Then I increase the size of the factors. When students use this strategy, they are applying the distributive property, distributing the multiplication over addends that are friendlier numbers. However, I don't focus at this time on formalizing the name and generalization of the distributive property; rather, I focus on their experience with using the idea of splitting.

3. Multiply mentally by multiples of ten—twenty, thirty, forty, and so on.

For 7×50, for example, students may think of 50 as 5×10, then multiply 7×5 to get 35, and then multiply 35×10 for the answer of 350. When they do this, students are actually changing the problem from 7×50 to $7 \times (5 \times 10)$ and then applying the associative property to solve the problem by thinking of it as $(7 \times 5) \times 10$. As with the other ideas, I give students enough experiences for them to see the patterns and become skilled at using them.

Order of Operations

Q. Our grade-level objectives include teaching the order of operations. I've been using the sentence "Please excuse my dear Aunt Sally" to teach this. Is there another way that will help my students understand as well as remember the right order to use? —*Grade 6*

A. Ah, the order of operations. The sentence you mention may be as good as anything for helping students remember. But that said, along with remembering, students should at least realize why such a convention is needed to avoid confusion. Point out that the value of an expression like $3 + 4 \times 5$ can be either 35 or 23, depending on whether you do $(3 + 4) \times 5$ or $3 + (4 \times 5)$. The order of operations defines what to do if there isn't any punctuation and avoids the problem of having two possible answers.

After receiving your question, I checked with several colleagues and then tried a lesson with fifth graders called *Four Strikes and You're Out*. I didn't tell the students that the idea came from a book written for a lower grade level but instead just told them the name. Trent protested, "But you're only supposed to have three strikes."

I responded, "Let's play the game once with four strikes and then see if a three-strike version would be better." I introduced the investigation as suggested in the book, by writing on the board:

_____ _____ + _____ _____ = _____ _____

0 1 2 3 4 5 6 7 8 9

I explained the rules, "You choose a digit from zero to nine and I'll cross it off the list. Then I'll write the digit in the problem wherever it appears. If the digit isn't in my problem, you get a strike. See

The game of *Four Strikes and You're Out* appears in *Teaching Arithmetic: Lessons for Addition and Subtraction, Grades 2–3* (Tank and Zolli 2001).

if you can figure out my problem before you get four strikes." I had written the problem—24 + 48 = 72—on a piece of paper that only I could see. "There are many possible problems," I added, "but you have to guess the one that I've selected." The students were successful. The best part was when they had partially solved the problem—24 + 4_ = _2—and reasoned to figure out the remaining digits.

Now that they understood how to play, I chose an example that led us to talk about the order of operations. I wrote on the board:

_____ + _____ × _____ = _____ _____

0 1 2 3 4 5 6 7 8 9

On my paper, I had written 1 + 5 × 7 = 36. I purposely left out parentheses, which certainly would have clarified the problem, so that I could talk about the order of operations. There was a protest when the problem came to this: 1 + 5 × ___ = ___6. "You have to write the six on the left side, too," Andy said. "It has to be thirty-six." He was thinking that 1 + 5 was 6, and that 6 × 6 was 36.

"No, what I've written matches the equation on my paper," I responded. After some more guesses, the students finally got the equation. Then there was some outrage, which gave me the opportunity to talk about the order of operations and the use of parentheses. We then played several more rounds of the game that gave them practice with applying the rules.

The students decided that they needed all four strikes, so I didn't change that rule of the game.

Patterns

Q. I've always given my students experiences with snapping cubes together and describing the repeating patterns in the colors they use. I'm wondering about the purpose of doing the sort of repeating patterns I've been doing. And is it OK to stop there or should I also give them experiences with growing patterns? —Grade 1

A. Involving students in making and describing patterns provides them with important and valuable mathematical experiences, and both repeating patterns and growth patterns have their place. One important similarity between patterns that repeat and patterns that grow is that both kinds of patterns provide the wherewithal to generalize and make predictions beyond the information currently available. For example, if you have a repeating red-blue-red-blue-red-blue cube pattern (*ababab* . . .), or a pattern that goes yellow-yellow-green-yellow-yellow-green (*aabaabaab* . . .), you can use the repeating aspect of the pattern to predict the color of cubes that are farther along in the train. For example, young students can extend the patterns to figure out the color of the tenth cube, while older students can think about what color the hundredth cube will be. In the same way, if you have a pattern that grows, such as the number of wheels on any number of tricycles, once you see the pattern of the number of wheels for one tricycle, two tricycles, three tricycles, and so on (3, 6, 9, 12, 15, . . .), you can predict the number of wheels you need for ten or one hundred tricycles. Young students may have to draw the tricycles and count the wheels; older students can think about multiplying by three.

Actually, both kinds of patterns deal with repeating, though in different ways. For the cube patterns, it's the color of the cubes that repeats in an orderly way. For the tricycles, the pattern that repeats in an orderly way is the relationship between the number of wheels and the number of tricycles—there are three wheels for every tricycle.

Is it enough to give first graders experiences only with repeating patterns? I don't think so. I think that one aspect of the mathematical experiences that we provide students should be to help them develop flexibility in their thinking. I wouldn't want students to encounter only repeating patterns and think that these constitute the full world of what patterns offer. A second reason for incorporating growth patterns is because they involve students with problem-solving experiences that help the development of their numerical reasoning. In this way, work with growth patterns supports students' work with numbers. And along with developing flexibility and supporting numerical reasoning, thinking about growth patterns is important for building a foundation for the development of students' algebraic thinking.

For more about patterns, see "Problem-Solving Investigations: Patterns and Algebraic Thinking" in Part 2 on page 241.

Patterns and Addition

Q. I tried a variation on Snap It, *an investigation in the "Beginning Number Concepts" section of* About Teaching Mathematics *(see page 327). I gave my students two colors of cubes and asked them to build different trains all with six cubes. I was hoping they would see the pattern of 0 + 5, 1 + 4, 2 + 3, and so on. They didn't! But they liked building the trains. Any ideas about what I might do differently to help them see this pattern?* —Grades 1–2

A. I had a similar experience when I asked second graders to build different two-color trains with seven cubes each. (I asked them to build trains, not towers, and place them flat on their desks. I've found that this avoids the toppling that typically happens with towers.) My goal was the same as yours except for the number 7—I wanted to focus students on the different pairs of addends for the number 7 and see the pattern of addends that you described for the number 6. And my experience was also the same as yours—the students didn't discover the pattern.

Also, many of the students enjoyed building trains with alternating colors (for example, *RBRBRBR* or *RRBBRRB*) rather than keep the red and blue portions of their trains together, as I had envisioned. And no one built a train that was all red or all blue; not only were they following my direction to build two-color trains, but I don't think they found a one-color train particularly interesting.

Here's what I did to reveal the pattern after they had built their trains. I called on a student to hold up one train and describe it, and I modeled how to describe the train another way, with an addition equation. I continued with other students doing the same, creating a list of equations, like this:

$1 + 5 + 1 = 7$

$3 + 4 = 7$

$6 + 1 = 7$

$5 + 2 = 7$

$1 + 1 + 1 + 1 + 1 + 1 + 1 = 7$

Then we played a game I called *What's a Matching Train?* I pointed to an equation on the list and the students would see if they had a matching train. If they did, they would hold it up for everyone to see (and check). This investigation reinforced for students how the trains they had physically constructed with the cubes could be mathematically represented with equations. When I pointed to $3 + 4 = 7$, some students held up a train with three red and four blue cubes and others held up a train with four red and three blue cubes. We talked about how both of these possibilities were OK.

Then, to reveal the pattern that you mentioned, I did a follow-up investigation, *What's a Matching Equation?* I explained, "This time I'm going to walk around the room and pick up trains that fit a pattern I'm thinking about. For each train, you'll tell me the matching equation and I'll write it on the board. As we continue, see if you can figure out my pattern. One thing you need to know is that for this pattern, the first number in the equation should always match the red cubes in the train I pick."

I walked around the room, chose a train that had six red cubes and one blue cube, held it up, and had the students talk with their partners about what a matching equation might be. I called on a student to report and wrote on the board $6 + 1 = 7$. I repeated this, next choosing a train that had five red cubes and two blue cubes, and writing $5 + 2 = 7$. I continued until I had recorded equations for six trains.

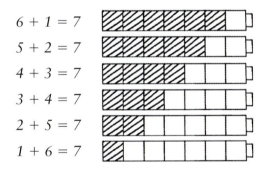

$6 + 1 = 7$

$5 + 2 = 7$

$4 + 3 = 7$

$3 + 4 = 7$

$2 + 5 = 7$

$1 + 6 = 7$

I asked the students what patterns they noticed, both in the list of equations and in the trains, and I gave all who wanted to a chance to report. They noticed that in the equations, the first numbers went down, the second numbers went up, and every equation ended with a seven. They commented that the trains had a zigzag pattern and looked like a staircase.

I asked them what equation I might write next if I wanted to follow the pattern. After they talked in pairs, I called on a student to report, and I added $0 + 7 = 7$ to the list. We talked about the matching train having seven blue cubes. Then we added an equation to the top of the list—$7 + 0 = 7$.

Patterns in Multiples

Q. Year after year, as part of my multiplication instruction, I teach my students to find the patterns in the multiples of sixes, eights, and so on. Why do we teach students to do this? —Grade 3

A. I think there are several reasons for asking students to find patterns in the multiples of sixes, eights, and so on. One is that the exploration reinforces for students that mathematics is, in large part, based on patterns, and the search for patterns in all areas helps us better understand mathematical ideas. A more specific benefit is that when looking for patterns in multiples, students are getting experience with those particular multiples, thus helping build their mathematical intuition as well as helping them become more familiar with these basic facts.

Rounding

Q. Rounding is very confusing for my students. Is there anything that I can do to help them? —Grade 4

A. Rounding is a skill we rely on often. We round when we decide how much tip to leave for a meal in a restaurant, budget money for a trip, and figure out how many rolls of wallpaper we need or how much fertilizer to mix for the garden. On our government tax forms, we round amounts to dollars and eliminate the cents.

In a fundamental way, rounding relates to estimating. In our daily lives, we always understand the purpose of rounding, and we rely on interpreting situations to figure out what makes sense. While students' daily needs aren't the same as ours, the instruction they receive in school about rounding should engage them in the same ways—interpreting situations and figuring out answers when being exact isn't essential.

Rules by themselves won't lead to understanding or develop adequate skills. It's important first for students to have many and varied experiences estimating and rounding. Here are some ideas that have worked for me.

Friendly Numbers
I talk with students about "friendly" numbers. "They're numbers that are easy to think about," I tell them. Then I ask a variety of questions. Following are samples.

What are some examples of numbers that you think are friendly?
Typically students choose 1, 5, 10, and 100; older students include 25 and 1000. I ask them to explain the reasons for their choices. I point out that 1, 10, 100, and 1000 are landmark numbers for our number system, and we discuss why.

Which do you think is friendlier, seventy-three or seventy?
Typically students agree that seventy is friendlier. "You get to

seventy by counting by tens," Alan told me, "but you can't get to seventy-three that way." We count by tens—ten, twenty, thirty, forty, and so on—and I identify these friendly numbers as multiples of ten.

What's a friendly number that's close to fifty-seven? One hundred thirteen? Four hundred eighty-seven?

Multiple answers are possible for questions like these, so I'm sure to have students explain their reasoning. For example, Robert thought that 113 was close to 100, but Lindsay argued that it was closer to 110, which was also a friendly number. I pointed out that if you were thinking about the hundreds part of the number, then 113 was closer to 100 than 200, but if you were thinking about the tens part, then 113 was closer to 110 than 120.

Then, for individual assignments, I give students "closer to" problems, choosing numbers that are appropriate for the students. Then I talk more with the class about rounding numbers to the closest ten or the closest hundred. Following are examples.

Is 163 closer to 160 or 165?

Is 163 closer to 160 or 170?

Is 163 closer to 100 or 200?

Is 163 closer to 150 or 200?

Mental Math Problems

I use regular classroom routines to present problems to the class that encourage them to round numbers and make estimates. We talk both about their solutions and how they reasoned. I phrase some questions so that they have one right answer. For example:

Eighteen students bought milk for lunch. Did we collect more or less than $10?

If everyone in the class took out four books from the library, would we take out more or less than one hundred books altogether?

I phrase other questions so more than one right answer are possible. For example:

I measured the hallway and it is 94 feet plus some more inches. About how long is it?

Some students think that 94 feet is a good estimate, some say 95 feet, and others vote for 100 feet.

Some questions suggest longer investigations. For example:

About how much do you think our class spends on milk in a week?

About how much does our year's supply of pencils cost?

About how many buttons do we have altogether?

About how many letters are there altogether in our first names? Our last names? Our first and last names together?

Connecting to the Language of Rounding

Once students are comfortable answering questions like the ones in the previous section, I address rounding directly. One way I've done this is to write on the board a number in the hundreds, for example, 138. Then I ask two questions:

What friendly number that ends in zero is closest to 138?

What friendly number that ends in two zeros is closest to 138?

I repeat this with other numbers between 100 and 900.

Then I introduce the typical language of rounding. I tell them that "rounding a number" means "finding a friendly number that is close to your original number." I explain how "ends in a zero" relates to tens while "ends in two zeros" relates to hundreds. To give them practice, I ask the same kinds of questions I did before, this time rephrasing to use the standard language of rounding.

Supporting Small-Group Work

Q. How can I get my students to participate in and enjoy group work? —Middle School

A. I began teaching as a middle school math teacher and taught eighth graders for six years. For the first few years, my classroom lessons followed a standard format: I'd go over the homework from the night before, teach a new lesson, give some class work to check that students understood, and finally assign homework for them to do that night. Within this format, I used the inquiry or discovery approach that I had learned in my teacher preparation, posing questions during lessons to lead students to new understandings and skills. Students sat at individual desks, and during the whole-group part of the lessons, only one of the students or I was talking. When I assigned class work, students worked by themselves and I circulated, giving help to individuals as needed. Sometimes, this part of the lesson was particularly hectic if many students needed help.

My teaching life began to change after I attended a workshop at a math conference where a teacher presented how she organized her students into groups of four and allowed them to work together. I was intrigued and tried it during the part of my lessons when students were doing class work. What a difference! Now, because students were working together on assignments instead of individually, the lesson wasn't as hectic because students were able to help one another. The room was noisier, for sure, but the noise was mostly productive noise. Of course, from time to time, I had to interrupt the students and ask that they all lower their voices, but this problem was overshadowed by the involvement I observed.

After that, group work became a staple of my classroom instruction. I began having students sit in groups all of the time and using small-group work during my whole-class instruction. Previously in my lessons, I'd pose a question to the class and allow wait time to give students a chance to think and raise their hands; then I'd call on a student to respond. Now, after posing a question and allowing time for students to think about it on their own, before I'd call on someone to respond, I'd ask them to "turn and talk" in their groups. The room would burst with conversation as students shared their thinking with one another. Then, after a few moments, I'd interrupt them and ask for someone to report to the entire class. Discussions became much more lively, and more students were engaged.

Some days, after going over the homework but before teaching a whole-class lesson, I'd assign a problem for students to work on first in groups. In this way, students had the chance to interact with the ideas I was planning to teach, which better prepared them for the lesson. At times, I'd ask them to work individually on the problem but to feel free to ask others in their group for help. Other times, I'd give them a problem to solve jointly, expecting each to contribute as much as possible.

Then I began using groups even for going over their homework assignments from the night before, beginning class by asking students in groups to compare their work and talk about any disagreements. Then we'd discuss differences they couldn't resolve. As the groups talked, I circulated and checked off who had and hadn't completed the assignments. A particular benefit was that students who hadn't completed assignments were still involved because they were able to participate in the small-group discussion.

Over the years, I've found small-group work to be invaluable for supporting student learning, maximizing student involvement, reducing isolation among individual students, and establishing a classroom environment that values student thinking, reasoning, and participation. I communicate these ideas to the students so that they understand why I'm expecting them to be productive group members. Also, over the years, I've honed my skills at successfully managing small-group work so that my math instruction goes as smoothly as possible. The following are some tips.

Make the rules clear.

Present the rules, explain them, post them, and review them often, especially just before students' beginning experiences with working in groups. I've changed the rules from time to time, but here is a good starting set:

1. You are responsible for your own work and behavior.

2. You must be willing to help any group member who asks.

3. You may ask the teacher for help only when everyone in your group has the same question.

The first rule isn't new, but I think it's useful to discuss it in the context of group work. Students now have a new option when doing their work; that is, to ask a group member for help. I clarify the second rule by pointing out the benefit that they all have willing helpers available at all times, without having to wait for help from me. The third rule is an incredible boon for helping with procedural as well as learning questions. Typically when I gave an assignment for students to do individually, I'd have to dash about and review or clarify what students were to do. Now students had to rely on their group first before receiving help from me. At the beginning, staying true to the third rule was the most difficult for me because I worried about not being responsive to my students' needs. However, following this rule and being disciplined about not giving group help until all hands were raised resulted in students becoming more independent as they learned to rely on one another.

Identify a procedure for establishing and changing groups.

Teachers have reported different ways to put students into groups. Some do it randomly, such as identifying groups with playing cards—ace, 2, 3, and so on—for as many groups as needed. Select the corresponding cards, distribute the cards, and have the students reorganize. Some teachers make the assignments themselves, setting up groups that they think will work well together. Other teachers, at times, let students select with whom they would like to work. Whatever system you use, be sure it's clear to the students. Also, it's helpful to let students know when you'll change groups—weekly, monthly, at report periods, when you start a new unit, or for some other reason.

Start with partner work.

It's easier for some students to stay on task when they are working with just one other classmate. Then, after they have some experience working in pairs, you can give them the opportunity to work in larger groups. To make the transition from partner to group work, choose a problem for which they clearly see the benefit of having more people available to contribute. For example, collecting data for a probability investigation is easier when more students are cooperating. Or read below to learn about *The Consecutive Sums Problem*. Also, there have been classes for which I've stuck just with partner work because I found that this was more effective and supportive for the particular students involved.

Choose first experiences carefully.

For their first experience, give students a problem to work on that will be accessible to all of them and will also engage their interest. I have several favorites for students' initial experiences with group work. One is *The Consecutive Sums Problem*, a problem for them to work on jointly. To introduce the problem, first establish that consecutive numbers are numbers that go in order—for example, 1, 2, 3, 4 or 11, 12, 13. Then ask, *How can we write nine as the sum of consecutive numbers?* The typical response is 5 + 4 (or 4 + 5, which you should consider to be the same). Record this, and then underneath write another solution:

$$9 = 5 + 4$$
$$9 = 2 + 3 + 4$$

Then ask the students, in their groups, to find all the ways to write each number from 1 to 25 as the sum of consecutive numbers. Tell them that some numbers are impossible, but don't reveal which; rather, challenge them to find the pattern of those numbers. (They are the powers of 2—2, 4, 8, 16, and so on.) Give them large sheets of newsprint or chart paper for recording. Ask them to look for patterns about which numbers can be written in only one way (such as 5), in two ways (such as 9), or in more ways.

For a more detailed description of *The Consecutive Sums Problem*, see "Planning Whole-Class Lessons with Problem-Solving Investigations" in Part 2 on page 139.

Have an extension ready for groups that finish quickly.

Groups will finish at different times, so it's good to have a challenge planned for those that work more quickly. For *The Consecutive Sums Problem*, if a group finishes work to your satisfaction, ask the group to predict how many ways thirty-six can be written as the sum of consecutive numbers. As a further extension, ask the group to predict for any number.

Lead whole-class discussions.

After groups have had a chance to complete an assignment you've given, be sure to have them present their ideas in a whole-class discussion. Use their work to teach ideas that are important to the curriculum. For example, *The Consecutive Sums Problem* gives you a way to discuss the powers of two—the numbers that are not possible to represent as the sums of consecutive numbers— and to use exponents to represent these numbers: 2^1, 2^2, 2^3, 2^4, and so on.

Subtraction

Q. My second graders have difficulty counting up to subtract. They seem to equate counting up with addition. How can I help students so they don't have to count backward? —Grade 2

A. In general, subtraction is hard for students. I think this is because there are several different meanings of subtraction, each of which relates to a different situation but all of which can be represented the same way arithmetically. One is the traditional take-away meaning, which has a built-in action: *You have seven pencils and give away four of them. How many do you have left?* Another is a how-many-more interpretation, which has no action but calls for comparing part of a set to the entire set: *I have three pencils but I need six pencils. How many more do I need?* And a third is a comparing meaning, which also has no action but calls for finding the difference between two sets: *You have seven pencils and I have five. How many more pencils do you have than I do?* Also confusing is that two of the meanings use the language of "how many more," one involving finding the difference between two sets and the other involving increasing one set to get to another number.

I agree that counting backward isn't a useful strategy for students to use for any of the subtraction situations. For many years, I assumed that because students could count forward, they could automatically count backward. But it doesn't seem to be so. (This makes sense when I realize that although I know the alphabet really well, I can't easily say the letters backward from Z to A!)

It's useful for students to be introduced to examples of each of the different situations, and it's helpful for them not only to figure out answers but also to explain how they reason. Typically, they will draw on different strategies for different situations. Also, working with situations helps students develop mental models that they can later apply to abstract problems.

Another important goal is for students to see how addition and subtraction are related, that the how-many-more and comparing situations, for example, can be represented both as subtraction

$(6 - 3 = ?)$ or as addition $(3 + ? = 6)$. In this way, counting up or counting backward both work, and students should be encouraged to choose a method that fits the situation, that is easy to use, and that makes sense.

Test Prep

Q. Do you believe in test prep? If so, what do you do? —Grade 5

A. All students benefit from being prepared to take high-stakes tests. What's important to me is that I relate any test prep to students' math learning. I've had success using a type of investigation I call hands-on-the-table math. Here's how I did this a few years ago when I was teaching fifth graders on a part-time basis, using the practice test booklet we were given. Here is one of the examples from the booklet:

> *Amy is paid $4 per hour for her first 10 hours of work one week. She earned $8 per hour for an additional 6 hours of overtime work. Which number sentence would you use to determine how much money Amy earned for the week?*
>
> *A. (16 + 12) = x*
>
> *B. [(4 × 10) + (8 × 6)] = x*
>
> *C. (10 + 6) (4 + 8) = x*
>
> *D. [(4 × 10) + (8 + 6)] = x*

I copied on the board just the first sentence from this test question:

> *Amy is paid $4 per hour for her first 10 hours of work one week.*

(Note: Sometimes I used an overhead projector and ahead of time wrote the entire problem on a transparency. Then I'd merely show this sentence, covering up the rest.)

Then I asked, "What do you know so far?" I gave everyone who wanted to respond the chance to do so. Then I wrote the next sentence underneath:

> *She earned $8 per hour for an additional 6 hours of overtime work.*

I asked, "What do you know now?" Again, I let all who were interested respond.

Then I asked, "What do you think the question is?"

For this problem, the general consensus was "How much money did Amy earn?" I gave the students time to figure out the answer, allowing them to talk with a partner, but doing it as hands-on-the-table math. That is, they had to figure mentally, without paper and pencil. I had several students explain how they figured out that Amy earned $88.

Then I wrote on the board the actual question from the text sample:

> *Which number sentence would you use to determine how much money Amy earned for the week?*

The students were surprised by the question. I asked them to talk with their partners about what might be a number sentence for figuring out how much money Amy earned (still without paper and pencil). After a few moments, I interrupted them and asked to hear their ideas. As students reported, I recorded their suggestions on the board.

I then wrote on the board the choices from the test sample:

A. *(16 + 12) = x*

B. *[(4 × 10) + (8 × 6)] = x*

C. *(10 + 6) (4 + 8) = x*

D. *[(4 × 10) + (8 + 6)] = x*

I said, "Talk with your partner about which you think is the correct answer." The students identified B.

Then we discussed why the others didn't work. They pointed out that in D, there was a plus sign where there should have been a times sign. For C, some of the students weren't familiar with the convention for multiplication shown by the expressions in the two parentheses without a times sign, and this gave me the chance to talk about it with them. And for A, they giggled when a student pointed out that sixteen was the sum of the hours Amy worked, and twelve was the sum of four dollars and eight dollars.

After a discussion like this one, I talk with the students about how this experience differs from what they'll face when they take the standardized test. I tell them that on the test the good news is that they'll have paper and pencil to do their figuring. I also tell them that the not so good news is that they won't have the chance to talk about their ideas with a partner or discuss them with the class.

I repeated this same experience for one or two problems a day for several weeks. This helped prepare students for the format of the test items, and it also focused them on paying attention to the information given and the questions asked.

Timed Tests

Q. What about using timed tests to help students learn their basic facts? —Grade 4

A. Teachers who use timed tests believe that the tests help students learn basic facts. This makes no instructional sense. Students who perform well under time pressure display their skills. Students who have difficulty with skills, or who work more slowly, run the risk of reinforcing wrong learning under pressure. In addition, students can become fearful and negative toward their math learning.

Also, timed tests do not measure students' understanding. Teachers concerned with the results of timed tests necessarily maintain a vigorous and steady program of drill and practice. The danger in this pedagogical focus is that an instructional emphasis on memorizing does not guarantee the needed attention to understanding. It doesn't ensure that students will be able to use the facts in problem-solving situations. Furthermore, it conveys to students that memorizing is the way to mathematical power, rather than learning to think and reason to figure out answers.

Students benefit from many and varied opportunities to apply their computation and numerical reasoning skills. An instructional approach based on developing students' thinking and reasoning should address broader goals for arithmetic competency than mere computational facility. Students should be required to analyze problem situations, decide on the operations needed, choose appropriate numbers, perform needed calculations, and evaluate results. Arithmetic practice that focuses on isolated numerical exercises alone doesn't prepare students to apply their skills to unique and diverse problems.

One challenge of teaching arithmetic is to emphasize the mathematical practices so that students learn to explore, justify, represent, solve, discuss, use, investigate, describe, develop, and predict. These actions are the heart of doing mathematics and should be incorporated into arithmetic drill and practice.

Multiplication and Division Word Problems

Q. Do you have a strategy for multiplication and division word problems? Code words can be fickle. Any help would be greatly appreciated. —Grades 3–4

A. I agree that relying on code words isn't a wise pedagogical strategy. Instead of focusing on particular words, our teaching challenge is to help students make sense of a situation and then connect it to the appropriate operation or operations. Addition situations generally relate to putting groups together. Subtraction situations can be taking groups apart, taking away, comparing two groups, or thinking about how many more are needed.

For multiplication and division, the key is dealing with equal-size groups. While addition problems can involve combining quantities of different sizes, multiplication calls for combining several groups of the same size. Division calls for either figuring out how many groups there are (with each group being the same size) or how many there are in each equal-size group.

Some problems can be interpreted by more than one operation. For example: *Mary, Luis, and Rory each decorated four eggs. How many eggs did they decorate altogether?* A child can represent this situation mathematically as $4 + 4 + 4 = ?$ or as $3 \times 4 = ?$ I want students to be able to use both representations and also to know when multiplication wouldn't be appropriate; for example: *Mary decorated three eggs, Luis decorated five, and Rory decorated two. How many eggs did they decorate altogether?* Multiplication doesn't work here; there aren't equal-size groups to combine.

Some addition and subtraction situations can also be interpreted and represented in more than one way. For example: *Sally has six birthday candles, but she needs ten. How many more does she need?* Students may represent this situation as addition ($6 + ? = 10$) or with subtraction ($10 - 6 = ?$).

Representing situations with appropriate operations is only one aspect of solving word problems. The other is performing the calculation to get the correct answer. A child may write *10 − 6* and then add or count on to arrive at a solution. Or a child who writes *3 × 4* may think, "Two fours are eight and four more make twelve." Computation strategies differ, especially when students are encouraged to figure mentally, which I think is a valuable skill for them to develop.

References

Professional References

Benezet, Louis. 1936. "The Teaching of Arithmetic I, II, III: The Story of an Experiment." *Journal of the National Education Association.*

Bresser, Rusty, Carolyn Felux, Kathy Melanese, and Christine Sphar. 2009. *Supporting English Language Learners in Math Class: A Multimedia Professional Learning Resource, Grades K–5.* Sausalito, CA: Math Solutions.

Burns, Marilyn. 1995. *Writing in Math Class: A Resource for Grades 2–8.* Sausalito, CA: Math Solutions.

———. 1996. *50 Problem-Solving Lessons: The Best from 10 Years of Math Solutions Newsletters, Grades 1–6.* Sausalito, CA: Math Solutions.

———. 2010. *Teaching Arithmetic: Lessons for Multiplying and Dividing Fractions.* Sausalito, CA: Math Solutions.

Burns, Marilyn, and Carrie De Francisco. 2002. *Teaching Arithmetic: Lessons for Decimals and Percents.* Sausalito, CA: Math Solutions.

Burns, Marilyn, and Cathy Humphreys. 1990. *A Collection of Math Lessons from Grades 6 Through 8.* Sausalito, CA: Math Solutions.

Burns, Marilyn, and Leyani von Rotz. 2002. *Lessons for Algebraic Thinking: Grades K–2.* Sausalito, CA: Math Solutions.

Burns, Marilyn, and Maryann Wickett. 2001. *Teaching Arithmetic: Lessons for Extending Multiplication, Grades 4–5.* Sausalito, CA: Math Solutions.

———. 2003. *Teaching Arithmetic: Lessons for Extending Division, Grades 4–5.* Sausalito, CA: Math Solutions.

California State Department of Education. 1987. *Mathematics Model Curriculum Guide: Kindergarten Through Grade Eight.* Sacramento: Author.

Chapin, Suzanne H., and Arthur Johnson. 2006. *Math Matters: Understanding the Math You Teach.* 2d ed. Sausalito, CA: Math Solutions.

Chapin, Suzanne H., Catherine O'Connor, and Nancy Canavan Anderson. 2013. *Classroom Discussions in Math: A Teacher's Guide for Using Math Talk Moves to Support the Common Core and More: A Multimedia Resource.* 3d ed. Sausalito, CA: Math Solutions.

Crawford, Jane. 2011. *Why Can't I Have Everything? Teaching Today's Children to Be Financially and Mathematically Savvy, Grades Pre-K–2.* Sausalito, CA: Math Solutions.

Dacey, Linda, Jayne Bamford Lynch, and Rebeka Eston Salemi. 2013. *How to Differentiate Your Math Instruction: Lessons, Ideas, and Videos with Common Core Support, Grades K–5: A Multimedia Resource.* Sausalito, CA: Math Solutions.

Hawkins, David. 1983. "Nature Closely Observed." *Daedalus* 112 (2): 65–89.

Joyner, Jeane, and Mari Muri. 2011. *INFORMative Assessment: Formative Assessment to Improve Math Achievement, Grades K–6.* Sausalito, CA: Math Solutions.

Lappan, Glenda. No date. "Knowing What We Teach and Teaching What We Know." http://nctm.org/news/pastpresident/1999-11president.htm.

National Governors Association Center for Best Practices and Council of Chief State School Officers. 2010. *Common Core State Standards for Mathematics.* Washington, DC: NGA Center and CCSSO. www.corestandards.org

O'Brien, Thomas C., and Shirley A. Casey. 1983. "Children Learning Multiplication Part I." *School Science and Mathematics* 83 (5): 407–412.

Parrish, Sherry. 2010, 2014. *Number Talks: Helping Children Build Mental Math and Computation Strategies, Updated with Common Core Connections.* Sausalito, CA: Math Solutions.

Petersen, Jamee. 2013. *Math Games for Independent Practice: Games to Support Math Workshops and More.* Sausalito, CA: Math Solutions.

Raphel, Annette. 2000. *Math Homework That Counts, Grades 4–6.* Sausalito, CA: Math Solutions.

Schuster, Lainie, and Nancy Canavan Anderson. 2005. *Good Questions for Math Teaching: 5–8.* Sausalito, CA: Math Solutions.

Sullivan, Peter, and Pat Lilburn. 2002. *Good Questions for Math Teaching: K–6.* Sausalito, CA: Math Solutions.

Tank, Bonnie, and Lynne Zolli. 2001. *Teaching Arithmetic: Lessons for Addition and Subtraction, Grades 2–3.* Sausalito, CA: Math Solutions.

Wickett, Maryann, Katharine Kharas, and Marilyn Burns. 2002. *Lessons for Algebraic Thinking: Grades K–2.* Sausalito, CA: Math Solutions.

Zinsser, William. 1988. *Writing to Learn.* New York: Harper & Row.

Children's Books

Baker, Keith. 1999. *Quack and Count*. New York: Voyager Books.

Burns, Marilyn. 1975. *The I Hate Mathematics! Book*. Covelo, CA: The Yolla Bolly Press.

———. 1990. *The $1.00 Word Riddle Book*. Sausalito, CA: Math Solutions.

———. 1997. *Spaghetti and Meatballs for All! A Mathematical Story*. New York: Scholastic.

Carle, Eric. 1991. *Rooster's Off to See the World*. New York Simon and Schuster Books for Young Readers.

———. 1992. *Draw Me a Star*. New York: Penguin Putnam Books for Young Readers.

Cleary, Beverly. 1968. *Ramona the Pest*. New York: William Morrow.

Crews, Donald. 1986. *Ten Black Dots*. New York: Greenwillow.

Goldstone, Bruce. 2001. *Ten Friends*. New York: Henry Holt.

Hillman, Ben. 2007. *How Big Is It? A Big Book All About Bigness*. New York: Scholastic.

———. 2008a. *How Fast Is It? A Zippy Book All About Speed*. New York: Scholastic.

———. 2008b. *How Strong Is It? A Mighty Book All About Strength*. New York: Scholastic.

———. 2009. *How Weird Is It? A Freaky Book All About Strangeness*. New York: Scholastic.

Hong, Lily Toy. 1993. *Two of Everything*. New York: Albert Whitman and Company.

Hutchins, Pat. 1982. *1 Hunter*. New York: Greenwillow.

———. 1986. *The Doorbell Rang*. New York: Greenwillow.

Lindbergh, Reeve. 1987. *The Midnight Farm*. New York: Dial Books for Young Readers.

Mahy, Margaret. 1987. *17 Kings and 42 Elephants*. New York: Dial Books for Young Readers.

Morozumi, Atsuko. 1996. *One Gorilla*. New York: Mirasol.

Myller, Rolf. 1962, 1990. *How Big Is a Foot?* New York: Yearling.

Neuschwander, Cindy. 1998. *Amanda Bean's Amazing Dream*. New York: Scholastic.

Pinczes, Elinor J. 1995. *A Remainder of One*. Boston: Houghton Mifflin.

———. 1999. *One Hundred Hungry Ants*. Boston: Houghton Mifflin.

Sayre, April Pulley, and Jeff Sayre. 2006. *One Is a Snail, Ten Is a Crab: A Counting by Feet Book*. Somerville, MA: Candlewick Press.

To find a complete list of children's books featured in the Math, Literature, and Nonfiction series, see mathsolutions.com/documents/lessons_chart-2.pdf.

For a complete list of children's books featured in *Math Reads*, see http://teacher.scholastic.com/products/math-concepts-skills/math-reads/math-books-topics.htm.

Index

Reproducibles can be downloaded from mathsolutions.com/atm4theditionreproducibles.

List of Investigations

The investigations marked with an asterisk (*) include About the Mathematics commentary written by the author. These explanations were written in response to queries from teachers asking for math help with particular problems.

Continued from copyright page.

The publisher would like to acknowledge the following resources for adapted material:

Pages 89, 484: *Four Strikes and You're Out* lesson adapted from *Teaching Arithmetic: Addition and Subtraction, Grades 2–3* (Tank and Zolli 2001).

Page 96: *Target 300* adapted from *Teaching Arithmetic: Lessons for Extending Multiplication* (Wickett and Burns 2001).

Page 229: *Pool Hall Math* lesson adapted from Mathematics: A Human Endeavor (Jacobs 1994).

Page 299: *A Mathematical Tug-of-War* lesson adapted from *Math for Smarty Pants* (Burns 1982).

Page 299: *Digit Place* lesson adapted from *Make It Simpler* (Meyer and Sallee 1983).

Page 343: Assessment adapted from *Mathematics Their Way* (Baratta-Lorton 1976).

Page 384: *The Factor Game* appears in *Prime Time: Factors and Multiples* (Lappan, Fey, Fitzgerald, Friel, and Phillips 1998).

Page 405: Another version of *How Many Beans?* appears in *Developing Number Sense, Grades 3–6* (Bresser and Holtzman 1999).

Page 407: *Hit the Target (Version 1)* appears in *Developing Number Sense, Grades 3–6* (Bresser and Holtzman 1999).

Page 437: Assessment 4 appears in "Communicating About Fractions with Pattern Blocks" (Caldwell 1995).

Page 451: *Sense or Nonsense* lesson appears in *Problem Solving in Mathematics: In-Service Guide* (Brannan and Schaaf 1983) and is shown being taught in the video *Mathematics: For Middle School, Part 3* (Burns 1989).

Pages 453: *What Percent Is Shaded?* lesson adapted from *Problem Solving in Mathematics: In-Service Guide* (Brannan and Schaaf 1983).

Page 458: The *Warehouse* problem appears in *Thinking Mathematically* (Mason, Burton, and Stacey 1982).